Willie Cassidy
Albany

Willie Cassidy
Albany
N. Y

Willie Cassidy

The Student's Specimens of English Literature.

CHOICE SPECIMENS

OF

ENGLISH LITERATURE;

SELECTED FROM THE CHIEF ENGLISH WRITERS,
AND ARRANGED CHRONOLOGICALLY.

BY

THOMAS B. SHAW, A. M.,

AND

WILLIAM SMITH, LL. D.

ADAPTED TO

THE USE OF AMERICAN STUDENTS,

BY

BENJAMIN N. MARTIN, D.D., L.H.D.,

PROFESSOR OF PHILOSOPHY AND LOGIC IN THE UNIVERSITY OF THE CITY OF NEW YORK.

NEW YORK:
SHELDON AND COMPANY,
498 AND 500 BROADWAY.
1870.

Stereotyped at the Boston Stereotype Foundry, 19 Spring Lane.

PREFACE

TO THE ENGLISH EDITION.

THE following extracts from the Chief English Writers were selected by the late Mr. Shaw to accompany his History of English Literature, and are divided into the same number of chapters, that they may be read with the biographical and critical account of each author. They present Specimens of all the chief English Writers from the earliest times to the present century. In making these Selections, two objects have been chiefly kept in view: first, the illustration of the style of each Writer by some of the most striking or characteristic specimens of his works; and, secondly, the choice of such passages as are suitable, either from their language or their matter, to be read in schools or committed to memory.

W. S.

PREFACE

TO THE AMERICAN EDITION.

IN furnishing to American students an edition of Dr. Shaw's "Specimens of English Literature," which should be adapted to their wants, the Editor deems it proper to state what changes have been made in the volume.

It appeared, upon examination, that, even with Dr. William Smith's additions to the original work of Dr. Shaw, some of the best English writers were not represented in the selections. As it seemed desirable to make the representation of approved authors as complete as a moderate limit would allow, it became necessary to revise the whole work; and, in order to gain space for a more extended view, to omit whatever was of inferior interest. It was found, too, that many passages, either not of the highest merit, of needless length, or unsuitable to be read in seminaries, might with advantage be abbreviated, or exchanged for others.

By these methods, it became possible, without increasing the size, materially to extend the scope of the work. While no important writer represented in the original has been excluded from this reprint, opportunity has been gained, by judicious condensation, to present to the reader specimens of the following list of English authors not included in the English edition, viz.: *Algernon Sydney*, *Ray*, *John Howe*, *Sir Isaac Newton*, *Doddridge*, *Watts*, *Bishop Butler*, *Bentham*, *Foster*, *Chalmers*, *Pollok*, *Hallam*, *Mrs. Hemans*, *Mrs. Browning*, *Hugh Miller*, *Edward Irving*, *Macaulay*, *Hazlitt*, and *Hood*.

In addition to the changes involved in this more enlarged representation, alterations have been made upon some one or other of the following grounds.

Passages containing Greek or Latin quotations have generally been omitted, as embarrassing in seminaries in which the ancient classics are not studied: an extract has occasionally been stricken out on the score of coarseness and bad taste: others of questionable truth, or of doubtful morality, have been either omitted or abridged; and prosaic or sombre passages have been exchanged for those of a more poetic or cheerful cast. A few brief foot-notes have also been added. The number, however, of such changes is not so great as to affect the identity of the two works; and has not seemed to require any other than this general acknowledgment.

The Editor indulges the hope that, while the changes which have been introduced will impart to the work an increased interest, they will not be found to impair at all its representative character; and that an improved tone, both of taste and of sentiment, in the selections, will justify the alterations with which it is now submitted to the American public.

B. N. M.

CONTENTS.

CHAPTER I.

Anglo-Saxon, Semi-Saxon, and Old English Literature.

CHAPTER II.

The Age of Chaucer.

CHAPTER III.

From the Death of Chaucer to the Age of Elizabeth, A. D. 1400–1558.

CHAPTER IV.

THE ELIZABETHAN POETS (INCLUDING THE REIGN OF JAMES I.).

CHAPTER V.

THE NEW PHILOSOPHY AND PROSE LITERATURE IN THE REIGNS OF ELIZABETH AND JAMES I.

CHAPTER VI.

THE DAWN OF THE DRAMA.

CHAPTER VII.

SHAKSPEARE, 1564–1616.

CHAPTER VIII.

THE SHAKSPEARIAN DRAMATISTS.

CHAPTER IX.

THE SO-CALLED METAPHYSICAL POETS.

CHAPTER X.

Theological Writers of the Civil War and the Commonwealth.

CHAPTER XI.

John Milton, 1608–1674.

CHAPTER XII.

The Age of the Restoration.

CHAPTER XIII.

The Second Revolution.

CHAPTER XIV.

Pope, Swift, and the Poets in the Reigns of Queen Anne, George I., and George II.

CHAPTER XV.

The Essayists.

CHAPTER XVI.

The Great Novelists.

CHAPTER XVII.

Historical, Moral, Political, and Theological Writers of the Eighteenth Century.

CHAPTER XVIII.

The Dawn of Romantic Poetry.

CHAPTER XIX.

Walter Scott.

CHAPTER XX.

Byron, Moore, Shelley, Keats, and Campbell.

CHAPTER XXI.

Wordsworth, Coleridge, Southey, and other Modern Poets.

CHAPTER XXII.

Letter Writers and Modern Essayists, with Prose Writers of the Nineteenth Century.

CHAPTER XXIII.

ORATORS.

INDEX OF AUTHORS.

CHOICE

SPECIMENS OF ENGLISH LITERATURE.

CHAPTER I.

ANGLO-SAXON, SEMI-SAXON, AND OLD ENGLISH LITERATURE.

A.—ANGLO-SAXON.

1.—CAEDMON, A. D. 650. *The Creation.* (Manual, p. 26.)

(From Guest's English Rhythms, vol. ii. p. 32.)

Ne wæs her tha giet, nymthe heolster-sceado,	Ne had there here as yet, save the vault-shadow,
Wiht geworden; ác thes wida grund	Aught existed; but this wide abyss
Stod deop and dim — drihtne fremde,[1]	Stood deep and dim — strange to its Lord,
Idel[2] and únnyt.	Idle[2] and useless.
On thone eagum wlat	On it with eyes glanc'd
Stith-frihth cining, and tha stowe beheold	The stalwart king, and the place beheld
Dreama lease. Geseah deorc gesweorc	All joyless. He saw dark cloud
Semian[3] sinnihte, sweart under roderum,	Lour with lasting night, swart under heaven,
Wonn[4] and weste; oth thæt theos woruld-gesceaft	Wan[4] and waste; till this world's creation
Thurh word gewearth wuldor-cyninges.	Rose through the word of the glory-King.
Her ærest gesceop éce drihten	Here first shap'd the eternal Lord
(Helm eall-wihta!) heofon and eorthan;	(Head of all things!) heaven and earth;
Rodor arærde, and this rume land	Sky he rear'd, and this wide land
Gestathelode — strangum mihtum,	He 'stablish'd — by his strong might,
Frea ælmihtig!	Lord Almighty!
Folde was tha gyt	Earth was not as yet
Græs-úngrene; gár-secg theahte,	Green with grass; ocean cover'd,

1 *Fremde* has a double ending in the nominative — one vowel, the other consonantal.

2 *Idel*, A. S., barren, idle. Deserts *idle*. — *Othello*. *Idle* pebbles. — *Lear*.

3 *Seman* is the active verb; *semian*, I believe, is always neuter. In Caedmon 4.

4 *Wan*, in the sense of dismal, was long known to our poetry:

Min is the drenching in the sea so *wan*. — *Chaucer*, *Knightes Tale*.

Sweart synnihte, side and wide,

Wonne wægas.

Tha wæs wuldor-torht,

Heofon-weardes gast ofer hólm boren,

Miclum spedum.

Metod engla heht,

(Lifes brytta) leoht forth cuman

Ofer rumne grúnd. Rathe wæs gefylled

Heah-cininges hǽs — him wæs halig leoht,

Ofer wéstenne, swa se wyrhta bebead.

Swart with lasting night, wide and far,

Wan pathways.

Then glory-bright,

Was the spirit of Heaven's-Guard o'er the water borne,

With mighty speed.

Bade the Angel-maker,

(The Life-dispenser) light to come forth

O'er the wide abyss. Quick was fulfill'd

The high King's hest — round him was holy light,

Over the waste, as the Maker bade.

---

2. KING ALFRED. *Ohther's Narrative, in Translation of Boëthius.* (Manual, p. 28.)

(From Marsh's Origin and History of the English Language, pp. 125–128.)

Fela spella him sædon tha Beormas, ægther ge of hyra agenum lande ge of thæm lande the ymb hy utan wæron; ac he nyste hwæt thæs sothes wær, forthæm he hit sylf ne geseah. Tha Finnas him thuhte, and tha Beormas spræcon neah an getheode. Swithost he for thyder, to-eacan thæs landes sceawunge, for thæm hors-hwælum, forthæm hi habbath swythe æthele ban on hyra tothum, tha teth hy brohton sume thæm cynincge: and hyra hyd bith swythe god to scip-rapum. Se hwæl bith micle læssa thonne othre hwalas, ne bith he lengra thonne syfan elna lang; ac on his agnum lande is se betsta hwæl-huntath, tha beoth eahta and feowertiges elna lange, and tha mæstan fiftiges elna lange; thara he sæde thæt he syxa sum ofsloge syxtig on twam dagum. He was swythe spedig man on thæm æhtum the heora speda on beoth, thæt is on wild-deorum. He hæfde tha-gyt, tha he thone cyningc sohte, tamra deora unbebohtra syx hund. Tha deor hi hatath hranas, thara wæron syx stæl-hranas, tha beoth swythe dyre mid Finnum, for-thæm hy fod tha wildan hranas mid.

Many things him told the Beormas, both of their own land and of the land that around them about were; but he wist-not what (of-) the sooth was, for-that he it self not saw. The Finns him thought, and the Beormas spoke nigh one language. Chiefliest he fared thither, besides the land's seeing, for the horse-whales, for-that they have very noble bones in their teeth, these teeth they brought some (to-) the king: and their hide is very good for ship-ropes. This whale is much less that other whales, not is he longer than seven ells long; but in his own land is the best whale-hunting, they are eight and forty ells long, and the largest fifty ells long; (of-) these he said that he (of-) six some slew sixty in two days. He was (a) very wealthy man in the ownings that their wealth in is, that is in wild-deer. He had yet, when he the king sought, (of-) tame deer unsold six hundred. These deer they hight reins, (of-) them were six stale-reins, these are very dear with (the) Finns, for-that they catch the wild reins with (them).

3. King Alfred. *Translation of the Pastorale of St. Gregory.* (Manual, p. 28.)

(From Wright's Biographia Britannica Literaria, Anglo-Saxon period, p. 397.)

Ælfred kyning hateth gretung Wulfsige bisceop his worthum luflice and freondlice, and the cythan hate, thæt me com swithe oft on ge-mynd, hwylce witan geo wæron geond Angel-cyn, ægther ge godcundra hada ge woruldcundra, and hu ge-sæliglica tida tha wæron geond Angle-cyn, and hu tha cyningas the thone anweald hæfdon thæs folces, Gode and his æryndwritum hyrsumodon; and hu hi ægther ge heora sybbe ge heora sydo, and ge heora anweald innan borde gehealdon and eac ut hira ethel rymdon; and hu him tha speow, ægther ge mid wige ge mid wisdome; and eac tha godcundan hadas hu georne hi wæron ægther ge ymbe lara ge ymbe leornunga, and ymbe ealle tha theowdomas thi hy Gode sceoldon, and hu man ut on borde wisdome and lare hider on land sohte, and hu we hi nu sceoldon ute begitan, gif we hi habban sceoldon. Swa clæne heo wæs othfeallen on Angel-cynne thæt swithe feawa wæron beheonan Humbre the hira thenunge cuthon understandan on Englisc, oththe furthon an ærendge-writ of Ledene on Englisc areccan; and ic wene thæt naht monige be-geondan Humbre næron. Swa feawa heora wæron, thæt ic furthon anne ænlepne ne mæg gethencan besuthan Thamise tha tha ic to rice feng. Gode ælmightigum sy thane, thæt we nu ænigne an steal habbath lareowa. For tham ic the beode, thæt thu do swa ic ge-lyfe thæt thu wille, thæt thu the thissa woruld thinga to tham ge-æmtige, swa thu oftost mæge, thæt thu thone wisdome the the God sealde thær thær thu hine befæstan mæge befæst. Gethenc hwilce witu us tha becomon for thisse woruld, tha tha we hit na hwæther ne selfe ne lufedon, ne

Alfred the king greets affectionately and friendly bishop Wulfsige his worthy, and I bid thee know, that it occurred to me very often in my mind, what kind of wise men there formerly were throughout the English nation, as well of the spiritual degree as of laymen, and how happy times there were then among the English people, and how the kings who then had the government of the people obeyed God and his Evangelists, and how they both in their peace and in their war, and in their government, held them at home, and also spread their nobleness abroad, and how they then flourished as well in war as in wisdom; and also the religious orders how earnest they were both about doctrine and about learning, and about all the services that they owed to God; and how people abroad came hither to this land in search of wisdom and teaching, and how we now must obtain them from without if we must have them. So clean it was ruined amongst the English people, that there were very few on this side the Humber who could understand their service in English, or declare forth an epistle out of Latin into English; and I think that there were not many beyond the Humber. So few such there were, that I cannot think of a single one to the south of the Thames when I began to reign. To God Almighty be thanks, that we now have any teacher in stall. Therefore I bid thee that thou do as I believe thou wilt, that thou, who pourest out to them these worldly things as often as thou mayest, that thou bestow the wisdom which God gave thee wherever thou mayest bestow it. Think what kind of punishments shall come to us for this world, if eac othrum mannum ne lyfdon. Thone naman anne we lufdon thæt we Cristene wæron, and swithe feawa tha theawas. Tha ic this eal ge-munde, tha ge-mund ic eac hu ic ge-seah ær tham the hit eal for-heregod wære and for-bærned, hu tha circan geond eal Angel-cyn stodon mathma and boca ge-fylled, and eac micel mæniu Godes theawa, and tha swithe lytle feorme thara boca wiston, for tham the hi hira nan thing ongitan ne mihton, for tham the hi næron on hira agenge theode awritene. Swilce hi cwædon ure yldran, tha the thas stowa ær heoldon, hi lufedon wisdome, and thurh thone hi begeton welan and us læfdon.

we neither loved it ourselves nor left it to other men. We have loved only the name of being Christians, and very few the duties. When I thought of all this, then I thought also how I saw, before it was all spoiled and burnt, how the churches throughout all the English nation were filled with treasures and books, and also with a great multitude of God's servants, and yet they knew very little fruit of the books, because they could understand nothing of them, because they were not written in their own language; as they say our elders, who held these places before them, loved wisdom, and through it obtained weal and left it to us.

B.—SEMI-SAXON.

4. LAYAMON. *Brut*, 1150–1250. *The Dream of Arthur.* (Manual, p. 32.)

(From Sir F. Madden's Edition, vol. iii. pp. 118–121.)

To niht a mine slepe,	To-night in my sleep (bed),
Ther ich laei on bure,	Where I lay in chamber,
Mei maette a sweuen;	I dreamt a dream,—
Ther uore ich ful sari aem.	Therefore I am "full" sorry.
Me imette that mon me hof	I dreamt that men raised (set) me
Uppen are halle.	Upon a hall;
Tha halle ich gon bestriden,	The hall I gan bestride,
Swulc ich wolde riden	As *if* I would ride;
Alle tha lond tha ich ah	All the lands that I possessed (had),
Alle ich ther ouer sah.	All I there overlooked (them saw).
And Walwain sat biuoren me;	And Walwain sate before me;
Mi sweord he bar an honde.	My sword he bare in hand.
Tha com Moddred faren ther	Then approached Modred there,
Mid unimete uolke.	With innumerable folk;
He bar an his honde	He bare in his hand
Ane wiax stronge.	A "battle"-axe (most) strong;
He bigon to hewene	He began to hew
Hardliche swithe,	Exceeding hardily;
And tha postes for-heou alle	And the posts all hewed in pieces,
Tha heolden up the halle.	That held up the hall.
Ther ich isey Wenheuer eke,	There I saw Wenhaver eke (the queen),
Wimmonen leofuest me:	"Dearest of women to me";
Al there muche halle rof	All the mickle hall roof
Mid hire honden heo to-droh.	With her hand she drew down;

Tha halle gon to haelden,	The hall gan to tumble,
And ich haeld to grunden,	And I tumbled to *the* ground,
That mi riht aerm to-brac.	*So* that my right arm brake in pieces,—
Tha seide Modred, Haue that!	Then said Modred, "Have that!"
Adun ueol tha halle	Down fell the hall;
And Walwain gon to ualle,	And Walwain gan to fall (was fallen),
And feol a there eorthe;	And fell on the earth;
His aermes brekeen beine.	His arms both brake.
And ich igrap mi sweord leofe	And I. grasped my dear (good) sword
Mid mire leoft honde,	With my left hand,
And smaet of Modred is haft,	And smote of Modred his head,
That hit wond a thene ueld;	*So* that it rolled on the field.
And tha quene ich al to-smathde,	And the queen I "cut all in pieces
Mid deore mine sweorde,	With my dear sword,
And seodthen ich heo adun sette	And afterwards I" set "her" down
In ane swarte putte.	In a black pit.
And al mi uolc riche	And all my good people
Sette to fleme,	Set to flight,
That nuste ich under Criste	*So* that I knew not under Christ,
Whar heo bicomen weoren.	Where (that) they were gone.
Buten mi seolf ich gond atstonden	But myself I gan stand
Uppen ane wolden	Upon a weald,
And ich ther wondrien agon	"And I there gan to wander
Wide yeond than moren.	Wide over the moors";
Ther ich isah gripes	There I saw gripes,
And grisliche fugheles.	And grisly (wondrous) fowls!
Tha com an guldene leo	Then approached a golden lion
Lithen ouer dune.	Over *the* down;—
Deoren swithe hende,	"A beast most fair,
Tha ure Drihten make.	That our Lord made";—
Tha leo me orn foren to,	The (this) lion ran towards (quickly to) me,
And iueng me bi than midle,	And took "me" by the middle,
And forth hire gun yeongen	And forth gan her move (he gan me carry),
And to there sae wende.	And to the sea went.
And ich isaeh thae vthen	"And I saw the waves
I there sae driuen;	Drive in the sea";
And the leo i than ulode	And the lion in the flood
Iwende with me seolue.	Went with myself.
Tha wit i sae comen,	When we came in *the* sea,
Tha vthen me hire binomen.	The waves took her from me;
Com ther an fisc lithe,	*But* there approached (came swimming) a fish,
And fereden me to londe.	And brought me to land;—
Tha wes ich al wet,	Then was I all wet,
And weri of soryen, and seoc.	"And" weary "from sorrow," and (very) sick.
Tha gon ich iwakien	When I gan to wake,
Swithe ich gon to quakien;	Greatly (then) gan I to quake;
Tha gon ich to binien	"Then gan I to tremble
Swule ich al fur burne.	As if I all burnt with fire."
And swa ich habbe al niht	And so (thus) I have all night

Of mine sweuene swithe ithoht;	Of my dream much thought;
For ich what to iwisse	For I wot (all) with certainty,
Agan is all mi blisse;	Gone is all my bliss,
For a to mine liue	For ever in my life
Soryen ich not driye.	Sorrow I must endure!
Wale that ich nabbe here	Alas! that I have (had) not here
Wenhauer mine quene!	Wenhaver, my queen!

---

5. *The Ormulum.* (Manual, p. 33.)

(Edited by Dr. White, Oxford, 1852.)

Nu, brotherr Wallterr, brotherr min	Now, brother Walter, brother mine
Affterr the flaeshes kinde;	After the flesh's kind (or nature);
Annd brotherr min i Crisstenn-dom	And brother mine in Christendom (or Christ's kingdom)
Thurrh fulluhht and thurrh trow-wthe;	Through baptism and through truth;
Annd brotherr min i Godess hus,	And brother mine in God's house,
Yet o the thride wise,	Yet on (in) the third wise, [both
Thurrh thatt witt hafenn takenn ba	Though that we two have taken
An reghellboc to folghenn,	One rule-book to follow,
Unnderr kanunnkess had and lif,	Under canonic's (canon's) rank and life,
Swa summ Sant Awwstin sette;	So as St. Austin set (or ruled);
Ich hafe don swa summ thu badd	I have done so as thou bade
Annd forthedd te thin wille;	And performed thee thine will (wish);
Ice hafe wennd inntill Ennglissh	I have wended (turned) into English
Goddspelless hallghe lare,	Gospel's holy lore,
Affterr thatt little witt tatt me	After that little wit that me
Min Drihhtin hafethth lenedd.	My Lord hath lent.

C.—OLD ENGLISH, 1250–1350.

6. HENRY III. *Proclamation in* A. D. 1258.

(From Marsh's Origin and History of the English Language, pp. 192, 193.)

Henr', thurg Godes fultume King on Engleneloande, lhoaverd on Irloand, duk' on Norm', on Aquitain', and eorl on Aniow, send igretinge to all hise halde ilaerde and ilaewede on Huntendon' schir'.	Henry, by the grace of God king in (of) England, lord in (of) Ireland, duke in (of) Normandy, in (of) Aquitaine, and earl in (of) Anjou, sends greeting to all his lieges, clerk and lay, in Huntingdonshire.
Thaet witen ge wel alle, thaet we willen and unnen, thaet thaet ure raedesmen alle other the moare dael of heom, thaet beoth ichosen thurg us and thurg thaet loandes	This know ye well all, that we will and grant that what our councillors, all or the major part of them, who are chosen by us and by the land's people in our king-

<table>
<tr><td>folk on ure kuneriche, habbeth idon and schullen don in the worthnesse of Gode and on ure treowthe for the freme of the loande thurg the besigte of than toforeniseide redesmen, beo stedefaest and ilestinde in alle thinge a buten aende, and we hoaten alle ure treowe in the treowthe, that heo us ogen, thaet heo stedefaestliche healden and swerien to healden and to werien the isetnesses, thaet beon imakede and beon to makien thurg than toforeniseide raedesmen other thurg the moare dael of heom alswo alse hit is biforen iseid, and thaet aehc other helpe thaet for to done bi than ilche othe agenes alle men rigt for to done and to foangen, and noan ne nime of loande ne of egte, where-thurg this besigte muge beon ilet other iwersed on onie wise and gif oni other onie cumen her ongenes, we willen and hoaten, thaet alle ure treowe heom healden deadliche ifoan, and for thaet we willen, thaet this beo stedefaest and lestinde, we senden gew this writ open iseined with ure seel to halden amanges gew ine hord.</td><td>dom, have done and shall do, to the honor of God and in allegiance to us, for the good of the land, by the ordinance of the aforesaid councillors, be steadfast and permanent in all things, time without end, and we command all our lieges by the faith that they owe us, that they steadfastly hold, and swear to hold and defend the regulations that are made and to be made by the aforesaid councillors, or by the major part of them, as is before said, and that each help others this to do, by the same oath, against all men, right to do and to receive, and that none take of land or goods, whereby this ordinance may be let or impaired in any wise, and if any [sing.] or any [plural] transgress here against, we will and command that all our lieges them hold as deadly foes, and because we will that this be steadfast and permanent, we send you these letters patent sealed with our seal, to keep among you in custody.</td></tr>
<tr><td>Witnesse usselven aet Lunden' thane egtetenthe day on the monthe of Octobr' in the two and fowertigthe geare of ure cruninge.
And this wes idom aetforen ure isworene redesmen:</td><td>Witness ourself at London the eighteenth day in the month of October in the two and fortieth year of our coronation.
And this was done before our sworn councillors:</td></tr>
<tr><td>[here follow the signatures of several *redesmen* or councillors]</td><td>[Signatures]</td></tr>
<tr><td>and aetforen othre moge.
And al on tho ilche worden is isend in to aeurihce othre shcire ouer al thaere kuneriche on Engleneloande and ek in tel Irelonde.</td><td>and before other nobles [?]
And all in the same words is sent into every other shire over all the kingdom in (of) England and also into Ireland.</td></tr>
</table>

---

7. *King Alisaunder.* (Manual, p. 34.)

(From Guest's History of English Rhythms, vol. ii. p. 142.)

<table>
<tr><td>Averil is merry, and longith the day;
Ladies loven solas and play;
Swaynes justes; knyghtis turnay;</td><td>April is merry, and length'neth the day;
Ladies love solace and play;
Swains the jousts; knights the tournay;</td></tr>
</table>

Syngeth the nyghtyngale; gredeth theo jay;	Singeth the nightingale; screameth the jay;
The hote sunne chongeth the clay;	The hot sun changeth the clay;
As ye well yseen may.	As ye well may see.

—*Alisaunder*, 140.

---

8. *Havelok.* (Manual, p. 34.)

(From Guest's History of English Rhythms, vol. ii. pp. 142–145.)

Hwan he was hosled and shriven,	When he was housled and shriven,
His quiste maked, and for him given,	His bequests made, and for him given,
His knictes dede he alle site,	His knights he made all sit,
For thorw them he wolde wite,	For from them would he know,
Hwo micte yeme hise children yunge,	Who should keep his children young,
Till that he couthen speken wit tunge,	Till they knew how to speak with tongue,
Speken, and gangen, on horse riden,	To speak, and walk, and ride on horse,
Knictes and sweynes bi hete[1] siden.	Knights and servants by their side.
He spoken there offe — and chosen sone	They spoke thereof — and chosen soon
A riche man was, that, under mone,	Was a rich man, that, under moon,
Was the trewest that he wende —	Was the truest that they knew —
Godard, the kinges oune frende;	Godard, the king's own friend;
And seyden, he moucthe hem best loke	And said they, *he* might best them keep
Yif that he hem undertoke,	If their charge he undertook,
Till hise sone mouthe bere	Till his son might bear
Helm on heued, and leden ut here,	Helm on head, and lead out host,
(In his hand a spere stark)	(In his hand a sturdy spear)
And king ben maked of Denmark.	And king of Denmark should be made.

1 This is clearly a mistake for *here*.

---

9. Robert of Gloucester. (Manual, p. 33.)

Thuse come lo! Engelond into Normannes honde,	Thus came lo! England into Normans'-hand.
And the Normans ne couthe speke tho bote her owe speche,	And the Normans not could speak then but their own speech,
And speke French as dude atom, and here chyldren dude al so teche;	And spake French as (they) did at home, and their children did all so teach:
So that heymen of thys lond, that of her blod come,	So that high men of this land, that of their blood come,
Holdeth alle thulke speche that hii of hem nome.	Hold all the same speech that they of them took;
Vor bote a man couthe French me tolth of hym wel lute;	For but a man know French men tell (reckon) of him well little:

Ac lowe men holdeth to Englyss and to her kunde speche yute.	But low men hold to English and to their natural speech yet.
Ich wene ther ne be man in world contreyes none	I wen there not be man in world countries none
That ne holdeth to her kunde speche, bot Engelond one.	That not holdeth to their natural speech but England (al-) one.
Ac wel me wot vor to conne both wel yt ys;	But well I wot for to know both well it is:
Vor the more that a man con, the more worth he ys.	For the more that a man knows, the more worth he is.

---

10. Robert Mannyng or Robert of Brunne.

(Manual, p. 33.)

Lordynges, that be now here,	Lords, that be now here,
If ye wille listene & lere	If ye will listen and learn
All the story of Inglande,	All the story of England,
Als Robert Mannyng wryten it fand,	As Robert Mannyng found it written,
& on Inglysch has it schewed,	And in English has shewed it,
Not for the lerid bot for the lewed,	Not for the learned but for the unlearned,
For tho that in this land wonn,	For those that in this land dwell,
That the Latyn no Frankys conn,	That know not Latin nor French,
For to haf solace & gamen	In order to have solace and enjoyment
In felawschip when thai sitt samen.	In fellowship when they sit together.

CHAPTER II.

THE AGE OF CHAUCER.

11. *The Vision of Piers Ploughman*, 1350. (Manual, p. 54.)

SATIRE OF LAWYERS.

Yet hoved[1] ther an hundred
In howves[2] of selk,
Sergeantz it bi-semed
That serveden at the barre,
Pleteden for penyes
And poundes the lawe;
And noght for love of our Lord
Unlose hire lippes ones.
Thow myghtest bettre meete myst
On Malverne hilles,
Than gete a mom of hire mouth,
Til moneie be shewed.

1 *hoved*, waited. 2 *howves*, hooks or caps.

12. JOHN GOWER, d. 1408. *Confessio Amantis*. (Manual, p. 56, seq.)

TALE OF THE COFFERS OR CASKETS.

From the Fifth Book.

In a Cronique thus I rede:
Aboute a king, as must nede,
Ther was of knyghtès and squiers
Gret route, and eke of officers:
Some of long time him hadden served,
And thoughten that they haue deserved
Avancèment, and gon withoute:
And some also ben of the route,
That comen but a while agon,
And they avanced were anon.
These oldè men upon this thing,
So as they durst, ageyne the king

Among hemself[1] compleignen ofte:
But there is nothing said so softe,
That it ne comith out at laste:
The king it wiste, and als so faste,
As he which was of high prudènce:
He shope therfore an evidence
Of hem[2] that pleignen in the cas,
To knowe in whose defalte it was;
And all within his owne entent,
That non ma wistè what it ment.
Anon he let two cofres make
Of one semblance, and of one make,
So lich,[3] that no lif thilke throwe,
That one may fro that other knowe:
They were into his chamber brought,
But no man wot why they be wrought,
And natheles the king hath bede
That they be set in privy stede,
As he that was of wisdom slih;
Whan he therto his time sih,[4]
All privĕly, that none it wiste
His ownè hondes that one chiste
Of fin gold, and of fin perie,[5]
The which out of his tresorie
Was take, anon he fild full;
That other cofre of straw and mull[6]
With stones meynd[7] he fild also:
Thus be they full bothè two.
  So that erliche[8] upon a day
He had within, where he lay,
Ther should be tofore his bed
A bord up set and fairè spred:
And than he let the cofres fette[9]
Upon the bord, and did hem sette.
He knewe the names well of tho,[10]
The whiche agein him grutched so,
Both of his chambre and of his halle,
Anon and sent for hem alle;
And seidè to hem in this wise.
  There shall no man his hap despise:
I wot well ye have longe served,
And God wot what ye have deserved;
But if it is along on me
Of that ye unavanced be,
Or elles if it belong on yow,

1 Themselves. 2 Them. 3 Like. 4 Saw. 5 Jewels, or precious stones. 6 Rubbish. 7 Mingled. 8 Early. 9 Fetched. 10 Those.

The sothè shall be proved now:
To stoppè with your evil word,
Lo! here two cofres on the bord;
Chese which you list of bothè two;
And witeth well that one of tho
Is with tresor so full begon,
That if ye happè therupon
Ye shall be richè men for ever:
Now chese,[11] and take which you is lever,
But be well ware ere that ye take,
For of that one I undertake
Ther is no maner good therein,
Wherof ye mighten profit winne.
Now goth [12] together of one assent,
And taketh your avisement;
For, but I you this day avance,
It stant upon your ownè chance,
Al only in defalte of grace;
So shall be shewed in this place
Upon you all well afyn,[13]
That no defaltè shal be myn.
  They knelen all, and with one vois
The king they thonken of this chois:
And after that they up arise,
And gon aside, and hem avise,
And at lastè they accorde
(Wherof her [14] talè to recorde
To what issue they be falle)
A knyght shall spekè for hem alle:
He kneleth doun unto the king,
And seith that they upon this thing,
Or for to winne, or for to lese,[15]
Ben all avised for to chese.
  Tho [16] toke this knyght a yerd [17] on honde,
And goth there as the cofres stonde,
And with assent of everychone [18]
He leith his yerde upon one,
And seith [19] the king how thilke same
They chese in reguerdon [20] by name,
And preith him that they might it have.
  The king, which wolde his honor save,
Whan he had heard the common vois,
Hath granted hem her owne chois,
And toke hem therupon the keie;
But for he woldè it were seie [21]

11 Choose. 12 Go. 13 At last. 14 Their. 15 Lose. 16 Then. 17 A rod. 18 Every one. 19 Sayeth to the king. 20 As their reward. 21 Seen.

What good they have as they suppose,
He bad anon the cofre unclose,
Which was fulfild with straw and stones:
Thus be they served all at ones.
  This king than, in the samè stede,
Anon that other cofre undede,
Where as they sihen gret richesse,
Wel morè than they couthen gesse.
  Lo! seith the king, now may ye se
That ther is no defalte in me;
Forthy[22] my self I wol aquite,
And bereth ye your ownè wite[23]
Of that[24] fortune hath you refused.
  Thus was this wise king excused:
And they lefte off her evil speche,
And mercy of her king beseche.

22 Therefore. 23 Blame. 24 *i. e.* that which.

---

13. Chaucer, 1328–1400. (Manual, p. 35, seq.)

From the Prologue to the Canterbury Tales.

Whannè that April with his shourès sote[1]
The droughte of March hath perced to the rote,[2]
And bathed every veine in swiche[3] licour,
Of whiche vertùe engendred is the flour;
Whan Zephirus eke with his sotè brethe
Enspired hath in every holt and hethe
The tendre croppès, and the yongè sonne
Hath in the Ram his halfè cours yronne,[4]
And smalè foulès maken melodie,
That slepen allè night with open eye,
So priketh hem[5] nature in hir[6] corages;[7]
Than longen folk to gon on pilgrimages,
And palmeres for to seken strangè strondes,
To servè[8] halweys[9] couthe[10] in sondry londes;
And specially, from every shirès ende
Of Englelond, to Canterbury they wende,[11]
The holy blisful martyr for to seke,
That hem hath holpen, whan that they were seke.[12]
  Befelle, that; in that seson on a day,
In Southwerk at the Tabard as I lay,
Redy to wenden on my pilgrimage
To Canterbury with devoute coràge,

1 Sweet. 2 Root. 3 Such. 4 Run. 5 Them. 6 Their. 7 Inclination. 8 To keep. 9 Holidays. 10 Known. 11 Go. 12 Sick.

At night was come into that hostelrie
Wel nine and twenty in a compagnie
Of sondry folk, by aventure yfalle [13]
In felawship, and pilgrimes were they alle,
That toward Canterbury wolden [14] ride.
The chambres and the stables weren wide,
And wel we weren esed attè beste.
  And shortly, whan the sonne was gon to reste,
So hadde I spoken with hem everich on [15]
That I was of hir felawship anon,
And madè forword erly for to rise,
To take oure way ther as I you devise.
  But natheles, while I have time and space,
Or that I forther in this talè pace,
Me thinketh it accordant to resòn,
To tellen you alle the condition
Of eche of hem, so as it semed me,
And whiche they weren, and of what degre;
And eke in what araie that they were inne:
And at a knight than wol I firste beginne.

13 Fallen. 14 Would. 15 Every one.

The Knight.

A Knight ther was, and that a worthy man,
That fro the timè that he firste began
To riden out, he loved Chevalrie,
Trouthe and honòur, fredom and curtesie.
Ful worthy was he in his lordès werre,[1]
And therto hadde he ridden, no man ferre,[2]
As wel in Cristendom as in Hethenesse,
And ever honoured for his worthinesse.
  At Alisandre he was whan it was wonne.
Ful often time he hadde the bord [3] begonne [4]
Aboven allè nations in Pruce.
In Lettowe hadde he reysed [5] and in Ruce,
No cristen man so ofte of his degre.
In Gernade at the siege eke hadde he be
Of Algesir, and ridden in Belmarie.
At Leyès was he, and at Satalie,
Whan they were wonne; and in the Grete see
At many a noble armee hadde he be.
At mortal batailles hadde he ben fiftene,
And foughten for our faith at Tramissène
In listès thries, and ay slain his fo.
This ilkè worthy knight hadde ben alsò

1 War. 2 Farther. 3 4 Been placed at the head of the table. 5 Travelled.

Sometimè with the Lord of Palatie,
Agen another hethen in Turkie:
And evermore he hadde a sovereine pris.[6]
And though that he was worthy he was wise,
And of his port as meke as is a mayde.
He never yet no vilanie ne sayde
In alle his lif, unto no manere wight.
He was a veray parfit gentil knight.
But for to tellen you of his araie,
His hors was good, but he ne was not gaie.
Of fustian he wered a gipòn,[7]
Allè besmotred[8] with his habergeon,[9]
For he was late ycome fro his viàge,
And wentè for to don his pilgrimage.

6 Praise. 7 Wore a short cassock. 8 Smutted. 9 Coat of mail.

The Prioress.

Ther was alsò a Nonne, a Prioresse,
That of hire smiling was full simple and coy;
Hire gretest othe n'as but by Seint Eloy;
And she was cleped[1] Madame Eglentine.
Ful wel she sangè the service devine,
Entuned in hire nose ful swetely;
And Frenche she spake ful fayre and fetisly,[2]
After the scole of Stratford attè Bowe,
For Frenche of Paris was to hire unknowe.
At metè was she wel ytaughte withalle;
She lette no morsel from her lippès fall,
Ne wette hire fingres in hire saucè depe.
Wel coude she carie a morsel, and wel kepe
Thattè no drope ne fell upon hire brest.
In curtesie was sette ful moche hire lest.[3]
Hire over lippè wiped she so clene,
That in hire cuppè was no ferthing sene[4]
Of gresè, whan she dronken hadde hire draught.
Ful semèly after her mete she raught.[5]
And sikerly she was of grete disport,
And ful plesànt, and amiable of port,
And peined[6] hire to contrefeten[7] chere
Of court, and ben estatelich of manère,
And to ben holden digne[8] of reverence.
But for to speken of hire conscience,
She was so charitable and so pitoùs,
She woldè wepe if that she saw a mous

1 Called. 2 Neatly. 3 Her pleasure. 4 Smallest spot. 5 Rose. 6 Took pains. 7 To imitate. 8 Worthy.

Caughte in a trappe, if it were ded or bledde.
Of smalè houndès hadde she, that she fedde
With rosted flesh, and milk, and wastel brede.
But sore wept she if on of hem were dede,
Or if men smote it with a yerdè[9] smert,[10]
And all was conscience and tendre herte.
  Full semely hire wimple ypinched was;
Hire nose tretìs;[11] hire eyen grey as glas;
Hire mouth ful smale, and therto soft and red;
But sikerly she hadde a fayre forehèd.
It was almost a spannè brode I trowe;
For hardily she was not undergrowe.[12]
  Ful fetise[13] was hire cloke, as I was ware.
Of smale coràll aboute hire arm she bare
A pair of bedès, gauded all with grene;
And theron heng a broche of gold ful shene,
On whiche was first ywriten a crouned A,
And after, *Amor vincit omnia.*

9 Stick. 10 Smartly, adv. 11 Straight. 12 Of low stature. 13 Neat.

THE FRIAR.

A Frere ther was, a wanton and a mery,
A Limitour, a ful solempnè man.
In all the ordres foure is none that can[1]
So muche of daliance and fayre langàge.
He hadde ymade ful many a mariàge
Of yongè wimmin, at his owen cost.
Until his ordre he was a noble post.
Ful wel beloved, and familier was he
With frankeleins over all in his contrèe,
And eke with worthy wimmen of the toun:
For he had power of confession,
As saide himselfè, more than a curàt,
For of his ordre he was licenciat.
Ful swetely herde he confession,
And plesant was his absolution.
He was an esy man to give penànce,
Ther as he wiste to han[2] a good pitànce:
For unto a poure[3] ordre for to give
Is signè that a man is well yshrive.[4]
For if he gave, he dorstè[5] make avant,
He wistè that a man was repentànt.
For many a man so hard is of his herte,
He may not wepe although him sorè smerte.
Therfòre in stede of weping and praières,
Men mote give silver to the pourè freres.

1 Knew. 2 Have. 3 Poor. 4 Shriven. 5 Durst make a boast.

His tippet was ay farsed[6] ful of knives,
And pinnès, for to given fayrè wives.
And certainly he hadde a mery note.
Wel coude he singe and plaien on a rote.[7]
Of yeddinges[8] he bare utterly the pris.
His nekke was whitè as the flour de lis.
Therto he strong was as a champioun,
And knew wel the tavèrnes in every toun,
And every hosteler and gay tapstère,
Better than a lazar or a beggère.
For unto swiche a worthy man as he
Accordeth nought, as by his facultè,
To haven[9] with sike lazars acquaintànce.
It is not honest, it may not avànce,
As for to delen with no swiche pouràille,[10]
But all with riche, and sellers of vitàille.
And over all, ther as profit shuld arise,
Curteis he was, and lowly of servìse.
Ther n' as no man no wher so vertuous.
He was the beste beggèr in all his hous:
And gave a certain fermè[11] for the grant,
Non of his bretheren came in his haunt.
For though a widewe haddè but a shoo,
(So plesant was his *in principio*)
Yet wold he have a ferthing or he went.
His pourchas[12] was wel better than his rent,
And rage he coude as it hadde ben a whelp,
In lovèdayes,[13] ther coude he mochel help.
For ther was he nat like a cloisterere,
With thredbare cope, as is a poure scolere,
But he was like a maister or a pope.
Of double worsted was his semicope,[14]
That round was as a belle out of the presse.
Somwhat he lisped for his wantonnesse,
To make his English swete upon his tonge;
And in his harping, whan that he hadde songe,
His eyen twinkeled in his hed aright,
As don the sterrès in a frosty night.
This worthy limitour was cleped Hubèrd.

6 Stuffed. 7 A stringed instrument. 8 Story telling. 9 Have. 10 Poor people. 11 Farm. 12 Purchase. 13 Days appointed for the amicable settlement of differences. 14 Half cloak.

The Doctor of Physic.

With us ther was a Doctour of Phisike,
In all this world ne was ther non him like
To speke of phisike, and of surgerie:

For he was grounded in astronomie.
He kept his patient a ful gret del
In hourès by his magike natural.
Wel coude he fortunen [1] the ascendent [2]
Of his imàges for his patient.
He knew the cause of every maladie,
Were it of cold, or hote, or moist, or drie,
And wher engendred, and of what humoùr,
He was a veray parfite practisour.
The cause yknowe, and of his harm the rote,[3]
Anon he gave to the sikè man his bote.[4]
Ful redy hadde he his apothecaries
To send him draggès,[5] and his lettuaries,[6]
For eche of hem made other for to winne;
Hir frendship n'as not newè to beginne.
Wel knew he the old Esculapius,
And Dioscorides, and eke Rufùs;
Old Hippocras, Hali, and Gallien,
Serapion, Rasis, and Avicen;
Averrois, Damascene, and Constantin;
Bernard, and Gatisden, and Gilbertin.
Of his diete mesùrable was he,
For it was of no superfluitee,
But of gret nourishing, and digestible.
His studie was but litel on the Bible.
In sanguin [7] and in perse [8] he clad was alle
Lined with taffata, and with sendalle.[9]
And yet he was but esy of dispence: [10]
He kepte that he wan [11] in the pestilence.
For golde in phisike is a cordial;
Therfore he loved gold in special.

1 Make fortune. 2 The ascendant. 3 Root. 4 Remedy. 5 Drugs. 6 Electuaries. 7 Blood-red color. 8 Sky-colored, or bluish grey. 9 Thin silk. 10 Expense. 11 Gained, got.

THE MILLER.

The Miller was a stout carl for the nones,
Ful bigge he was of braun, and eke of bones;
That proved wel, for over all ther he came,
At wrastling he wold bere away the ram.[1]
He was short shuldered brode, a thikkè gnarre,[2]
Ther n'as no dore, that he n'olde heve of barre,
Or breke it at a renning with his hede.
His berd as any sowe or fox was rede,
And therto brode, as though it were a spade.
Upon the cop [4] right of his nose he hade

1 The prize. 2 A hard knot in a tree. 3 A running. 4 Top.

A wert, and theron stode a tufte of heres,
Rede as the bristles of a sowès eres.
His nosè-thirlès [5] blackè were and wide.
A swerd and bokeler bare he by his side.
His mouth as widè was as a forneis.
He was a jangler,[6] and a goliardeis,[7]
And that was most of sinne, and harlotries.
Wel coude he stelen corne, and tollen thries.
And yet he had a thomb [8] of gold parde.[9]
A white cote and a blew hode wered he.
A baggèpipe wel coude he blowe and soune,
And therwithall he brought us out of toune.

5 Nostrils. 6 Prater. 7 Buffoon. 8 9 He was as honest as other millers, though he had, according to the proverb, like every miller, a thumb of gold.

---

14. John Barbour, d. A. D. 1396. (See Manual, p. 51.)

Apostrophe to Freedom.

[Old Orthography.]

A! fredome is a nobill thing!
Fredome mayse man to haiff liking!
Fredome all solace to man giffis:
He levys at ese that frely levys!
A noble hart may haiff nane ese,
Na ellys nocht that may him plese,
Gyff fredome failythe: for fre liking
Is yearnyt our all othir thing.
Na he, that ay hase levyt fre,
May nocht knaw weill the propyrte,
The angyr, na the wretchyt dome,
That is cowplyt to foule thyrldome.
Bot gyff he had assayit it,
Then all perquer he suld it wyt;
And suld think fredome mar to pryse
Than all the gold in warld that is.

[Modern Orthography.]

Ah! Freedom is a noble thing!
Freedom makes men to have liking! [1]
Freedom all solace to man gives:
He lives at ease that freely lives!
A noble heart may have none ease,
Na elsé nought that may him please,
If freedom faileth: for free liking
Is yearnéd [2] oure [3] all other thing.
Na he, that aye has livéd free,
May not know well the property,[4]
The anger, na the wretched doom,
That it coupléd to foul thyrldom. [5]
But if he had assayéd it,
Then all perquer [6] he should it wit; [7]
And should think freedom more to prize
Than all the gold in world that is.

1 Pleasure. 2 Desired. 3 Over, above. 4 Peculiar state or condition. 5 Thraldom. 6 Exactly. 7 Know.

15. CHAUCER (*Prose*). *Tale of Melibœus* (from the Parson's Tale).

COUNSEL OF PRUDENCE.

Whan dame Prudence, ful debonairly and with gret pacience, had herd all that hire husbonde liked for to say, than axed she of him licence for to speke, and sayde in this wise. My lord, (quod she) as to your first reson, it may lightly ben answerd: for I say that it is no folie to chaunge conseil whan the thing is chaunged, or elles whan the thing semeth otherwise than it semed afore. And moreover I say, though that ye have sworne and behight[1] to performe your emprise, and nevertheles ye weive to performe thilke same emprise by just cause, men shuld not say therfore ye were a lyer, ne forsworn: for the book sayth, that the wise man maketh no lesing,[2] when he turneth his corage[3] for the better. And al be it that your emprise be established and ordeined by gret multitude of folk, yet thar[4] you not accomplish thilke ordinance but[5] you liketh: for the trouthe of thinges, and the profit, ben rather founden in fewe folk that ben wise and ful of reson, than by gret multitude of folk, ther[6] every man cryeth and clattereth what him liketh: sothly[7] swiche[8] multitude is not honest. As to the second reson, wheras ye say, that alle women ben wicke: save your grace, certes ye despise alle women in this wise, and he that all despiseth, as saith the book, all displeseth. And Senek saith, that who so wol have sapience, shal no man dispreise, but he shal gladly teche the science that he can, without presumption or pride: and swiche thinges as he nought can, he shal not ben ashamed to lere[9] hem, and to enquere of lesse folke than himself.

1 Promised. 2 Lie. 3 Heart. 4 It behooveth. 5 Unless. 6 Where. 7 Truly. 8 Such. 9 Learn them.

---

16. SIR JOHN DE MANDEVILLE, 1300–1371. (Manual, p. 54.)

And therfore I schalle telle zou, what the Soudan tolde me upon a day, in his Chambre. He leet voyden out of his Chambre alle maner of men, Lordes and othere: for he wolde speke with me in Conseille. And there he askede me, how the Cristene men governed hem in oure Contree. And I seyde him, Righte wel: thonked be God. And he seyde me, Treulyche, nay: for zee Cristene men ne recthen righte noghte how untrewly to serve God. Ze scholde zeven ensample to the lewed peple, for to do wel; and zee zeven hem ensample to don evylle. For the Comownes, upon festyfulle dayes, whan thei scholden gon to Chirche to serve God, than gon thei to Tavernes, and ben there in glotony, alle the day and alle nyghte, and eten and drynken, as Bestes that have no resoun, and wite not whan thei have y now. And also the Cristene men enforcen hem, in alle maneres that thei mowen, for to fighte, and for to desceyven that on that other. And there with alle thei ben so proude, that thei knowen not how to ben clothed; now long, now schort, now streyt, now large, now swerded, now daggered, and in all manere gyses. Thei scholden ben symple, meke and trewe, and fulle of Almes dede, as Jhesu was, in whom thei trowe: but thei ben alle the contrarie, and evere enclyned to the Evylle, and to don evylle. And thei ben so coveytous, that for a lytylle Sylver, thei sellen here Doughtres, here Sustres and here owne Wyfes, to putten hem to Leccherie. And on with drawethe the Wif of another: and non of hem holdethe Feythe to another: but thei defoulen here Lawe, that Jhesu Crist betook hym to kepe, for here Salvacioun. And thus for here Synnes, han thei lost alle this Lond, that wee holden. For, for hire Synnes here God hathe taken hem in to oure Hondes, noghte only be Strengthe of our self, but for here Synnes. For wee knowen wel in verry sothe, that whan zee serve God, God wil helpe zou: and whan he is with zou, no man may be azenst you. And that knowe we wel, be oure Prophecyes, that Cristene men schulle wynnen azen this Lond out of oure Hondes, whan thei serven God more devoutly. But als longe als thei ben of foule and of unclene Lyvnge, (as thei ben now) wee have no drede of hem, in no kynde: for here God wil not helpen hem in no wise. And than I asked him, how he knew the State of Cristene men. And he answerde me, that he knew alle the state of the Comounes also, be his Messangeres, that he sente to alle Londes, in manere as thei weren Marchauntes of precyous Stones, of Clothes of Gold and of othere thinges; for to knowen the manere of every Contree amonges Cristene men. And than he leet clepe in alle the Lordes, that he made voyden first out of his Chambre; and there he schewed me 4, that weren grete Lordes in the Contree, that tolden me of my Contree, and of many othere Cristene Contrees, als wel as thei had ben of the same Contree; and thei spak Frensche righte wel; and the Sowdan also, where of I had gret Marvaylle. Allas! that it is gret sclaundre to oure Feythe and to oure Lawe, whan folk that ben with outen Lawe, schulle repreven us and undernemen us of oure Synnes. And thei that scholden ben converted to Crist and to the Lawe of Jhesu, be oure gode Ensamples and be oure acceptable Lif to God, and so converted to the Lawe of Jhesu Crist, ben thorghe oure Wykkednesse and evylle lyvynge, fer fro us and Straungeres fro the holy and verry Beleeve, schulle thus appelen us and holden us for wykkede Lyveres and cursed. And treuly thei sey sothe. For the Sarazines ben gode and feythfulle. For thei kepen entierly the Cōmaundement of the Holy Book Alkaron, that God sente hem be his Messager Machomet; to the whiche, as thei seyne, seynt Gabrielle the Aungel often tyme tolde the wille of God.

17. WICLIFFE, A. D. 1324–1384. (Manual, p. 58.)

MATTHEW'S GOSPEL, CHAP. VIII.

Forsothe when Jhesus hadde comen doun fro the hil, many cumpanyes folewiden hym. And loo! a leprouse man cummynge worshipide hym, sayinge; Lord, gif thou wolt, thou maist make me clene. And Jhesus holdynge forthe the hond, touchide hym sayinge, I wole; be thou maad clene. And anoon the lepre of hym was clensid. And Jhesus saith to hym; See, say thou to no man; but go, shewe thee to prestis, and offre that gifte that Moyses comaundide, into witnessing to hem. Sothely when he hadde entride in to Capharnaum, centurio neigide to hym preyinge hym, And said, Lord, my child lyeth in the hous sike on the palsie, and is yuel tourmentid. And Jhesus saith to hym, I shal cume, and shal hele hym. And centurio answerynge saith to hym, Lord, I am not worthi, that thou entre vndir my roof; but oonly say bi word, and my child shall be helid. For whi and I am a man ordeynd vnder power, hauynge vndir me knigtis; and I say to this, Go, and he goth; and to an other, Come thou, and he cometh; and to my seruaunt, Do thou this thing, and he doth. Sothely Jhesus, heerynge these thingis, wondride, and saide to men suynge hym: Trewly I saye to you I fond nat so grete feith in Yrael. Sothely Y say to you, that manye shulen come fro the est and west, and shulen rest with Abraham and Ysaac and Jacob in the kyngdam of heuenes; forsothe the sonys of the rewme shulen be cast out into vttremest derknessis; there shal be weepynge, and beetynge togidre of teeth. And Jhesus saide to centurio, Go; and as thou hast bileeued be it don to thee. And the child was helid fro that houre. And when Jhesus hadde comen in to the hous of Symond Petre, he say his wyues moder liggynge, and shakun with feueris. And he touchide hir hond, and the feuer lefte hir: and she roose, and seruyde hem. Sothely whan the euenyng was maad, thei brougte to hym many hauynge deuelys: and he castide out spiritis by word, and helide alle hauynge yuel; that it shulde be fulfillid, that thing that was said by Ysaie, the prophete, sayinge, He toke oure infirmytees, and bere oure sykenessis. Sothely Jhesus seeynge many cumpanyes about hym, bad *his disciplis* go ouer the water. And oo scribe, *or a man of lawe*, commynge to, saide to hym, Maistre, I shal sue thee whidir euer thou shalt go. And Jhesus said to hym, Foxis han dichis, *or borowis*, and briddis of the eir *han* nestis; but mannes sone hath nat wher he reste his heued. Sotheli an other of his disciplis saide to hym, Lord, suffre me go first and birye my fadir. Forsothe Jhesus saide to hym, Sue thou me, and late dede men birye her dead men. And Jhesu steyinge vp in to a litel ship, his disciplis sueden him. And loo! a grete steryng was made in the see, so that the litil ship was hilid with wawis; but he slepte. And his disciplis camen nig to hym, and raysiden hym, sayinge, Lord, saue vs: we perishen. And Jhesus seith to hem, What ben yee of litil feith agast? Thanne he rysynge comaundide to the wyndis and the see, and a grete pesiblenesse is maad. Forsothe men wondreden, sayinge: What manere *man* is *he* this, for the wyndis and the see obeishen to hym. And whan Jhesus hadde comen ouer the water in to the cuntre of men of Genazereth twey men hauynge deuelis runnen to hym, goynge out fro birielis, ful feerse, *or wickid*, so that no man migte passe by that wey. And loo! thei crieden, sayinge, What to vs and to thee, Jhesu the sone of God? hast thou comen hidir before the tyme for to tourmente vs? Sothely a floc, *or droue*, of many hoggis lesewynge was nat fer from hem. But the deuelis preyeden him, seyinge, gif thou castist out vs hennes, sende vs in to the droue of hoggis. And he saith to hem, Go yee. And thei goynge out wente in to the hoggis; and loo! in a greet bire al the droue wente heedlynge in to the see, and thei ben dead in watris. Forsothe the hirdes fledden awey, and cummynge in to the citee, tolden alle these thingis; and of hem that hadden the fendis. And loo! al the citee wente ageinis Jhesu, metynge hym; and hym seen, thei preiden *hym*, that he shulde pass fro her coostis.

CHAPTER III.

FROM THE DEATH OF CHAUCER TO THE AGE OF ELIZABETH.
A. D. 1400-1558.

A.—SCOTTISH POETS.

18. JAMES I. 1394–1437. (Manual, p. 60.)

From the King's Quair (Quire or Book).

ON HIS BELOVED.

The longè dayès and the nightès eke,
I would bewail my fortune in this wise,
For which, again [1] distress comfort to seek
My custom was, on mornès, for to rise
Early as day: O happy exercise!
By thee come I to joy out of tormènt;
But now to purpose of my first intent.

Bewailing in my chamber, thus alone,
Despaired of all joy and remedy,
For-tired of my thought, and woe begone;
And to the window gan I walk in hye,[2]
To see the world and folk that went forby;
As for the time (though I of mirthis food
Might have no more) to look it did me good.

Now was there made fast by the touris wall
A garden fair; and in the corners set
An herbere [3] green; with wandis long and small
Railed about and so with treeìs set
Was all the place, and hawthorn hedges knet,
That life was none (a) walking there forby
That might within scarce any wight espy.

* * * * * *

Of her array the form gif[4] I shall write,
Toward her golden hair, and rich attire,

1 Against. 2 Haste. 3 Herbary, or garden of simples.

In fret wise couched with pearlis white,
And greatè balas[5] lemyng[6] as the fire;
With many an emerant and faire sapphìre,
And on her head a chaplet fresh of hue,
Of plumys parted red and white and blue.

About her neck, white as the fyr amaille,[7]
A goodly chain of small orfevyrie,[8]
Whereby there hang a ruby without fail
Like to a heart yshapen verily,
That as a spark of lowe[9] so wantonly
Seemèd burnyng upon her whitè throat;
Now gif there was good parly God it wote.

And for to walk that freshè mayè's morrow,
An hook she had upon her tissue white,
That goodlier had not been seen toforrow,[10]
As I suppose, and girt she was a lyte[11]
Thus halfling[12] loose for haste; to such delight
It was to see her youth in goodlihead,
That for rudeness to speak thereof I dread.

In her was youth, beauty with humble port,
Bounty, richess, and womanly feature:
(God better wote than my pen can report)
Wisdom largèss, estate and cunning sure,
In a word in deed, in shape and countenance,
That nature might no more her childe avance.

5 Rubies. 6 Burning. 7 Mr. Ellis conjectures that this is an error, for *fair email*, i. e. enamel. 8 Goldsmith's work. 9 Fire. 10 Heretofore. 11 A little. 12 Half.

---

19. William Dunbar, about 1465–1520. (Manual, p. 60.)

From the Dance of the Seven Deadly Sins.

Ire, Pride, and Envy.

And first of all in dance was Pryd,
With hair wyl'd bak, bonet on side,[1]
  Like to mak vaistie wainis;[2]
And round about him, as a quheill,[3]
Hang all in rumpilis to the heill,[4]
  His kethat for the nanis.[5]
Mony proud trompour with him trippit,[6]
Throw skaldan fyre ay as they skippit,[7]
  They girnd with hyddous granis.[8]

1 With hair combed back (and) bonnet to one side. 2 Likely to make wasteful wants. 3 Like a wheel. 4 Hung all in rumples to the heel. 5 His cassock for the nonce. 6 Many a proud impostor with him tripped. 7 Through scalding fire as they skipped. 8 They grinned with hideous groans.

Then Ire cam in with sturt and strife,[9]
His hand was ay upon his knyfe,
  He brandeist lyk a beir;
Bostaris, braggaris, and burganeris,[10]
After him passit into pairis,[11]
  All bodin in feir of weir.[12]
In jakkis stryppis and bonnettis of steil,[13]
Thair leggis were chenyiet to the heill,[14]
  Frawart was thair affeir.[15]
Sum upon uder with brands beft,[16]
Some jaggit uthers to the heft[17]
  With knyves that scherp coud scheir.[18]

Next in the dance followit Invy,[19]
Fild full of feid and fellony,[20]
  Hid malice and dispyte,
For privy haterit that tratour trymlet;[21]
Him followit mony freik dissymlit,[22]
  With fenyiet wordis quhyte.[23]
And flattereris into menis faces,[24]
And backbyteris of sundry races[25]
  To ley that had delyte,[26]
With rownaris of false lesingis;[27]
Allace, that courtis of noble kingis[28]
  Of thame can nevir be quyte.[29]

9 Then Ire came with trouble and strife. 10 Boasters, braggarts, and bullies, 11 After him passed in pairs. 12 All arrayed in feature of war. 13 In coats of armor and bonnets of steel. 14 Their legs were chained to the heel. (Probably it means covered with iron net-work.) 15 Froward was their aspect. 16 Some struck upon others with brands. 17 Some stuck others to the hilt. 18 With knives that sharply could mangle. 19 Followed Envy. 20 Filled full of quarrel and felony. 21 For privy hatred that traitor trembled. 22 Him followed many a dissembling renegado. 23 With feigned words fair or white. 24 And flatterers to men's faces. 25 And backbiters of sundry races. 26 To lie that had delight. 27 With spreaders of false lies. 28 Alas that courts of noble kings. 29 Of them can never be rid.

---

20. SIR DAVID LYNDSAY. 1490–1557. (Manual, p. 69.)

MELDRUM'S DUEL WITH THE ENGLISH CHAMPION TALBART.

Then clariouns and trumpets blew,
And weiriours[1] many hither drew;
On eviry side come[2] mony man
To behald wha the battel wan.
The field was in the meadow green,
Quhare everie man micht weil be seen:
The heraldis put tham sa in order,
That na man past within the border,

1 Warriors. 2 Came.

Nor preissit[3] to com within the green,
Bot heraldis and the campiouns keen;
The order and the circumstance
Wer lang to put in remembrance.
Quhen thir twa nobill men of weir
Wer weill accounterit in their geir,
And in thair handis strong burdounis,[4]
Than trumpettis blew and clariounis,
And heraldis cryit hie on hicht,
Now let thame go — God shaw[5] the richt.
Than trumpettis blew triumphantly,
And thay twa campiouns eagerlie,
They spurrit their hors with spier on breist,
Pertly to prief[6] their pith they preist.[7]
That round rink-room[8] was at utterance,
Bot Talbart's hors with ane mischance
He outterit,[9] and to run was laith;[10]
Quharof Talbart was wonder wraith.[11]
The Squyer furth his rink[12] he ran,
Commendit weill with every man,
And him discharget of his speir
Honestlie, like ane man of weir.
The trenchour[13] of the Squyreis speir
Stak still into Sir Talbart's geir;
Than everie man into that steid[14]
Did all beleve that he was dede.
The Squyer lap richt haistillie
From his coursour[15] deliverlie,
And to Sir Talbart made support,
And humillie[16] did him comfort.
When Talbart saw into his schield
Ane otter in ane silver field,
This race, said he, I sair may rew,
For I see weill my dreame was true;
Methocht yon otter gart[17] me bleid,
And buir[18] me backwart from my sted;
But heir I vow to God soverane,
That I sall never just[19] agane.
And sweitlie to the Squiyre said,
Thou knawis[20] the cunning[21] that we made,
Quhilk[22] of us twa suld tyne[23] the field,
He suld baith hors and armour yield
Till him[24] that wan, quhairfore I will
My hors and harness geve thé till.

3 Pressed. 4 Spears. 5 Shew. 6 Prove. 7 Tried. 8 Course-room. 9 Swerved from the course. 10 Loath. 11 Wroth. 12 Course. 13 Head of the spear. 14 In that situation. 15 Courser. 16 Humbly. 17 Made. 18 Bore. 19 Joust. 20 Thou knowest. 21 Agreement or understanding. 22 Which. 23 Lose. 24 To him.

Then said the Squyer, courteouslie,
Brother, I thank you hartfullie;
Of you, forsooth, nothing I crave,
For I have gotten that I would have.

B.—ENGLISH POETS.

21. JOHN SKELTON, d. 1529. (Manual, p. 65.)

ATTACK UPON WOLSEY.

But this mad Amalek
Like to a Mamelek,[1]
He regardeth lords
No more than potshords;
He is in such elation
Of his exaltation,
And the supportation
Of our sovereign lord,
That, God to record,[2]
He ruleth all at will,
Without reason or skill;[3]
Howbeit the primordial
Of his wrětched original,
And his base progeny,[4]
And his greasy genealogy,
He came of the sank royal[5]
That was cast out of a butcher's stall.

. . . .

He would dry up the streams
Of nine kings' reams,[6]
All rivers and wells,
All water that swells;
For with us he so mells[7]
That within England dwells,
I wold he were somewhere else;
For else by and by
He will drink us so dry,
And suck us so nigh,
That men shall scantly
Have penny or halfpenny.
God save his noble grave,
And grant him a place
Endless to dwell
With the devil of hell!

1 Mamaluke. 2 Witness. 3 Regard to propriety. 4 Progenitorship? 5 Sanguo royal, blood royal. 6 Realms. 7 Meddles.

For, an he were there,
We need never fear
Of the feindes blake;
For I undertake
He wold so brag and crake,
That he wold than make
The devils to quake,
To shudder and to shake,
Like a fire-drake,[8]
And with a coal rake
Bruise them on a brake,[9]
And bind them to a stake,
And set hell on fire
At his own desire.
He is such a grim sire,
And such a potestolate,[10]
And such a potestate,
That he wold brake the brains
Of Lucifer in his chains,
And rule them each one
In Lucifer's trone.[11]

8 Fiery dragon. 9 Engine of torture. 10 "Equivalent, I suppose, to legatee."—*Dyce.* 11 Throne.

---

22. Sir Thomas Wyatt. 1503–1541. (Manual, p. 66.)

To his Beloved.

Forget not yet the tried intent
Of such a truth as I have meant;
My great travail so gladly spent,
Forget not yet!

Forget not yet when first began
The weary life, ye know since whan,
The suit, the service, none tell can;
Forget not yet!

Forget not yet the great assays,
The cruel wrong, the scornful ways,
The painful patience in delays,
Forget not yet!

Forget not!—Oh! forget not this,
How long ago hath been, and is
The mind that never meant amiss,
Forget not yet!

Forget not then thine own approv'd,
The which so long hath thee so lov'd,
Whose steadfast faith yet never mov'd,
Forget not this!

---

23. EARL OF SURREY. 1517–1547. (Manual, p. 66.)

A PRISONER IN WINDSOR CASTLE, HE REFLECTS ON PAST HAPPINESS.

So cruel prison how could betide, alas!
As proud Windsor? Where I in lust and joy,
With a king's son, my childish years did pass,
In greater feast than Priam's sons of Troy;
Where each sweet place returns a taste full sour.
The large green courts, where we were wont to hove,
With eyes upcast unto the maiden's tower,
And easy sighs, such as folk draw in love.
The stately seats, the ladies bright of hue,
The dances short, long tales of great delight;
With words and looks that tigers could but rue,
When each of us did plead the other's right.
The palm play,[1] where dèsported[2] for the game,
With dazed eyes oft we, by gleams of love,
Have miss'd the ball, and got sight of our dame,
To bait her eyes, which kept the leads above.
The gravell'd ground, with sleeves tied on the helm,
On foaming horse with swords and friendly hearts;
With cheer as though one should another whelm,
Where we have fought, and chased oft with darts.
With silver drops the meads yet spread for ruth;
In active games of nimbleness and strength,
Where we did strain, trained with swarms of youth,
Our tender limbs that yet shot up in length.
The secret groves, which oft we made resound
Of pleasant plaint, and of our ladies praise;
Recording soft what grace each one had found,
What hope of speed, what dread of long delays.
The wild forèst, the clothed holts with green;
With reins avail'd,[3] and swift ybreathed horse,
With cry of hounds, and merry blasts between,
Where we did chase the fearful hart of force.
The void walls eke that harbour'd us each night:
Wherewith, alas! revive within my breast
The sweet accord, such sleeps as yet delight;
The pleasant dreams, the quiet bed of rest;

1 Tennis-court. 2 Stripped. 3 Shortened.

The secret thoughts, imparted with such trust;
The wanton talk, the divers change of play;
The friendship sworn, each promise kept so just,
Wherewith we past the winter nights away.
And with this thought the blood forsakes the face;
The tears berain my cheeks of deadly hue:
The which, as soon as sobbing sighs, alas!
Upsupped have, thus I my plaint renew:
O place of bliss! renewer of my woes!
Give me account, where is my noble fere?[4]
Whom in thy walls thou didst each night enclose;
To other lief:[5] but unto me most dear.
Echo, alas! that doth my sorrow rue,
Returns thereto a hollow sound of plaint.
Thus I alone, where all my freedom grew,
In prison pine, with bondage and restraint:
And with remembrance of the greater grief,
To banish the less, I find my chief relief.

4 Companion. 5 Beloved.

---

24. Description of Spring.

The soote[1] season, that bud and bloom forth brings,
With green hath clad the hill, and eke the vale,
The nightingale with feathers new she sings;
The turtle to her make[2] hath told her tale.
Summer is come, for every spray now springs.
The hart hath hung his old head on the pale;
The buck in brake his winter coat he flings;
The fishes fleet with new repaired scale;
The adder all her slough away she flings;
The swift swallow pursueth the flies small;
The busy bee her honey now she mings;[3]
Winter is worn that was the flower's bale.[4]
And thus I see among these pleasant things
Each care decays, and yet my sorrow springs.

1 Sweet. 2 Mate. 3 Mingles. 4 Destruction.

---

25. Thomas, Lord Vaux. (Manual, p. 70.)

Upon his White Hairs.

These hairs of age are messengers
Which bid me fast repent and pray;
They be of death the harbingers,
That doth prepare and dress the way:
Wherefore I joy that you may see
Upon my head such hairs to be.

They be the lines that lead the length
How far my race was for to run;
They say my youth is fled with strength,
And how old age is well begun;
The which I feel, and you may see
Such lines upon my head to be.

They be the strings of sober sound,
Whose music is harmonical;
Their tunes declare a time from ground
I came, and how thereto I shall:
Wherefore I love that you may see
Upon my head such hairs to be.

God grant to those that white hairs have,
No worse them take than I have meant;
That after they be laid in grave,
Their souls may joy their lives well spent;
God grant, likewise, that you may see
Upon my head such hairs to be.

C.—ENGLISH PROSE.

26. CAXTON, d. 1491. (Manual, p. 59.)

INTRODUCTION TO THE MORTE D'ARTHUR.

After that I had accomplysshed and fynysshed dyuers hystoryes as wel of contemplacyon as of other hystoryal and worldly actes of grete conquerours & prynces. And also certeyn bookes of ensaumples and doctryne. Many noble and dyuers gentylmen of thys royame of Englond camen and demaunded me many and oftymes, wherfore that I haue not do made & enprynte the noble hystorye of the saynt greal, and of the moost renomed crysten Kyng. Fyrst and chyef of the thre best crysten and worthy, kyng Arthur, whyche ought moost to be remembred emonge vs englysshe men tofore al other crysten kynges. For it is notoyrly knowen thorugh the vnyuersal world, that there been ix worthy & the best that euer were. That is to wete thre paynyms, thre Jewes and thre crysten men. As for the paynyms they were tofore the Incarnacyon of Cryst, whiche were named, the fyrst Hector of Troye, of whome thystorye is comen bothe in balade and in prose. The second Alysaunder the grete, & the thyrd Julyus Cezar Emperour of Rome of whome thystoryes ben wel kno and had. And as for the thre Jewes whyche also were tofore thyncarnacyon of our lord of whome the fyrst was Duc Josue whyche brought the chyldren of Israhel in to the londe of byheste. The second Dauyd kyng of Jherusalem, & the thyrd Judas Machabeus of these thre the byble reherceth al theyr noble hystoryes & actes. And sythe the sayd Incarnacyon haue ben thre noble crysten men stalled and admytted thorugh the vnyuersal world in to the nombre of the ix beste & worthy, of whome was fyrst the noble Arthur whose noble actes I purpose to wryte in thys present book here folowyng. The second was Charlemayn or Charles the grete, of whome thystorye is had in many places bothe in frensshe and englysshe, and the thyrd and last was Godefray of boloyn, of whose actes & life I made a book vnto thexcellent prynce and kyng of noble memorye kyng Edward the fourth, the sayd noble Jentylmen instantly requyred me temprynte thystorye of the sayd noble kyng and conquerour king Arthur, and of his knyghtes wyth thystorye of the saynt greal, and of the deth and endyng of the sayd Arthur. Afferm-yng that I ouzt rather tenprynet his actes and noble feates, than of godefroye of boloyne, or any of the other eyght, consyderyng that he was a man born wythin this royame and kyng and Emperour of the same.

---

27. Lord Berners's Froissart. (Manual, p. 62.)

Anon after the dethe of the pope Gregory, the cardynalles drew them into the conclaue, in the palays of saynt Peter. Anone after, as they were entred to chose a pope, acordyng to their vsage, such one as shuld be good and profytable for holy churche, the romayns assembled thē togyder in a great nombre, and came into the bowrage of saynt Peter: they were to the nombre of xxx. thousand what one and other, in the entent to do yuell, if the mater went nat accordynge to their appetytes. And they came oftentymes before the conclaue, and sayd, Harke, ye sir cardynalles, delyuer you atones, and make a pope; ye tary to longe; if ye make a romayne, we woll nat chaung him; but yf ye make any other, the romayne people and counsayles woll nat take hym for pope, and ye putte yourselfe all in aduenture to be slayne. The cardynals, who were as than in the danger of the romayns, and herde well those wordes, they were nat at their ease, nor assured of their lyues, and so apeased them of their yre as well as they myght with fayre wordes; but somoche rose the felony of the romayns, y[t] suche as were next to y[e] conclaue, to thentent to make the cardynalles afrayde, and to cause them to cōdiscende the rather to their opinyons, brake vp the dore of the conclaue, whereas the cardynalles were. Than the cardynalles went surely to haue been slayne, and so fledde away to saue their lyues, some one waye and some another; but the romayns were nat so content, but toke them and put them togyder agayn, whether they wolde or nat. The cardynalles than seynge thēselfe in the daunger of the romayns, and in great parell of their lyues, agreed among themselfe, more for to please the people than for any deuocyon; howbeit, by good electyon they chase an holy man, a cardynall of the romayne nacion, whome pope Vrbayne the fyfte had made cardynall, and he was called before, the cardynall of saynt Peter. This electyon pleased greatly y[e] romayns, and so this good man had all the ryghtes that belonged to the papalite; howebeit he lyued nat but thre dayes after, and I shall shewe you why. The romayns, who desyred a pope of their owne nacion, were so ioyfull of this newe pope, y[t] they toke hym, who was a hundred yere of age, and sette hym on a whyte mule, and so ledde him vp and doune through ye cytie of Rome, exaltyng him, and shewyng howe they had vãquesshed the cardynals, seyng they had a pope romayn accordyng to their owne ententes, in so moche that the good holy man was so sore traueyled that he fell syck, and so dyed the thyrde daye, and was buryed in the churche of saynt Peter, and there he lyethe. —*Reprint of* 1812, vol. i. pp. 510, 511.

---

28. TYNDALE, d. 1536. (Manual, p. 62.)

MATTHEW'S GOSPEL, CHAP. VIII.

When Jesus was come downe from the mountayne, moch people folowed him. And lo, there cam a lepre, and worsheped him saynge, Master, if thou wylt, thou canst make me clene. He putt forthe his hond and touched him saynge: I will, be clene, and immediatly his leprosy was clensed. And Jesus said vnto him. Se thou tell no man, but go and shewe thysilf to the preste and offer the gyfte, that Moses commaunded to be offred, in witnes to them. When Jesus was entred in to Capernaum, there cam vnto him a certayne Centurion, besechyng him And saynge: Master, my servaunt lyeth sicke att home off the palsye, and is grevously payned. And Jesus sayd vnto him. I will come and cure him. The Centurion answered and saide: Syr I am not worthy that thou shuldest com vnder the rofe of my housse, but speake the worde only and my servaunt shalbe healed. For y also my selfe am a man vndre power, and have sowdeeres vndre me, and y saye to one, go, and he goeth: and to anothre, come, and he cometh: and to my servaunt, do this, and he doeth it. When Jesus herde these saynges: he marveyled, and said to them that folowed him: Verely y say vnto you, I have not founde so great fayth: no, not in Israell. I say therfore vnto you, that many shall come from the eest and weest, and shall rest with Abraham, Ysaac and Jacob, in the kyngdom of heven: And the children of the kingdom shalbe cast out in to the vtmoost dercknes, there shalbe wepinge and gnasshing of tethe. Then Jesus said vnto the Centurion, go thy waye, and as thou hast believed so be it vnto the. And his servaunt was healed that same houre. And Jesus went into Peters housse, and saw his wyves mother lyinge sicke of a fevre, And he thouched her hande, and the fevre leeft her; and she arose, and ministred vnto them. When the even was come they brought vnto him many that were possessed with devylles, And he cast out the spirites with a word, and healed all that were sicke, To fulfill that whiche was spoken by Esay the prophet sainge: He toke on him oure infirmytes, and bare oure sicknesses. When Jesus saw moche people about him, he commaunded to go over the water. And there cam a scribe and said vnto him: master, I woll folowe the whythersumever thou goest. And Jesus said vnto him: the foxes have holes, and the byrddes of the aier have nestes, but the sonne of man hath not whereon to leye his heede: Anothre that was one of hys disciples seyd vnto him: master suffre me fyrst to go and burye my father. But Jesus said vnto him: folowe me, and let the deed burie their deed. And he entred in to a shyppe, and his disciples folowed him, And lo there arose a greate storme in the see, in so moche, that the shippe was hyd with waves, and he was aslepe. And his disciples cam vnto him, and awoke him, sayinge: master, save us, we perishe. And he said vnto them: why are ye fearfull, o ye endewed with lytell faithe? Then he arose, and rebuked the wyndes and the see, and there folowed a greate calme. And men marveyled and said: what man is this, that bothe wyndes and see obey him? And when he was come to the other syde, in to the countre off the gergesens, there met him two possessed of devylls, which cam out off the graves, and were out off measure fearce, so that no man myght go by that waye. And lo they cryed out saynge: O Jesu the sonne off God, what have we to do with the? art thou come hyther to torment vs before the tyme [be come]? There was a good waye off from them a greate heerd of swyne fedinge. Then the devyls besought him saynge: if thou cast vs out, suffre vs to go oure waye into the heerd of swyne. And he said vnto them: go youre wayes: Then went they out, and departed into the heerd of swyne. And lo, all the heerd of swyne was caryed with violence hedlinge into the see, and perisshed in the water. Then the heerdmen fleed, and went there ways into the cite, and tolde every thinge, and what had fortuned vnto them that were possessed of the devyls. And lo, all the cite cam out, and met Jesus. And when they sawe him they besought him, to depart out off there costes.

---

29. Hugh Latimer, d. 1555. (Manual, p. 62.)

(From his Sermons.)

I can not go to my boke for pore folkes come vnto me, desirynge me that I wyll speake y[t] theyr matters maye be heard. I trouble my Lord of Canterburye, & beynge at hys house nowe and then I walke in the garden lokyng in my boke, as I canne do but little good at it. But some thynge I muste nedes do to satisfye thys place.

I am no soner in the garden and haue red a whyle, but by and by commeth there some or other knocking at the gate.

Anone cometh my man and sayth: Syr, there is one at the gate woulde speake wyth you. When I come there, then is it some or other that desireth me that I wyll speake that hys matter might be heard, & that he hath layne thys longe at great costes and charges, and can not once haue hys matter come to the hearing, but amõg all other, one especially moued me at thys time to speake.

Thys it is syr: A gentylwoman came to me and tolde me, that a greate man kepeth certaine landes of hyrs from hyr and wilbe hyr tenaunte in the spite of hyr tethe. And that in a whole twelue moneth she coulde not gette but one daye for the hearynge of hyr matter, and the same daye when the matter shoulde be hearde, the greate manne broughte on hys syde a greate syghte of Lawyers for hys counsayle, the gentilwoman had but one mā of lawe: and the great man shakes him so, so that he cā [not] tell what to do, so that when the matter came to the poynte, the Judge was a meane to the gentylwoman that she wold let the great mā haue a quietnes in hyr Lande. I beseche your grace that ye wyll loke to these matters.

---

30. SIR THOMAS MORE, 1480–1535. (Manual, p. 61.)

DESCRIPTION OF RICHARD III.

Richarde, the thirde sonne of Richarde, Duke of York, was in witte and courage egall with his two brothers, in bodye and prowesse farre vnder them bothe, little of stature, ill fetured of limmes, croke backed, his left shoulder much higher than his right, hard fauoured of visage, and such as is in states called warlye, in other menne otherwise, he was malicious, wrathfull, enuious, and from afore his birth, euer frowarde. . . . None euill captaine was hee in the warre, as to whiche his disposicion was more metely then for peace. Sundrye victories hadde hee, and sommetime ouerthrowes, but neuer in defaulte as for his owne parsone, either of hardinesse or polytike order, free was hee called of dyspence, and sommewhat aboue hys power liberall, with large giftes hee get him vnstedfaste frendeshippe, for whiche hee was fain to pil and spoyle in other places, and get him stedfast hatred. Hee was close and secrete, a deepe dissimuler, lowlye of counteynaunce, arrogant of heart, outwardly coumpinable where he inwardely hated, not letting to kisse whome hee thoughte to kyll: dispitious and cruell, not for euill will alway, but after for ambicion, and either for the suretie or encrease of his estate. Frende and foo was muche what indifferent, where his aduantage grew, he spared no mans deathe, whose life withstoode his purpose. He slewe with his owne handes king Henry the sixt, being prisoner in the Tower, as menne constantly saye, and that without commaundement or knoweledge of the king, whiche woulde vndoubtedly yf he had entended that thinge, haue appointed that boocherly office, to some other then his owne borne brother.

31. Roger Ascham, 1515–1568. (Manual, p. 64.)

(From the School Master.)

And one example, whether love or feare doth worke more in a childe, for vertue and learning, I will gladlie report: which maie be hard with some pleasure, and folowed with more profit. Before I went into Germanie, I came to Brodegate in Lecetershire, to take my leave of that noble Ladie Jane Grey, to whom I was exceding moch beholdinge. Hir parentes, the Duke and the Duches, with all the houshould, Gentlemen and Gentlewomen, were huntinge in the Parke: I founde her, in her Chamber, readinge Phædon Platonis in Greeke, and that with as moch delite, as som jentleman wold read a merie tale in Bocase. After salutation, and dewtie done, with som other taulke, I asked hir, whie she wold leese soch pastime in the Parke? smiling she answered me: I wisse, all their sporte in the Parke is but a shadoe to that pleasure, that I find in Plato: Alas good folke, they never felt, what trewe pleasure ment. And howe came you Madame, quoth I, to this deepe knowledge of pleasure, and what did chieflie allure you unto it: seinge, not many women, but verie fewe men have atteined thereunto? I will tell you, quoth she, and tell you a troth, which perchance ye will mervell at. One of the greatest benefites, that ever God gave me, is, that he sent me so sharpe and severe Parentes, and so jentle a scholemaster. For when I am in presence either of father or mother, whether I speake, kepe silence, sit, stand, or go, eate, drinke, be merie, or sad, be sowyng, plaiyng, dauncing, or doing anie thing els, I must do it, as it were, in soch weight, mesure, and number, even so perfitelie, as God made the world, or else I am so sharplie taunted, so cruellie threatened, yea presentlie some tymes, with pinches, nippes, and bobbes, and other waies, which I will not name, for the honor I beare them, so without measure misordered, that I thinke my selfe in hell, till tyme cum, that I must go to M. Elmer, who teacheth me so jentlie, so pleasantlie, with soch faire allurementes to learning, that I thinke all the tyme nothing, whiles I am with him. And when I am called from him, I fall on weeping, because, what soever I do els, but learning, is ful of grief, trouble, feare, and whole misliking unto me: And thus my booke, hath bene so moch my pleasure, and bringeth dayly to me more pleasure and more, that in respect of it, all other pleasures, in very deede, be but trifles and troubles unto me. I remember this talke gladly, both bicause it is so worthy of memorie, and bicause also, it was the last talke that ever I had, and the last tyme, that ever I saw that noble and worthie Ladie.

D.—BALLADS.

32. *The Ancient Ballad of Chevy Chase.* (Manual, pp. 67–69.)

Sir Philip Sydney, in his Discourse of Poetry, speaks of this Ballad in the following words:—"I never heard the old song of Piercy and Douglas, that I found not my heart more moved than with a trumpet; and yet it is sung by some blind crowder with no rougher voice than rude stile; which being so evil apparelled in the dust and cobweb of that uncivil age, what would it work trimmed in the gorgeous eloquence of Pindar?"

THE FIRST FIT.[1]

The Persè owt[2] of Northombarlande,
And a vowe to God mayd he,
That he wolde hunte in the mountayns
Off Chyviat within dayes thre,
In the mauger[3] of dougtè Dogles,
And all that ever with him be.

The fattiste hartes in all Cheviat
He sayd he wold kill, and cary them away:
Be my feth, sayd the dougheti Doglas agayn,
I wyll let[4] that hontyng yf that I may.

Then the Persè owt of Banborowe cam,
With him a myghtye meany;[5]
With fifteen hondrith archares bold;
The wear chosen out of shyars thre.

This begane on a Monday at morn
In Cheviat the hillys so he;
The chyld may rue that ys un-born,
It was the mor pittè.

The dryvars thorowe the woodes went
For to reas the dear;
Bomen bickarte uppone the bent[6]
With ther browd aras cleare.

Then the wyld thorowe the woodes went
On every syde shear:

1 Fit is a part or division of a song. 2 Out. 3 In spite of. 4 Hinder. 5 Company. 6 Field.

Grea-hondes thorowe the greves glent
  For to kyll thear dear.

The begane in Chyviat the hyls above
  Yerly on a monnyn day;
Be that it drewe to the oware [7] off none
  A hondrith fat hartes ded ther lay.

The blewe a mort uppone the bent,
  The semblyd on sydis shear;
To the quyrry [8] then the Persè went
  To se the bryttlynge off the deare.

He sayd, It was the Duglas promys
  This day to meet me hear;
But I wyste he wold faylle verament:
  A gret oth the Persè swear.

At the laste a squyar of Northombelonde
  Lokyde at his hand full ny,
He was war [9] ath the doughetie Doglas comynge:
  With him a mightè meany.

Both with spear, byll,[10] and brande: [11]
  Yt was a myghti sight to se,
Hardyar men both off hart nar hande
  Were not in Christiantè.

The wear twenty hondrith spear-men good
  Withouten any fayle;
The wear borne a-long be the watter a Twydè,
  Yth [12] bowndes of Tividale.

Leave off the brytlyng of the dear, he sayde,
  And to your bowys look ye tayk good heed;
For never sithe ye wear on your mothars borne
  Had ye never so mickle need.

The dougheti Dogglas on a stede
  He rode att his men beforne;
His armor glytteryde as dyd a glede; [13]
  A bolder barne was never born.

Tell me 'what' men ye ar, he says,
  Or whos men that ye be:
Who gave youe leave to hunte in this
  Chyviat chays in the spyt of me?

7 Hour. 8 Quarry. 9 Aware. 10 Battle-axe. 11 Sword. 12 In the. 13 A red-hot coal.

The first mane that ever him an answear mayd,
 Yt was the good lord Persè:
We wyll not tell the 'what' men we ar, he says,
 Nor whos men that we be;
But we wyll hount hear in this chays
 In the spyte of thyne, and of the.

The fattiste hartes in all Chyviat
 We have kyld, and cast[14] to carry them a-way.
Be my troth, sayd the doughtè Dogglas agayn,
 Ther-for the ton[15] of us shall de this day.

Then sayd the doughtè Doglas
 Unto the lord Persè:
To kyll all thes giltless men,
 A-las! it wear great pittè.

But, Persè, thowe art a lord of lande,
 I am a yerle[16] callyd within my contre;
Let all our men uppone a parti stande;
 And do the battell off the and of me.

Now Cristes cors on his crowne, sayd the lord Persè,
 Who-soever ther-to says nay.
Be my troth, doughtè Doglas, he says,
 Thow shalt never se that day;

Nethar in Ynglonde, Skottlonde, nar France,
 Nor for no man of a woman born,
But and fortune be my chance,
 I dar met him on man for on.

Then bespayke a squyar off Northombarlonde,
 Ric. Wytharynton was him nam;
It shall never be told in Sothe-Ynglonde,
 To kyng Herry the fourth for sham.

I wat[17] youe byn[18] great lordes twaw,
 I am a poor squyar of lande;
I will never se my captayne fyght on a fylde,
 And stande my-selffe, and looke on,
But whyll I may my weppone welde,
 I wyll not 'fayl' both harte and hande.

That day, that day, that dredfull day;
 The first fit here I fynde.
And youe wyll here any mor athe hountyng athe Chyviat,
 Yet ys ther mor behynde.

14 Mean. 15 One. 16 Earl. 17 Know. 18 Are.

THE SECOND FIT.

The Yngglishe men hade ther bowys yebent,
The hartes were good yenoughe;
The first of arros that the shote off,
Seven skore spear-men the sloughe.[19]

Yet bydys the yerle Doglas uppon the bent
A captayne good yenoughe,
And that was sene verament,
For he wrought hom both woo and wouche.[20]

The Dogglas pertyd his ost in thre,
Like a cheffe cheften [21] off pryde,
With suar [22] speares of myghttè tre
The cum in on every syde.

Thrughe our Ynglishe archery
Gave many a wounde full wyde;
Many a doughete the garde to dy,
Which ganyde [23] them no pryde.

The Ynglishe men let thear bowys be,
And pulde [24] owt brandes that wer bright;
It was a hevy syght to se
Bryght swordes on basnites [25] lyght.

Thorowe ryche male, and myne-ye-ple
Many sterne the stroke downe streight:
Many a freyke [26] that was full free,
That undar foot dyd lyght.

At last the Duglas and the Persè met,
Lyk to captayns of myght and mayne;
The swapte togethar tyll the both swat
With swordes, that wear of fyn myllàn.

Thes worthè freckys for to fyght
Ther-to the wear full fayne,
Tyll the bloode owte off their basnites sprente,[27]
As ever dyd heal [28] or rayne.

Holde the, Persè, sayd the Doglas,
And i' feth I shall the brynge
Wher thowe shalte have a yerls wagis
Of Jamy our Scottish kynge.

19 Slew. 20 Mischief. 21 Chieftain. 22 Heavy. 23 Gained. 24 Pulled.
25 Helmets. 26 Fellow. 27 Sprung. 28 Hail.

Thoue shalte have thy ransom fre,
I hight[29] the hear this thinge,
For the manfullyste man yet art thowe,
That ever I conqueryd in filde fightyng.

Nay 'then' sayd the lord Persè,
I tolde it the beforne,
That I wolde never yeldyde be
To no man of a woman born.

With that ther cam an arrowe hastely
Forthe off a mightie wane,[30]
Hit hathe strekene the yerle Duglas
In at the brest bane.

Thoroue lyvar and longs bathe[31]
The sharp arrowe ys gane,
That never after in all his lyffe days,
He spayke mo wordes but ane,
That was, Fyghte ye, my merry men whyllys[32] ye may,
For my lyff days ben[33] gan.

The Persè leanyde[34] on his brande,
And sawe the Duglas de;[35]
He tooke the dede man be the hande,
And sayd, Wo ys me for the!

To have sayvde thy lyffe I wold have pertyd[36] with
My landes for years thre,
For a better man of hart, nare of hande
Was not in all the north countrè.

Of all that se[37] a Skottishe knyght,
Was callyd Sir Hewe the Mongonbyrry,
He sawe the Duglas to the deth was dyght;[38]
He spendyd[39] a spear a trusti tre:

He rod uppon a corsiare
Throughe a hondrith archery;
He never styntyde[40] nar never blane,[41]
Tyll he cam to the good lord Persè.

He set uppone the lord Persè
A dynte that was full soare;
With a suar spear of a myghtè tre
Clean thorow the body he the Persè bore,

[29] Entreat. [30] Ane, one, *sc.* man. [31] Both. [32] Whilst. [33] Are. [34] Leaned. [35] Die. [36] Parted. [37] Saw. [38] Put. [39] Grasped. [40] Stopped. [41] Staid.

Athe[42] tothar syde, that a man myght se,
A large cloth yard and mare:
Towe bettar captayns wear nat in Christiantè,
Then that day slain were ther.

An archar off Northomberlonde
Say slean was the lord Persè,
He bar a bende-bow in his hande,
Was made off trusti tre:

An arow, that a cloth yarde was lang,
To th' hard stele haylde[43] he;
A dynt, that was both sad and sore,
He sat on Sir Hewe the Mongon-byrry.

The dynt yt was both sad and sar,
That he of Mongon-byrry sete;
The swane-fethars, that his arrowe bar,[44]
With his hart blood the wear wete.

Ther was never a freake wone foot wolde fle,
But still in stour[45] dyd stand,
Heawying on yche othar, whyll the myght dre,
With many a bal-ful brande.

This battell begane in Chyviat
An owar[46] befor the none,
And when even song bell was rang
The battell was nat half done.

The tooke 'on' on ethar hand
Be the lyght off the mone;
Many hade no strength for to stande,
In Chyviat the hyllys aboun.[47]

Of fifteen hondrith archers of Ynglonde
Went away but fifti and thre;
Of twenty hondrith spear-men of Skotlonde,
But even five and fifti:

But all wear slayne Cheviat within:
The hade no strengthe to stand on hie;
The chylde may rue that ys un-borne,
It was the mor pittè.

Thear was slayne with the lord Persè
Sir John of Agerstone,
Sir Roge the hinde Hartly,
Sir Wyllyam the bolde Hearone.

42 At the. 43 Hauled. 44 Bore. 45 Fight. 46 Hour. 47 Above.

Sir Jorg the worthè Lovele
  A knight of great renowen,
Sir Raff the rych Rugbè
  With dyntes wear beaten dowene.

For Wetharryngton my harte was wo,
  That ever he slayne shulde be;
For when both his leggis wear hewyne in to,
  Yet he knyled and fought on hys kne.

Ther was slayne with the dougheti Douglas
  Sir Hewe the Mongon-byrry,
Sir Davye Lwdale, that worthè was,
  His sistars son was he:

Sir Charles a Murrè, in that place,
  That never a foot wolde fle;
Sir Hewe Maxwell, a lorde he was,
  With the Duglas dyd he dey.

So on the morrowe the mayde them byears
  Off byrch, and hasell so 'gray;'
Many wedous with wepyng tears
  Cam to fach [48] ther makys a-way.

Tivydale may carpe [49] off care,
  Northombarlond may mayk grat mone,
For towe such captayns, as slayne wear thear,
  On the march perti shall never be none.

Wordeys commen to Edden burrowe,
  To Jamy the Skottishe kyng,
That dougheti Duglas, lyff-tenant of the Merches,
  He lay slean Chyviot with-in.

His handdes did he weal [50] and wryng,
  He sayd, Alas, and woe ys me!
Such another captayn Skotland within,
  He sayd, y-feth shud never be.

Worde ys commyn to lovly Londone
  Till the fourth Harry our kyng,
That lord Persè, leyff-tennante of the Merchis,
  He lay slayne Chyviat within.

God have merci on his soll, sayd kyng Harry,
  Good lord, yf thy will it be!

[48] Fetch. [49] Lament. [50] Wail.

I have a hondrith captayns in Ynglonde,
  As good as ever was hee:
But Persè, and I brook[51] my lyffe,
  Thy deth well quyte[52] shall be.

As our noble kyng made his a-vowe,
  Lyke a noble prince of renowen,
For the deth of the lord Persè,
  He dyd the battel of Hombyll-down:

Wher syx and thritte[53] Skottish knyghtes
  On a day wear beaten down:
Glendale glytteryde on ther armor bryght,
  Over castill, towar, and town.

This was the hontynge off the Cheviat;
  That tear begane this spurn:
Old men that knowen the grownde well yenoughe,
  Call it the Battell of Otterburn.

At Otterburn began this spurne
  Uppon a monnyn day:
Ther was the dougghtè Doglas slean,
  The Persè never went away

Ther was never a tym on the march partes
  Sen[54] the Doglas and the Persè met,
But yt was marvele, and the redde blude ronne not,
  As the reane doys in the stret.

Jhesue Christ our balys bete,
  And to the blys us brynge!
Thus was the hountynge of the Chevyat:
  God send us all good ending!

51 Enjoy. 52 Paid. 53 Thirty. 54 Since.

---

33. *The more modern Ballad of Chevy Chase.*

This form of the Ballad was probably written not much later than the time of Queen Elizabeth. It is the one criticised by Addison in the 'Spectator,' Nos. 70 and 74.

God prosper long our noble king,
  Our lives and safetyes all;
A woefull hunting once there did
  In Chevy-Chace befall;

To drive the deere with hound and horne,
  Erle Percy took his way;
The child may rue that is unborne,
  The hunting of that day.

The stout Erle of Northumberland
  A vow to God did make,
His pleasure in the Scottish woods
  Three summers days to take;

The cheefest harts in Chevy-Chace
  To kill and beare away.
These tydings to Erle Douglas came,
  In Scottland where he lay:

Who sent Erle Percy present word,
  He wold prevent his sport.
The English Erle, not fearing that,
  Did to the woods resort

With fifteen hundred bow-men bold;
  All chosen men of might,
Who knew full well in time of neede
  To ayme their shafts arright.

The gallant greyhounds swiftly ran,
  To chase the fallow deere:
On munday they began to hunt
  Ere day-light did appeare;

And long before high noone they had
  An hundred fat buckes slaine;
Then having dined, the drovyers went
  To rouze the deare againe.

The bow-men mustered on the hills,
  Well able to endure;
Theire backsides all, with speciall care,
  That day were guarded sure.

The hounds ran swiftly through the woods,
  The nimble deere to take,
That with their cryes the hills and dales
  An eccho shrill did make.

Lord Percy to the quarry went,
  To view the slaughter'd deere:
Quoth he, "Erle Douglas promised
  This day to meet me heere:

But if I thought he wold not come,
  Noe longer wold I stay."
With that, a brave younge gentleman
  Thus to the Erle did say:

"Loe, yonder doth Erle Douglas come,
  His men in armour bright;
Full twenty hundred Scottish speres
  All marching in our sight;

All men of pleasant Tivydale,
  Fast by the river Tweede:"
"O, cease your sports," Erle Percy said,
  "And take your bowes with speede:

And now with me, my countrymen,
  Your courage forth advance;
For there was never champion yett,
  In Scotland or in France,

That ever did on horsebacke come,
  But if my hap it were,
I durst encounter man for man,
  With him to break a spere."

Erle Douglas on his milke-white steede,
  Most like a baron bold,
Rode formost of his company,
  Whose armour shone like gold.

"Show me," sayd hee, "whose men you bee,
  That hunt soe boldly heere,
That, without my consent, doe chase
  And kill my fallow-deere."

The first man that did answer make,
  Was noble Percy hee;
Who sayd, "Wee list not to declare,
  Nor shew whose men wee bee:

Yet wee will spend our deerest blood,
  Thy cheefest harts to slay."
Then Douglas swore a solempne oathe,
  And thus in rage did say,

"Ere thus I will out-braved bee,
  One of us two shall dye:
I know thee well, an erle thou art;
  Lord Percy, soe am I.

But trust me, Percy, pittye it were,
  And great offence to kill
Any of these our guiltlesse men,
  For they have done no ill.

Let thou and I the battell trye,
  And set our men aside."
"Accurst bee he," Erle Percy sayd,
  By whome this is denyed."

Then stept a gallant squier forth,
  Witherington was his name,
Who said, "I wold not have it told
  To Henry our king for shame,

That ere my captaine fought on foote,
  And I stood looking on,
You bee two erles," sayd Witherington,
  "And I, a squier alone:

Ile doe the best that doe I may,
  While I have power to stand:
While I have power to weeld my sword,
  Ile fight with hart and hand."

Our English archers bent their bowes,
  Their harts were good and trew;
Att the first flight of arrowes sent,
  Full four-score Scots they slew.

[1] [Yet bides Earl Douglas on the bent,
  As Chieftain stout and good.
As valiant Captain, all unmov'd
  The shock he firmly stood.

His host he parted had in three,
  As Leader ware and try'd,
And soon his spearmen on their foes
  Bare down on every side.

Throughout the English archery
  They dealt full many a wound:
But still our valiant Englishmen
  All firmly kept their ground:

1 The four stanzas here inclosed in Brackets, which are borrowed chiefly from the ancient Copy, are offered to the Reader instead of the following lines, which occur in the Editor's folio MS.:—

To drive the deere with hound and horne,
  Douglas bade on the bent;
Two captaines moved with mickle might,
  Their speres to shivers went.

And throwing strait their bows away,
They grasp'd their swords so bright:
And now sharp blows, a heavy shower,
On shields and helmets light.]

They closed full fast on everye side,
Noe slacknes there was found;
And many a gallant gentleman
Lay gasping on the ground.

O Christ! it was a griefe to see,
And likewise for to heare,
The cries of men lying in their gore,
And scattered here and there.

At last these two stout erles did meet,
Like captaines of great might:
Like lyons wood, they layd on lode,
And made a cruell fight:

They fought untill they both did sweat,
With swords of tempered steele;
Until the blood, like drops of rain,
They trickling downe did feele.

"Yeeld thee, Lord Percy," Douglas sayd;
"In faith I will thee bringe,
Where thou shalt high advanced bee
By James our Scottish king:

Thy ransome I will freely give,
And this report of thee,
Thou art the most couragious knight,
That ever I did see."

"Noe, Douglas," quoth Erle Percy then,
"Thy proffer I doe scorne;
I will not yeelde to any Scott,
That ever yett was borne."

With that, there came an arrow keene
Out of an English bow,
Which struck Erle Douglas to the heart,
A deepe and deadlye blow:

Who never spake more words than these,
"Fight on, my merry men all;
For why, my life is at an end;
Lord Percy sees my fall."

Then leaving liffe, Erle Percy tooke
  The dead man by the hand;
And said, "Erle Douglas, for thy life
  Wold I had lost my land.

O Christ! my verry hart doth bleed
  With sorrow for thy sake;
For sure, a more redoubted knight
  Mischance cold never take."

A knight amongst the Scotts there was,
  Which saw Erle Douglas dye,
Who streight in wrath did vow revenge
  Upon the Lord Percye:

Sir Hugh Mountgomery was he call'd,
  Who, with a spere most bright,
Well-mounted on a gallant steed,
  Ran fiercely through the fight;

And past the English archers all,
  Without all dread or feare;
And through Earl Percyes body then
  He thrust his hatefull spere;

With such a vehement force and might
  He did his body gore,
The staff ran through the other side
  A large cloth-yard, and more.

So thus did both these nobles dye,
  Whose courage none could staine:
An English archer then perceiv'd
  The noble erle was slaine;

He had a bow bent in his hand,
  Made of a trusty tree;
An arrow of a cloth-yard long
  Up to the head drew hee:

Against Sir Hugh Mountgomerye,
  So right the shaft he sett,
The grey goose-winge that was thereon,
  In his harts bloode was wett.

This fight did last from breake of day,
  Till setting of the sun;
For when they rung the evening-bell,
  The battel scarce was done.

With stout Erle Percy, there was slaine,
  Sir John of Egerton,
Sir Robert Ratcliff, and Sir John,
  Sir James that bold barròn:

And with Sir George and stout Sir James,
  Both knights of good account,
Good Sir Ralph Raby there was slaine
  Whose prowesse did surmount.

For Witherington needs must I wayle,
  As one in doleful dumpes;
For when his leggs were smitten off,
  He fought upon his stumpes.

And with Erle Douglas, there was slaine
  Sir Hugh Mountgomerye,
Sir Charles Murray, that from the field
  One foote wold never flee.

Sir Charles Murray, of Ratcliff, too,
  His sisters sonne was hee;
Sir David Lamb, so well esteem'd,
  Yet saved cold not bee.

And the Lord Maxwell in like case
  Did with Erle Douglas dye:
Of twenty hundred Scottish speres,
  Scarce fifty-five did flye.

Of fifteen hundred Englishmen,
  Went home but fifty-three;
The rest were slaine in Chevy-Chase,
  Under the greene woode tree.

Next day did many widdowes come,
  Their husbands to bewayle;
They washt their wounds in brinish teares,
  But all wold not prevayle.

Theyr bodyes bathed in purple gore,
  They bare with them away:
They kist them dead a thousand times,
  Ere they were cladd in clay.

The newes was brought to Eddenborrow,
  Where Scottlands king did raigne,
That brave Erle Douglas suddenlye
  Was with an arrow slaine:

"O, heavy newes," King James did say,
  "Scottland may witnesse bee,
I have not any captaine more
  Of such account as hee."

Like tydings to King Henry came,
  Within as short a space,
That Percy of Northumberland
  Was slaine at Chevy-Chese:

"Now, God be with him," said our king,
  "Sith it will noe better bee;
I trust I have, within my realme,
  Five hundred as good as hee:

Yett shall not Scotts, nor Scotland say,
  But I will vengeance take:
I'll be revenged on them all,
  For brave Erle Percyes sake."

This vow full well the king perform'd
  After, at Humbledowne;
In one day, fifty knights were slayne,
  With lords of great renowne:

And of the rest, of small account,
  Did many thousands dye:
Thus endeth the hunting of Chevy-Chase,
  Made by the Erle Percy.

God save our king, and bless this land
  With plentye, joy, and peace;
And grant henceforth, that foule debate
  'Twixt noblemen may cease.

---

34. *Sir Patrick Spens.*

The king sits in Dunfermline town,
  Drinking the blude-red wine;
"O whare[1] will I get a skeely[2] skipper,
  To sail this new ship o' mine!" —

O up and spake an eldern knight,
  Sat at the king's right knee, —
"Sir Patrick Spens is the best sailor,
  That ever sail'd the sea."

1 Where. 2 Skilful.

Our king has written a braid letter,
  And seal'd it with his hand,
And sent it to Sir Patrick Spens,
  Was walking on the strand.

"To Noroway, to Noroway,
  To Noroway o'er the faem;
The king's daughter of Noroway,
  'Tis thou maun bring her hame."—

The first word that Sir Patrick read.
  Sae loud loud laughed he:
The neist[3] word that Sir Patrick read,
  The tear blinded his e'e.

"O wha is this has done this deed,
  And tauld the king o' me,
To send us out, at this time of the year,
  To sail upon the sea?

Be it wind, be it weet, be it hail, be it sleet,
  Our ship must sail the faem;
The king's daughter of Noroway,
  'Tis we must fetch her hame."

They hoysed their sails on Monenday morn,
  Wi' a' the speed they may;
They ha'e landed in Noroway,
  Upon a Wodensday.

They hadna been a week, a week,
  In Noroway, but twae,
When that the lords o' Noroway
  Began aloud to say—

"Ye Scottishmen spend a' our king's goud,
  And a' our queenis fee."—
"Ye lie, ye lie, ye liars loud!
  Fu' loud I hear ye lie;

For I ha'e brought as much white monie,
  As gane my men and me,
And I ha'e brought a half-fou[4] of gude red goud,
  Out o'er the sea wi' me.

Make ready, make ready, my merry-men a'!
  Our gude ship sails the morn."—
"Now, ever alake, my master dear,
  I fear a deadly storm!

3 Next. 4 Bushel.

I saw the new moon, late yestreen,
  Wi' the auld moon in her arm;
And, if we gang to sea, master,
  I fear we'll come to harm."

They hadna sail'd a league, a league,
  A league but barely three,
When the lift grew dark, and the wind blew loud,
  And gurly grew the sea.

The ankers brak, and the topmasts lap,
  It was sic a deadly storm;
And the waves cam o'er the broken ship,
  Till a' her sides were torn.

"O where will I get a gude sailor,
  To take my helm in hand,
Til I get up to the tall top-mast,
  To see if I can spy land?"

"O here am I, a sailor gude,
  To take the helm in hand,
Till you go up to the tall top-mast;
  But I fear you'll ne'er spy land." —

He hadna gane a step, a step,
  A step but barely ane,
When a boult flew out of our goodly ship,
  And the salt sea it came in.

"Gae, fetch a web o' the silken claith,
  Another o' the twine,
And wap them into our ship's side,
  And let nae the sea come in."

They fetch'd a web o' the silken claith,
  Another o' the twine,
And they wapp'd them round that gude ship's side,
  But still the sea came in.

O laith, laith, were our gude Scots lords
  To weet[5] their cork-heel'd shoon![6]
But lang or[7] a' the play was play'd,
  They wat their hats aboon.[8]

Any mony was the feather bed,
  That floated on the faem;
And mony was the gude lord's son,
  That never mair cam hame.

[5] To wet. [6] Shoes. [7] Before. [8] Above.

The ladyes wrang their fingers white,
  The maidens tore their hair,
A' for the sake of their true loves, —
  For them they'll see nae mair.

O lang, lang, may the ladyes sit,
  Wi' their fans into their hand,
Before they see Sir Patrick Spens
  Come sailing to the strand!

And lang, lang, may the maidens sit,
  With their goud kaims[9] in their hair,
A' waiting for their ain dear loves!
  For them they'll see nae mair.

Half owre, half owre to Aberdour,
  'Tis fifty fathoms deep,
And there lies gude Sir Patrick Spens,
  Wi' the Scots lords at his feet!

[9] Combs.

---

35. *The Two Corbies.*

There were two corbies sat on a tree,
Large and black as black might be;
And one the other gan say,
Where shall we go and dine to-day?
Shall we go dine by the wild salt sea?
Shall we go dine 'neath the greenwood tree?

As I sat on the deep sea sand,
I saw a fair ship nigh at land,
I waved my wings, I bent my beak,
The ship sunk, and I heard a shriek;
There they lie, one, two, and three,
I shall dine by the wild salt sea.

Come, I will show ye a sweeter sight,
A lonesome glen, and a new-slain knight;
His blood yet on the grass is hot,
His sword half-drawn, his shafts unshot,
And no one kens that he lies there,
But his hawk, his hound, and his lady fair.

His hound is to the hunting gane,
His hawk to fetch the wild fowl hame,

His lady's away with another mate,
So we shall make our dinner sweet;
Our dinner's sure, our feasting free,
Come, and dine by the greenwood tree.

Ye shalt sit on his white hause-bane,[1]
I will pick out his bony blue een;
Ye'll take a tress of his yellow hair,
To theak yere nest when it grows bare;
The gowden[2] down on his young chin
Will do to sewe my young ones in.

O, cauld and bare will his bed be,
When winter storms sing in the tree;
At his head a turf, at his feet a stone,
He will sleep nor hear the maiden's moan;
O'er his white bones the birds shall fly,
The wild deer bound, and foxes cry.

1 The neck-bone — a phrase for the neck. 2 Golden.

CHAPTER IV.

THE ELIZABETHAN POETS (INCLUDING THE REIGN OF JAMES I.).

---

36. GEORGE GASCOIGNE. 1530–1577. (Manual, p. 71.)

THE VANITY OF THE BEAUTIFUL.

They course the glass, and let it take no rest;
They pass and spy who gazeth on their face;
They darkly ask whose beauty seemeth best;
They hark and mark who marketh most their grace;
They stay their steps, and stalk a stately pace;
They jealous are of every sight they see;
They strive to seem, but never care to be.

* * * * * *

What grudge and grief our joys may then suppress,
To see our hairs, which yellow were as gold,
Now grey as glass; to feel and find them less;
To scrape the bald skull which was wont to hold
Our lovely locks with curling sticks controul'd;
To look in glass, and spy Sir Wrinkle's chair
Set fast on fronts which erst were sleek and fair.

* * * * * *

---

37. THOMAS SACKVILLE, LORD BUCKHURST. (Manual, p. 72.)

ALLEGORICAL PERSONAGES IN HELL.

From the Induction to the Mirrour for Magistrates.

And first within the porch and jaws of Hell
Sat deep Remorse of Conscience, all besprent
With tears; and to herself oft would she tell
Her wretchedness, and cursing never stent[1]

1 Stopped.

To sob and sigh; but ever thus lament
With thoughtful care, as she that all in vain
Would wear and waste continually in pain.

Her eyes unstedfast, rolling here and there,
Whirl'd on each place, as place that vengeance brought,
So was her mind continually in fear,
Toss'd and tormented by the tedious thought
Of those detested crimes which she had wrought:
With dreadful cheer and looks thrown to the sky,
Wishing for death, *and yet she could not die.*

Next saw we Dread, all trembling how he shook,
With foot uncertain proffer'd here and there;
Benumm'd of speech, and with a ghastly look,
Search'd every place, all pale and dead for fear;
His cap upborn with staring of his hair,
Stoyn'd[2] and amazed at his shade for dread,
And fearing greater dangers than was need.

And next within the entry of this lake
Sat fell Revenge, gnashing her teeth for ire,
Devising means how she may vengeance take,
Never in rest till she have her desire;
But frets within so far forth with the fire
Of wreaking flames, that now determines she
To die by death, or veng'd by death to be.

When fell Revenge, with bloody foul pretence,
Had shewed herself, as next in order set,
With trembling limbs we softly parted thence,
Till in our eyes another sight we met,
When from my heart a sigh forthwith I fet,[3]
Rewing, alas! upon the woeful plight
Of Misery, that next appear'd in sight.

His face was lean and some-deal pin'd away,
And eke his handes consumed to the bone,
But what his body was I cannot say;
For on his carcass raiment had he none,
Save clouts and patches, pieced one by one;
With staff in hand, and scrip on shoulders cast,
His chief defence against the winters blast.

His food, for most, was wild fruits of the tree;
Unless sometime some crumbs fell to his share,
Which in his wallet long, God wot, kept he,

2 Astonished. 3 Fetched.

As on the which full daintily would he fare.
His drink the running stream, his cup the bare
Of his palm closed, his bed the hard çold ground;
To this poor life was Misery ybound.

---

38. Edmund Spenser, 1553–1599. (Manual, pp. 73–78.)

From the Faëry Queen.

Una and the Lion. Book I., Canto 3.

One day, nigh wearie of the yrkesome way,
From her unhastie beast she did alight;
And on the grasse her dainty limbs did lay
In secrete shadow, far from all mens sight;
From her fayre head her fillet she undight,[1]
And layd her stole aside: Her angels face,
As the great eye of heaven, shyned bright,
And make a sunshine in the shady place;
Did ever mortall eye behold such heavenly grace?

It fortuned, out of the thickest wood
A ramping lyon rushed suddeinly,
Hunting full greedy after salvage blood:
Soone as the royall Virgin he did spy,
With gaping mouth at her ran greedily,
To have attonce devourd her tender corse:
But to the pray when as he drew more ny,
His bloody rage aswaged with remorse,
And, with the sight amazd, forgat his furious forse.

Instead thereof he kist her wearie feet,
And lickt her lilly hands with fawning tong;
As[2] he her wronged innocence did weet.[3]
O how can beautie maister the most strong,
And simple truth subdue avenging wrong!
Whose yielded pryde and proud submission,
Still dreading death, when she had marked long,
Her hart gan melt in great compassion;
And drizling teares did shed for pure affection.

"The lyon, lord of everie beast in field,"
Quoth she, "his princely puissance doth abate,
And mightie proud to humble weake does yield,
Forgetfull of the hungry rage, which late
Him prickt, in pittie of my sad estate:—
But he, my lyon, and my noble lord,

1 Undight—took off. 2 As—as if. 3 Weet—understand.

How does he find in cruell hart to hate
Her, that him lov'd, and ever most adord
As the god of my life? why hath he me abhord?"

Redounding[4] tears did choke th' end of her plaint,
Which softly echoed from the neighbour wood;
And, sad to see her sorrowfull constraint,
The kingly beast upon her gazing stood;
With pittie calmd, downe fell his angry mood,
At last, in close hart shutting up her payne,
Arose the Virgin borne of heavenly brood,
And to her snowy palfrey got agayne,
To seek her strayed Champion if she might attayne.

The lyon would not leave her desolate,
But with her went along, as a strong gard
Of her chast person, and a faythfull mate
Of her sad troubles and misfortunes hard:
Still, when she slept, he kept both watch and ward;
And, when she wakt, he wayted diligent,
With humble service to her will prepard:
From her fayre eyes he took commandément,
And ever by her lookes conceived her intent.

4 Redounding—flowing.

---

39. Prince Arthur. Book I., Canto 7.

At last she chaunced by good hap to meet
A goodly Knight, faire marching by the way,
Together with his Squyre, arrayed meet:
His glitterand armour shined far away,
Like glauncing light of Phœbus brightest ray;
From top to toe no place appeared bare,
That deadly dint of steele endanger may:
Athwart his brest a bauldrick brave he ware,
That shind, like twinkling stars, with stones most pretious rare:

And, in the midst thereof, one pretious stone
Of wondrous worth, and eke of wondrous mights,
Shapt like a Ladies head, exceeding shone,
Like Hesperus emongst the lesser lights,
And strove for to amaze the weaker sights:
Thereby his mortall blade full comely hong
In yvory sheath, ycarv'd with curious slights,[1]
Whose hilts were burnisht gold; and handle strong
Of mother perle; and buckled with a golden tong.

1 Slights—devices.

His haughtie helmet, horrid all with gold,
Both glorious brightnesse and great terrour bredd:
For all the crest a dragon did enfold
With greedie pawes, and over all did spredd
His golden winges; his dreadfull hideous hedd,
Close couched on the bever, seemd to throw
From flaming mouth bright sparckles fiery redd,
That suddeine horrour to faint hartes did show;
And scaly tayle was stretcht adowne his back full low.

---

40. Belphœbe. Book II., Canto 3.

Her face so faire, as flesh it seemed not,
But hevenly pourtraict of bright angels hew,
Cleare as the skye, withouten blame or blot,
Through goodly mixture of complexions dew;
And in her cheekes the vermeill red did shew
Like roses in a bed of lillies shed,
The which ambrosiall odours from them threw,
And gazers sence with double pleasure fed,
Hable to heale the sicke and to revive the ded.

In her faire eyes two living lamps did flame,
Kindled above at th' Hevenly Makers light,
And darted fyrie beames out of the same,
So passing persant,[1] and so wondrous bright,
That quite bereavd the rash beholders sight;
In them the blinded god his lustful fyre
To kindle oft assayd, but had no might;
For, with dredd maiestie and awfull yre
She broke his wanton darts, and quenched bace desyre.

Her yvoire forhead, full of bountie brave,
Like a broad table did itselfe dispred,
For Love his loftie triumphes to engrave,
And write the battailes of his great godhed:
All good and honour might therein be red;
For there their dwelling was. And, when she spake,
Sweete wordes, like dropping honny, she did shed;
And twixt the perles and rubins[2] softly brake
A silver sound, that heavenly musicke seemd to make.

1 Persant—piercing. 2 Rubins—rubies.

---

41. The Care of Angels over Men. Book II., Canto 8.

And is there care in heaven? And is there love
In heavenly spirits to these creatures bace,
That may compassion of their evils move?

There is: — else much more wretched were the cace
Of men then beasts: But O! th' exceeding grace
Of Highest God that loves his creatures so,
And all his workes with mercy doth embrace,
That blessed Angels he sends to and fro,
To serve to wicked man, to serve his wicked foe!

How oft do they their silver bowers leave
To come to succour us that succour want!
How oft do they with golden pineons cleave
The flitting[1] skyes, like flying pursuivant,
Against fowle feendes to ayd us militant!
They for us fight, they watch and dewly ward,
And their bright squadrons round about us plant;
And all for love and nothing for reward:
O, why should Hevenly God to men have such regard!

1 Yielding.

---

42. THE SEASONS. Book VII., Canto 7.

So forth issew'd the Seasons of the yeare:
First, lusty Spring all dight[1] in leaves of flowres
That freshly budded and new bloosmes did beare,
In which a thousand birds had built their bowres,
That sweetly sung to call forth paramours;
And in his hand a iavelin he did beare,
And on his head (as fit for warlike stoures[2])
A guilt[3] engraven morion[4] he did weare;
That as some did him love, so others did him feare.

Then came the iolly Sommer, being dight
In a thin silken cassock colored greene,
That was unlyned all, to be more light:
And on his head a girlond well beseene
He wore, from which, as he had chauffed[5] been,
The sweat did drop; and in his hand he bore
A bowe and shaftes, as he in forrest greene
Had hunted late the libbard[6] or the bore,
And now would bathe his limbes with labor heated sore.

Then came the Autumne all in yellow clad,
As though he ioyed in his plentious store,
Laden with fruits that made him laugh, full glad
That he had banisht hunger, which to-fore
Had by the belly oft him pinched sore:

1 Adorned. 2 Encounters. 3 Gilded. 4 Helmet. 5 Chafed, heated. 6 Leopard.

Upon his head a wreath, that was enrold
With ears of corne of every sort, he bore;
And in his hand a sickle he did holde,
To reape the ripened fruits the which the earth had yold.[7]

Lastly, came Winter cloathed all in frize,
Chattering his teeth for cold that did him chill;
Whilst on his hoary beard his breath did freese,
And the dull drops, that from his purpled bill[8]
As from a limbeck[9] did adown distill:
In his right hand a tipped staffe he held,
With which his feeble steps he stayed still;
For he was faint with cold, and weak with eld;[10]
That scarce his loosed limbes he able was to weld.[11]

7 Yielded. 8 Nose. 9 Retort. 10 Old age. 11 Wield, move.

---

43. Sonnet LXXXVIII.

Like as the culver,[1] on the bared bough,
Sits mourning for the absence of her mate,
And in her songs sends many a wishful vow
For his return that seems to linger late;
So I alone, now left disconsolate,
Mourn to myself the absence of my love,
And, wand'ring here and there, all desolate,
Seek with my plaints to match that mournful dove:
Ne joy of aught that under heaven doth hove,[2]
Can comfort me but her own joyous sight,
Whose sweet aspect both God and man can move,
In her unspotted pleasures to delight.
Dark is my day, whiles her fair light I miss,
And dead my life, that wants such lively bliss.

1 Dove. 2 Hover, or stay.

---

44. Sir Philip Sydney. 1554–1586. (Manual, p. 78.)

For Extracts from his Prose Works, see next Chapter.

Sonnet to Sleep.

Come, sleep, O sleep, the certain knot of peace,
The baiting-place of wit, the balm of woe,
The poor man's wealth, the prisoner's release,
Th' indifferent judge between the high and low!
With shield of proof, shield me from out the prease
Of those fierce darts Despair at me doth throw:

O make me in those civil wars to cease!
I will good tribute pay if thou do so.
Take thou of me smooth pillows, sweetest bed
A chamber deaf to noise, and blind to light;
A rosy garland, and a weary head;
And if these things, as being thine by right,
Move not thy heavy grace, thou shalt in me,
Livelier than elsewhere Stella's image see.

SIR WALTER RALEIGH. 1552-1618.

For Extracts from his Prose Works, see next Chapter.

45. A PASSIONATE SHEPHERD TO HIS LOVE.

By Christopher Marlowe.

Come live with me and be my love,
And we will all the pleasures prove
That grove or valley, hill or field,
Or wood and steepy mountain yield.

Where we will sit on rising rocks,
And see the shepherds feed their flocks
By shallow rivers, to whose falls
Melodious birds sing madrigals.

Pleased will I make thee beds of roses,
And twine a thousand fragrant posies;
A cap of flowers and rural kirtle,
Embroider'd all with leaves of myrtle.

A jaunty gown of finest wool,
Which from our pretty lambs we pull;
And shoes lined choicely for the cold,
With buckles of the purest gold:

A belt of straw and ivy buds,
With coral clasps and amber studs;
If these, these pleasures can thee move,
Come live with me, and be my love.

THE NYMPH'S REPLY TO THE PASSIONATE SHEPHERD.

By Sir Walter Raleigh.

If all the world and Love were young,
And truth on every Shepherd's tongue,
These pleasures might my passion move
To live with thee, and be thy love.

But fading flowers in every field,
To winter floods their treasures yield;
A honey'd tongue — a heart of gall,
Is Fancy's spring, but Sorrow's fall.

Thy gown, thy shoes, thy beds of roses,
Thy cap, thy kirtle, and thy posies,
Are all soon wither'd, broke, forgotten,
In Folly ripe, in Reason rotten.

Thy belt of straw, and ivy-buds,
Thy coral clasps, and amber studs,
Can me with no enticements move,
To live with thee, and be thy love.

But could Youth last, could Love still breed;
Had joys no date, had Age no need;
Then those delights my mind might move
To live with thee, and be thy love.

The Soul's Errand.

This beautiful poem appeared anonymously in "Davison's Poetical Rhapsody," in 1608. It has been ascribed to Sir Walter Raleigh by many able critics.

Go, Soul, the Body's guest,
  Upon a thankless errand;
Fear not to touch the best;
  The truth shall be thy warrant.
Go, since I needs must die,
And give them all the lie.

Go, tell the Court it glows,
  And shines like painted wood;
Go, tell the Church it shows
  What's good, but does no good.
If Court and Church reply,
Give Court and Church the lie.

Tell Potentates, they live
  Acting, but oh! their actions
Not loved, unless they give;
  Nor strong, but by their factions.
If Potentates reply,
Give Potentates the lie.

Tell men of high condition,
  That rule affairs of state,

Their purpose is ambition;
  Their practice only hate.
And if they do reply,
Then give them all the lie.

Tell those that brave it most,
  They beg for more by spending,
Who, in their greatest cost,
  Seek nothing but commending.
And if they make reply,
Spare not to give the lie.

Tell Zeal it lacks devotion;
  Tell Love it is but lust;
Tell Time it is but motion;
  Tell Flesh it is but dust:
And wish them not reply,
For thou must give the lie.

Tell Age it daily wasteth;
  Tell Honor how it alters;
Tell Beauty that it blasteth;
  Tell Favor that she falters:
And as they do reply,
Give every one the lie.

Tell Wit how much it wrangles
  In fickle points of niceness;
Tell Wisdom she entangles
  Herself in over-wiseness:
And if they do reply,
Then give them both the lie.

Tell Physic of her boldness;
  Tell Skill it is pretension;
Tell Charity of coldness;
  Tell Law it is contention:
And if they yield reply,
Then give them still the lie.

Tell Fortune of her blindness;
  Tell Nature of decay;
Tell Friendship of unkindness;
  Tell Justice of delay:
And if they do reply,
Then give them all the lie.

Tell Arts they have no soundness,
  But vary by esteeming;

Tell Schools they lack profoundness,
  And stand too much on seeming.
If Arts and Schools reply,
Give Arts and Schools the lie.

Tell Faith it's fled the city;
  Tell how the Country erreth;
Tell Manhood, shakes off pity;
  Tell Virtue, least preferreth.
And if they do reply,
Spare not to give the lie.

So, when thou hast, as I
  Commanded thee, done blabbing;
Although to give the lie
  Deserves no less than stabbing;
Yet stab at thee who will,
No stab the Soul can kill.

---

46. Samuel Daniel. 1562–1619. (Manual, p. 80.)

Richard II. on the Morning before his Murder.

From the Third Book of the Civil Wars.

The morning of that day which was his last
After a weary rest, rising to pain,
Out at a little grate his eyes he cast
Upon those bordering hills and open plain,
Where others' liberty makes him complain
The more his own, and grieves his soul the more,
Conferring [1] captive crowns with freedom poor.

O happy man, saith he, that lo I see,
Grazing his cattle in those pleasant fields,
If he but knew his good. How blessed he
That feels not what affliction greatness yields!
Other than what he is he would not be,
Nor change his state with him that sceptre wields.
Thine, thine is that true life: that is to live
To rest secure, and not rise up to grieve.

Thou sitt'st at home safe by thy quiet fire,
And hear'st of others' harms, but fearest none,
And there thou tell'st of kings, and who aspire,
Who fall, who rise, who triumph, who do moan.

1 Comparing.

Perhaps thou talk'st of me, and dost inquire
Of my restraint, why here I live alone,
And pitiest this my miserable fall;
For pity must have part—envy not all.

Thrice happy you that look as from the shore,
And have no venture in the wreck you see;
No interest, no occasion to deplore
Other men's travels, while yourselves sit free.
How much doth your sweet rest make us the more
To see our misery and what we be:
Whose blinded greatness, ever in turmoil,
Still seeking happy life, makes life a toil.

MICHAEL DRAYTON. 1563–1631. (Manual, pp. 80, 81.)

From the Nymphidia.

47. PIGWIGGEN ARMING.

And quickly arms him for the field,
A little cockle-shell his shield,
Which he could very bravely wield,
        Yet could it not be pierced:
His spear a bent both stiff and strong,
And well near of two inches long:
The pile was of a horse-fly's tongue,
        Whose sharpness nought reversed.

And puts him on a coat of mail,
Which was of a fish's scale,
That when his foe should him assail,
        No point should be prevailing.
His rapier was a hornet's sting,
It was a very dangerous thing;
For if he chanc'd to hurt the king,
        It would be long in healing.

His helmet was a beetle's head,
Most horrible and full of dread,
That able was to strike one dead,
        Yet it did well become him:
And for a plume, a horse's hair,
Which being tossed by the air,
Had force to strike his foe with fear,
        And turn his weapon from him.

Himself he on an earwig set,
Yet scarce he on his back could get,
So oft and high he did curvet,
Ere he himself could settle:
He made him turn, and stop, and bound,
To gallop, and to trot the round,
He scarce could stand on any ground,
He was so full of mettle.

---

48. From the Poly-olbion.—Song XIII.

When Phœbus lifts his head out of the winter's wave,
No sooner doth the earth her flowery bosom brave,
At such time as the year brings on the pleasant spring,
But hunts-up, to the morn, the feath'red sylvans sing:
And in the lower grove, as on the rising knoll,
Upon the highest spray of every mounting pole,
Those quiristers are percht with many a speckled breast.
Then from her burnisht gate the goodly glitt'ring east
Gilds every lofty top, which late the humorous night
Bespangled had with pearl, to please the morning's sight:
On which the mirthful quires, with their clear open throats,
Unto the joyful morn so strain their warbling notes,
That hills and vallies ring, and even the echoing air
Seems all compos'd of sounds, about them everywhere.

---

49. Sir John Davies. 1570–1626. (Manual, p. 81.)

From the Nosce Teipsum.

As spiders, touch'd, seek their web's inmost part;
As bees, in storms, back to their hives return;
As blood in danger gathers to the heart;
As men seek towns when foes the country burn:

If aught can teach us aught, affliction's looks
(Making us pry into ourselves so near),
Teach us to know ourselves beyond all books,
Or all the learned schools that ever were.

She within lists my ranging mind hath brought,
That now beyond myself I will not go:
Myself am centre of my circling thought:
Only myself I study, learn, and know.

I know my body's of so frail a kind,
As force without, fevers within can kill;
I know the heavenly nature of my mind,
But 'tis corrupted both in wit and will.

I know my soul hath power to know all things,
Yet is she blind and ignorant in all;
I know I'm one of nature's little kings,
Yet to the least and vilest things am thrall.

I know my life's a pain, and but a span;
I know my sense is mock'd in every thing:
And, to conclude, I know myself a man,
Which is a proud and yet a wretched thing.

---

50. JOHN DONNE. 1573–1631. (Manual, p. 82.)

FROM HIS ELEGIES.

Language, thou art too narrow and too weak
To ease us now; great sorrows cannot speak.
If we could sigh our accents, and weep words,
Grief wears, and lessens, that tears breath affords.
Sad hearts, the less they seem, the more they are;
So guiltiest men stand mutest at the bar;
Not that they know not, feel not their estate,
But extreme sense hath made them desperate.
Sorrow! to whom we owe all that we be,
Tyrant in the fifth and greatest monarchy,
Was't that she did possess all hearts before
Thou hast killed her, to make thy empire more?
Knew'st thou some would, that knew her not, lament,
As in a deluge perish the innocent?
Was't not enough to have that palace won,
But thou must raze it too, that was undone?
Had'st thou stay'd there, and looked out at her eyes,
All had adored thee, that now from thee flies;
For they let out more light than they took in;
They told not when, but did the day begin.
She was too sapphirine and clear for thee;
Clay, flint, and jet now thy fit dwellings be.
Alas, she was too pure, but not too weak;
Whoe'er saw crystal ordnance but would break?
And, if we be thy conquest, by her fall
Thou hast lost thy end; in her we perish all:
Or, if we live, we live but to rebel,
That know her better now, who knew her well.

51. Bishop Hall. 1574–1656. (Manual, p. 83.)

From the Satires.

Seest thou how gaily my young master goes,
Vaunting himself upon his rising toes;
And pranks his hand upon his dagger's side;
And picks his glutted teeth since late noon-tide?
'Tis Ruffio: Trow'st thou where he din'd to-day?
In sooth I saw him sit with Duke Humfrày.[1]
Many good welcomes, and much gratis cheer,
Keeps he for every straggling cavalier.
And open house, haunted with great resort;
Long service mixt with musical disport.
Many fair yonker with a feather'd crest,
Chooses much rather be his shot-free guest,
To fare so freely with so little cost,
Than stake his twelvepence to a meaner host.
Hadst thou not told me, I should surely say
He touch'd no meat of all this live-long day,
For sure methought, yet that was but a guess,
His eyes seem'd sunk for very hollowness,
But could he have (as I did it mistake)
So little in his purse, so much upon his back?
So nothing in his maw? yet seemeth by his belt,
That his gaunt gut no too much stuffing felt.
Seest thou how side it hangs beneath his hip?
Hunger and heavy iron makes girdles slip.
Yet for all that, how stiffly struts he by,
All trapped in the new-found bravery.
The nuns of new-won Calais his bonnet lent,
In lieu of their so kind a conquerment.
What needed he fetch that from farthest Spain,
His grandame could have lent with lesser pain?
Though he perhaps ne'er pass'd the English shore,
Yet fain would counted be a conqueror.
His hair, French-like, stares on his frighted head,
One lock amazon-like dishevelled,
As if he meant to wear a native cord,
If chance his fates should him that bane afford.
All British bare upon the bristled skin,
Close notched is his beard both lip and chin;
His linen collar labyrinthian set,

1 The phrase of dining with Duke Humphry arose from St. Paul's being the general resort of the loungers of those days, many of whom, like Hall's gallant, were glad to beguile the thoughts of dinner with a walk in the middle aisle, where there was a tomb, by mistake supposed to be that of Humphry, Duke of Gloucester.

Whose thousand double turnings never met:
His sleeves half hid with elbow pinionings,
As if he meant to fly with linen wings.
But when I look, and cast mine eyes below,
What monster meets mine eyes in human shew?
So slender waist with such an abbot's loin,
Did never sober nature sure conjoin.
Lik'st a straw scare-crow in the new-sown field,
Rear'd on some stick, the tender corn to shield.
Or if that semblance suit not every deal,
Like a broad shake-fork with a slender steel.
* * * * * *

---

52. ROBERT SOUTHWELL. 1560–1595. (Manual, p. 85.)

TIMES GO BY TURNS.

The loppèd tree in time may grow again,
  Most naked plants renew both fruit and flower;
The sorriest wight may find release of pain,
  The driest soil suck in some moistening shower:
Time goes by turns, and chances change by course,
From foul to fair, from better hap to worse.

The sea of fortune doth not ever flow,
  She draws her favors to the lowest ebb:
Her tides have equal times to come and go;
  Her loom doth weave the fine and coarsest web:
No joy so great but runneth to an end,
No hap so hard but may in fine amend.

Not always fall of leaf, nor ever spring;
  Not endless night, yet not eternal day:
The saddest birds a season find to sing,
  The roughest storm a calm may soon allay.
Thus, with succeeding turns, God tempereth all,
That man may hope to rise, yet fear to fall.

A chance may win that by mischance was lost;
  That net that holds no great, takes little fish;
In some things all, in all things none are cross'd;
  Few all they need, but none have all they wish.
Unmingled joys here to no man befall;
Who least, hath some; who most, hath never all.

53. Giles Fletcher. (Manual, p. 84.)

From Christ's Victory in Heaven.

Justice Addressing the Creator.

Upon two stony tables, spread before her,
She leant her bosom, more than stony hard;
There slept th' impartial judge and strict restorer
Of wrong or right, with pain or with reward;
There hung the score of all our debts — the card
Where good, and bad, and life, and death, were painted:
Was never heart of mortal so untainted,
But, when that scroll was read, with thousand terrors fainted.

Witness the thunder that Mount Sinai heard,
When all the hill with fiery clouds did flame,
And wand'ring Israel, with the sight afear'd,
Blinded with seeing, durst not touch the same,
But like a wood of shaking leaves became.
On this dead Justice, she, the living law,
Bowing herself with a majestic awe,
All heaven, to hear her speech, did into silence draw.

* * * * *

---

54. William Drummond. 1585–1649. (Manual, p. 87.)

On Sleep.

Sleep, Silence' child, sweet father of soft rest,
  Prince, whose approach peace to all mortals brings,
  Indifferent host to shepherds and to kings,
Sole comforter of minds with grief oppress'd;
  Lo, by thy charming rod, all breathing things
Lie slumbering, with forgetfulness possess'd,
  And yet o'er me to spread thy drowsy wings
Thou spar'st, alas! who cannot be thy guest.
  Since I am thine, O come, but with that face
To inward light, which thou art wont to show,
With feigned solace ease a true-felt woe;
  Or if, deaf god, thou do deny that grace,
Come as thou wilt, and what thou wilt bequeath;
I long to kiss the image of my death.

CHAPTER V.

THE NEW PHILOSOPHY AND PROSE LITERATURE IN THE REIGNS OF ELIZABETH AND JAMES I.

---

55. SIR PHILIP SYDNEY. 1554–1586. (Manual, p. 78.)

(For his Poetry, see page 79.)

From the Defence of Poesy.

IN PRAISE OF POETRY.

Now therein — (that is to say, the power of at once teaching and enticing to do well) — now therein, of all sciences — I speak still of human and according to human conceit — is our poet the monarch. For he doth not only show the way, but giveth so sweet a prospect into the way, as will entice any man to enter into it. Nay, he doth, as if your journey should lie through a fair vineyard, at the very first give you a cluster of grapes, that, full of that taste, you may long to pass further. He beginneth not with obscure definitions, which must blur the margent with interpretations, and load the memory with doubtfulness; but he cometh to you with words set in delightful proportion, either accompanied with, or prepared for, the well-enchanting skill of music; and with a tale, forsooth, he cometh unto you with a tale which holdeth children from play, and old men from the chimney-corner; and pretending no more, doth intend the winning of the mind from wickedness to virtue, even as the child is often brought to take most wholesome things, by hiding them in such other as have a pleasant taste. For even those hard-hearted evil men, who think virtue a school name, and know no other good but *indulgere genio*, and therefore despise the austere admonitions of the philosopher, and feel not the inward reason they stand upon, yet will be content to be delighted; which is all the good-fellow poet seems to promise; and so steal to see the form of goodness — which, seen, they cannot but love ere themselves be aware, as if they had taken a medicine of cherries. By these, therefore, examples and reasons, I think it may be manifest that the poet, with that same hand of delight, doth draw the mind more effectually than any other art doth. And so a conclusion not unfitly ensues, that as virtue is the most excellent resting-place for all worldly learning to make an end of, so poetry, being the most familiar to teach it, and most princely to move towards it, in the most excellent work is the most excellent workman.

Since, then, poetry is of all human learning the most ancient, and of most fatherly antiquity, as from whence other learnings have taken their beginnings; — Since it is so universal that no learned nation doth despise it, no barbarous nation is without it; — Since both Roman and Greek gave such divine names unto it, the one of prophesying, the other of making; and that, indeed, that name of making is fit for it, considering that whereas all other arts retain themselves within their subject, and receive, as it were, their being from it, — the poet, only, bringeth his own stuff, and doth not learn a conceit out of the matter, but maketh matter for a conceit; — Since, neither his description nor end containing any evil, the thing described cannot be evil; — Since his effects be so good as to teach goodness and delight the learners of it; — Since therein (namely, in moral doctrine, the chief of all knowledge) he doth not only far pass the historian, but, for instructing, is well nigh comparable to the philosopher, and for moving, leaveth him behind; — Since the Holy Scripture (wherein there is no uncleanness) hath whole parts in it poetical, and that even our Saviour Christ vouchsafed to use the flowers of it; — Since all its kinds are not only in their united forms, but in their severed dissections fully commendable: — I think — (*and I think I think rightly*) — the laurel crown appointed for triumphant captains, doth worthily, of all other learnings, honor the poet's triumph.

---

56. Sir Walter Raleigh. 1552–1618. (Manual, p. 89.)

(For his Poetry, see page 80.)

From the History of the World.

The Folly of Ambition and Power of Death.

If we seek a reason of the succession and continuance of boundless ambition in mortal men, we may add, that the kings and princes of the world have always laid before them the actions, but not the ends of those great ones which preceded them. They are always transported with the glory of the one, but they never mind the misery of the other, till they find the experience in themselves. They neglect the advice of God while they enjoy life, or hope it, but they follow the counsel of death upon his first approach. It is he that puts into man all the wisdom of the world without speaking a word, which God, with all the words of his law, promises, or threats, doth not infuse. Death, which hateth and destroyeth man, is believed; God, which hath made him and loves him, is always deferred. "I have considered," saith Solomon, "all the works that are under the sun, and, behold, all is vanity and vexation of spirit;" but who believes it, till death tells it us? It was death, which, opening the conscience of

Charles V., made him enjoin his son Philip to restore Navarre, and King Francis I. of France to command that justice should be done upon the murderers of the Protestants in Merindol and Cabrieres, which till then he neglected. It is therefore death alone that can suddenly make man to know himself. He tells the proud and insolent that they are but abjects, and humbles them at the instant, makes them cry, complain, and repent, yea, even to hate their forepassed happiness. He takes the account of the rich, and proves him a beggar, a naked beggar, which hath interest in nothing but in the gravel that fills his mouth. He holds a glass before the eyes of the most beautiful, and makes them see therein their deformity and rottenness, and they acknowledge it.

O eloquent, just, and mighty death! whom none could advise, thou hast persuaded; what none could advise, thou hast persuaded; what none hath dared, thou hast done; and whom all the world hath flattered, thou only hast cast out of the world and despised; thou hast drawn together all the far-stretched greatness, all the pride, cruelty, and ambition of man, and covered it all over with these two narrow words, *hic jacet!*

---

57. RICHARD HOOKER. 1553–1598. (Manual, p. 91.)

From the Ecclesiastical Polity.

THE NECESSITY AND MAJESTY OF LAW.

The stateliness of houses, the goodliness of trees, when we behold them, delighteth the eye; but that foundation which beareth up the one, that root which ministreth unto the other nourishment and life, is in the bosom of the earth concealed; and if there be occasion at any time to search into it, such labor is then more necessary than pleasant, both to them which undertake it, and for the lookers on. In like manner, the use and benefit of good laws all that live under them may enjoy with delight and comfort, albeit the grounds and first original causes from whence they have sprung be unknown, as to the greatest part of men they are.

Since the time that God did first proclaim the edicts of his law upon the world, heaven and earth have hearkened unto his voice, and their labor hath been to do his will. *He made a law for the rain;* he gave his *decree unto the sea, that the waters should not pass his commandment.* Now, if nature should intermit her course, and leave altogether, though it were for a while, the observation of her own laws; if those principal and mother elements of the world, whereof all things in this lower world are made, should lose the qualities which now they have; if the frame of that heavenly arch erected over our heads should loosen and dissolve itself; if celestial spheres should forget their wonted motions, and by irregular volubility turn themselves any way as it might happen; if the prince of the lights of heaven, which now, as a giant, doth run his unwearied course, should, as it were, through a languishing faintness, begin to stand and to rest himself; if the moon should wander from her beaten way, the times and seasons of the year blend themselves by disordered and confused mixture, the winds breathe out their last gasp, the clouds yield no rain, the earth be defected of heavenly influence, the fruits of the earth pine away, as children at the withered breasts of their mother, no longer able to yield them relief; what would become of man himself, whom these things do now all serve? See we not plainly, that obedience of creatures unto the law of nature is the stay of the whole world?

Of Law there can be no less acknowledged than that her seat is the bosom of God; her voice the harmony of the world. All things in heaven and earth do her homage; the very least as feeling her care, and the greatest as not exempted from her power. Both angels and men, and creatures of what condition soever, though each in different sort and manner, yet all with uniform consent, admiring her as the mother of their peace and joy.

FRANCIS BACON. 1561–1626. (Manual, pp. 92–104.)

From the Essays.

58. OF STUDIES.

Studies serve for delight, for ornament, and for ability. Their chief use for delight, is in privateness and retiring; for ornament, is in discourse; and for ability, is in the judgment and disposition of business; for expert men can execute, and perhaps judge of particulars, one by one: but the general counsels, and the plots and marshalling of affairs come best from those that are learned. To spend too much time in studies, is sloth; to use them too much for ornament, is affectation; to make judgment wholly by their rules, is the humor of a scholar: they perfect nature, and are perfected by experience: for natural abilities are like natural plants, that need pruning by study; and studies themselves do give forth directions too much at large, except they be bounded in by experience. Crafty men contemn studies, simple men admire them, and wise men use them; for they teach not their own use; but that is a wisdom without them, and above them, won by observation. Read not to contradict and confute, nor to believe and take for granted, nor to find talk and discourse, but to weigh and consider. Some books are to be tasted, others to be swallowed, and some few to be chewed and digested; that is, some books are to be read only in parts; others to be read, but not curiously; and some few to be read wholly, and with diligence and attention. Some books also may be read by deputy, and extracts made of them by others; but that would be only in the less important arguments and the meaner sort of books; else distilled books are, like common distilled waters, flashy things. Reading maketh a full man; conference a ready man; and writing an exact man; and, therefore, if a man write little, he had need have a great memory; if he confer little, he had need have a present wit; and if he read little, he had need have much cunning, to seem to know that he doth not. Histories make men wise; poets, witty; the mathematics, subtile; natural philosophy, deep; moral, grave; logic and rhetoric, able to contend.

---

59. Of Adversity.

But to speak in a mean, the virtue of prosperity is temperance, the virtue of adversity is fortitude, which in morals is the more heroical virtue. Prosperity is the blessing of the Old Testament, adversity is the blessing of the New, which carrieth the greater benediction, and the clearer revelation of God's favor. Yet even in the Old Testament, if you listen to David's harp, you shall hear as many hearse-like airs as carols; and the pencil of the Holy Ghost hath labored more in describing the afflictions of Job than the felicities of Solomon. Prosperity is not without many fears and distastes; and adversity is not without comforts and hopes. We see in needle-works and embroideries, it is more pleasing to have a lively work upon a sad and solemn ground, than to have a dark and melancholy work upon a lightsome ground: judge, therefore, of the pleasure of the heart by the pleasure of the eye. Certainly virtue is like precious odors, most fragrant when they are incensed, or crushed: for prosperity doth best discover vice, but adversity doth best discover virtue.

---

60. Of Discourse.

Some in their discourse desire rather commendation of wit, in being able to hold all arguments, than of judgment, in discerning what is true; as if it were a praise to know what might be said, and not what should be thought. Some have certain common-places and themes, wherein they are good, and want variety: which kind of poverty is for the most part tedious, and, when it is once perceived, ridiculous. The honorablest part of talk is to give the occasion; and again to moderate and pass to somewhat else, for then a man leads the dance. It is good in discourse, and speech of conversation, to vary and intermingle speech of the present occasion with arguments, tales with reasons, asking of questions with telling of opinions, and jest with earnest; for it is a dull thing to tire, and as we say now, to jade anything too far. As for jest, there be certain things which ought to be privileged from it; namely, religion, matters of state, great persons, any man's present business of importance, and any case that deserveth pity; yet there be some that think their wits have been asleep, except they dart out somewhat that is piquant, and to the quick; that is a vein which would be bridled. And, generally, men ought to find the difference between saltness and bitterness. Certainly, he that hath a satirical vein, as he maketh others afraid of his wit, so he had need be afraid of others' memory. He that questioneth much, shall learn much, and content much; but especially if he apply his questions to the skill of the persons whom he asketh; for he shall give them occasion to please themselves in speaking, and himself shall continually gather knowledge; but let his questions not be troublesome, for that is fit for a poser; and let him be sure to leave other men their turns to speak: nay, if there be any that would reign and take up all the time, let him find means to take them off, and to bring others on, as musicians use to do with those that dance too long galliards. If you dissemble sometimes your knowledge of that you are thought to know, you shall be thought, another time, to know that you know not. Speech of a man's self ought to be seldom, and well-chosen.

---

61. Atheism Ignoble.

I had rather believe all the fables in the Legend, and the Talmud, and the Alcoran, than that this universal frame is without a Mind. And therefore God never wrought miracle to convince Atheism; because his ordinary works convince it. It is true that a little philosophy inclineth man's mind to Atheism; but depth in philosophy bringeth men's minds about to Religion: for, while the mind of man looketh upon second causes scattered, it may sometimes rest in them, and go no farther; but, when it beholdeth the chain of them, confederate and linked together, it must needs fly to Providence and Deity. The Scripture saith, "The fool hath said in his heart, there is no God;" it is not said, "The fool hath thought in his heart:" so as he rather saith it by rote to himself, as that he would have, than that he can thoroughly believe it or be persuaded of it. For none deny there is a God, but those for whom it maketh that there were no God. But the great Atheists, indeed, are hypocrites, which are ever handling holy things, but without feeling. They that deny a God, destroy man's nobility: for certainly man is of kin to the beasts by his body: and, if he be not akin to God by his spirit, he is a base and ignoble creature. It destroys likewise magnanimity and the raising of human nature: for, take an example of a dog, and mark what a generosity and courage he will put on when he finds himself maintained by a man, who to him is instead of a God or Melior Natura: which courage is manifestly such, as that creature, without that confidence of a better nature than his own, could never attain. So man, when he resteth and assureth himself upon Divine protection and favour, gathereth a force and faith, which human nature in itself could not obtain. Therefore, as Atheism is in all respects hateful, so in this, that it depriveth human nature of the means to exalt itself above human frailty.

From the Introduction to "The Great Restauration."

62. Design of the Inductive Philosophy.

The sixth and last part of our work, to which all the rest are subservient, is to lay down that philosophy which shall flow from the just, pure, and strict inquiry hitherto proposed. But to perfect this, is beyond both our abilities and our hopes, yet we shall lay the foundations of it, and recommend the superstructure to posterity. We design no contemptible beginning to the work; and anticipate that the fortune of mankind will lead it to such a termination as is not possible for the present race of men to conceive. The point in view is not only the contemplative happiness, but the whole fortunes, and affairs, and power, and works, of men. For man being the minister and interpreter of nature, acts and understands so far as he has observed of the order, the works, and mind, of nature, and can proceed no farther; for no power is able to loose or break the chain of causes, nor is nature to be conquered but by submission: whence those twin intentions, human knowledge and human power, are really coincident; and the greatest hinderance to works, is the ignorance of causes.

The capital precept for the whole undertaking is this, that the eye of the mind be never taken off from things themselves, but receive their images truly as they are. And God forbid that ever we should offer the dreams of fancy for a model of the world; but rather in his kindness vouchsafe to us the means of writing a revelation and true vision of the traces and moulds of the Creator in his creatures.

May thou, therefore, O Father, who gavest the light of vision as the first fruit of creation, and who hast spread over the fall of man the light of thy understanding as the accomplishment of thy works, guard and direct this work, which, issuing from thy goodness, seeks in return thy glory! When thou hadst surveyed the works which thy hands had wrought, all seemed good in thy sight, and thou restedst. But when man turned to the works of his hands, he found all vanity and vexation of spirit, and experienced no rest. If, however, we labour in thy works, thou wilt make us to partake of thy vision and sabbath; we, therefore, humbly beseech thee to strengthen our purpose, that thou mayst be willing to endow thy family of mankind with new gifts, through our hands; and the hands of those in whom thou shalt implant the same spirit.

From the Advancement of Learning. Book I. § 6.

63. The Benefit of Learning.

If it be objected, that learning takes up much time, which might be better employed, I answer that the most active or busy men have many vacant hours, while they expect the tides and returns of business; and then the question is, how those spaces of leisure shall be filled up, whether with pleasure or study? Demosthenes being taunted by Æschines, a man of pleasure, that his speeches smelt of the lamp, very pertly retorted, "There is great difference between the objects which you and I pursue by lamp-light." No fear, therefore, that learning should displace business, for it rather keeps and defends the mind against idleness and pleasure, which might otherwise enter to the prejudice both of business and learning.

For the allegation that learning should undermine the reverence due to laws and government, it is a mere calumny, without shadow of truth; for to say that blind custom of obedience should be a safer obligation than duty, taught and understood, is to say that a blind man may tread surer by a guide than a man with his eyes open can by a light. And, doubtless, learning makes the mind gentle and pliable to government, whereas ignorance renders it churlish and mutinous; and it is always found that the most barbarous, rude, and ignorant times have been most tumultuous, changeable, and seditious.

From the Advancement of Learning. Close of Book I.

64. The Dignity of Literature.

To conclude, the dignity and excellence of knowledge and learning is what human nature most aspires to for the securing of immortality, which is also endeavoured after by raising and ennobling families, by buildings, foundations, and monuments of fame, and is in effect the bent of all other human desires. But we see how much more durable the monuments of genius and learning are than those of the hand. The verses of Homer have continued above five and twenty hundred years without loss, in which time numberless palaces, temples, castles, and cities have been demolished and are fallen to ruin. It is impossible to have the true pictures or statues of Cyrus, Alexander, Cæsar, or the great personages of much later date, for the originals cannot last, and the copies must lose life and truth; but the images of men's knowledge remain in books, exempt from the injuries of time, and capable of perpetual renovation. Nor are these properly called images; because they generate still, and sow their seed in the minds of others, so as to cause infinite actions and opinions in succeeding ages. If, therefore, the invention of a ship was thought so noble, which carries commodities from place to place and consociateth the remotest regions in participation of their fruits, how much more are letters to be valued, which, like ships, pass through the vast ocean of time, and convey knowledge and inventions to the remotest ages? Nay, some of the philosophers who were most immersed in the senses, and denied the immortality of the soul, yet allowed that whatever motions the spirit of man could perform without the organs of the body might remain after death, which are only those of the understanding and not of the affections, so immortal and incorruptible a thing did knowledge appear to them. And thus having endeavored to do justice to the cause of knowledge, divine and human, we shall leave Wisdom to be justified of her children.

Advancement of Learning. Book III., chap. II.

65. VINDICATION OF NATURAL THEOLOGY.

Divine philosophy is a science, or rather the rudiments of a science, derivable from God by the light of nature, and the contemplation of his creatures; so that with regard to its object, it is truly divine; but with regard to its acquirement, natural. The bounds of this knowledge extend to the confutation of atheism, and the ascertaining the laws of nature, but not to the establishing of religion. And, therefore, God never wrought a miracle to convert an atheist, because the light of nature is sufficient to demonstrate a deity; but miracles were designed for the conversion of the idolatrous and superstitious, who acknowledged a God, but erred in their worship of him — the light of nature being unable to declare the will of God, or assign the just form of worshipping him. For as the power and skill of a workman are seen in his works, but not his person, so the works of God express the wisdom and omnipotence of the Creator, without the least representation of his image. And in this particular, the opinion of the heathens differed from the sacred verity, as supposing the world to be the image of God, and man a little image of the world. The Scripture never gives the world that honour, but calls it the work of his hands; making only man the image of God. And, therefore, the being of a God, that he governs the world, that he is all-powerful, wise, prescient, good, a just rewarder and punisher, and to be adored, may be shown and enforced from his works; and many other wonderful secrets, with regard to his attributes, and much more as to his dispensation and government over the universe, may also be solidly deduced, and made appear from the same. And this subject has been usefully treated by several.

ROBERT BURTON. 1576–1640. (Manual, p. 104.)

From the Anatomy of Melancholy.

66. PHILAUTIA, OR SELF-LOVE, A CAUSE OF MELANCHOLY.

Now the common cause of this mischief ariseth from ourselves or others: we are active and passive. It proceeds inwardly from ourselves, as we are active causes, from an overweening conceit we have of our good parts, own worth (which indeed is no worth), our bounty, favour, grace, valour, strength, wealth, patience, meekness, hospitality, beauty, temperance, gentry, knowledge, wit, science, art, learning, our excellent gifts and fortunes, for which (Narcissus-like) we admire, flatter, and applaud ourselves, and think all the world esteems so of us; and, as deformed women easily believe those that tell them they be fair, we are too credulous of our own good parts and praises, too well persuaded of ourselves. We brag and vendicate our own works, and scorn all others in respect of us. . . . That which Tully writ to Atticus long since, is still in force — *there was never yet true poet or orator, that thought any other better than himself.* And such, for the most part, are your princes, potentates, great philosophers, historiographers, authors of sects or heresies, and all our great scholars, as Hierom defines: *a natural philosopher is glory's creature, and a very slave of rumour, fame, and popular opinion:* and, though they write *de contemptu gloriæ*, yet (as he observes) they will put their names to their books.

---

67. The Power of Love.

Bocace hath a pleasant tale to this purpose, which he borrowed from the Greeks, and which Beroaldus hath turned into Latine, Bebelius into verse, of Cymon and Iphigenia. This Cymon was a fool, a proper man of person, and the governor of Cyprus son, but a very ass; insomuch that his father being ashamed of him, sent him to a farm-house he had in the country, to be brought up; where by chance, as his manner was, walking alone, he espied a gallant young gentlewoman named Iphigenia, a burgomaster's daughter of Cyprus, with her maid, by a brook side, in a little thicket. *When Cymon saw her, he stood leaning on his staffe, gaping on her immovable, and in a maze:* at last he fell so far in love with the glorious object, that he began to rouze himself up; to bethink what he was; would needs follow her to the city, and for her sake began to be civil, to learn to sing and dance, to play on instruments, and got all those gentleman-like qualities and complements, in a short space, which his friends were most glad of. In brief, he became from an idiot and a clown, to be one of the most complete gentlemen in Cyprus; did many valorous exploits, and all for the love of Mistress Iphigenia. In a word I may say this much of them all, let them be never so clownish, rude and horrid, Grobians and sluts, if once they be in love, they will be most neat and spruce. 'Tis all their study, all their business, how to wear their clothes neat, to be polite and terse, and to set out themselves. No sooner doth a young man see his sweetheart coming, but he smugs up himself, pulls up his cloak, now fallen about his shoulders, ties his garters, points, sets his band, cuffs, slicks his hair, twires his beard, &c

68. Lord Herbert of Cherbury. 1581–1648. (Manual, p. 105.)

From Life of Henry VIII.

Sir Thomas More, Lord Chancellor of England, after divers suits to be discharged of his place — which he had held two years and a half — did at length by the king's good leave resign it. The example whereof being rare, will give me occasion to speak more particularly of him. Sir Thomas More, a person of sharp wit, and endued besides with excellent parts of learning (as his works may testify), was yet (out of I know not what natural facetiousness) given so much to jesting, that it detracted no little from the gravity and importance of his place, which, though generally noted and disliked, I do not think was enough to make him give it over in that merriment we shall find anon, or retire to a private life. Neither can I believe him so much addicted to his private opinions as to detest all other governments but his own Utopia, so that it is probable some vehement desire to follow his book, or secret offence taken against some person or matter — among which perchance the king's new intended marriage, or the like, might be accounted — occasioned this strange counsel; though, yet, I find no reason pretended for it but infirmity and want of health. Our king hereupon taking the seal, and giving it, together with the order of knighthood, to Thomas Audley, Speaker of the Lower House, Sir Thomas More, without acquainting any body with what he had done, repairs to his family at Chelsea, where after a mass celebrated, the next day, in the church, he comes to his lady's pew, with his hat in his hand — an office formerly done by one of his gentlemen — and says: "Madam, my lord is gone." But she thinking this at first to be but one of his jests, was little moved, till he told her sadly, he had given up the great seal; whereupon she speaking some passionate words he called his daughters then present to see if they could not spy some fault about their mother's dressing; but they after search saying they could find none, he replied: "Do you not perceive that your mother's nose standeth somewhat awry?" — of which jeer the provoked lady was so sensible, that she went from him in a rage. Shortly after, he acquainted his servants with what he had done, dismissing them also to the attendance of some other great personages, to whom he had recommended them. For his fool, he bestowed him on the lord-mayor during his office, and afterwards on his successors in that charge. And now coming to himself, he began to consider how much he had left, and finding that it was not above one hundred pounds yearly in lands, besides some money, he advised with his daughters how to live together. But the grieved gentlewomen — who knew not what to reply, or indeed how to take these jests — remained astonished, he says: "We will begin with the slender diet of the students of the law, and if that will not hold out, we will take such commons as they have at Oxford; which, yet, if our purse will not stretch to maintain, for our last refuge we will go a begging, and at every man's door sing together a Salve Regina to get alms." But these jests were thought to have in them more levity than to be taken everywhere for current; he might have quitted his dignity without using such sarcasms, and betaken himself to a more retired and quiet life without making them or himself contemptible. And certainly whatsoever he intended hereby, his family so little understood his meaning, that they needed some more serious instructions. So that I cannot persuade myself for all this talk, that so excellent a person would omit at fit times to give his family that sober account of his relinquishing this place, which I find he did to the Archbishop Warham, Erasmus, and others.

---

69. THOMAS HOBBES. 1588–1679. (Manual, p. 105.)

From the Treatise on Human Nature.

EMULATION AND ENVY.

Emulation is *grief* arising from seeing *one's self exceeded* or excelled by his *concurrent*, together with *hope* to *equal* or exceed him in time to come, by his own ability. But, *envy* is the same *grief* joined with *pleasure* conceived in the imagination of some *ill* fortune that may befall him.

LAUGHTER.

There is a passion that hath *no name;* but the sign of it is that distortion of the countenance which we call *laughter*, which is always *joy:* but what joy, what we think, and wherein we triumph when we laugh, is not hitherto declared by any. That it consisteth in *wit*, or, as they call it, in the *jest*, experience *confuteth:* for men laugh at mischances and indecencies, wherein there lieth no wit nor jest at all. And forasmuch as the same thing is no more ridiculous when it groweth stale or usual, whatsoever it be that moveth laughter, it must be *new* and *unexpected.* Men laugh often, especially such as are greedy of applause from everything they do well, at their *own* actions performed never so little beyond their own expectations; as also at their own *jests:* and in this case it is manifest, that the passion of laughter proceedeth from a *sudden conception* of some *ability* in himself that laugheth. Also men laugh at the *infirmities* of others, by comparison wherewith their own abilities are set off and illustrated. Also men laugh at *jests*, the *wit* whereof always consisteth in the elegant *discovering* and conveying to our minds some *absurdity* of *another:* and in this case also the passion of laughter proceedeth from the *sudden* imagination of our own odds and eminency: for what is else the recommending of ourselves to our own good opinion, by comparison with another man's infirmity or absurdity? For when a jest is broken upon ourselves, or friends of whose dishonour we participate, we never laugh thereat. I may therefore conclude, that the passion of laughter is nothing else but *sudden glory* arising from some sudden *conception* of some *eminency* in ourselves, by *comparison* with the *infirmity* of others, or with our own formerly: for men laugh at the follies of themselves past, when they come suddenly to remembrance, except they bring with them any present dishonour. It is no wonder therefore that men take heinously to be laughed at or derided, that is, triumphed over. Laughter *without offence*, must be at *absurdities* and infirmities *abstracted* from persons, and when all the company may laugh together: for laughing to one's self putteth all the rest into jealousy and examination of themselves. Besides, it is vain glory, and an argument of little worth, to think the infirmity of another, sufficient matter for his triumph.

WEEPING.

The passion opposite hereunto, whose signs are another distortion of the face with tears, called *weeping*, is the *sudden falling out with* ourselves, or sudden conception of defect; and therefore *children* weep often; for seeing they think that every thing ought to be given them which they desire, of necessity every repulse must be a check of their expectation, and puts them in mind of their too much weakness to make themselves masters of all they look for. For the same cause *women* are more apt to weep than men, as being not only more accustomed to have their wills, but also to measure their powers by the power and love of others that protect them. Men are apt to weep that prosecute revenge, when the revenge is suddenly stopped or frustrated by the repentance of their adversary; and such are the tears of *reconciliation*. Also revengeful men are subject to this passion upon the beholding those men they pity, and suddenly remember they cannot help. Other weeping in men proceedeth for the most part from the same cause it proceedeth from in women and children.

ADMIRATION AND CURIOSITY.

Forasmuch as all *knowledge* beginneth from *experience*, therefore also *new experience* is the beginning of *new knowledge*, and the increase of experience the beginning of the increase of knowledge. Whatsoever therefore happeneth new to a man, giveth him matter of *hope* of *knowing* somewhat that he knew *not before*. And this hope and expectation of future knowledge from anything that happeneth new and strange, is that passion which we commonly call *admiration;* and the same considered as appetite, is called *curiosity*, which is appetite of knowledge. As in the discerning of faculties, *man leaveth* all community with *beasts* at the faculty of *imposing names;* so also doth he surmount their nature at this *passion* of *curiosity*. For when a beast seeth anything new and strange to him, he considereth it so far only as to discern whether it be likely to serve his turn, or hurt him, and accordingly approacheth nearer to it, or fleeth from it: whereas man, who in most events remembereth in what manner they were caused and begun, looketh for the cause and beginning of everything that ariseth new unto him. And from this passion of admiration and curiosity, have arisen not only the invention of names, but also supposition of such causes of all things as they thought might produce them. And from this beginning is derived all *philosophy;* as *astronomy* from the admiration of the course of heaven; *natural philosophy* from the strange effects of the elements and other bodies. And from the degrees of curiosity, proceed also the degrees of knowledge amongst men: for, to a man in the chase of riches or authority (which in respect of knowledge are but sensuality), it is a diversity of little pleasure, whether it be the motion of the sun or the earth that maketh the day, or to enter into other contemplations of any strange accident, otherwise than whether it conduce or not to the end he pursueth. Because *curiosity* is *delight,* therefore also *novelty* is so, but especially that novelty from which a man conceiveth an *opinion* true or false of *bettering* his own estate; for, in such case, they stand affected with the hope that all gamesters have while the cards are shuffling.

CHAPTER VI.

THE DAWN OF THE DRAMA.

CHRISTOPHER MARLOWE. 1563?–1593. (Manual, p. 126.)

70. FROM EDWARD II.

Murder of the King.

Berkley Castle. The King is left alone with Lightborn, a murderer.

Edw. Who's there? what light is that? wherefore comest thou?
Light. To comfort you, and bring you joyful news.
Edw. Small comfort finds poor Edward in thy looks.
Villain, I know thou comest to murder me.
Light. To murder you, my most gracious lord?
Far is it from my heart to do you harm.
The queen sent me to see how you were used,
For she relents at this your misery:
And what eyes can refrain from shedding tears,
To see a king in this most piteous state?
Edw. Weep'st thou already? list awhile to me,
And then thy heart, were it as Gurney's[1] is,
Or as Matrevis,[1] hewn from the Caucasus,
Yet will it melt, ere I have done my tale.
This dungeon where they keep me is a sink
Wherein the filth of all the castle falls.
Light. O villains!
Edw. And there, in mire and puddle have I stood
This ten days' space; and lest that I should sleep,
One plays continually upon a drum.
They give me bread and water, being a king;
So that, for want of sleep and sustenance,
My mind 's distemper'd, and my body 's numb'd,
And whether I have limbs or no, I know not.
O, would my blood drop out from every vein,
As doth this water from my tatter'd robes!
Tell Isabel the queen, I look'd not thus,
When for her sake I ran at tilt in France,
And there unhorsed the duke of Cleremont.

1 His keepers.

Light. O, speak no more, my lord! this breaks my heart.
Lie on this bed, and rest yourself awhile.
Edw. These looks of thine can harbour naught but death:
I see my tragedy written in thy brows.
Yet stay awhile, forbear thy bloody hand,
And let me see the stroke before it comes,
That even then when I shall lose my life,
My mind may be more steadfast on my God.
Light. What means your highness to mistrust me thus?
Edw. What mean'st thou to dissemble with me thus?
Light. These hands were never stained with innocent blood,
Nor shall they now be tainted with a king's.
Edw. Forgive my thought, for having such a thought.
One jewel have I left, receive thou this.
Still fear I, and I know not what 's the cause,
But every joint shakes as I give it thee.
O, if thou harbour'st murder in thy heart,
Let this gift change thy mind, and save thy soul.
Know that I am a king: O, at that name
I feel a hell of grief. Where is my crown?
Gone, gone, and do I still remain alive?
Light. You 're overwatch'd, my lord; lie down and rest.
Edw. But that grief keeps me waking, I should sleep;
For not these ten days have these eyelids closed.
Now as I speak they fall, and yet with fear
Open again. O, wherefore sitt'st thou here?
Light. If you mistrust me, I 'll be gone, my lord.
Edw. No, no, for if thou mean'st to murder me,
Thou wilt return again; and therefore stay.
Light. He sleeps.
Edw. O, let me not die; yet stay, O, stay awhile.
Light. How now, my lord?
Edw. Something still buzzeth in mine ears,
And tells me if I sleep I never wake;
This fear is that which makes me tremble thus.
And therefore tell me, wherefore art thou come?
Light. To rid thee of thy life; Matrevis, come.
Edw. I am too weak and feeble to resist:
Assist me, sweet God, and receive my soul.

---

71. FROM DOCTOR FAUSTUS.

FAUSTUS *alone. The clock strikes eleven.*

Faust. O Faustus,
Now hast thou but one bare hour to live,
And then thou must be damn'd perpetually.

Stand still, you ever-moving spheres of heaven,
That time may cease and midnight never come.
Fair nature's Eye, rise, rise again, and make
Perpetual day: or let this hour be but
A year, a month, a week, a natural day,
That Faustus may repent and save his soul.
O lente lente currite noctis equi.
The stars move still, time runs, the clock will strike,
The Devil will come, and Faustus must be damn'd.
O, I will leap to heaven: who pulls me down?
See where Christ's blood streams in the firmament:
One drop of blood will save me: O, my Christ,
Rend not my heart for naming of my Christ.
Yet will I call on him: O spare me, Lucifer.
Where is it now? 'tis gone;
And see, a threatening arm, and angry brow.
Mountains and hills, come, come, and fall on me,
And hide me from the heavy wrath of heaven.
No? then will I headlong run into the earth:
Gape earth. O no, it will not harbour me.
You stars that reign'd at my nativity,
Whose influence have allotted death and hell,
Now draw up Faustus like a foggy mist
Into the entrails of yon labouring cloud;
That when you vomit forth into the air,
My limbs may issue from your smoky mouths,
But let my soul mount and ascend to heaven.

The watch strikes.

O half the hour is past: 'twill all be past anon.
O if my soul must suffer for my sin,
Impose some end to my incessant pain.
Let Faustus live in hell a thousand years,
A hundred thousand, and at the last be saved:
No end is limited to damnéd souls.
Why wert thou not a creature wanting soul?
Or why is this immortal that thou hast?
O Pythgoras' Metempsychosis! were that true,
This soul should fly from me, and I be changed
Into some brutish beast.
All beasts are happy, for when they die,
Their souls are soon dissolved in elements:
But mine must live still to be plagued in hell.
Curst be the parents that engender'd me:
No, Faustus, curse thyself, curse Lucifer,
That hath deprived thee of the joys of heaven.

The clock strikes twelve.

It strikes, it strikes; now, body, turn to air,
Or Lucifer will bear thee quick to hell.
O soul, be changed into small water drops,
And fall into the ocean; ne'er be found.

Thunder, and enter the devils.

O mercy, Heaven! look not so fierce on me.
Adders and serpents, let me breathe awhile:
Ugly hell gape not; come not, Lucifer:
I 'll burn my books: O, Mephostophilis!

* * * * * * * *

CHAPTER VII.

SHAKSPEARE, 1564–1616.

(Manual, pp. 128–151.)

A.—COMEDIES.

From As You Like It.

72. *The World a Stage.*—Act II. Sc. 7.

Jaques. All the world 's a stage,
And all the men and women merely players:
They have their exits, and their entrances;
And one man in his time plays many parts,
His acts being seven ages. At first, the infant,
Mewling and puking in the nurse's arms:
Then, the whining school-boy, with his satchel,
And shining morning face, creeping like snail
Unwillingly to school: and then, the lover,
Sighing like furnace, with a woful ballad
Made to his mistress' eyebrow: then, a soldier,
Full of strange oaths, and bearded like the pard,
Jealous in honor, sudden and quick in quarrel,
Seeking the bubble reputation
E'en in the cannon's mouth: and then, the justice,
In fair round belly, with good capon lined,
With eyes severe, and beard of formal cut,
Full of wise saws and modern instances,
And so he plays his part: The sixth age shifts
Into the lean and slippered pantaloon;
With spectacles on nose, and pouch on side;
His youthful hose well saved, a world too wide
For his shrunk shank; and his big, manly voice,
Turning again toward childish treble, pipes
And whistles in his sound: Last scene of all,
That ends this strange, eventful history,
Is second childishness, and mere oblivion;
Sans teeth, sans eyes, sans taste, sans everything.

From MEASURE FOR MEASURE.

73. *The Abuse of Authority.* — Act II. Sc. 2.

Isabella. O, it is excellent
To have a giant's strength; but it is tyrannous
To use it like a giant.
* * * * * * *
Could great men thunder
As Jove himself does, Jove would ne'er be quiet,
For every pelting, petty officer
Would use his heaven for thunder: nothing but thunder.
Merciful Heaven!
Thou rather, with thy sharp and sulphurous bolt,
Splitt'st the unwedgeable and gnarlèd oak,
Than the soft myrtle: But man, proud man,
Dressed in a little brief authority;
Most ignorant of what he 's most assured, —
His glassy essence, — like an angry ape,
Plays such fantastic tricks before high Heaven,
As make the angels weep: who, with our spleens,
Would all themselves laugh mortal.

From THE MERCHANT OF VENICE.

74. *Mercy.* — Act IV. Sc. 1.

Portia. The quality of mercy is not strained;
It droppeth as the gentle rain from heaven
Upon the place beneath: it is twice blessed;
It blesseth him that gives and him that takes:
'T is mightiest in the mightiest; it becomes
The thronèd monarch better than his crown;
His sceptre shows the force of temporal power,
The attribute to awe and majesty,
Wherein doth sit the dread and fear of kings;
But mercy is above this sceptred sway;
It is enthronèd in the hearts of kings,
It is an attribute to God himself;
And earthly power doth then show likest God's
When mercy seasons justice. Therefore, Jew,
Though justice be thy plea, consider this —
That in the course of justice, none of us
Should see salvation: we do pray for mercy;
And that same prayer doth teach us all to render
The deeds of mercy.

From A MIDSUMMER NIGHT'S DREAM.

75. *Oberon's Vision.* — Act II. Sc. 2.

Obe. My gentle Puck, come hither: Thou remember'st
Since once I sat upon a promontory,
And heard a mermaid, on a dolphin's back,
Uttering such dulcet and harmonious breath,
That the rude sea grew civil at her song;
And certain stars shot madly from their spheres,
To hear the sea-maid's music.
Puck. I remember.
Obe. That very time I saw (but thou couldst not),
Flying between the cold moon and the earth,
Cupid all armed; a certain aim he took
At a fair vestal, thronéd by the west;
And loosed his love-shaft smartly from his bow,
As it should pierce a hundred thousand hearts:
But I might see young Cupid's fiery shaft
Quenched in the chaste beams of the watery moon;
And the imperial votaress passed on,
In maiden meditation, fancy-free.[1]
Yet marked I where the bolt of Cupid fell:
It fell upon a little western flower, —
Before, milk-white; now, purple with love's wound, —
And maidens call it love-in-idleness.
Fetch me that flower; the herb I showed thee once;
The juice of it on sleeping eyelids laid,
Will make or man or woman madly dote
Upon the next live creature that it sees.
Fetch me this herb: and be thou here again,
Ere the leviathan can swim a league.
Puck. I'll put a girdle round about the earth
In forty minutes.

1 Queen Elizabeth.

---

76. *The Power of Imagination.* — Act. V. Sc. 1.

Theseus. I never may believe
These antique fables, nor these fairy toys.
Lovers and madmen have such seething brains,
Such shaping fantasies, that apprehend
More than cool reason ever comprehends.
The lunatic, the lover, and the poet,
Are of imagination all compact:
One sees more devils than vast hell can hold —

That is the madman: the lover, all as frantic,
Sees Helen's beauty in a brow of Egypt:
The poet's eye, in a fine frenzy rolling,
Doth glance from heaven to earth, from earth to heaven,
And, as imagination bodies forth
The forms of things unknown, the poet's pen
Turns them to shapes, and gives to airy nothing
A local habitation and a name.
Such tricks hath strong imagination;
That, if it would but apprehend some joy,
It comprehends some bringer of that joy;
Or, in the night, imagining some fear,
How easy is a bush supposed a bear!

B.—HISTORICAL PLAYS.

From KING JOHN.

77. *Lamentation of Constance.* — Act III. Sc. 4.

K. Philip. Bind up your hairs.
Const. Yes, that I will; And wherefore will I do it?
I tore them from their bonds; and cried aloud,
O that these hands could so redeem my son,
As they have given these hairs their liberty!
But now I envy at their liberty,
And will again commit them to their bonds
Because my poor child is a prisoner.
And, father cardinal, I have heard you say,
That we shall see and know our friends in heaven:
If that be true, I shall see my boy again;
For, since the birth of Cain, the first male child,
To him that did but yesterday suspire,
There was not such a gracious creature born.
But now will canker sorrow eat my bud,
And chase the native beauty from his cheek,
And he will look as hollow as a ghost;
As dim and meagre as an ague's fit;
And so he'll die; and, rising so again,
When I shall meet him in the court of heaven
I shall not know him: therefore never, never
Must I behold my pretty Arthur more.
Pandulph. You hold too heinous a respect of grief.
Const. He talks to me that never had a son.
K. Phi. You are as fond of grief as of your child.
Const. Grief fills the room up of my absent child,
Lies in his bed, walks up and down with me,

Puts on his pretty looks, repeats his words,
Remembers me of all his gracious parts,
Stuffs out his vacant garments with his form;
Then, have I reason to be fond of grief.
Fare you well: had you such a loss as I,
I could give better comfort than you do. —
I will not keep this form upon my head,
[*Tearing off her head-dress.*
When there is such disorder in my wit.
O Lord! my boy, my Arthur, my fair son!
My life, my joy, my food, my all the world!
My widow-comfort, and my sorrows' cure!

From KING RICHARD III.

78. *Clarence's Dream.* — Act. I. Sc. 4.

CLARENCE *and* BRAKENBURY.

Brak. Why looks your grace so heavily to-day?
Clar. O, I have passed a miserable night,
So full of fearful dreams, of ugly sights,
That, as I am a Christian faithful man,
I would not spend another such a night,
Though 'twere to buy a world of happy days;
So full of dismal terror was the time.
Brak. What was your dream, my lord? I pray you, tell me.
Clar. Methought that I had broken from the Tower,
And was embarked to cross to Burgundy;
And in my company my brother Gloster:
Who from my cabin tempted me to walk
Upon the hatches; there we looked toward England,
And cited up a thousand heavy times,
During the wars of York and Lancaster,
That had befallen us. As we paced along
Upon the giddy footing of the hatches,
Methought that Gloster stumbled; and, in falling,
Struck me, that thought to stay him, overboard,
Into the tumbling billows of the main.
O Lord! methought what pain it was to drown!
What dreadful noise of water in mine ears!
What sights of ugly death within mine eyes!
Methought I saw a thousand fearful wracks;
A thousand men that fishes gnawed upon;
Wedges of gold, great anchors, heaps of pearl,
Inestimable stones, unvalued jewels,
All scattered in the bottom of the sea.

Some lay in dead men's skulls; and in those holes
Where eyes did once inhabit there were crept,
As 'twere in scorn of eyes, reflecting gems,
That wooed the slimy bottom of the deep,
And mocked the dead bones that lay scattered by.

Brak. Had you such leisure in the time of death
To gaze upon these secrets of the deep?

Clar. Methought I had; and often did I strive
To yield the ghost: but still the envious flood
Stopped in my soul, and would not let it forth
To find the empty, vast, and wandering air:
But smothered it within my panting bulk,
Which almost burst to belch it in the sea.

Brak. Awaked you not in this sore agony?

Clar. No, no, my dream was lengthened after life:
O, then began the tempest to my soul!
I passed, methought, the melancholy flood
With that sour ferryman which poets write of,
Unto the kingdom of perpetual night.
The first that there did greet my stranger soul
Was my great father-in-law, renownéd Warwick;
Who spake aloud, — "What scourge for perjury
Can this dark monarchy afford false Clarence?"
And so he vanished: Then came wandering by
A shadow like an angel, with bright hair
Dabbled in blood; and he shrieked out aloud, —
"Clarence is come, — false, fleeting, perjured Clarence, —
That stabbed me in the field by Tewksbury; —
Seize on him, furies, take him unto torment!" —
With that, methought, a legion of foul fiends
Environed me, and howléd in mine ears
Such hideous cries, that, with the very noise
I trembling waked, and, for a season after,
Could not believe but that I was in hell;
Such terrible impression made my dream.

Brak. No marvel, lord, though it affrighted you;
I am afraid, methinks, to hear you tell it.

Clar. O, Brakenbury, I have done these things, —
That now give evidence against my soul, —
For Edward's sake; and see how he requites me!
O God! if my deep prayers cannot appease thee,
But thou wilt be avenged on my misdeeds,
Yet execute thy wrath on me alone:
O, spare my guiltless wife and my poor children!
I pray thee, gentle keeper, stay by me;
My soul is heavy, and I fain would sleep.

From KING HENRY VIII.

79. *Wolsey and Cromwell.* — Act III. Sc. 2.

Wol. Farewell, a long farewell, to all my greatness!
This is the state of man: To-day he puts forth
The tender leaves of hopes, to-morrow blossoms,
And bears his blushing honors thick upon him;
The third day comes a frost, a killing frost;
And, — when he thinks, good easy man, full surely
His greatness is a ripening, — nips his root,
And then he falls, as I do. I have ventured,
Like little wanton boys that swim on bladders,
This many summers in a sea of glory,
But far beyond my depth: my high-blown pride
At length broke under me; and now has left me,
Weary, and old with service, to the mercy
Of a rude stream, that must forever hide me.
Vain pomp and glory of this world, I hate ye;
I feel my heart new opened: O, how wretched
Is that poor man that hangs on princes' favors!
There is, betwixt that smile we would aspire to,
That sweet aspect of princes, and their ruin,
More pangs and fears than wars or women have;
And when he falls, he falls like Lucifer,
Never to hope again. — * * *
* * * Why, how now, Cromwell?
Crom. I have no power to speak, sir.
Wol. What, amazed
At my misfortunes? can thy spirit wonder
A great man should decline? Nay, an you weep,
I am fallen indeed.
Crom. How does your grace?
Wol. Why, well;
Never so truly happy, my good Cromwell.
I know myself now; and I feel within me
A peace above all earthly dignities,
A still and quiet conscience. The king has cured me,
I humbly thank his grace; and from these shoulders,
These ruined pillars, out of pity, taken
A load would sink a navy, too much honor:
O, 'tis a burden, Cromwell, 'tis a burden,
Too heavy for a man that hopes for heaven.
* * * * * * *
Cromwell, I did not think to shed a tear
In all my miseries; but thou hast forced me
Out of thy honest truth to play the woman.

Let's dry our eyes: and thus far hear me, Cromwell;
And when I am forgotten, as I shall be,
And sleep in dull, cold marble, where no mention
Of me more must be heard of, say I taught thee;
Say Wolsey — that once trod the ways of glory,
And sounded all the depths and shoals of honor —
Found thee a way, out of his wrack, to rise in;
A sure and safe one, though thy master missed it.
Mark but my fall, and that that ruined me.
Cromwell, I charge thee, fling away ambition;
By that sin fell the angels; how can man then,
The image of his Maker, hope to win by't?
Love thyself last; cherish those hearts that hate thee;
Corruption wins not more than honesty.
Still in thy right hand carry gentle peace,
To silence envious tongues. Be just, and fear not:
Let all the ends thou aim'st at be thy country's,
Thy God's, and truth's; then if thou fall'st, O Cromwell,
Thou fall'st a blessèd martyr. Serve the king;
And — Prithee, lead me in:
There take an inventory of all I have,
To the last penny; 'tis the king's: my robe,
And my integrity to heaven, is all
I dare now call my own. O Cromwell, Cromwell,
Had I but served my God with half the zeal
I served my king, he would not in mine age
Have left me naked to mine enemies.

---

80. *Death of Queen Katharine.* — Act IV. Sc. 2.

KATHARINE *and* CAPUCIUS.

Kath. Sir, I most humbly pray you to deliver
This to my lord the king.
Cap. Most willing, madam.
Kath. In which I have commended to his goodness
The model of our chaste loves, his young daughter:
The dews of heaven fall thick in blessings on her! —
Beseeching him to give her virtuous breeding;
(She is young, and of a noble, modest nature;
I hope she will deserve well;) and a little
To love her for her mother's sake, that loved him,
Heaven knows how dearly. My next poor petition
Is, that his noble grace would have some pity
Upon my wretched women, that so long
Have followed both my fortunes faithfully:
Of which there is not one, I dare avow,

(And now I should not lie,) but will deserve,
For virtue, and true beauty of the soul,
For honesty, and decent carriage,
A right good husband, let him be a noble;
And, sure, those men are happy that shall have them.
The last is, for my men; — they are the poorest,
But poverty could never draw them from me; —
That they may have their wages duly paid them,
And something over to remember me by;
If heaven had pleased to have given me longer life,
And able means, we had not parted thus.
These are the whole contents: — And, good my lord,
By that you love the dearest in this world,
As you wish Christian peace to souls departed,
Stand these poor people's friend, and urge the king
To do me this last right.

Cap. By heaven, I will;
Or let me lose the fashion of a man!

Kath. I thank you, honest lord. Remember me
In all humility unto his highness:
Say, his long trouble now is passing
Out of this world: tell him, in death I blessed him,
For so I will. — Mine eyes grow dim. — Farewell,
My lord. — Griffith, farewell. — Nay, Patience,
You must not leave me yet, I must to bed;
Call in more women. — When I am dead, good wench,
Let me be used with honor; strew me over
With maiden flowers, that all the world may know
I was a chaste wife to my grave: embalm me,
Then lay me forth: although unqueened, yet like
A queen, and daughter to a king, inter me.
I can no more.

C.—TRAGEDIES.

From HAMLET.

81. *Hamlet and the Ghost.* — Act I. Sc. 4.

HAMLET, HORATIO, *and* MARCELLUS.

Enter GHOST.

Hor. Look, my lord, it comes!

Ham. Angels and ministers of grace defend us! —
Be thou a spirit of health, or goblin damned,
Bring with thee airs from heaven, or blasts from hell,
Be thy intents wicked, or charitable,

Thou comest in such a questionable shape,
That I will speak to thee; I'll call thee, Hamlet,
King, father, royal Dane: O, answer me:
Let me not burst in ignorance! but tell,
Why thy canonized bones, hearsed in death,
Have burst their cerements! why the sepulchre,
Wherein we saw thee quietly in-urned,
Hath oped his ponderous and marble jaws,
To cast thee up again! What may this mean,
That thou, dead corse, again, in complete steel,
Revisit'st thus the glimpses of the moon,
Making night hideous; and we fools of nature,
So horridly to shake our disposition,
With thoughts beyond the reaches of our souls?
Say, why is this? wherefore? what should we do?

Hor. It beckons you to go away with it,
As if it some impartment did desire
To you alone.

Mar. Look, with what courteous action
It wafts you to a more removéd ground:
But do not go with it.

Hor. No, by no means.

Ham. It will not speak; then will I follow it.

Hor. Do not, my lord.

Ham. It wafts me still:—
Go on, I'll follow thee.
Where wilt thou lead me? speak, I'll go no further.

Ghost. Mark me.

Ham. I will.

Ghost. My hour is almost come,
When I to sulphurous and tormenting flames
Must render up myself.

Ham. Alas, poor ghost!

Ghost. Pity me not, but lend thy serious hearing
To what I shall unfold.

Ham. Speak, I am bound to hear.

Ghost. So art thou to revenge, when thou shalt hear.

Ham. What?

Ghost. I am thy father's spirit;
Doomed for a certain term to walk the night;
And, for the day, confined to fast in fires,
Till the foul crimes, done in my days of nature,
Are burnt and purged away. But that I am forbid
To tell the secrets of my prison-house,
I could a tale unfold, whose lightest word
Would harrow up thy soul; freeze thy young blood;
Make thy two eyes, like stars, start from their spheres;

Thy knotted and combinéd locks to part,
And each particular hair to stand an end,
Like quills upon the fretful porcupine;
But this eternal blazon must not be
To ears of flesh and blood:—List, Hamlet, O list!—
If thou didst ever thy dear father love,—
Ham. O heaven!
Ghost. Revenge his foul and most unnatural murther.

---

82. *Hamlet's Soliloquy on Death.*—Act III. Sc. 1.

Ham. To be, or not to be, that is the question:
Whether 'tis nobler in the mind, to suffer
The slings and arrows of outrageous fortune,
Or to take arms against a sea of troubles,
And by opposing end them? To die,—to sleep,—
No more; and, by a sleep, to say we end
The heart-ache, and the thousand natural shocks
That flesh is heir to,—'tis a consummation
Devoutly to be wished. To die,—to sleep;—
To sleep! perchance to dream;—ay, there's the rub;
For in that sleep of death what dreams may come,
When we have shuffled off this mortal coil,
Must give us pause: there's the respect,
That makes calamity of so long life:
For who would bear the whips and scorns of time,
The oppressor's wrong, the proud man's contumely,
The pangs of disprized love, the law's delay,
The insolence of office, and the spurns
That patient merit of the unworthy takes,
When he himself might his quietus make
With a bare bodkin? Who would these fardels bear,
To grunt and sweat under a weary life;
But that the dread of something after death,
The undiscovered country, from whose bourn
No traveller returns, puzzles the will;
And makes us rather bear those ills we have,
Than fly to others that we know not of?
Thus conscience does make cowards of us all;
And thus the native hue of resolution
Is sicklied o'er with the pale cast of thought;
And enterprises of great pith and moment,
With this regard, their currents turn awry,
And lose the name of action.

From JULIUS CÆSAR.

83. *Mark Antony's Oration over the dead body of Cæsar.*
Act III. Sc. 2.

Ant. Friends, Romans, countrymen, lend me your ears;
I come to bury Cæsar, not to praise him.
The evil that men do lives after them;
The good is often interrèd with their bones:
So let it be with Cæsar. The noble Brutus
Hath told you Cæsar was ambitious:
If it were so, it was a grievous fault;
And grievously hath Cæsar answered it.
Here, under leave of Brutus and the rest,
(For Brutus is an honorable man;
So are they all, all honorable men;)
Come I to speak in Cæsar's funeral.
* * * * * * *
If you have tears, prepare to shed them now.
You all do know this mantle: I remember
The first time ever Cæsar put it on;
'Twas on a summer's evening, in his tent,
That day he overcame the Nervii:—
Look! in this place ran Cassius' dagger through:
See, what a rent the envious Casca made:
Through this, the well-belovèd Brutus stabbed;
And, as he plucked his cursèd steel away,
Mark how the blood of Cæsar followed it,
As rushing out of doors, to be resolved
If Brutus so unkindly knocked, or no;
For Brutus, as you know, was Cæsar's angel:
Judge, O you gods, how dearly Cæsar loved him!
This was the most unkindest cut of all:
For when the noble Cæsar saw him stab,
Ingratitude, more strong than traitors' arms,
Quite vanquished him: then burst his mighty heart;
And, in his mantle muffling up his face,
Even at the base of Pompey's statue,
Which all the while ran blood, great Cæsar fell.
O, what a fall was there, my countrymen!
Then I, and you, and all of us fell down,
Whilst bloody treason flourished over us.
O, now you weep; and, I perceive, you feel,
The dint of pity: these are gracious drops.
Kind souls, what weep you, when you but behold
Our Cæsar's vesture wounded. Look you here,
Here is himself, marred, as you see, with traitors.
* * * * * * * *

Good friends, sweet friends, let me not stir you up
To such a sudden flood of mutiny.
They that have done this deed are honorable;
What private griefs they have, alas! I know not,
That made them do it; they are wise and honorable,
And will, no doubt, with reasons answer you.
I come not, friends, to steal away your hearts;
I am no orator, as Brutus is;
But as you know me all, a plain blunt man,
That loves my friend; and that they know full well
That gave me public leave to speak of him.
For I have neither wit, nor words, nor worth,
Action, nor utterance, nor the power of speech,
To stir men's blood: I only speak right on;
I tell you that which you yourselves do know;
Show you sweet Cæsar's wounds, poor, poor dumb mouths,
And bid them speak for me: But were I Brutus,
And Brutus Antony, there were an Antony
Would ruffle up your spirits, and put a tongue
In every wound of Cæsar, that should move
The stones of Rome to rise and mutiny.

From MACBETH.

84. *Macbeth's Irresolution before the Murder of Duncan.*
Act I. Sc. 7.

Macb. If it were done, when 'tis done, then 'twere well
It were done quickly: If the assassination
Could trammel up the consequence, and catch,
With his surcease, success; that but this blow
Might be the be-all and the end-all, here,
But here, upon this bank and shoal of time,
We'd jump the life to come. — But in these cases,
We still have judgment here; that we but teach
Bloody instructions, which, being taught, return
To plague the inventor: This even-handed justice
Commends the ingredients of our poisoned chalice
To our own lips. He's here in double trust:
First, as I am his kinsman and his subject,
Strong both against the deed: then, as his host,
Who should against his murtherer shut the door,
Not bear the knife myself. Besides, this Duncan
Hath borne his faculties so meek, hath been
So clear in his great office, that his virtues
Will plead like angels, trumpet-tongued, against
The deep damnation of his taking-off:

And pity, like a naked new-born babe,
Striding the blast, or heaven's cherubim, horsed
Upon the sightless couriers of the air,
Shall blow the horrid deed in every eye,
That tears shall drown the wind. — I have no spur
To prick the sides of my intent, but only
Vaulting ambition, which o'erleaps itself,
And falls on the other.

---

85. *Witches.* — Act IV. Sc. I.

A dark Cave. In the middle, a Caldron boiling. Thunder.

Enter the three Witches.

1st Witch. Thrice the brinded cat hath mewed.
2nd Witch. Thrice; and once the hedge-pig whined.
3rd Witch. Harpier cries: — 'Tis time, 'tis time.
1st Witch. Round about the caldron go;
In the poisoned entrails throw.
Toad, that under cold stone,
Days and nights hast thirty-one
Sweltered venom sleeping got,
Boil thou first i' the charmèd pot!
All. Double, double, toil and trouble;
Fire burn, and caldron bubble.
2nd Witch. Fillet of a fenny snake,
In the caldron boil and bake:
Eye of newt, and toe of frog,
Wool of bat, and tongue of dog,
Adder's fork, and blind-worm's sting,
Lizard's leg, and owlet's wing,
For a charm of powerful trouble;
Like a hell-broth boil and bubble.
All. Double, double, toil and trouble;
Fire burn, and caldron bubble.

D. — SONGS.

86. Ariel's Song.

Where the bee sucks, there suck I;
In a cowslip's bell I lie:
There I couch when owls do cry,
On the bat's back I do fly
After summer merrily:
Merrily, merrily, shall I live now,
Under the blossom that hangs on the bough.

The Tempest. Act V. Sc. 1.

87. The Fairy to Puck.

Over hill, over dale,
  Thorough bush, thorough brier,
Over park, over pale,
  Thorough flood, thorough fire,
I do wander everywhere,
Swifter than the moon's sphere;
And I serve the fairy queen,
To dew her orbs upon the green:
The cowslips tall her pensioners be;
In their gold coats spots you see;
Those be rubies, fairy favors,
In those freckles live their savors:
I must go seek some dew-drops here,
And hang a pearl in every cowslip's ear.

Midsummer Night's Dream. Act II. Sc. 1.

---

88. Sonnet XCIX.

The forward violet thus did I chide; —
Sweet thief, whence didst thou steal thy sweet that smells,
If not from my love's breath? The purple pride
Which on thy soft cheek for complexion dwells,
In my love's veins thou hast too grossly dyed.
The lily I condemnéd for thy hand,
And buds of marjoram had stolen thy hair:
The roses fearfully on thorns did stand,
One blushing shame, another white despair;
A third, nor red nor white, had stolen of both,
And to his robbery had annexed thy breath;
But for his theft, in pride of all his growth
A vengeful canker eat him up to death.
  More flowers I noted, yet I none could see,
  But sweet or color it had stolen from thee.

CHAPTER VIII.

THE SHAKSPEARIAN DRAMATISTS.

BEN JONSON. 1573–1637. (Manual, p. 152.)

89. FROM THE SAD SHEPHERD; OR, A TALE OF ROBIN HOOD.

Alken, an old Shepherd, instructs Robin Hood's men how to find a Witch, and how she is to be hunted.

Alken. Within a gloomy dimble[1] she doth dwell,
Down in a pit o'ergrown with brakes and briars,
Close by the ruins of a shaken abbey,
Torn with an earthquake down unto the ground,
'Mongst graves, and grots, near an old charnel-house,
Where you shall find her sitting in her fourm,
As fearful, and melancholic, as that
She is about; with caterpillars' kells,
And knotty cobwebs, rounded in with spells.
Then she steals forth to relief, in the fogs,
And rotten mists, upon the fens and bogs,
Down to the drownèd lands of Lincolnshire;
To make ewes cast their lambs, swine eat their farrow;
The housewife's tun not work, nor the milk churn;
Writhe children's wrists, and suck their breath in sleep;
Get vials of their blood; and where the sea
Casts up his slimy ooze, search for a weed
To open locks with, and to rivet charms,
Planted about her, in the wicked seat
Of all her mischiefs, which are manifold.
* * * * * * *
The venomed plants
Wherewith she kills; where the sad mandrake grows,
Whose groans are deathful; the dead numbing nightshade;
The stupefying hemlock; adder's tongue,
And martegan;[2] the shrieks of luckless owls,
We hear, and croaking night-crows in the air;
Green-bellied snakes; blue fire-drakes in the sky;
And giddy flitter-mice[3] with leather wings;

1 Dingle, or dell. 2 A kind of lily. 3 Bats.

The scaly beetles, with their habergeons
That make a humming murmur as they fly;
There, in the stocks of trees, white fays do dwell,
And span-long elves that dance about a pool,
With each a little changeling in their arms:
The airy spirits play with falling stars,
And mount the sphere of fire, to kiss the moon;
While she sits reading by the glowworm's light,
Or rotten wood, o'er which the worm hath crept,
The baneful schedule of her nocent charms,
And binding characters, through which she wounds
Her puppets, the *Sigilla*[4] of her witchcraft.
All this I know, and I will find her for you;
And show you her sitting in her fourm; I'll lay
My hand upon her; make her throw her scut
Along her back, when she doth start before us.
But you must give her law; and you shall see her
Make twenty leaps and doubles, cross the paths,
And then squat down beside us.

[4] Seals, or talismans.

---

90. FROM SEJANUS.

Sejanus, the morning he is condemned by the Senate, receives some tokens which presage his death.

SEJANUS, POMPONIUS, MINUTIUS, TERENTIUS, &c.

Ter. Are these things true?
Min. Thousands are gazing at it in the streets.
Sej. What's that?
Ter. Minutius tells us here, my lord,
That a new head being set upon your statue,
A rope is since found wreathed about it! and
But now a fiery meteor in the form
Of a great ball was seen to roll along
The troubled air, where yet it hangs unperfect,
The amazing wonder of the multitude.
Sej. No more. —
Send for the tribunes: we will straight have up
More of the soldiers for our guard. Minutius,
We pray you go for Cotta, Latiaris,
Trio the consul, or what senators
You know are sure, and ours. You, my good Natta,
For Laco, provost of the watch. Now, Satrius,
The time of proof comes on. Arm all our servants,
And without tumult. You, Pomponius,
Hold some good correspondence with the consul·

Attempt him, noble friend. These things begin
To look like dangers, now, worthy my fates.
Fortune, I see thy worst: let doubtful states
And things uncertain hang upon thy will;
Me surest death shall render certain still.

* * * * * * *

If you will, destinies, that after all
I faint now ere I touch my period,
You are but cruel; and I already have done
Things great enough. All Rome hath been my slave;
The senate sat an idle looker-on,
And witness of my power; when I have blushed
More to command, than it to suffer; all
The fathers have sat ready and prepared
To give me empire, temples, or their throats,
When I would ask them; and (what crowns the top)
Rome, senate, people, all the world, have seen
Jove but my equal, Cæsar but my second.
'Tis then your malice, Fates, who (but your own)
Envy and fear to have any power long known.

BEAUMONT, 1586–1615, and FLETCHER, 1576–1625. (Manual, p. 157.)

91. FROM THE FAITHFUL SHEPHERDESS.

Clorin, a Shepherdess, watching by the grave of her Lover, is found by a Satyr.

Clor. Hail, holy earth, whose cold arms do embrace
The truest man that ever fed his flocks
By the fat plains of fruitful Thessaly.
Thus I salute thy grave, thus do I pay
My early vows, and tribute of mine eyes,
To thy still loved ashes: thus I free
Myself from all ensuing heats and fires
Of love: all sports, delights, and jolly games,
That shepherds hold full dear, thus put I off.
Now no more shall these smooth brows be begirt
With youthful coronals, and lead the dance.
No more the company of fresh fair maids
And wanton shepherds be to me delightful:
Nor the shrill pleasing sound of merry pipes
Under some shady dell, when the cool wind
Plays on the leaves: all be far away,
Since thou art far away, by whose dear side
How often have I sat crowned with fresh flowers
For summer's queen, whilst every shepherd's boy

Puts on his lusty green, with gaudy hook,
And hanging script of finest cordevan!
But thou art gone, and these are gone with thee,
And all are dead but thy dear memory:
That shall outlive thee, and shall ever spring,
Whilst there are pipes, or jolly shepherds sing.
And here will I, in honor of thy love,
Dwell by thy grave, forgetting all those joys
That former times made precious to mine eyes,
Only remembering what my youth did gain
In the dark hidden virtuous use of herbs.
That will I practise, and as freely give
All my endeavors, as I gained them free.
Of all green wounds I know the remedies
In men or cattle, be they stung with snakes,
Or charmed with powerful words of wicked art;
Or be they lovesick, or through too much heat
Grown wild, or lunatic; their eyes, or ears,
Thickened with misty film of dulling rheum:
These I can cure, such secret virtue lies
In herbs applied by a virgin's hand.
My meat shall be what these wild woods afford,
Berries and chestnuts, plantains, on whose cheeks
The sun sits smiling, and the lofty fruit
Pulled from the fair head of the straight-grown pine.
On these I'll feed with free content and rest,
When night shall blind the world, by thy side blessed.

A Satyr enters.

Satyr. Thorough yon same bending plain
That flings his arms down to the main,
And through these thick woods have I run,
Whose bottom never kissed the sun.
Since the lusty spring began,
All to please my master Pan,
Have I trotted without rest
To get him fruit; for at a feast
He entertains this coming night
His paramour the Syrinx bright:
But behold a fairer sight!
By that heavenly form of thine,
Brightest fair, thou art divine,
Sprung from great immortal race
Of the gods, for in thy face
Shines more awful majesty,
Than dull weak mortality
Dare with misty eyes behold,
And live: therefore on this mould

Lowly do I bend my knee
In worship of thy deity.
Deign it, goddess, from my hand
To receive whate'er this land
From her fertile womb doth send
Of her choice fruits; and but lend
Belief to that the Satyr tells,
Fairer by the famous wells
To this present day ne'er grew,
Never better, nor more true.
Here be grapes, whose lusty blood
Is the learnéd poet's good;
Sweeter yet did never crown
The head of Bacchus; nuts more brown
Than the squirrels' teeth that crack them,
Deign, O fairest fair, to take them,
For these, black-eyed Driopé
Hath oftentimes commanded me
With my clasped knee to climb.
See how well the lusty time
Hath decked their rising cheeks in red,
Such as on your lips is spread.
Here be berries for a queen,
Some be red, some be green;
These are of that luscious meat
The great god Pan himself doth eat:
All these, and what the woods can yield,
The hanging mountain, or the field,
I freely offer, and ere long
Will bring you more, more sweet and strong;
Till when, humbly leave I take,
Lest the great Pan do awake,
That sleeping lies in a deep glade,
Under a broad beech's shade.
I must go, I must run,
Swifter than the fiery sun.

---

92. From the Two Noble Kinsmen.

Palamon and Arcite, repining at their hard condition, in being made captives for life in Athens, derive consolation from the enjoyment of each other's company in prison.

Pal. O cousin Arcite,
Where is Thebes now? where is our noble country?
Where are our friends and kindreds? never more
Must we behold those comforts, never see
The hardy youths strive for the games of honor,

Hung with the painted favors of their ladies
Like tall ships under sail; then start amongst them,
And as an east wind leave them all behind us
Like lazy clouds, whilst Palamon and Arcite,
Even in the wagging of a wanton leg,
Outstripped the people's praises, won the garlands
Ere they have time to wish them ours. O, never
Shall we two exercise, like twins of honor,
Our arms again, and feel our fiery horses
Like proud seas under us; our good swords now,
(Better the red-eyed god of war ne'er wore)
Ravished our sides, like age, must run to rust,
And deck the temples of those gods that hate us,
These hands shall never draw them out like lightning
To blast whole armies more.

Arc. No, Palamon,
Those hopes are prisoners with us; here we are,
And here the graces of our youths must wither
Like a too timely spring; here age must find us,
And (which is heaviest) Palamon, unmarried;
The sweet embraces of a loving wife
Loaden with kisses, armed with thousand Cupids,
Shall never clasp our necks, no issue know us,
No figures of ourselves shall we e'er see,
To glad our age, and like young eagles teach them
Boldly to gaze against bright arms, and say,
"Remember what your fathers were, and conquer."
The fair-eyed maids shall weep our banishments,
And in their songs curse ever-blinded Fortune,
Till she for shame see what a wrong she has done
To youth and nature. This is all our world:
We shall know nothing here, but one another;
Hear nothing, but the clock that tells our woes.
The vine shall grow, but we shall never see it:
Summer shall come, and with her all delights,
But dead-cold winter must inhabit here still.

Pal. 'Tis too true, Arcite. To our Theban hounds,
That shook the agéd forest with their echoes,
No more now must we halloo, no more shake
Our pointed javelins, whilst the angry swine
Flies like a Parthian quiver from our rages,
Struck with our well-steeled darts. All valiant uses
(The food and nourishment of noble minds)
In us two here shall perish: we shall die
(Which is the curse of honor) lastly
Children of grief and ignorance.

93. Philip Massinger. 1584–1640. (Manual, p. 161.)

From the Virgin Martyr.

Angelo, an Angel, attends Dorothea as a Page.

Angelo. Dorothea. *The time, midnight.*

Dor. My book and taper.
Ang. Here, most holy mistress.
Dor. Thy voice sends forth such music, that I never
Was ravished with a more celestial sound.
Were every servant in the world like thee,
So full of goodness, angels would come down
To dwell with us: thy name is *Angelo*,
And like that name thou art. Get thee to rest;
Thy youth with too much watching is oppressed.
Ang. No, my dear lady. I could weary stars,
And force the wakeful moon to lose her eyes,
By my late watching, but to wait on you.
When at your prayers you kneel before the altar,
Methinks I'm singing with some quire in heaven,
So blest I hold me in your company.
Therefore, my most loved mistress, do not bid
Your boy, so serviceable, to get hence;
For then you break his heart.
Dor. Be nigh me still, then.
In golden letters down I'll set that day,
Which gave thee to me. Little did I hope
To meet such worlds of comfort in thyself,
This little, pretty body, when I coming
Forth of the temple, heard my beggar-boy,
My sweet-faced, godly beggar-boy, crave an alms,
Which with glad hand I gave, with lucky hand;
And when I took thee home, my most chaste bosom
Methought was filled with no hot wanton fire,
But with a holy flame, mounting since higher,
On wings of cherubims, than it did before.
Ang. Proud am I that my lady's modest eye
So likes so poor a servant.
Dor. I have offered
Handfuls of gold but to behold thy parents.
I would leave kingdoms, were I queen of some,
To dwell with thy good father; for, the son
Bewitching me so deeply with his presence,
He that begot him must do't ten times more.
I pray thee, my sweet boy, show me thy parents:
Be not ashamed.
Ang. I am not: I did never

Know who my mother was; but, by yon palace,
Filled with bright heavenly courtiers, I dare assure you,
And pawn these eyes upon it, and this hand,
My father is in heaven; and, pretty mistress,
If your illustrious hour-glass spend his sand
No worse, than yet it doth, upon my life,
You and I both shall meet my father there,
And he shall bid you welcome.

Dor. A blessèd day.

---

94. JOHN FORD. 1586–1639. (Manual, p. 162.)

FROM THE LOVER'S MELANCHOLY.

Contention of a Bird and a Musician.

Passing from Italy to Greece, the tales
Which poets of an elder time have feigned
To glorify their Tempé, bred in me
Desires of visiting that paradise.
To Thessaly I came, and living private,
Without acquaintance of more sweet companions
Than the old inmates to my love, my thoughts,
I day by day frequented silent groves
And solitary walks. One morning early
This accident encountered me: I heard
The sweetest and most ravishing contention
That art or nature ever were at strife in.
A sound of music touched mine ears, or rather
Indeed entranced my soul: as I stole nearer,
Invited by the melody, I saw
This youth, this fair-faced youth, upon his lute
With strains of strange variety and harmony
Proclaiming (as it seemed) so bold a challenge
To the clear quiristers of the woods, the birds,
That as they flocked about him, all stood silent,
Wondering at what they heard. I wondered too.
A nightingale,
Nature's best skilled musician, undertakes
The challenge; and, for every several strain
The well-shaped youth could touch, she sung her down;
He could not run division with more art
Upon his quaking instrument, than she
The nightingale did with her various notes
Reply to.
Some time thus spent, the young man grew at last
Into a pretty anger; that a bird,

Whom art had never taught cliffs, moods, or notes,
Should vie with him for mastery, whose study
Had busied many hours to perfect practice:
To end the controversy, in a rapture
Upon his instrument he plays so swiftly,
So many voluntaries, and so quick,
That there was curiosity and cunning,
Concord in discord, lines of differing method
Meeting in one full centre of delight.
The bird (ordained to be
Music's first martyr) strove to imitate
These several sounds: which when her warbling throat
Failed in, for grief down dropped she on his lute
And brake her heart. It was the quaintest sadness,
To see the conqueror upon her hearse
To weep a funeral elegy of tears.
He looks upon the trophies of his art,
Then sighed, then wiped his eyes, then sighed, and cried,
"Alas! poor creature, I will soon revenge
This cruelty upon the author of it.
Henceforth this lute, guilty of innocent blood,
Shall never more betray a harmless peace
To an untimely end:" and in that sorrow,
As he was pashing it against a tree,
I suddenly stepped in.

---

95. John Webster. Fl. 1623. (Manual, p. 163.)

From the Duchess of Malfy.

The Duchess's marriage with Antonio being discovered, her brother Ferdinand shuts her up in a prison, and torments her with various trials of studied cruelty. By his command, Bosola, the instrument of his devices, shows her the bodies of her husband and children counterfeited in wax, as dead.

Bos. He doth present you this sad spectacle,
That now you know directly they are dead,
Hereafter you may wisely cease to grieve
For that which cannot be recovered.
Duch. There is not between heaven and earth one wish
I stay for after this: it wastes me more
Than were 't my picture fashioned out of wax,
Stuck with a magical needle, and then buried
In some foul dunghill; and 'yond's an excellent property
For a tyrant, which I would account mercy.
Bos. What's that?
Duch. If they would bind me to that lifeless trunk,
And let me freeze to death.

Bos. Come, you must live.
Leave this vain sorrow.
Things being at the worst begin to mend.
The bee,
When he hath shot his sting into your hand,
May then play with your eyelid.
Duch. Good comfortable fellow,
Persuade a wretch that's broke upon the wheel
To have all his bones new set; entreat him live
To be executed again. Who must despatch me?
I account this world a tedious theatre,
For I do play a part in't 'gainst my will.
Bos. Come, be of comfort; I will save your life.
Duch. Indeed I have not leisure to attend
So small a business.
I will go pray. — No: I'll go curse.
Bos. O fie!
Duch. I could curse the stars!
Bos. O fearful.
Duch. And those three smiling seasons of the year
Into a Russian winter: nay, the world
To its first chaos.
Plagues (that make lanes through largest families)
Consume them![1]
Let them like tyrants
Ne'er be remembered but for the ill they've done!
Let all the zealous prayers of mortified
Churchmen forget them!
Let heaven a little while cease crowning martyrs,
To punish them! go, howl them this; and say, I long to bleed:
It is some mercy when men kill with speed.

[1] Her brothers.

---

96. JAMES SHIRLEY. 1594–1666. (Manual, p. 164.)

FROM THE LADY OF PLEASURE.

Sir Thomas Bornewell expostulates with his Lady on her extravagance and love of pleasure.

BORNEWELL. ARETINA, *his lady.*

Are. I am angry with myself;
To be so miserably restrained in things,
Wherein it doth concern your love and honor
To see me satisfied.

Bor. In what, Aretina,
Dost thou accuse me? have I not obeyed
All thy desires, against mine own opinion;
Quitted the country, and removed the hope
Of our return, by sale of that fair lordship
We lived in: changed a calm and retired life
For this wild town, composed of noise and charge?
Are. What charge, more than is necessary
For a lady of my birth and education?
Bor. I am not ignorant how much nobility
Flows in your blood, your kinsmen great and powerful
In the state; but with this lose not your memory
Of being my wife; I shall be studious,
Madam, to give the dignity of your birth
All the best ornaments which become my fortune;
But would not flatter it, to ruin both,
And be the fable of the town, to teach
Other men wit by loss of mine, employed
To serve your vast expenses.
Are. Am I then
Brought in the balance? so, sir.
Bor. Though you weigh
Me in a partial scale, my heart is honest;
And must take liberty to think, you have
Obeyed no modest counsel to effect,
Nay, study ways of pride and costly ceremony;
Your change of gaudy furniture, and pictures,
Of this Italian master, and that Dutchman's;
Your mighty looking-glasses, like artillery
Brought home on engines; the superfluous plate
Antic and novel; vanities of tires,
Fourscore pound suppers for my lord your kinsman,
Banquets for the other lady, aunt, and cousins;
And perfumes that exceed all; train of servants,
To stifle us at home, and show abroad
More motley than the French, or the Venetian,
About your coach, whose rude postilion
Must pester every narrow lane, till passengers
And tradesmen curse your choking up their stalls,
And common cries pursue your ladyship
For hindering of their market.
Are. Have you done, sir.
Bor. I could accuse the gaiety of your wardrobe,
And prodigal embroideries, under which,
Rich satins, plushes, cloth of silver, dare
Not show their own complexions; your jewels,
Able to burn out the spectators' eyes,

And show like bonfires on you by the tapers:
Something might here be spared, with safety of
Your birth and honor, since the truest wealth
Shines from the soul, and draws up just admirers.
I could urge something more.

Are. Pray, do. I like
Your homily of thrift.

Bor. I could wish, madam,
You would not game so much.

Are. A gamester, too!

Bor. But are not come to that repentance yet,
Should teach you skill enough to raise your profit;
You look not through the subtilty of cards,
And mysteries of dice, nor can you save
Charge with the box, buy petticoats and pearls,
And keep your family by the precious income;
Nor do I wish you should: my poorest servant
Shall not upbraid my tables, nor his hire
Purchased beneath my honor: you make play
Not a pastime, but a tyranny, and vex
Yourself and my estate by it.

Are. Good, proceed.

Bor. Another game you have, which consumes more
Your fame than purse, your revels in the night,
Your meetings, called the ball, to which appear
As to the court of pleasure, all your gallants
And ladies, thither bound by a subpœna
Of Venus and small Cupid's high displeasure:
'Tis but the family of Love, translated
Into more costly sin; there was a play on it;
And had the poet not been bribed to a modest
Expression of your antic gambols in it,
Some darks had been discovered; and the deeds too;
In time he may repent, and make some blush,
To see the second part danced on the stage.
My thoughts acquit you for dishonoring me
By any foul act; but the virtuous know,
'Tis not enough to clear ourselves, but the
Suspicions of our shame.

Are. Have you concluded
Your lecture?

Bor. I have done, and howsoever
My language may appear to you, it carries
No other than my fair and just intent
To your delights, without curb to their modest
And noble freedom.

Are. I'll not be so tedious
In my reply, but, without art or elegance,

Assure you I keep still my first opinion;
And though you veil your avaricious meaning
With handsome names of módesty and thrift,
I find you would intrench and wound the liberty
I was born with. Were my desires unprivileged
By example; while my judgment thought them fit,
You ought not to oppose; but when the practice
And tract of every honorable lady
Authorize me, I take it great injustice
To have my pleasures circumscribed and taught me.

CHAPTER IX.

THE SO-CALLED METAPHYSICAL POETS.

---

97. GEORGE WITHER. 1588–1667. (Manual, p. 167.)

THE STEADFAST SHEPHERD.

Hence away, thou Siren, leave me,
  Pish! unclasp these wanton arms;
Sugared wounds can ne'er deceive me,
  (Though thou prove a thousand charms).
      Fie, fie, forbear;
      No common snare
  Can ever my affection chain:
      Thy painted baits,
      And poor deceits,
  Are all bestowed on me in vain.
    *   *   *   *   *   *
Leave me then, you Sirens, leave me;
  Seek no more to work my harms:
Crafty wiles cannot deceive me,
  Who am proof against your charms:
      You labor may
      To lead astray
  The heart, that constant shall remain;
      And I the while
      Will sit and smile
  To see you spend your time in vain.

---

98. FRANCIS QUARLES. 1592–1644. (Manual, p. 167.)

O THAT THOU WOULDST HIDE ME IN THE GRAVE, THAT THOU WOULDST KEEP ME IN SECRET UNTIL THY WRATH BE PAST.

Ah! whither shall I fly? what path untrod
Shall I seek out to escape the flaming rod
Of my offended, of my angry God?

Where shall I sojourn? what kind sea will hide
My head from thunder? where shall I abide,
Until his flames be quenched or laid aside?

What if my feet should take their hasty flight,
And seek protection in the shades of night?
Alas! no shades can blind the God of light.

What if my soul should take the wings of day,
And find some desert? if she springs away,
The wings of Vengeance clip as fast as they.

What if some solid rock should entertain
My frighted soul? can solid rocks restrain
The stroke of Justice and not cleave in twain?

Nor sea, nor shade, nor shield, nor rock, nor cave,
Nor silent deserts, nor the sullen grave,
What flame-eyed Fury means to smite, can save.

'Tis vain to flee; till gentle Mercy show
Her better eye, the farther off we go,
The swing of Justice deals the mightier blow.

Th' ingenuous child, corrected, doth not fly
His angry mother's hand, but clings more nigh,
And quenches with his tears her flaming eye.

Great God! there is no safety here below;
Thou art my fortress, thou that seem'st my foe;
'Tis thou, that strik'st the stroke, must guard the blow.

---

99. George Herbert. 1593–1632. (Manual, p. 168.)

Sunday.

O day most calm, most bright!
The fruit of this, the next world's bud;
Th' indorsement of supreme delight,
Writ by a friend, and with his blood;
The couch of time; care's balm and bay;
The week were dark, but for thy light;—
Thy torch doth show the way.

The other days and thou
Make up one man; whose face thou art,
Knocking at heaven with thy brow:
The worky days are the back-part;
The burden of the week lies there,
Making the whole to stoop and bow,
Till thy release appear.

Man had straight forward gone
To endless death. But thou dost pull
And turn us round, to look on one,
Whom, if we were not very dull,
We could not choose but look on still;
Since there is no place so alone,
The which he doth not fill.

Sundays the pillars are
On which heaven's palace archéd lies:
The other days fill up the spare
And hollow room with vanities.
They are the fruitful bed and borders
In God's rich garden; that is bare,
Which parts their ranks and orders.

The Sundays of man's life,
Threaded together on time's string,
Make bracelets to adorn the wife
Of the eternal, glorious King.
On Sunday, heaven's gate stands ope;
Blessings are plentiful and rife;
More plentiful than hope.

* * * * * * * *

Thou art a day of mirth:
And, where the week-days trail on ground,
Thy flight is higher, as thy birth.
O, let me take thee at the bound,
Leaping with thee from seven to seven;
Till that we both, being tossed from earth,
Fly hand in hand to heaven!

---

100. RICHARD CRASHAW. 1620–1650. (Manual, p. 168.)

LINES ON A PRAYER-BOOK SENT TO MRS. R.

Lo! here a little volûme, but large book,
(Fear it not, sweet,
It is no hypocrite,)
Much larger in itself than in its look.
It is, in one rich handful, heaven and all —
Heaven's royal hosts encamped thus small;
To prove that true, schools used to tell,
A thousand angels in one point can dwell.

It is love's great artillery,
Which here contracts itself, and comes to lie
Close couched in your white bosom, and from thence,

As from a snowy fortress of defence,
Against the ghostly foe to take your part,
And fortify the hold of your chaste heart.
It is the armory of light:
Let constant use but keep it bright,
You'll find it yields
To holy hands and humble hearts,
More swords and shields
Than sin hath snares or hell hath darts.

Only be sure
The hands be pure
That hold these weapons, and the eyes
Those of turtles, chaste and true,
Wakeful and wise,
Here is a friend shall fight for you.
Hold but this book before your heart,
Let prayer alone to play his part.
But O! the heart
That studies this high art
Must be a sure housekeeper
And yet no sleeper.

Dear soul, be strong,
Mercy will come ere long,
And bring her bosom full of blessings—
Flowers of never-fading graces,
To make immortal dressings,
For worthy souls whose wise embraces
Store up themselves for Him who is alone
The spouse of virgins, and the virgin's son.

---

101. Robert Herrick. 1591–1674. (Manual, p. 169.)

Song.

Gather the rose-buds while ye may,
Old Time is still a flying;
And this same flower that smiles to-day
To-morrow will be dying.

The glorious lamp of heaven, the sun,
The higher he's a getting,
The sooner will his race be run,
And nearer he's to setting.

The age is best which is the first,
When youth and blood are warmer;
But being spent, the worse and worst
Times still succeed the former.

Then be not coy, but use your time,
  And, whilst ye may, go marry;
For having lost but once your prime,
  You may forever tarry.

To Meadows.

Fair daffodils, we weep to see
You haste away so soon;
As yet, the early-rising sun
Has not attained its moon.
          Stay, stay
Until the hasting day
          Has run
But to the even song;
And having prayed together, we
Will go with you along.

We have short time to stay as you,
We have as short a spring;
As quick a growth to meet decay,
As you or any thing.
          We die,
As your hours do, and dry
          Away,
Like to the summer's rain,
Or as the pearls of morning's dew,
Ne'er to be found again.

---

102. Sir John Suckling. 1609–1641. (Manual, p. 169.)

Song.

Out upon it, I have loved
  Three whole days together;
And am like to love three more,
  If it prove fair weather.

Time shall melt away his wings,
  Ere he shall discover
In the whole wide world again
  Such a constant lover.

But the spite on't is, no praise
  Is due at all to me:
Love with me had made no stays,
  Had it any been but she.

Had it any been but she,
  And that very face,
There had been at least ere this
  A dozen dozen in her place.

---

103. Sir Richard Lovelace. 1618–1658. (Manual, p. 169.)

To Althea from Prison.

When love with unconfinéd wings
  Hovers within my gates,
And my divine Althea brings
  To whisper at my gates;
When I lie tangled in her hair,
  And fettered with her eye,
The birds that wanton in the air,
  Know no such liberty.

When flowing cups run swiftly round
  With no allaying Thames,
Our careless heads with roses crowned,
  Our hearts with loyal flames;
When thirsty grief in wine we steep,
  When healths and draughts go free,
Fishes, that tipple in the deep,
  Know no such liberty.

When, linnet-like, confinéd I
  With shriller note shall sing
The mercy, sweetness, majesty,
  And glories of my king;
When I shall voice aloud how good
  He is, how great should be,
Th' enlargéd winds that curl the flood,
  Know no such liberty.

Stone walls do not a prison make,
  Nor iron bars a cage,
Minds innocent and quiet, take
  That for an hermitage:
If I have freedom in my love,
  And in my soul am free,
Angels alone, that soar above,
  Enjoy such liberty.

104. THOMAS CAREW. 1589–1639. (Manual, pp. 170 and 86.)

SONG.

Ask me no more, where Jove bestows,
When June is past, the fading rose;
For in your beauties orient deep
These flowers, as in their causes, sleep.

Ask me no more, whither do stray
The golden atoms of the day;
For, in pure love, heaven did prepare
Those powders to enrich your hair.

Ask me no more, whither doth haste
The nightingale, when May is past;
For in your sweet dividing throat
She winters, and keeps warm her note.

Ask me no more, where those stars light,
That downwards fall in dead of night;
For in your eyes they sit, and there
Fixed become, as in their sphere.

Ask me no more, if east or west,
The phœnix builds her spicy nest;
For unto you at last she flies,
And in your fragrant bosom dies.

---

105. WILLIAM BROWNE. 1590–1645. (Manual, p. 171.)

EVENING.

As in an evening when the gentle air
Breathes to the sullen night a soft repair,
I oft have sat on Thames' sweet bank to hear
My friend with his sweet touch to charm mine ear.
When he hath played (as well he can) some strain
That likes me, straight I ask the same again,
And he as gladly granting, strikes it o'er
With some sweet relish was forgot before:
I would have been content if he would play,
In that one strain to pass the night away;
But fearing much to do his patience wrong,
Unwillingly have asked some other song:

So in this differing key though I could well
A many hours but as few minutes tell,
Yet lest mine own delight might injure you
(Though loath so soon) I take my song anew.

---

106. William Habington. 1605–1654. (Manual, p. 171.)

Cupio Dissolvi.

My God! if 'tis thy great decree
That this must the last moment be
  Wherein I breathe this air;
My heart obeys, joyed to retreat
From the false favors of the great,
  And treachery of the fair.

When thou shalt please this soul t' enthrone
Above impure corruption;
  What should I grieve or fear,
To think this breathless body must
Become a loathsome heap of dust,
  And ne'er again appear.

For in the fire when ore is tried,
And by that torment purified,
  Do we deplore the loss?
And when thou shalt my soul refine,
That it thereby may purer shine,
  Shall I grieve for the dross?

---

107. Edmund Waller. 1605–1687. (Manual, p. 171.)

Song.

Go, lovely rose!
  Tell her that wastes her time and me,
That now she knows
  When I resemble her to thee,
  How sweet and fair she seems to be.

Tell her that's young,
  And shuns to have her graces spied,
That hadst thou sprung
  In deserts, where no men abide,
  Thou must have uncommended died.

Small is the worth
  Of beauty from the light retired:
Bid her come forth,
  Suffer herself to be desired,
  And not blush so to be admired.

Then die! that she
  The common fate of all things rare
May read in thee,
  How small a part of time they share
  That are so wondrous sweet and fair.

On a Girdle.

That which her slender waist confined
Shall now my joyful temples bind:
No monarch but would give his crown,
His arms might do what this has done.
  It was my heaven's extremest sphere,
The pale which held that lovely deer.
My joy, my grief, my hope, my love,
Did all within this circle move!
  A narrow compass! and yet there
Dwelt all that's good, and all that's fair;
Give me but what this ribbon bound,
Take all the rest the sun goes round.

---

108. Sir William Davenant. 1605–1668. (Manual, p. 172.)

From "Gondibert."

Character of Birtha.

To Astragon, heaven for succession gave
  One only pledge, and Birtha was her name;
Whose mother slept, where flowers grew on her grave,
  And she succeeded her in face and fame.

She ne'er saw courts, yet courts could have undone
  With untaught looks and an unpractised heart;
Her nets, the most prepared could never shun;
  For nature spread them in the scorn of art.

She never had in busy cities been,
  Ne'er warmed with hopes, nor e'er allayed with fears;
Not seeing punishment, could guess no sin;
  And sin not seeing, ne'er had use of tears.

But here her father's precepts gave her skill,
  Which with incessant business filled the hours;
In Spring, she gathered blossoms for the still;
  In Autumn, berries; and in Summer, flowers.

And as kind nature with calm diligence
  Her own free virtue silently employs,
Whilst she, unheard, does ripening growth dispense,
  So were her virtues busy without noise.

Whilst her great mistress, Nature, thus she tends,
  The busy household waits no less on her;
By secret law, each to her beauty bends;
  Though all her lowly mind to that prefer.

---

109. Sir John Denham. 1615–1668. (Manual, p. 173.)

From "Cooper's Hill."

The Thames.

My eye, descending from the Hill, surveys
Where Thames among the wanton valleys strays.
Thames! the most loved of all the Ocean's sons,
By his old sire, to his embraces runs,
Hasting to pay his tribute to the sea,
Like mortal life to meet eternity;
Though with those streams he no resemblance hold,
Whose foam is amber, and their gravel gold:
His genuine and less guilty wealth t' explore,
Search not his bottom, but survey his shore,
O'er which he kindly spreads his spacious wing
And hatches plenty for th' ensuing spring;
Nor then destroys it with too fond a stay,
Like mothers which their infants overlay;
Nor with a sudden and impetuous wave,
Like profuse kings, resumes the wealth he gave.
No unexpected inundations spoil
The mower's hopes, nor mock the ploughman's toil;
But godlike his unwearied bounty flows;
First loves to do, then loves the good he does.
Nor are his blessings to his banks confined,
But free and common as the sea or wind;
When he, to boast or to disperse his stores,
Full of the tributes of his grateful shores,
Visits the world, and in his flying tours
Brings home to us, and makes both Indies ours;
Finds wealth where 'tis, bestows it where it wants,

Cities in deserts, woods in cities, plants.
So that to us no thing, no place, is strange,
While his fair bosom is the world's exchange.
O, could I flow like thee, and make thy stream
My great example, as it is my theme!
Though deep yet clear, though gentle yet not dull,
Strong without rage, without o'erflowing full.

ABRAHAM COWLEY. 1618–1667. (Manual, p. 174.)

110. HYMN TO LIGHT.

Hail! active Nature's watchful life and health!
Her joy, her ornament, and wealth!
Hail to thy husband, Heat, and thee!
Thou the world's beauteous bride, the lusty bridegroom he!

Say, from what golden quivers of the sky
Do all thy wingéd arrows fly?
Swiftness and Power by birth are thine;
From thy great Sire they come, thy Sire, the Word Divine.

Thou in the moon's bright chariot, proud and gay,
Dost thy bright wood of stars survey,
And all the year dost with thee bring
Of thousand flowery lights thine own nocturnal spring.

Thou, Scythian-like, dost round thy lands above
The Sun's gilt tent forever move,
And still, as thou in pomp dost go,
The shining pageants of the world attend thy show.

---

111. CHARACTER OF CROMWELL.

What can be more extraordinary than that a person of mean birth, no fortune, no eminent qualities of body, which have sometimes, or of mind, which have often, raised men to the highest dignities, should have the courage to attempt, and the happiness to succeed in, so improbable a design as the destruction of one of the most ancient and most solidly-founded monarchies upon the earth? That he should have the power or boldness to put his prince and master to an open and infamous death; to banish that numerous and strongly-allied family; to do all this under the name and wages of a parliament; to trample upon them too as he pleased, and spurn them out of doors when he grew weary of them; to raise up a new and unheard-of monster out of their ashes; to stifle that in the very infancy, and set up himself above all things that ever were called sovereign in England; to oppress all his enemies by arms, and all his friends afterwards by artifice; to serve all parties patiently for a while, and to command them victoriously at last; to overrun each corner of the three nations, and overcome with equal facility both the riches of the south and the poverty of the north; to be feared and courted by all foreign princes, and adopted a brother to the gods of the earth; to call together parliaments with a word of his pen, and scatter them again with the breath of his mouth; to be humbly and daily petitioned that he would please to be hired, at the rate of two millions a year, to be the master of those who had hired him before to be their servant; to have the estates and lives of three kingdoms as much at his disposal as was the little inheritance of his father, and to be as noble and liberal in the spending of them; and lastly (for there is no end of all the particulars of his glory), to bequeath all this with one word to his posterity; to die with peace at home, and triumph abroad; to be buried among kings, and with more than regal solemnity; and to leave a name behind him, not to be extinguished, but with the whole world; which, as it is now too little for his praises, so might have been too for his conquests, if the short line of his human life could have been stretched out to the extent of his immortal designs?

CHAPTER X.

THEOLOGICAL WRITERS OF THE CIVIL WAR AND THE COMMONWEALTH.

112. John Hales. 1584–1656. (Manual, p. 177.)

Peace in the Church.

He that shall look into the acts of Christians as they are recorded by more indifferent writers, shall easily perceive that all that were Christians were not saints. But this is the testimony of an enemy. Yea, but have not our friends taken up the same complaint? Doubtless, if it had been the voice and approbation of the bridegroom, that secular state and authority had belonged to the church, either of due or of necessity, the friends of the bridegroom hearing it would have rejoiced at it: but it is found they have much sorrowed at it. St. Hilary, much offended with the opinion, that even orthodox bishops of his time had taken up that it was a thing very necessary for the church to lay hold on the temporal sword, in a tract of his against Auxentius, the Arian bishop of Milan, thus plainly bespeaks them:— "And first of all, I must needs pity the labor of our age, and bewail the fond opinions of the present times, by which men suppose the arm of flesh can much advantage God, and strive to defend by secular ambition the church of Christ. I beseech you, bishops, you that take yourselves so to be, whose authority in preaching of the Gospel did the apostles use? By the help of what powers preached they Christ, and turned almost all nations from idols to God? Took they unto themselves any honor out of princes' palaces, who, after their stripes, amidst their chains in prison, sung praises unto God? Did St. Paul, when he was made a spectacle in the theatre, summon together the churches of Christ by the edicts and writs of kings? It is likely he had the safe conduct of Nero, or Vespasian, or Decius, through whose hate unto us the confession of the faith grew famous. Those men who maintained themselves with their own hands and industry, whose solemn meetings were in parlors and secret closets, who travelled through villages and towns, and whole countries by sea and land, in spite of the prohibition of kings and councils."

113. William Chillingworth. 1602–1644. (Manual, p. 178.)

The Religion of Protestants.

When I say the religion of Protestants is, in prudence, to be preferred before yours,[1] I do not understand the doctrine of Luther, or Calvin, or Melancthon; nor the Confession of Augusta[2] or Geneva; nor the Catechism of Heidelberg; nor the Articles of the Church of England; no, nor the harmony of Protestant confessions; but that wherein they all agree, and which they all subscribe with a greater harmony, as the perfect rule of their faith and actions, — that is, THE BIBLE. The BIBLE — I say the BIBLE only — is the religion of Protestants! Whatsoever else they believe besides it, and the plain, irrefragable, indubitable consequences of it, well may they hold it as a matter of opinion: but, as matter of faith and religion, neither can they, with coherence to their own grounds, believe it themselves, nor require the belief of it of others, without most high and most schismatical presumption. I, for my part, after a long and (as I verily believe and hope) impartial search of "the true way to eternal happiness," do profess plainly that I cannot find any rest to the sole of my foot but upon this Rock only. I see plainly, and with my own eyes, that there are popes against popes; councils against councils; some fathers against others; the same fathers against themselves; a consent of fathers of one age against a consent of fathers of another age; the Church of one age against the Church of another age. Traditive interpretations of Scripture are pretended, but there are few or none to be found. No tradition, but only of Scripture, can derive itself from the Fountain, but may be plainly proved either to have been brought in, in such an age after Christ, or that in such an age it was not in. In a word, there is no sufficient certainty, but of Scripture only, for any considering man to build upon. This, therefore, and this only, I have reason to believe: this I will profess; according to this I will live; and for this, if there be occasion, I will not only willingly, but even gladly, lose my life, though I should be sorry that Christians should take it from me. Propose me anything out of this Book, and require whether I believe it or no, and seem it never so incomprehensible to human reason, I will subscribe it with hand and heart, as knowing no demonstration can be stronger than this: — God hath said so; therefore it is true. In other things I will take no man's liberty of judgment from him, neither shall any man take mine from me. I will think no man the worse man, nor the worse Christian; I will love no man the less for differing in opinion from me. And what measure I mete to others, I expect from them again. I am fully assured that God does not, and therefore that man ought not, to require any more of any man than this, to believe the Scripture to be

1 The Roman Catholic. 2 Augsburg.

God's Word; to endeavor to find the true sense of it; and to live according to it.

This is the religion which I have chosen, after a long deliberation; and I am verily persuaded that I have chosen wisely, much more wisely, than if I had guided myself according to your Church's authority.

---

114. Sir Thomas Browne. 1605–1682. (Manual, p. 178.)

Thoughts on Death and Immortality.

From the "Hydriotaphia."

In a field of Old Walsingham, not many months past, were digged up between forty and fifty urns, deposited in a dry and sandy soil, not a yard deep, not far from one another: not all strictly of one figure, but most answering these described; some containing two pounds of bones, distinguishable in skulls, ribs, jaws, thigh-bones, and teeth, with fresh impressions of their combustion; besides, the extraneous substances, like pieces of small boxes, or combs handsomely wrought, handles of small brass instruments, brazen nippers, and in one some kind of opal.

That these were the urns of Romans, from the common custom and place where they were found, is no obscure conjecture; not far from a Roman garrison, and but five miles from Brancaster, set down by ancient record under the name of Brannodunum; and where the adjoining town, containing seven parishes, in no very different sound, but Saxon termination, still retains the name of Burnham; which being an early station, it is not improbable the neighbor parts were filled with habitations, either of Romans themselves, or Britons Romanized, which observed the Roman customs. * * * *

What song the sirens sang, or what name Achilles assumed when he hid himself among women, though puzzling questions, are not beyond all conjecture. What time the persons of these ossuaries entered the famous nations of the dead, and slept with princes and counsellors, might admit a wide solution. But who were the proprietaries of these bones, or what bodies these ashes made up, were a question above antiquarianism; not to be resolved by man, not easily perhaps by spirits, except we consult the provincial guardians, or tutelary observators. Had they made as good provision for their names, as they have done for their relics, they had not so grossly erred in the art of perpetuation. But to subsist in bones, and be but pyramidally extant, is a fallacy in duration. * * * *

But the iniquity of oblivion blindly scattereth her poppy, and deals with the memory of men without distinction to merit of perpetuity. Who can but pity the founder of the pyramids? Herostratus lives, that burnt the temple of Diana! *he* is almost lost that built it. Time hath spared the epitaph of Adrian's horse, confounded that of himself. In vain we compute our felicities by the advantage of our good names, since bad have equal durations; and Thersites is like to live as long as Agamemnon, without the favor of the everlasting register. Who knows whether the best of men be known, or whether there be not more remarkable persons forgot, than any that stand remembered in the known account of time? The first man had been as unknown as the last, and Methuselah's long life had been his only chronicle.

There is nothing strictly immortal but immortality. Whatever hath no beginning, may be confident of no end. All others have a dependent being, and within the reach of destruction, which is the peculiar of that necessary essence that cannot destroy itself, and the highest strain of omnipotency, to be so powerfully constituted, as not to suffer even from the power of itself. . But the sufficiency of Christian immortality frustrates all earthly glory, and the quality of either state after death makes a folly of posthumous memory.

Man is a noble animal, splendid in ashes, and pompous in the grave; solemnizing nativities and deaths with equal lustre.

---

115. THOMAS FULLER. 1608–1661. (Manual, p. 179.)

THE GOOD SCHOOLMASTER.

From the "Holy State."

There is scarce any profession in the commonwealth more necessary, which is so slightly performed. The reasons whereof I conceive to be these: — First, young scholars make this calling their refuge; yea, perchance, before they have taken any degree in the university, commence schoolmasters in the country, as if nothing else were required to set up this profession but only a rod and a ferula. Secondly, others who are able, use it only as a passage to better preferment, to patch the rents in their present fortune, till they can provide a new one, and betake themselves to some more gainful calling. Thirdly, they are disheartened from doing their best with the miserable reward which in some places they receive, being masters to their children and slaves to their parents. Fourthly, being grown rich they grow negligent, and scorn to touch the school but by the proxy of the usher. But see how well our schoolmaster behaves himself.

His genius inclines him with delight to his profession. God, of his goodness, hath fitted several men for several callings, that the necessity of Church and State, in all conditions, may be provided for. And thus God mouldeth some for a schoolmaster's life, undertaking it with desire and delight, and discharging it with dexterity and happy success.

He studieth his scholars' natures as carefully as they their books; and ranks their dispositions into several forms. And though it may seem difficult for him in a great school to descend to all particulars, yet experienced schoolmasters may quickly make a grammar of boys' natures.

He is able, diligent, and methodical in his teaching; not leading them rather in a circle than forwards. He minces his precepts for children to swallow, hanging clogs on the nimbleness of his own soul, that his scholars may go along with him.

He is moderate in inflicting deserved correction. Many a schoolmaster better answereth the name *paidotribe*[1] than *paidagogos*,[2] rather tearing his scholars' flesh with whipping, than giving them good education. No wonder if his scholars hate the Muses, being presented unto them in the shapes of fiends and furies.

Such an Orbilius mars more scholars than he makes. Their tyranny hath caused many tongues to stammer which spake plain by nature, and whose stuttering at first was nothing else but fears quavering on their speech at their master's presence, and whose mauling them about their heads hath dulled those who in quickness exceeded their master.

To conclude, let this, amongst other motives, make schoolmasters careful in their place — that the eminences of their scholars have commended the memories of their schoolmasters to posterity.

1 Boy-bruiser. 2 Boy-teacher.

---

116. Jeremy Taylor. 1613–1667. (Manual, p. 181.)

Marriage.

The dominion of a man over his wife is no other than as the soul rules the body; for which it takes a mighty care, and uses it with a delicate tenderness, and cares for it in all contingencies, and watches to keep it from all evils, and studies to make for it fair provisions, and very often is led by its inclinations and desires, and does never contradict its appetites, but when they are evil, and then also not without some trouble and sorrow; and its government comes only to this, it furnishes the body with light and understanding, and the body furnishes the soul with hands and feet; the soul governs, because the body cannot else be happy, but the government is no other than provision; as a nurse governs a child, when she causes him to eat, and to be warm, and dry, and quiet. And yet even the very government itself is divided; for man and wife in the family, are as the sun and moon in the firmament of heaven; he rules by day, and she by night, that is, in the lesser and more proper circles of her affairs, in the conduct of domestic provisions and necessary offices, and shines only by his light, and rules by his authority. And as the moon in opposition to the sun shines brightest; that is, then, when she is in her own circles and separate regions; so is the authority of the wife then most conspicuous, when she is separate and in her proper sphere; "in gynæceo," in the nursery and offices of domestic employment. But when she is in conjunction with the sun, her brother, that is, in that place and employment in which his care and proper offices are employed, her light is not seen, her authority hath no proper business.

But else there is no difference, for they were barbarous people, among whom wives were instead of servants; and it is a sign of weakness, to force the camels to kneel for their load because thou hast not strength and spirit enough to climb; to make the affections and evenness of a wife bend by the flexures of a servant, is a sign the man is not wise enough to govern when another is by. And as amongst men and women humility is the way to be preferred, so it is in husbands, they shall prevail by cession, by sweetness and counsel, and charity and compliance. So that we cannot discourse of the man's right, without describing the measures of his duty.

On Prayer.

Prayer is an action of likeness to the Holy Ghost, the Spirit of gentleness and dove-like simplicity; an imitation of the holy Jesus, whose spirit is meek, up to the greatness of the biggest example; and a conformity to God, whose anger is always just, and marches slowly, and is without transportation, and often hindered, and never hasty, and is full of mercy. Prayer is the peace of our spirit, the stillness of our thoughts, the evenness of recollection, the seat of meditation, the rest of our cares, and the calm of our tempest; prayer is the issue of a quiet mind, of untroubled thoughts, it is the daughter of charity, and the sister of meekness; and he that prays to God with an angry, that is, with a troubled and discomposed spirit, is like him that retires into a battle to meditate, and sets up his closet in the out-quarters of an army, and chooses a frontier garrison to be wise in. Anger is a perfect alienation of the mind from prayer, and therefore is contrary to that attention, which presents our prayers in a right line to God. For so have I seen a lark rising from his bed of grass, and soaring upwards, singing as he rises, and hopes to get to heaven, and climb above the clouds; but the poor bird was beaten back with the loud sighings of an eastern wind, and his motion made irregular and inconstant, descending more at every breath of the tempest than it could recover by the libration and frequent weighing of his wings; till the little creature was forced to sit down and pant, and stay till the storm was over; and then it made a prosperous flight, and did rise and sing as if it had learned music and motion from an angel, as he passed sometimes through the air about his ministries here below: so is the prayer of a good man: when his affairs have required business, and his business was matter of discipline, and his discipline was to pass upon a sinning person, or had a design of charity, his duty met with the infirmities of a man, and anger was its instrument, and the instrument became stronger than the prime agent, and raised a tempest, and overruled the man; and then his prayer was broken, and his thoughts were troubled, and his words went up towards a cloud, and his thoughts pulled them back again, and made them without intention, and the good man sighs for his infirmity, but must be content to lose the prayer, and he must recover it when his anger is removed, and his spirit is becalmed, made even as the brow of Jesus, and smooth like the heart of God; and then it ascends to heaven upon the wings of the holy dove, and dwells with God, till it returns, like the useful bee, loaden with a blessing and the dew of heaven.

ON CONTENT.

Since all the evil in the world consists in the disagreeing between the object and the appetite, as when a man hath what he desires not, or desires what he hath not, or desires amiss, he that composes his spirit to the present accident hath variety of instances for his virtue, but none to trouble him, because his desires enlarge not beyond his present fortune: and a wise man is placed in the variety of chances, like the nave or centre of a wheel in the midst of all the circumvolutions and changes of posture, without violence or change, save that it turns gently in compliance with its changed parts, and is indifferent which part is up, and which is down; for there is some virtue or other to be exercised whatever happens — either patience or thanksgiving, love or fear, moderation or humility, charity or contentedness.

It conduces much to our content, if we pass by those things which happen to our trouble, and consider that which is pleasing and prosperous; that, by the representation of the better, the worse may be blotted out.

It may be thou art entered into the cloud which will bring a gentle shower to refresh thy sorrows.

I am fallen into the hands of publicans and sequestrators, and they have taken all from me: what now? let me look about me. They have left me the sun and moon, fire and water, a loving wife, and many friends to pity me, and some to relieve me, and I can still discourse; and, unless I list, they have not taken away my merry countenance, and my cheerful spirit, and a good conscience; they still have left me the providence of God, and all the promises of the Gospel, and my religion, and my hopes of heaven, and my charity to them too: and still I sleep and digest, I eat and drink, I read and meditate, I can walk in my neighbor's pleasant fields, and see the varieties of natural beauties, and delight in all that in which God delights, that is, in virtue and wisdom, in the whole creation, and in God himself.

AGAINST ANGER.

1. Consider that anger is a professed enemy to counsel; it is a direct storm, in which no man can be heard to speak or call from without: for if you counsel gently, you are despised; if you urge it and be vehement, you provoke it more. Be careful, therefore, to lay

up beforehand a great stock of reason and prudent consideration, that, like a besieged town, you may be provided for, and be defensible from within, since you are not likely to be relieved from without. Anger is not to be suppressed but by something which is as inward as itself, and more habitual. To which purpose add that, 2. Of all passions it endeavors most to make reason useless. 3. That it is a universal passion, of an infinite object; for no man was ever so amorous as to love a toad; none so envious as to repine at the condition of the miserable; no man so timorous as to fear a dead bee; but anger is troubled at every thing, and every man, and every accident: and therefore, unless it be suppressed, it will make a man's condition restless. 4. If it proceeds from a great cause, it turns to fury; if from a small cause, it is peevishness: and so is always either terrible or ridiculous. 5. It makes a man's body monstrous, deformed, and contemptible; the voice horrid; the eyes cruel; the face pale or fiery; the gait fierce; the speech clamorous and loud. 6. It is neither manly nor ingenuous. 7. It proceeds from softness of spirit and pusillanimity; which makes, that women are more angry than men, sick persons more than the healthful, old men more than young, unprosperous and calamitous people than the blessed and fortunate. 8. It is a passion fitter for flies and insects, than for persons professing nobleness and bounty. 9. It is troublesome, not only to those that suffer it, but to them that behold it; there being no greater incivility of entertainment, than, for the cook's fault or the negligence of the servants, to be cruel, or outrageous, or unpleasant in the presence of guests. 10. It makes marriage to be a necessary and unavoidable trouble; friendships, and societies, and familiarities to be intolerable. 11. It multiplies the evils of drunkenness, and makes the levities of wine to run into madness. 12. It makes innocent jesting to be the beginning of tragedies. 13. It turns friendship into hatred; it makes a man lose himself, and his reason, and his argument in disputations. It turns the desires of knowledge into an itch of wrangling. It adds insolency to power. It turns justice into cruelty, and judgment into oppression. It changes discipline into tediousness and hatred of liberal institutions. It makes a prosperous man to be envied, and the unfortunate to be unpitied. It is a confluence of all the irregular passions: there is in it envy and sorrow, fear and scorn, pride and prejudice, rashness and inconsideration, rejoicing in evil, and a desire to inflict it, self-love, impatience, and curiosity. And, lastly, though it be very troublesome to others, yet it is most troublesome to him that hath it.

Comforting the Afflicted.

Certain it is, that as nothing can better do it, so there is nothing greater, for which God made our tongues, next to reciting His praises, than to minister comfort to a weary soul. And what greater measure can we have, than that we should bring joy to our brother, who with his dreary eyes looks to heaven and round about, and cannot find so much rest as to lay his eyelids close together — than that thy tongue should be tuned with heavenly accents, and make the weary soul to listen for light and ease; and when he perceives that there is such a thing in the world, and in the order of things, as comfort and joy, to begin to break out from the prison of his sorrows at the door of sighs and tears, and by little and little melt into showers and refreshment? This is glory to thy voice, and employment fit for the brightest angel. But so have I seen the sun kiss the frozen earth, which was bound up with the images of death, and the colder breath of the north; and then the waters break from their enclosures, and melt with joy, and run in useful channels; and the flies do rise again from their little graves in the walls, and dance a while in the air, to tell that their joy is within, and that the great mother of creatures will open the stock of her new refreshment, become useful to mankind, and sing praises to her Redeemer. So is the heart of a sorrowful man under the discourses of a wise comforter; he breaks from the despairs of the grave, and the fetters and chains of sorrow; he blesses God, and he blesses thee, and he feels his life returning; for to be miserable is death, but nothing is life but to be comforted; and God is pleased with no music from below so much as in the thanksgiving songs of relieved widows, of supported orphans, of rejoicing, and comforted, and thankful persons.

---

117. RICHARD BAXTER. 1615–1691. (Manual, p. 184.)

FROM THE "SAINTS' REST."

Rest! how sweet the sound! It is melody to my ears! It lies as a reviving cordial at my heart, and from thence sends forth lively spirits which beat through all the pulses of my soul! Rest, not as the stone that rests on the earth, nor as this flesh shall rest in the grave, nor such a rest as the carnal world desires. O blessed rest! when we rest not day and night, saying, "Holy, holy, holy, Lord God Almighty:" when we shall rest from sin, but not from worship; from suffering and sorrow, but not from joy! O blessed day! when I shall rest with God! when I shall rest in the bosom of my Lord! when my perfect soul and body shall together perfectly enjoy the most perfect God! when God, who is love itself, shall perfectly love me, and rest in this love to me, as I shall rest in my love to Him; and rejoice over me with joy, and joy over me with singing, as I shall rejoice in Him!

This is that joy which was procured by sorrow, that crown which was procured by the Cross. My Lord wept that now my tears might be wiped away; He bled that I might now rejoice; He was forsaken that I might not now be forsook; He then died that I might now live. O free mercy, that can exalt so vile a wretch! Free to me, though dear to Christ: free grace that hath chosen me, when thousands were forsaken. This is not like our cottages of clay, our prisons, our earthly dwellings. This voice of joy is not like our old complaints, our impatient groans and sighs; nor this melodious praise like the scoffs and revilings, or the oaths and curses, which we heard on earth. This body is not like that we had, nor this soul like the soul we had, nor this life like the life we lived. We have changed our place and state, our clothes and thoughts, our looks, language, and company. Before, a saint was weak and despised; but now, how happy and glorious a thing is a saint! Where is now their body of sin, which wearied themselves and those about them? Where are now our different judgments, reproachful names, divided spirits, exasperated passions, strange looks, uncharitable censures? Now are all of one judgment, of one name, of one heart, house, and glory. O sweet reconciliation! happy union! Now the Gospel shall no more be dishonored through our folly. No more, my soul, shalt thou lament the sufferings of the saints, or the church's ruins, or mourn thy suffering friends, nor weep over their dying beds or their graves. Thou shalt never suffer thy old temptations from Satan, the world, or thy own flesh. Thy pains and sickness are all cured; thy body shall no more burden thee with weakness and weariness; thy aching head and heart, thy hunger and thirst, thy sleep and labor, are all gone. O what a mighty change is this. From the dunghill to the throne! From persecuting sinners to praising saints! From a vile body to this which shines as the brightness of the firmament! From a sense of God's displeasure to the perfect enjoyment of Him in love! From all my fearful thoughts of death to this joyful life! Blessed change! Farewell sin and sorrow forever; farewell my rocky, proud, unbelieving heart; my worldly, sensual, carnal heart; and welcome my most holy, heavenly nature. Farewell repentance, faith, and hope; and welcome love, and joy, and praise. I shall now have my harvest without ploughing or sowing: my joy without a preacher or a promise: even all from the face of God Himself. Whatever mixture is in the streams, there is nothing but pure joy in the fountain. Here shall I be encircled with eternity, and ever live, and ever, ever praise the Lord. My face will not wrinkle, nor my hair be gray: for this corruptible shall have put on incorruption; and this mortal immortality; and death shall be swallowed up in victory. O death, where is now thy sting? O grave, where is thy victory? The date of my lease will no more expire, nor shall I trouble myself with thoughts of death, nor lose my joys through fear of losing them. When millions of ages are past, my glory is but beginning; and when millions more are past, it is no nearer ending. Every day is all noon, every month is harvest, every year is a jubilee, every age is a full manhood, and all this is one eternity. O blessed eternity! the glory of my glory, the perfection of my perfection.

118. JOSEPH HALL. 1574–1656. (Manual, p. 186.)

(For his Poetry, see page 57.)

THE PLEASURE OF STUDY.

I can wonder at nothing more than how a man can be idle, but of all others, a scholar; in so many improvements of reason, in such sweetness of knowledge, in such variety of studies, in such importunity of thoughts: other artisans do but practise, we still learn; others run still in the same gyre to weariness, to satiety; our choice is infinite; other labors require recreation; our very labor recreates our sports; we can never want either somewhat to do, or somewhat that we would do. How numberless are the volumes which men have written of arts, of tongues! How endless is that volume which God hath written of the world! wherein every creature is a letter, every day a new page. Who can be weary of either of these? To find wit in poetry; in philosophy profoundness; in mathematics acuteness; in history wonder of events; in oratory sweet eloquence; in divinity supernatural light and holy devotion; as so many rich metals in their proper mines; whom would it not ravish with delight? After all these, let us but open our eyes, we cannot look beside a lesson, in this universal book of our Maker, worth our study, worth taking out. What creature hath not his miracle? what event doth not challenge his observation? How many busy tongues chase away good hours in pleasant chat, and complain of the haste of night! What ingenious mind can be sooner weary of talking with learned authors, the most harmless and sweetest companions? Let the world contemn us; while we have these delights we cannot envy them; we cannot wish ourselves other than we are. Besides, the way to all other contentments is troublesome; the only recompense is in the end. But very search of knowledge is delightsome. Study itself is our life; from which we would not be barred for a world. How much sweeter then is the fruit of study, the conscience of knowledge? In comparison whereof the soul that hath once tasted it, easily contemns all human comforts.

---

119. OWEN FELTHAM. Circa 1610–1677. (Manual, p. 186.)

SEDULITY AND DILIGENCE.

There is no such prevalent workman as sedulity and diligence. A man would wonder at the mighty things which have been done by degrees and gentle augmentations. Diligence and moderation are the best steps whereby to climb to any excellency. Nay, it is rare if there be any other way. The heavens send not down their rain in floods, but by drops and dewy distillations. A man is neither good, nor wise, nor rich, at once: yet softly creeping up these hills, he shall every day better his prospect; till at last he gains the top. Now he learns a virtue, and then he damns [1] a vice. An hour in a day may much profit a man in his study, when he makes it stint and custom. Every year something laid up, may in time make a stock great. Nay, if a man does but save, he shall increase; and though when the grains are scattered, they be next to nothing, yet together they will swell the heap. He that has the patience to attend small profits, may quickly grow to thrive and purchase: they be easier to accomplish, and come thicker. So, he that from everything collects somewhat, shall in time get a treasury of wisdom. And when all is done, for man, this is the best way. It is for God, and for Omnipotency, to do mighty things in a moment: but, *degreeingly* to grow to greatness, is the course that He hath left for man.

1 Used in the Latin sense of *damno*, to condemn, to renounce.

---

120. Sir Thomas Overbury. 1581–1613. (Manual, p. 186.)

A Fair and Happy Milkmaid

Is a country wench, that is so far from making herself beautiful by art, that one look of hers is able to put all face-physic out of countenance. She knows a fair look is but a dumb orator to commend virtue, therefore minds it not. All her excellences stand in her so silently, as if they had stolen upon her without her knowledge. The lining of her apparel, which is herself, is far better than outsides of tissues; for though she be not arrayed in the spoil of the silkworm, she is decked in innocence, a far better wearing. She doth not, with lying long in bed, spoil both her complexion and conditions: nature hath taught her too, immoderate sleep is rust to the soul; she rises therefore with Chanticlere, her dame's cock, and at night makes the lamb her curfew. In milking a cow, and straining the teats through her fingers, it seems that so sweet a milk-press makes the milk whiter or sweeter; for never came almond-glore or aromatic ointment on her palm to taint it. The golden ears of corn fall and kiss her feet when she reaps them, as if they wished to be bound and led prisoners by the same hand that felled them. Her breath is her own, which scents all the year long of June, like a new-made haycock. She makes her hand hard with labor, and her heart soft with pity; and when winter evenings fall early, sitting at her merry wheel, she sings defiance to the giddy wheel of fortune. She doth all things with so sweet a grace, it seems ignorance will not suffer her to do ill, being her mind is to do well. She bestows her year's wages at next fair, and in choosing her garments, counts no bravery in the world like decency. The garden and beehive are all her physic and surgery, and she lives the longer for it. She dares go alone and unfold sheep in the night, and fears no manner of ill, because she means none; yet, to say truth, she is never alone, but is still accompanied with old songs, honest thoughts, and prayers, but short ones; yet they have their efficacy, in that they are not palled with ensuing idle cogitations. Lastly, her dreams are so chaste, that she dare tell them; only a Friday's dream is all her superstition; that she conceals for fear of anger. Thus lives she, and all her care is, she may die in the spring-time, to have store of flowers stuck upon her winding-sheet.

CHAPTER XI.

JOHN MILTON. 1608–1674. (Manual, p. 187–205.)

121. FROM THE HYMN OF THE NATIVITY.

It was the winter wild,
While the heaven-born child
  All meanly wrapt in the rude manager lies;
Nature, in awe to him,
Had doffed her gaudy trim,
  With her great Master so to sympathize;
It was no season then for her
To wanton with the sun, her lusty paramour.

No war, or battle's sound
Was heard the world around,
  The idle spear and shield were high up hung,
The hookéd chariot stood
Unstained with hostile blood;
  The trumpet spake not to the arméd throng;
And kings sat still with awful eye,
As if they surely knew their sovereign Lord was by.

But peaceful was the night,
Wherein the Prince of Light
  His reign of peace upon the earth began:
The winds, with wonder whist,
Smoothly the waters kissed,
  Whispering new joys to the mild ocean,
Who now hath quite forget to rave,
While birds of calm sit brooding on the charméd wave.

The stars, with deep amaze,
Stand fixed in steadfast gaze,
  Bending one way their precious influence;
And will not take their flight,
For all the morning light,
  Or Lucifer, that often warned them thence;
But in their glimmering orbs did glow,
Until their Lord himself bespake, and bid them go.

The shepherds on the lawn,
Or e'er the point of dawn,
  Sat simply chatting in a rustic row;
Full little thought they than,
That the mighty Pan
  Was kindly come to live with them below;
Perhaps their loves, or else their sheep,
Was all that did their silly thoughts so busy keep.

When such music sweet
Their hearts and ears did greet,
  As never was by mortal finger strook;
Divinely-warbled voice
Answering the stringéd noise,
  As all their souls in blissful rapture took:
The air, such pleasures loath to lose,
With thousand echoes still prolongs each heavenly close.

The oracles are dumb,
No voice or hideous hum
  Runs through the archéd roof in words deceiving.
Apollo from his shrine
Can no more divine,
  With hollow shriek the steep of Delphos leaving.
No nightly trance, or breathéd spell,
Inspires the pale-eyed priest from the prophetic cell.

The lonely mountains o'er
And the resounding shore,
  A voice of weeping heard and loud lament;
From haunted spring and dale,
Edged with poplar pale,
  The parting Genius is with sighing sent:
With flower-inwoven tresses torn,
The Nymphs, in twilight shade of tangled thickets, mourn.

In consecrated earth,
And on the holy hearth,
  The Lars and Lemures moan with midnight plaint;
In urns and altars round,
A drear and dying sound
  Affrights the Flamens at their service quaint;
And the chill marble seems to sweat,
While each peculiar power foregoes his wonted seat.

But see, the Virgin blessed
Hath laid her Babe to rest;
  Time is, our tedious song should here have ending:

Heaven's youngest-teemèd star
Hath fixed her polished car,
Her sleeping Lord with handmaid lamp attending;
And all about the courtly stable
Bright-harnessed angels sit in order serviceable.

---

122. From Comus.

Song.

Sweet Echo, sweetest nymph, that liv'st unseen
Within thy aery shell,
By slow Meander's margent green
And in the violet-embroidered vale,
Where the love-lorn nightingale
Nightly to thee her sad song mourneth well;
Canst thou not tell me of a gentle pair
That likest thy Narcissus are?
O if thou have
Hid them in some flowery cave,
Tell me but where,
Sweet queen of parley, daughter of the sphere!
So mayst thou be translated to the skies,
And give resounding grace to all heaven's harmonies.

Enter Comus.

Comus. Can any mortal mixture of earth's mould
Breathe such divine enchanting ravishment?
Sure something holy lodges in that breast,
And with these raptures moves the vocal air
To testify his hidden residence.
How sweetly did they float upon the wings
Of silence, through the empty-vaulted night,
At every fall smoothing the raven-down
Of darkness, till it smiled! I have oft heard
My mother Circe with the sirens three,
Amid the flowery-kirtled Naiades,
Culling their potent herbs and baleful drugs;
Who, as they sung, would take the prisoned soul,
And lap it in Elysium: Scylla wept,
And chid her barking waves into attention,
And fell Charybdis murmured soft applause:
Yet they in pleasing slumber lulled the sense,
And in sweet madness robbed it of itself;
But such a sacred and home-felt delight,
Such sober certainty of waking bliss,
I never heard till now. — I'll speak to her,

And she shall be my queen. — Hail, foreign wonder!
Whom certain these rough shades did never breed,
Unless the goddess that in rural shrine
Dwell'st here with Pan, or Sylvan: by blest song
Forbidding every bleak unkindly fog
To touch the prosperous growth of this tall wood.

---

123. FROM LYCIDAS.

Where were ye, Nymphs, when the remorseless deep
Closed o'er the head of your loved Lycidas?
For neither were ye playing on the steep,
Where your old bards, the famous Druids, lie,
Nor on the shaggy top of Mona high,
Nor yet where Deva spreads her wizard stream.
Ay me! I fondly dream!
Had ye been there — for what could that have done?
What could the Muse herself that Orpheus bore,
The Muse herself, for her enchanting son,
Whom universal Nature did lament,
When by the rout that made the hideous roar,
His gory visage down the stream was sent,
Down the swift Hebrus to the Lesbian shore?
  Alas! what boots it with uncessant care
To tend the homely, slighted shepherd's trade,
And strictly meditate the thankless Muse?
Were it not better done, as others use,
To sport with Amaryllis in the shade,
Or with the tangles of Neæra's hair?
Fame is the spur that the clear spirit doth raise,
(That last infirmity of noble mind)
To scorn delights, and live laborious days;
But the fair guerdon when we hope to find,
And think to burst out into sudden blaze,
Comes the blind Fury with the abhorréd shears,
And slits the thin-spun life. "But not the praise,"
Phœbus replied, and touched my trembling ears;
"Fame is no plant that grows on mortal soil,
Nor in the glistering foil
Set off to the world, nor in broad rumor lies;
But lives and spreads aloft by those pure eyes,
And perfect witness of all-judging Jove:
As he pronounces lastly on each deed,
Of so much fame in Heaven expect thy meed."

124. From L'Allegro.

Haste thee, Nymph, and bring with thee
Jest and youthful Jollity,
Quips and Cranks, and wanton Wiles,
Nods, and Becks, and wreathèd Smiles,
Such as hang on Hebe's cheek,
And love to live in dimple sleek;
Sport that wrinkled care derides,
And Laughter holding both his sides.
Come, and trip it, as you go,
On the light fantastic toe;
And in thy right hand lead with thee
The mountain-nymph, sweet Liberty;
And, if I give thee honor due,
Mirth, admit me of thy crew,
To live with her, and live with thee,
In unreprovèd pleasures free.
To hear the lark begin his flight,
And singing startle the dull Night,
From his watch-tower in the skies,
Till the dappled Dawn doth rise;
Then to come in spite of sorrow,
And at my window bid good morrow,
Through the sweet-brier or the vine,
Or the twisted eglantine:
While the cock, with lively din,
Scatters the rear of darkness thin,
And to the stack or the barn door
Stoutly struts his dames before.

* * * * * * *

And ever, against eating cares,
Lap me in soft Lydian airs,
Married to immortal verse;
Such as the meeting soul may pierce,
In notes, with many a winding bout
Of linkèd sweetness long drawn out,
With wanton heed and giddy cunning;
The melting voice through mazes running,
Untwisting all the chains that tie
The hidden soul of harmony;
That Orpheus' self may heave his head
From golden slumber on a bed
Of heaped Elysian flowers, and hear
Such strains as would have won the ear
Of Pluto, to have quite set free
His half-regained Eurydicè.
These delights if thou canst give,
Mirth, with thee I mean to live.

125. From Il Penseroso.

Come, pensive nun, devout and pure,
Sober, steadfast, and demure,
All in a robe of darkest grain,
Flowing with majestic train,
And sable stole of Cyprus lawn,
Over thy decent shoulders drawn.
Come, but keep thy wonted state,
With even step and musing gait;
And looks commèrcing with the skies,
Thy rapt soul sitting in thine eyes;
There, held in holy passion still,
Forget thyself to marble, till
With a sad leaden downward cast
Thou fix them on the earth as fast:
And join with thee calm Peace and Quiet,
Spare Fast, that oft with gods doth diet,
And hears the Musés in a ring
Aye round about Jove's altar sing:
And add to these retiréd Leisure,
That in trim gardens takes his pleasure.
But first, and chiefest, with thee bring
Him that yon soars on golden wing,
Guiding the fiery-wheeléd throne,
The cherub Contemplation;
And the mute Silence hist along,
'Less Philomel will deign a song,
In her sweetest, saddest plight,
Smoothing the rugged brow of Night,
While Cynthia checks her dragon yoke,
Gently o'er the accustomed oak:
Sweet bird, that shunn'st the noise of folly,
Most musical, most melancholy!
Thee, chantress, oft, the woods among,
I woo, to hear thy even-song;
And, missing thee, I walk unseen
On the dry smooth-shaven green
To behold the wandering moon,
Riding near her highest noon,
Like one that had been led astray
Through the heaven's wide pathless way;
And oft, as if her head she bowed,
Stooping through a fleecy cloud
Oft, on a plat of rising ground,
I hear the far-off Curfew sound,
Over some wide-watered shore,
Swinging slow with sullen roar.

FROM "PARADISE LOST."

126. EXORDIUM OF BOOK I.

Of man's first disobedience, and the fruit
Of that forbidden tree, whose mortal taste
Brought death into the world, and all our woe,
With loss of Eden, till one greater Man
Restore us, and regain the blissful seat,
Sing, heavenly Muse, that on the secret top
Of Oreb, or of Sinai, didst inspire
That Shepherd, who first taught the chosen seed,
In the beginning, how the Heavens and Earth
Rose out of Chaos: Or, if Sion hill
Delight thee more, and Siloa's brook that flowed
Fast by the oracle of God; I thence
Invoke thy aid to my adventurous song,
That with no middle flight intends to soar
Above the Aonian mount, while it pursues
Things unattempted yet in prose or rhyme.
And chiefly thou, O Spirit, that dost prefer
Before all temples the upright heart and pure,
Instruct me, for thou know'st; thou from the first
Wast present, and, with mighty wings outspread,
Dove-like satt'st brooding on the vast abyss
And mad'st it pregnant: what in me is dark
Illumine; what is low raise and support;
That to the height of this great argument
I may assert eternal Providence,
And justify the ways of God to men.

---

127. SATAN. (Book I.)

He scarce had ceased when the superior fiend
Was moving toward the shore: his ponderous shield,
Ethereal temper, massy, large and round,
Behind him cast; the broad circumference
Hung on his shoulders like the Moon, whose orb
Through optic glass the Tuscan artist views
At evening from the top of Fesolé,
Or in Valdarno, to descry new lands,
Rivers, or mountains in her spotty globe.
His spear, to equal which the tallest pine
Hewn on Norwegian hills, to be the mast
Of some great ammiral, were but a wand,
He walked with, to support uneasy steps

Over the burning marle, not like those steps
On Heaven's azure; and the torrid clime
Smote on him sore besides, vaulted with fire:
Nathless he so endured till on the beach
Of that inflamèd sea he stood, and called
His legions, angel forms, who lay entranced,
Thick as autumnal leaves that strew the brooks
In Vallombrosa, where the Etrurian shades,
High over-arched, embower; or scattered sedge
Afloat, when with fierce winds Orion armed
Hath vexed the Red-Sea coast, whose waves o'erthrew
Busiris and his Memphian chivalry,
While with perfidious hatred they pursued
The sojourners of Goshen, who beheld
From the safe shore their floating carcasses
And broken chariot wheels: so thick bestrewn,
Abject and lost lay these, covering the flood,
Under amazement of their hideous change.
He called so loud, that all the hollow deep
Of Hell resounded. "Princes, potentates,
Warriors, the flower of Heaven, once yours, now lost,
If such astonishment as this can seize
Eternal spirits; or have ye chosen this place,
After the toil of battle to repose
Your wearied virtue, for the ease you find
To slumber here, as in the vales of Heaven?
Or in this abject posture have ye sworn
T' adore the Conqueror? who now beholds
Cherub and seraph rolling in the flood
With scattered arms and ensigns, till anon
His swift pursuers, from Heaven-gates, discern
Th' advantage, and, descending, tread us down
Thus drooping, or with linkèd thunderbolts
Transfix us to the bottom of this gulf.
Awake, arise, or be forever fallen."

---

128. PANDEMONIUM. (Book I.)

Anon, out of the earth a fabric huge
Rose like an exhalation, with the sound
Of dulcet symphonies and voices sweet,
Built like a temple, where pilasters round
Were set, and Doric pillars overlaid
With golden architrave; nor did there want
Cornice or frieze, with bossy sculptures graven:
The roof was fretted gold. Not Babylon,

Nor great Alcairo, such magnificence
Equalled in all their glories, to enshrine
Belus or Serapis their gods, or seat
Their kings, when Egypt with Assyria strove
In wealth and luxury. The ascending pile
Stood fixed her stately height: and straight the doors,
Opening their brazen folds, discover, wide
Within, her ample spaces, o'er the smooth
And level pavement; from the archéd roof,
Pendent by subtle magic, many a row
Of starry lamps and blazing cressets, fed
With naphtha and asphaltus, yielded light
As from a sky.

---

129. Death and Satan. (Book II.)

The other shape,
If shape it might be called that shape had none
Distinguishable in member, joint, or limb;
Or substance might be called that shadow seemed,
For each seemed either: black it stood as night,
Fierce as ten furies, terrible as Hell,
And shook a dreadful dart; what seemed his head
The likeness of a kingly crown had on.
Satan was now at hand, and from his seat
The monster moving onward came as fast
With horrid strides; Hell trembled as he strode.
The undaunted fiend what this might be admired,
Admired, not feared; God and his Son except,
Created thing naught valued he, nor shunned;
And with disdainful look thus first began:
"Whence and what art thou, execrable shape,
That dar'st, though grim and terrible, advance
Thy miscreated front athwart my way
To yonder gates? through them I mean to pass,
That be assured, without leave asked of thee:
Retire, or taste thy folly, and learn by proof
Hell-born, not to contend with spirits of Heaven."
To whom the goblin full of wrath replied:
"Art thou that traitor-angel, art thou he,
Who first broke peace in Heaven, and faith, till then
Unbroken; and in proud rebellious arms
Drew after him the third part of Heaven's sons
Conjured against the Highest; for which both thou
And they, outcast from God, are here condemned
To waste eternal days in woe and pain?
And reckon'st thou thyself with spirits of Heaven,

Hell-doomed, and breath'st defiance here and scorn,
Where I reign king, and, to enrage thee more,
Thy king and lord? Back to thy punishment,
False fugitive, and to thy speed add wings,
Lest with a whip of scorpions I pursue
Thy lingering, or with one stroke of this dart
Strange horror seize thee, and pangs unfelt before."
  So spake the grisly terror, and in shape,
So speaking and so threatening, grew tenfold
More dreadful and deform. On the other side,
Incensed with indignation, Satan stood
Unterrified, and like a comet burned,
That fires the length of Ophiucus huge
In the arctic sky, and from his horrid hair
Shakes pestilence and war. Each at the head
Levelled his deadly aim; their fatal hands
No second stroke intend; and such a frown
Each cast at the other, as when two black clouds,
With Heaven's artillery fraught, come rattling on
Over the Caspian, then stand front to front,
Hovering a space, till winds the signal blow
To join their dark encounter in mid air:
So frowned the mighty combatants, that Hell
Grew darker at their frown; so matched they stood
For never but once more was either like
To meet so great a foe.

---

130. Invocation to Light. (Book III.)

Hail, holy Light, offspring of Heaven, first-born,
Or of the Eternal coeternal beam,
May I express thee unblamed? since God is light,
And never but in unapproachéd light
Dwelt from eternity, dwelt then in thee,
Bright effluence of bright essence increate.
Or hear'st thou rather, pure ethereal stream,
Whose fountain who shall tell? Before the Sun,
Before the Heavens thou wert, and at the voice
Of God, as with a mantle, didst invest
The rising world of waters dark and deep,
Won from the void and formless infinite.
Thee I revisit now with bolder wing,
Escaped the Stygian pool, though long detained
In that obscure sojourn, while, in my flight,
Through utter and through middle darkness borne,
With other notes than to the Orphéan lyre,
I sung of Chaos and eternal Night;

Taught by the heavenly Muse to venture down
The dark descent, and up to re-ascend,
Though hard and rare: thee I revisit safe,
And feel thy sovran vital lamp: but thou
Revisit'st not these eyes, that roll in vain
To find thy piercing ray, and find no dawn;
So thick a drop serene hath quenched their orbs,
Or dim suffusion veiled. Yet not the more
Cease I to wander, where the Muses haunt
Clear spring, or shady grove, or sunny hill,
Smit with the love of sacred song; but chief
Thee, Sion, and the flowery brooks beneath,
That wash thy hallowed feet, and warbling flow,
Nightly I visit: nor sometimes forget
Those other two, equalled with me in fate
So were I equalled with them in renown,
Blind Thamyris, and blind Mæonides,
And Tiresias, and Phineus, prophets old:
Then feed on thoughts, that voluntary move
Harmonious numbers; as the wakeful bird
Sings darkling, and in shadiest covert hid,
Tunes her nocturnal note. Thus with the year
Seasons return; but not to me returns
Day, or the sweet approach of even or morn,
Or sight of vernal bloom, or summer's rose,
Or flocks, or herds, or human face divine;
But cloud instead, and ever-during dark
Surrounds me, from the cheerful ways of men
Cut off, and for the book of knowledge fair
Presented with a universal blank
Of Nature's works, to me expunged and rased,
And wisdom at one entrance quite shut out.
So much the rather thou, celestial Light,
Shine inward, and the mind through all her powers
Irradiate: there plant eyes, all mist from thence
Purge and disperse, that I may see and tell
Of things invisible to mortal sight.

---

131. EDEN. (Book IV.)

Thus was this place
A happy rural seat of various view;
Groves whose rich trees wept odorous gums and balm;
Others whose fruit, burnished with golden rind,
Hung amiable, Hesperian fables true,
If true, here only, and of delicious taste:

Betwixt them lawns, or level downs, and flocks
Grazing the tender herb, were interposed;
Or palmy hillock, or the flowery lap
Of some irriguous valley spread her store,
Flowers of all hue, and without thorn the rose:
Another side, umbrageous grots and caves
Of cool recess, o'er which the mantling vine
Lays forth her purple grape, and gently creeps
Luxuriant; meanwhile murmuring waters fall
Down the slope hills, dispersed, or in a lake,
That to the fringéd bank with myrtle crowned
Her crystal mirror holds, unite their streams.
The birds their quire apply; airs, vernal airs,
Breathing the smell of field and grove, attune
The trembling leaves, while universal Pan,
Knit with the Graces and the Hours in dance,
Led on the eternal Spring.

---

132. Adam and Eve. (Book IV.)

Two of far nobler shape, erect and tall,
Godlike erect, with native honor clad,
In naked majesty seemed lords of all
And worthy seemed: for in their looks divine
The image of their glorious Maker shone,
Truth, wisdom, sanctitude severe and pure
(Severe, but in true filial freedom placed),
Whence true authority in men; though both
Not equal, as their sex not equal seemed;
For contemplation he and valor formed;
For softness she, and sweet attractive grace;
He for God only, she for God in him:
His fair large front and eye sublime declared
Absolute rule; and hyacinthine locks
Round from his parted forelock manly hung
Clustering, but not beneath his shoulders broad:
She, as a veil, down to the slender waist
Her unadornéd golden tresses wore
Dishevelled, but in wanton ringlets waved,
As the vine curls her tendrils, which implied
Subjection, but required with gentle sway,
And by her yielded, by him best received,
Yielded with coy submission, modest pride,
And sweet, reluctant, amorous delay.

133. Evening in Eden. (Book IV.)

Now came still Evening on, and Twilight gray
Had in her sober livery all things clad;
Silence accompanied; for beast and bird,
They to their grassy couch, these to their nests,
Were slunk, all but the wakeful nightingale:
She all night long her amorous descant sung;
Silence was pleased: now glowed the firmament
With living sapphires: Hesperus, that led
The starry host, rode brightest, till the Moon,
Rising in clouded majesty, at length
Apparent queen, unveiled her peerless light,
And o'er the dark her silver mantle threw.

---

134. Morning Prayer of Adam and Eve. (Book V.)

These are thy glorious works, Parent of good,
Almighty! Thine this universal frame,
Thus wondrous fair: Thyself how wondrous then,
Unspeakable! who sitt'st above these heavens
To us invisible, or dimly seen
In these thy lowest works; yet these declare
Thy goodness beyond thought, and power divine.
Speak, ye who best can tell, ye sons of light,
Angels: for ye behold him, and with songs
And choral symphonies, day without night,
Circle his throne rejoicing; ye in heaven,
On earth join all ye creatures to extol
Him first, him last, him midst, and without end.
Fairest of stars, last in the train of night,
If better thou belong not to the dawn,
Sure pledge of day, that crown'st the smiling morn
With thy bright circlet, praise him in thy sphere,
While day arises, that sweet hour of prime.
Thou sun, of this great world both eye and soul,
Acknowledge him thy greater; sound his praise
In thy eternal course, both when thou climb'st,
And when high noon hast gained, and when thou fall'st.
Moon, that now meet'st the orient sun, now fly'st,
With the fixed stars, fixed in their orb that flies;
And ye five other wandering fires, that move
In mystic dance not without song, resound
His praise, who out of darkness called up light.
Air, and ye elements, the eldest birth
Of nature's womb, that in quaternion run

Perpetual circle, multiform; and mix
And nourish all things; let your ceaseless change
Vary to our great Maker still new praise.
Ye mists and exhalations, that now rise
From hill or steaming lake, dusky or gray,
Till the sun paint your fleecy skirts with gold,
In honor to the world's great Author rise;
Whether to deck with clouds the uncolored sky,
Or wet the thirsty earth with falling showers,
Rising or falling, still advance his praise.
His praise, ye winds, that from four quarters blow,
Breathe soft or loud; and wave your tops, ye pines,
With every plant, in sign of worship wave.
Fountains, and ye that warble as ye flow,
Melodious murmurs, warbling tune his praise.
Join voices, all ye living souls: ye birds,
That, singing, up to heaven-gate ascend,
Bear on your wings and in your notes his praise.
Ye that in waters glide, and ye that walk
The earth, and stately tread, or lowly creep;
Witness if I be silent, morn or even,
To hill or valley, fountain or fresh shade,
Made vocal by my song, and taught his praise.
Hail, universal Lord! be bounteous still
To give us only good; and if the night
Have gathered aught of evil or concealed,
Disperse it, as now light dispels the dark.

FROM "PARADISE REGAINED."

135. ATHENS. (Book IV.)

Look once more, ere we leave this specular mount,
Westward, much nearer by south-west; behold
Where on the Ægean shore a city stands,
Built nobly; pure the air, and light the soil;
Athens, the eye of Greece, mother of arts
And eloquence, native to famous wits,
Or hospitable, in her sweet recess,
City, or suburban, studious walks and shades:
See there the olive grove of Academe,
Plato's retirement, where the Attic bird
Trills her thick-warbled notes the summer long;
There flowery hill Hymettus with the sound
Of bees' industrious murmur oft invites
To studious musing: there Ilissus rolls
His whispering stream: within the walls then view

The schools of ancient sages; his who bred
Great Alexander to subdue the world,
Lyceum there, and painted Stoa next:
There shalt thou hear and learn the secret power
Of harmony, in tones and numbers hit
By voice or hand; and various-measured verse,
Æolian charms and Dorian lyric odes,
And his who gave them breath, but higher sung,
Blind Melesigenes, thence Homer called,
Whose poem Phœbus challenged for his own:
Thence what the lofty grave tragedians taught
In chorus or iambic, teachers best
Of moral prudence, with delight received
In brief sententious precepts, while they treat
Of fate, and chance, and change in human life;
High actions, and high passions best describing:
Thence to the famous orators repair,
Those ancient, whose resistless eloquence
Wielded at will that fierce democratie,
Shook the arsenal, and fulmined over Greece
To Macedon and Artaxerxes' throne:
To sage Philosophy next lend thine ear,
From Heaven descended to the low-roofed house
Of Socrates; see there his tenement,
Whom, well inspired, the oracle pronounced
Wisest of men; from whose mouth issued forth
Mellifluous streams, that watered all the schools
Of Academics old and new, with those
Surnamed Peripatetics, and the sect
Epicurean, and the Stoic severe:
These here revolve, or, as thou likest, at home,
Till time mature thee to a kingdom's weight:
These rules will render thee a king complete
Within thyself; much more with empire joined.

FROM "SAMSON AGONISTES."

136. LAMENT OF SAMSON.

O loss of sight, of thee I most complain!
Blind among enemies, O worse than chains,
Dungeon, or beggary, or decrepit age!
Light, the prime work of God, to me is extinct,
And all her various objects of delight
Annulled, which might in part my grief have eased,
Inferior to the vilest now become
Of man or worm; the vilest here excel me:

They creep, yet see; I, dark in light, exposed
To daily fraud, contempt, abuse, and wrong,
Within doors or without, still as a fool,
In power of others, never in my own;
Scarce half I seem to live, dead more than half.
O dark, dark, dark, amid the blaze of noon,
Irrecoverably dark, total eclipse
Without all hope of day!
O first-created Beam, and thou great Word,
"Let there be light, and light was over all;"
Why am I thus bereaved thy prime decree?
The sun to me is dark,
And silent as the moon,
When she deserts the night,
Hid in her vacant interlunar cave.
Since light so necessary is to life,
And almost life itself, if it be true
That light is in the soul,
She all in every part; why was this sight
To such a tender ball as the eye confined,
So obvious and easy to be quenched?
And not, as feeling, through all parts diffused,
That she might look at will through every pore?
Then had I not been thus exiled from light,
As in the land of darkness, yet in light,
To live a life half dead, a living death,
And buried; but, O yet more miserable!
Myself my sepulchre, a moving grave;
Buried, yet not exempt,
By privilege of death and burial,
From worst of other evils, pains, and wrongs;
But made hereby obnoxious more
To all the miseries of life,
Life in captivity
Among inhuman foes.

From the Sonnets.

137. Sonnet on his own Blindness.

When I consider how my light is spent
  Ere half my days, in this dark world and wide,
  And that one talent which is death to hide,
Lodged with me useless, though my soul more bent
To serve therewith my Maker, and present
  My true account, lest He, returning, chide;
  "Doth God exact day-labor, light denied?"

I fondly ask: but Patience, to prevent
That murmur, soon replies, "God doth not need
Either man's work, or his own gifts; who best
Bear his mild yoke, they serve him best; his state
Is kingly; thousands at his bidding speed,
And post o'er land and ocean without rest:
They also serve who only stand and wait."

---

138. On the late Massacre in Piedmont.

Avenge, O Lord, thy slaughtered saints, whose bones
Lie scattered on the Alpine mountains cold;
Even them who kept thy truths so pure of old,
When all our fathers worshipped stocks and stones,
Forget not: in thy book record their groans
Who were thy sheep, and in their ancient fold
Slain by the bloody Piedmontese, that rolled
Mother with infant down the rocks. Their moans
The vales redoubled to the hills, and they
To heaven. Their martyred blood and ashes sow
O'er all the Italian fields, where still doth sway
The triple tyrant; that from these may grow
A hundred fold, who, having learned thy way,
Early may fly the Babylonian woe.

From the Areopagitica.

139. Argument for the Liberty of the Press.

I deny not but that it is of greatest concernment in the church and commonwealth to have a vigilant eye how books demean themselves, as well as men, and thereafter to confine, imprison, and do sharpest justice on them as malefactors, — for books are not absolutely dead things, but do contain a progeny of life in them to be as active as that soul was whose progeny they are; nay, they do preserve, as in a vial, the purest efficacy and extraction of that living intellect that bred them. I know they are as lively and as vigorously productive as those fabulous dragon's teeth; and, being sown up and down, may chance to spring up armed men. And yet, on the other hand, unless wariness be used, as good almost kill a man as kill a good book. Who kills a man kills a reasonable creature, God's image; but he who destroys a good book, kills reason itself; kills the image of God, as it were, in the eye. Many a man lives a burden to the earth; but a good book is the precious life-blood of a master-spirit, embalmed and treasured up on purpose to a life beyond life. It is true no age can restore a life, whereof, perhaps, there is no great loss; and revolutions of ages do not oft recover the loss of a rejected truth, for the want of which whole nations fare the worse. We should be wary, therefore, what persecution we raise against the living labors of public men, how we spill that seasoned life of man preserved and stored up in books, since we see a kind of homicide may be thus committed, — sometimes a martyrdom; and if it extend to the whole impression, a kind of massacre, whereof the execution ends not in the slaying of an elemental life, but strikes at the ethereal and fifth essence, — the breath of reason itself: slays an immortality rather than a life. * *

Lest some should persuade ye, Lords and Commons, that these arguments of learned men's discouragement at this your order are mere flourishes, and not real, I could recount what I have seen and heard in other countries, where this kind of inquisition tyrannizes: when I have sat among their learned men (for that honor I had), and been counted happy to be born in such a place of philosophic freedom, as they supposed England was, while themselves did nothing but bemoan the servile condition into which learning amongst them was brought; that this was it which had damped the glory of Italian wits; that nothing had been there written now these many years but flattery and fustian. There it was that I found and visited the famous Galileo, grown old, a prisoner to the inquisition, for thinking in astronomy otherwise than the Franciscan and Dominican licensers thought. And though I knew that England then was groaning loudest under the prelatical yoke, nevertheless I took it as a pledge of future happiness that other nations were so persuaded of her liberty. Yet it was beyond my hope that those worthies were then breathing in her air, who should be her leaders to such a deliverance, as shall never be forgotten by any revolution of time that this world hath to finish. Lords and Commons of England! consider what nation it is whereof ye are, and whereof ye are the governors; a nation not slow and dull, but of a quick, ingenious, and piercing spirit; acute to invent, subtle and sinewy to discourse, not beneath the reach of any point the highest that human capacity can soar to. Therefore the studies of learning in her deepest sciences have been so ancient and so eminent among us, that writers of good antiquity and able judgment have been persuaded that even the school of Pythagoras and the Persian wisdom took beginning from the old philosophy of this island. And that wise and civil Roman, Julius Agricola, who governed once here for Cæsar, preferred the natural wits of Britain, before the labored studies of the French. Behold now this vast city; a city of refuge, the mansion-house of liberty, encompassed and surrounded with his protection; the shop of war hath not there more anvils and hammers waking, to fashion out the plates and instruments of armed justice in defence of beleaguered truth, than there be pens and heads there, sitting by their studious lamps, musing, searching, revolving new notions and ideas, wherewith to present, as with their homage and their fealty, the approaching reformation; others as fast reading, trying all things, assenting to the force of reason and convincement. * *

This is a lively and cheerful presage of our happy success and victory. For as in a body when the blood is fresh, the spirits pure and vigorous, not only to vital, but to rational faculties, and those in the acutest and the pertest operations of wit and subtlety, it argues in what good plight and constitution the body is; so, when the cheerfulness of the people is so sprightly up as that it has not only wherewith to guard well its own freedom and safety, but to spare, and to bestow upon the solidest and sublimest points of controversy and new invention, it betokens us not degenerated, nor drooping to a fatal decay, by casting off the old and wrinkled skin of corruption, to outlive these pangs, and wax young again, entering the glorious ways of truth and prosperous virtue, destined to become great and honorable in these latter ages. Methinks I see in my mind a noble and puissant nation rousing herself like a strong man after sleep, and shaking her invincible locks; methinks I see her as an eagle, mewing her mighty youth, and kindling her undazzled eyes at the full midday beam; purging and unscaling her long-abused sight at the fountain itself of heavenly radiance; while the whole noise of timorous and flocking birds, with those also that love the twilight, flutter about, amazed at what she means, and, in their envious gabble, would prognosticate a year of sects and schisms. * * * *

Though all the winds of doctrine were let loose to play upon the earth, so Truth be in the field, we do injuriously, by licensing and prohibiting, to misdoubt her strength. Let her and falsehood grapple; who ever knew Truth put to the worst in a free and open encounter? Her confuting is the best and surest suppressing. He who hears what praying there is for light and clear knowledge to be sent down among us, would think of other matters to be constituted beyond the discipline of Geneva, framed and fabricked already to our hands. Yet when the new life which we beg for shines in upon us, there be who envy and oppose, if it come not first in at their casements. What a collusion is this, when, as we are exhorted by the wise man to use diligence, "to seek for wisdom as for hidden treasures," early and late, that another order shall enjoin us to know nothing but by statute! When a man hath been laboring the hardest labor in the deep mines of knowledge, hath furnished out his findings in all their equipage, drawn forth his reasons, as it were a battle ranged, scattered and defeated all objections in his way, calls out his adversary into the plain, offers him the advantage of wind and sun, if he please, only that he may try the matter by dint of argument; for his opponents then to skulk, to lay ambushments, to keep a narrow bridge of licensing where the challenger should pass, though it be valor enough in soldiership, is but weakness and cowardice in the wars of Truth. For who knows not that Truth is strong, next to the Almighty? She needs no policies, nor stratagems, nor licensings, to make her victorious; those are the shifts and the defences that error uses against her power; give her but room, and do not bind her when she sleeps.

ANDREW MARVELL. 1620–1678. (Manual, p. 205.)

140. THE NYMPH COMPLAINING FOR THE DEATH OF HER FAWN.

The wanton troopers riding by
Have shot my fawn, and it will die.
Ungentle men! they cannot thrive
Who killed thee. Thou ne'er didst alive
Them any harm; alas! nor could
Thy death to them do any good.
I'm sure I never wished them ill;
Nor do I for all this; nor will:
But, if my simple prayers may yet
Prevail with heaven to forget
Thy murder, I will join my tears,
Rather than fail. But, O my fears!
It cannot die so. Heaven's king
Keeps register of everything,
And nothing may we use in vain:
Even beasts must be with justice slain.
* * * * * * *
Inconstant Sylvio, when yet
I had not found him counterfeit,
One morning (I remember well),
Tied in this silver chain and bell,
Gave it to me: nay, and I know
What he said then: I'm sure I do.
Said he, "Look how your huntsman here
Hath taught a fawn to hunt his deer."
But Sylvio soon had me beguiled.
This waxéd tame while he grew wild,
And, quite regardless of my smart,
Left me his fawn, but took his heart.
Thenceforth I set myself to play
My solitary time away
With this, and very well content
Could so my idle life have spent;
For it was full of sport, and light
Of foot, and heart; and did invite
Me to its game; it seemed to bless
Itself in me. How could I less
Than love it? O, I cannot be
Unkind t' a beast that loveth me.
Had it lived long, I do not know
Whether it too might have done so

As Sylvio did; his gifts might be
Perhaps as false, or more, than he.
But I am sure, for aught that I
Could in so short a time espy,
Thy love was far more better than
The love of false and cruel man.

CHAPTER XII.

THE AGE OF THE RESTORATION.

---

141. SAMUEL BUTLER. 1612–1680. (Manual, pp. 207–212.)

FROM "HUDIBRAS."

HONOR.

Quoth he, "That honor's very squeamish,
That takes a basting for a blemish:
For what's more honorable than scars,
Or skin to tatters rent in wars?
Some have been beaten till they know
What wood a cudgel's of by th' blow;
Some kicked, until they can feel whether
A shoe be Spanish or neat's leather;
And yet have met, after long running,
With some whom they have taught that cunning,
The furthest way about, t' o'ercome,
I' th' end does prove the nearest home.
By laws of learned duellists,
They that are bruised with wood, or fists,
And think one beating may for once
Suffice, are cowards and poltroons;
But if they dare engage t' a second,
They're stout and gallant fellows reckoned.
Th' old Romans freedom did bestow;
Our princes worship with a blow:
King Pyrrhus cured his splenetic
And testy courtiers with a kick.
The Negus, when some mighty lord
Or potentate's to be restored,
And pardoned for some great offence,
With which he's willing to dispense,
First has him laid upon his belly,
Then beaten back and side t' a jelly;
That done, he rises, humbly bows,
And gives thanks for the princely blows;
Departs not meanly proud, and boasting

Of his magnificent rib-roasting.
The beaten soldier proves most manful,
That, like his sword, endures the anvil,
And justly's held more formidable,
The more his valor's malleable:
But he that fears a bastinado,
Will run away from his own shadow.

Caligula's Campaign in Britain.

So th' emperor Caligula,
That triumphed o'er the British sea,
Took crabs and oysters prisoners,
And lobsters, 'stead of cuirassiers;
Engaged his legions in fierce bustles,
With periwinkles, prawns, and muscles,
And led his troops with furious gallops,
To charge whole regiments of scallops;
Not like their ancient way of war,
To wait on his triumphal car;
But when he went to dine or sup,
More bravely ate his captives up,
And left all war, by his example,
Reduced to vict'ling of a camp well.

The Procession of the Skimmington.

And now the cause of all their fear
By slow degrees approached so near,
They might distinguish different noise
Of horns, and pans, and dogs, and boys,
And kettle-drums, whose sullen dub
Sounds like the hooping of a tub,
But when the sight appeared in view,
They found it was an antique show;
A triumph that, for pomp and state,
Did proudest Romans emulate:
For as the aldermen of Rome
Their foes at training overcome,
And not enlarging territory,
As some, mistaken, write in story,
Being mounted in their best array,
Upon a car, and who but they?
And followed with a world of tall lads,
That merry ditties trolled, and ballads,
Did ride with many a good-morrow,
Crying, Hey for our town, through the borough.

THE OPPOSITION IN THE LONG PARLIAMENT.

Are these the fruits o' th' protestation,
The prototype of reformation,
Which all the saints, and some, since martyrs,
Wore in their hats like wedding garters,
When 'twas resolvéd by their house
Six members' quarrel to espouse?
Did they for this draw down the rabble,
With zeal, and noises formidable;
And make all cries about the town
Join throats to cry the bishops down?
Who having round begirt the palace,
(As once a month they do the gallows,)
As members gave the sign about,
Set up their throats with hideous shout.
When tinkers bawled aloud, to settle
Church discipline, for patching kettle:
The oyster women locked their fish up,
And trudged away to cry No Bishop;
The mousetrap-men laid save-alls by,
And 'gainst evil counsellors did cry;
Botchers left old clothes in the lurch,
And fell to turn and patch the church;
Some cried the covenant, instead
Of pudding-pies, and gingerbread;
And some for brooms, old boots, and shoes,
Bawled out to purge the common's-house:
Instead of kitchen-stuff, some cry
A gospel-preaching ministry;
And some for old suits, coats, or cloak,
No surplices nor service-book.
A strange harmonious inclination
Of all degrees to reformation.

JOHN DRYDEN. 1631–1700. (Manual, pp. 212–221.)

FROM THE "ANNUS MIRABILIS."

142. LONDON AFTER THE FIRE.

Methinks already from this chymic flame,
 I see a city of more precious mould:
Rich as the town which gives the Indies name,
 With silver paved, and all divine with gold.

Already laboring with a mighty fate,
  She shakes the rubbish from her mounting brow,
And seems to have renewed her charter's date,
  Which Heaven will to the death of Time allow.

More great than human now, and more august,
  Now deified she from her fires does rise:
Her widening streets on new foundations trust,
  And opening into larger parts she flies.

Before, she like some shepherdess did show,
  Who sat to bathe her by a river's side;
Not answering to her fame, but rude and low,
  Nor taught the beauteous arts of modern pride.

Now like a maiden queen she will behold,
  From her high turrets, hourly suitors come;
The East with incense, and the West with gold,
  Will stand like suppliants to receive her doom.

The silver Thames, her own domestic flood,
  Shall bear her vessels like a sweeping train;
And often wind, as of his mistress proud,
  With longing eyes to meet her face again.

---

143. On Milton.

Three poets, in three distant ages born,
Greece, Italy, and England did adorn.
The first in loftiness of thought surpassed;
The next in majesty; in both the last.
The force of nature could no further go;
To make a third, she joined the other two.

From "Absalom and Achitophel."

144. Character of Shaftesbury (Achitophel).

Of these the false Achitophel was first;
A name to all succeeding ages cursed:
For close designs and crooked counsels fit,
Sagacious, bold, and turbulent of wit:
Restless, unfixed in principles and place;
In power unpleased, impatient of disgrace,
A fiery soul which, working out its way,
Fretted the pigmy body to decay,
And o'er informed its tenement of clay:
A daring pilot in extremity;

Pleased with the danger, when the waves went high
He sought the storms; but, for a calm unfit,
Would steer too nigh the sands to show his wit.
Great wits are sure to madness near allied,
And thin partitions do their bounds divide:
Else, why should he, with wealth and honors blest,
Refuse his age the needful hours of rest?
Punish a body which he could not please;
Bankrupt of life, yet prodigal of ease?

* * * * * * *

In friendship false, implacable in hate,
Resolved to ruin or to rule the state.
To compass this the triple bond he broke,
The pillars of the public safety shook,
And fitted Israel with a foreign yoke;
Then, seized with fear, yet still affecting fame,
Usurped a patriot's all-atoning name;
So easy still it proves, in factious times,
With public zeal to cancel private crimes.
How safe is treason, and how sacred ill,
Where none can sin against the people's will!
Where crowds can wink, and no offence be known,
Since in another's guilt they find their own!
Yet fame deserved no enemy can grudge;
The statesman we abhor, but praise the judge.
In Israel's courts ne'er sat an Abethdin
With more discerning eyes, or hands more clean,
Unbribed, unsought, the wretched to redress;
Swift of despatch and easy of access.
O, had he been content to serve the crown
With virtue only proper to the gown;
Or had the rankness of the soil been freed
From cockle, that oppressed the noble seed;
David for him his tuneful harp had strung.

* * * * * * * *

But wild Ambition loves to slide, not stand;
And Fortune's ice prefers to Virtue's land.
Achitophel, grown weary to possess
A lawful fame, a lasting happiness,
Disdained the golden fruit to gather free,
And lent the crowd his arm to shake the tree.
Now, manifest of crimes contrived long since,
He stood at bold defiance with his prince;
Held up the buckler of the people's cause
Against the crown, and skulked behind the laws.

145. Character of Zimri (Villiers, Duke of Buckingham).

Some of their chiefs were princess of the land;
In the first rank of these did Zimri stand:
A man so various, that he seemed to be
Not one, but all mankind's epitome:
Stiff in opinions, always in the wrong;
Was everything by starts, and nothing long;
But, in the course of one revolving moon,
Was chemist, fiddler, statesman, and buffoon.
Blest madman, who could every hour employ
With something new to wish, or to enjoy!
Railing and praising were his usual themes,
And both, to shew his judgment, in extremes;
So over violent, or over civil,
That every man with him was God or Devil.
In squandering wealth was his peculiar art;
Nothing went unrewarded but desert.
Beggared by fools, whom still he found too late;
He had his jest, and they had his estate.
He laughed himself from court, then sought relief
By forming parties, but could ne'er be chief;
For spite of him the weight of business fell
On Absalom, and wise Achitophel:
Thus, wicked but in will, of means bereft,
He left not faction, but of that was left.

---

146. Veni Creator Spiritus.

Creator Spirit, by whose aid
The World's foundations first were laid,
Come, visit every pious mind;
Come, pour thy joys on human kind;
From sin and sorrow set us free,
And make thy temples worthy Thee.

O Source of uncreated light,
The Father's promised Paraclete!
Thrice holy fount, thrice holy fire,
Our hearts with heavenly love inspire;
Come, and thy sacred unction bring,
To sanctify us while we sing.

Plenteous of grace, descend from high,
Rich in thy sevenfold energy!
Thou strength of his Almighty hand,
Whose power does heaven and earth command;

Proceeding Spirit, our defence,
Who dost the gifts of tongues dispense,
And crown'st thy gifts with eloquence.

Refine and purge our earthy parts;
But, O, inflame and fire our hearts!
Our frailties help, our vice control,
Submit the senses to the soul;
And when rebellious they are grown,
Then lay thine hand, and hold them down.

Chase from our minds the infernal foe,
And peace, the fruit of love, bestow;
And, lest our feet should step astray,
Protect and guide us in the way.

Make us eternal truths receive,
And practise all that we believe:
Give us Thyself, that we may see
The Father, and the Son, by Thee.

Immortal honor, endless fame,
Attend the Almighty Father's name!
The Saviour Son be glorified,
Who for lost man's redemption died!
And equal adoration be,
Eternal Paraclete, to Thee!

FROM "RELIGIO LAICI."

147. FAITH.

What then remains, but, waiving each extreme,
The tide of ignorance and pride to stem?
Neither so rich a treasure to forego;
Nor proudly seek beyond our power to know:
Faith is not built on disquisitions vain;
The things we must believe are few and plain.
But, since men will believe more than they need,
And every man will make himself a creed,
In doubtful questions 'tis the safest way
To learn what unsuspected ancients say:
For 'tis not likely we should higher soar
In search of Heaven, than all the church before:
Nor can we be deceived unless we see
The Scripture and the Fathers disagree.
If after all they stand suspected still—
For no man's faith depends upon his will—

'Tis some relief, that points not clearly known,
Without much hazard may be let alone:
And, after hearing what our church can say,
If still our reason runs another way,
That private reason 'tis more just to curb,
Than by disputes the public peace disturb:
For points obscure are of small use to learn,
But common quiet is mankind's concern.

---

148. Epistle to Congreve.

O that your brows my laurel had sustained!
Well had I been deposed, if you had reigned,
The father had descended for the son;
For only you are lineal to the throne.
Thus, when the state one Edward did depose,
A greater Edward in his room arose:
But now, not I, but poetry is cursed;
For Tom the second reigns like Tom the first.
But let them not mistake my patron's part,
Nor call his charity their own desert.
Yet this I prophesy: thou shalt be seen
(Though with some short parenthesis between)
High on the throne of wit, and, seated there,
Not mine, that's little, but thy laurel wear.
Thy first attempt an early promise made,
That early promise this has more than paid.
So bold, yet so judiciously you dare,
That your least praise is to be regular.
Time, place, and action, may with pains be wrought,
But genius must be born, and never can be taught.
This is your portion; this your native store;
Heaven, that but once was prodigal before,
To Shakspeare gave as much; she could not give him more.
  Maintain your post: that all the fame you need;
For 'tis impossible you should proceed.
Already I am worn with cares and age,
And just abandoning th' ungrateful stage:
Unprofitably kept at Heaven's expense,
I live a rent-charge on his providence;
But you, whom every Muse and Grace adorn,
Whom I foresee to better fortune born,
Be kind to my remains; and, O, defend,
Against your judgment, your departed friend!
Let not th' insulting foe my fame pursue,—
But shade those laurels which descend to you:
And take for tribute what these lines express:
You merit more; nor could my love do less.

FROM "THE COCK AND THE FOX."

149. DREAMS.

Dreams are but interludes which Fancy makes;
When monarch Reason sleeps, this mimic wakes:
Compounds a medley of disjointed things,
A mob of cobblers, and a court of kings:
Light fumes are merry, grosser fumes are sad:
Both are the reasonable soul run mad;
And many monstrous forms in sleep we see,
That neither were, nor are, nor ne'er can be.
Sometimes forgotten things long cast behind
Rush forward in the brain, and come to mind.
The nurse's legends are for truths received,
And the man dreams but what the boy believed.
Sometimes we but rehearse a former play,
The night restores our actions done by day;
As hounds in sleep will open for their prey.
In short, the farce of dreams is of a piece,
Chimeras all; and more absurd, or less.

---

150. ALEXANDER'S FEAST.

AN ODE IN HONOR OF ST. CECILIA'S DAY.

'Twas at the royal feast for Persia won
By Philip's warlike son;
Aloft in awful state
The godlike hero sate
On his imperial throne:
His valiant peers were placed around;
Their brows with roses and with myrtles bound
(So should desert in arms be crowned):
The lovely Thais, by his side,
Sate, like a blooming Eastern bride,
In flower of youth and beauty's pride.
Happy, happy, happy pair!
None but the brave,
None but the brave,
None but the brave deserves the fair.

Timotheus, placed on high
Amid the tuneful quire,
With flying fingers touched the lyre:
The trembling notes ascend the sky,
And heavenly joys inspire.
The song began — from Jove,
Who left his blissful seats above

(Such is the power of mighty love).
A dragon's fiery form belied the god,
Sublime on radiant spires he rode.

* * * * * * *

The listening crowd admire the lofty sound,
A present deity! they shout around:
A present deity! the vaulted roofs rebound:
With ravished ears
The monarch hears,
Assumes the god,
Affects to nod,
And seems to shake the spheres.

The praise of Bacchus then, the sweet musician sung:
Of Bacchus ever fair and ever young:
The jolly god in triumph comes;
Sound the trumpets; beat the drums;
Flushed with a purple grace,
He shows his honest face;
Now give the hautboys breath: he comes! he comes!
Bacchus, ever fair and young,
Drinking joys did first ordain;
Bacchus' blessings are a treasure,
Drinking is the soldier's pleasure:
Rich the treasure,
Sweet the pleasure;
Sweet is pleasure after pain.

Soothed with the sound, the king grew vain;
Fought all his battles o'er again;
And thrice he routed all his foes; and thrice he slew the slain.
The master saw the madness rise;
His glowing cheeks, his ardent eyes;
And, while he Heaven and Earth defied,
Changed his hand, and checked his pride.
He chose a mournful Muse,
Soft pity to infuse:
He sung Darius great and good,
By too severe a fate,
Fallen, fallen, fallen, fallen,
Fallen from his high estate,
And welt'ring in his blood;
Deserted, at his utmost need,
By those his former bounty fed:
On the bare earth exposed he lies,
With not a friend to close his eyes.
With downcast looks the joyless victor sate,

Revolving in his altered soul
The various turns of Chance below;
And, now and then, a sigh he stole;
And tears began to flow.

The mighty master smiled, to see
That love was in the next degree:
'Twas but a kindred sound to move,
For pity melts the mind to love.
Softly sweet, in Lydian measures,
Soon he soothed his soul to pleasures.
War, he sung, is toil and trouble;
Honor, but an empty bubble;
Never ending, still beginning,
Fighting still, and still destroying;
If the world be worth thy winning,
Think, O, think it worth enjoying:
Lovely Thais sits beside thee,
Take the good the gods provide thee!
The many rend the skies with loud applause;
So Love was crowned, but Music won the cause.
The prince, unable to conceal his pain,
Gazed on the fair
Who caused his care,
And sighed and looked, sighed and looked,
Sighed and looked, and sighed again:
At length, with love and wine at once oppressed,
The vanquished victor sunk upon her breast.

Now strike the golden lyre again:
A louder yet, and yet a louder strain.
Break his bands of sleep asunder,
And rouse him, like a rattling peal of thunder.
Hark, hark, the horrid sound
Has raised up his head!
As awaked from the dead,
And amazed, he stares around.
Revenge! revenge! Timotheus cries,
See the Furies arise:
See the snakes that they rear,
How they hiss in their hair,
And the sparkles that flash from their eyes.
Behold a ghastly band,
Each a torch in his hand!
Those are Grecian ghosts, that in battle were slain,
And unburied remain
Inglorious on the plain:

Give the vengeance due
To the valiant crew!
Behold how they toss their torches on high,
How they point to the Persian abodes,
And glittering temples of their hostile gods!
The princes applaud, with a furious joy;
And the king seized a flambeau with zeal to destroy;
Thaïs led the way,
To light him to his prey,
And, like another Helen, fired another Troy.

Thus, long ago,
Ere heaving bellows learned to blow
While organs yet were mute;
Timotheus, to his breathing flute,
And sounding lyre,
Could swell the soul to rage, or kindle soft desire.
At last divine Cecilia came,
Inventress of the vocal frame;
The sweet enthusiast, from her sacred store,
Enlarged the former narrow bounds,
And added length to solemn sounds,
With Nature's mother-wit, and arts unknown before.
Let old Timotheus yield the prize,
Or both divide the crown;
He raised a mortal to the skies,
She drew an angel down.

Dryden's Prose.

151. Chaucer and Cowley.

In the first place, as he is the father of English poetry, so I hold him in the same degree of veneration as the Grecians held Homer, or the Romans Virgil. He is a perpetual fountain of good sense, learned in all sciences, and therefore speaks properly on all subjects. As he knew what to say, so he knows also when to leave off; a continence which is practised by few writers, and scarcely by any of the ancients, excepting Virgil and Horace. One of our late great poets [1] is sunk in his reputation, because he could never forgive any conceit which came in his way; but swept, like a drag-net, great and small. There was plenty enough, but the dishes were ill sorted; whole pyramids of sweetmeats for boys and women, but little of solid meat for men. All this proceeded not from any want of knowledge, but of judgment. Neither did he want that in discerning the beauties and faults of other

[1] Cowley.

poets, but only indulged himself in the luxury of writing; and perhaps knew it was a fault, but hoped the reader would not find it. For this reason, though he must always be thought a great poet, he is no longer esteemed a good writer; and for ten impressions, which his works have had in so many successive years, yet at present a hundred books are scarcely purchased once a twelve-month; for, as my last Lord Rochester said, though somewhat profanely, Not being of God, he could not stand.

Chaucer followed nature everywhere; but was never so bold to go beyond her. It is true, I cannot go so far as he who published the last edition of him; for he would make us believe the fault is in our ears, and that there were really ten syllables in a verse, where we find but nine. But this opinion is not worth confuting; it is so gross and obvious an error, that common sense (which is a rule in everything but matters of faith and revelation) must convince the reader, that equality of numbers in every verse which we call heroic, was either not known, or not always practised in Chaucer's age. It were an easy matter to produce some thousands of his verses, which are lame for want of half a foot, and sometimes a whole one, and which no pronunciation can make otherwise. We can only say, that he lived in the infancy of our poetry, and that nothing is brought to perfection at the first. We must be children, before we grow men. There was an Ennius, and in process of time a Lucilius and a Lucretius, before Virgil and Horace. Even after Chaucer there was a Spenser, a Harrington, a Fairfax, before Waller and Denham were in being; and our numbers were in their nonage till these last appeared.

---

152. Shakspeare and Ben Jonson.

To begin, then, with Shakspeare. He was the man, who, of all modern, and perhaps ancient poets, had the largest and most comprehensive soul. All the images of nature were still present to him, and he drew them not laboriously, but luckily: when he describes anything, you more than see it — you feel it too. Those who accuse him to have wanted learning, give him the greater commendation: he was naturally learned; he needed not the spectacles of books to read nature; he looked inwards, and found her there. I cannot say he is everywhere alike; were he so, I should do him injury to compare him with the greatest of mankind. He is many times flat, insipid; his comic wit degenerating into clenches,[1] his serious swelling into bombast. But he is always great when some great occasion is presented to him. * * * *

The consideration of this made Mr. Hales of Eton say, that there was no subject of which any poet ever writ, but he would produce it much better done in Shakspeare; and however others are now gener-

1 An old word for *puns*.

ally preferred before him, yet the age wherein he lived, which had contemporaries with him, Fletcher and Jonson, never equalled them to him in their esteem; and in the last king's court, when Ben's reputation was at highest, Sir John Suckling, and with him the greater part of the courtiers, set our Shakspeare far above him.

As for Jonson, to whose character I am now arrived, if we look upon him while he was himself (for his last plays were but his dotages), I think him the most learned and judicious writer which any theatre ever had. He was a most severe judge of himself, as well as others. One cannot say he wanted wit, but rather that he was frugal of it. In his works you find little to retrench or alter. Wit, and language, and humor, also in some measure, we had before him; but something of art was wanting to the drama, till he came. He managed his strength to more advantage than any who preceded him. You seldom find him making love in any of his scenes, or endeavoring to move the passions; his genius was too sullen and saturnine to do it gracefully, especially when he knew he came after those who had performed both to such a height. Humor was his proper sphere; and in that he delighted most to represent mechanic people. He was deeply conversant in the ancients, both Greek and Latin, and he borrowed boldly from them; there is scarce a poet or historian among the Roman authors of those times, whom he has not translated in Sejanus and Catiline. But he has done his robberies so openly, that one may see he fears not to be taxed by any law. He invades authors like a monarch; and what would be theft in other poets, is only victory in him. With the spoils of these writers he so represents old Rome to us, in his rites, ceremonies, and customs, that if one of their poets had written either of his tragedies, we had seen less of it than in him. If there was any fault in his language, 'twas that he weaved it too closely and laboriously, in his comedies especially: perhaps, too, he did a little too much Romanize our tongue, leaving the words which he translated almost as much Latin as he found them; wherein, though he learnedly followed their language, he did not enough comply with the idiom of ours. If I would compare him with Shakspeare, I must acknowledge him the more correct poet, but Shakspeare the greater wit. Shakspeare was the Homer, or father of our dramatic poets: Jonson was the Virgil, the pattern of elaborate writing: I admire him, but I love Shakspeare.

Algernon Sidney. 1621–1684. (Manual, p. 206.)

From the "Discourses on Government."

153. Influence of Government on the Character of a People.

Men are valiant and industrious when they fight for themselves and their country. They prove excellent in all the arts of war and peace, when they are bred up in virtuous exercises, and taught by their fathers and masters to rejoice in the honors gained by them. They love their country when the good of every particular man is comprehended in the public prosperity, and the success of their achievements is improved to the general advantage. They undertake hazards and labor for the government, when it is justly administered; when innocence is safe, and virtue honored; when no man is distinguished from the vulgar, but such as have distinguished themselves by the bravery of their actions; when no honor is thought too great for those who do it eminently, unless it be such as cannot be communicated to others of equal merit. They do not spare their persons, purses, or friends, when the public powers are employed for the public benefit, and imprint the like affections in their children from their infancy. The discipline of obedience, in which the Romans were bred, taught them to command: and few were admitted to the magistracies of inferior rank, till they had given such proofs of their virtue as might deserve the supreme. Cincinnatus, Camillus, Papirius, Fabius Maximus, were not made dictators that they might learn the duties of the office, but because they were judged to be of such wisdom, valor, integrity, and experience, that they might be safely trusted with the highest powers; and, whilst the law reigned, not one was advanced to that honor who did not fully answer what was expected from him. By these means the city was so replenished with men fit for the greatest employments, that even in its infancy, when three hundred and six of the Fabii were killed in one day, the city did lament the loss, but was not so weakened to give any advantage to their enemies: and when every one of those who had been eminent before the second Punic war, Fabius Maximus only excepted, had perished in it, others arose in their places, who surpassed them in number, and were equal to them in virtue. The city was a perpetual spring of such men, as long as liberty lasted; but that was no sooner overthrown, than virtue was torn up by the roots: the people became base and sordid; the small remains of the nobility slothful and effeminate; and, their Italian associates becoming like to them, the empire, whilst it stood, was only sustained by the strength of foreigners. The Grecian virtue had the same fate, and expired with liberty. * * * It is absurd to impute this to the change of times; for time changes nothing; and nothing was changed in those times, but the government, and that changed all things. This is not accidental, but according to the rules given to nature by God, imposing upon all things a necessity of perpetually following their causes. Fruits are always of the same nature with the seeds and roots from which they come, and trees are known by the fruits they bear. As a man begets a man, and a beast a beast, that society of men which constitutes a government upon the foundation of justice, virtue, and the common good, will always have men to promote those ends, and that which intends the advancement of one man's desires and vanity will abound in those that will foment them.

JOHN RAY. 1628–1705. (Manual, p. 261.)

FROM "THE WISDOM OF GOD IN CREATION."

154. CIVILIZATION DESIGNED BY THE CREATOR.

I persuade myself that the bountiful and gracious Author of man's being and faculties, and all things else, delights in the beauty of his creation, and is well pleased with the industry of man in adorning the earth with beautiful cities and castles, with pleasant villages and country houses; with regular gardens and orchards, and plantations of all sorts of shrubs, and herbs, and fruits for meat, medicine, or moderate delight; with shady woods and groves, and walks set with rows of elegant trees; with pastures clothed with flocks, and valleys covered over with corn, and meadows burdened with grass, and whatever else differenceth a civil and well-cultivated region from a barren and desolate wilderness.

If a country thus planted and adorned, thus polished and civilized, thus improved to the height by all manner of culture for the support and sustenance, and convenient entertainment of innumerable multitudes of people, be not to be preferred before a barbarous and inhospitable Scythia, without houses, without plantations, without cornfields or vineyards, where the roving hordes of the savage and truculent inhabitants transfer themselves from place to place in wagons, as they can find pasture and forage for their cattle, and live upon milk, and flesh roasted in the sun at the pommels of their saddles; or a rude and unpolished America, peopled with slothful and naked Indians, instead of well built houses, living in pitiful huts and cabins, made of poles set endwise; then surely the brute beast's condition and manner of living, to which what we have mentioned doth nearly approach, is to be esteemed better than man's, and wit and reason was in vain bestowed on him.

JOHN BUNYAN. 1628–1688. (Manual, pp. 221–225.)

FROM "THE PILGRIM'S PROGRESS."

155. THE VALLEY OF HUMILIATION.

Now they began to go down the hill into the valley of humiliation. It was a steep hill, and the way was slippery; but they were very careful; so they got down pretty well. When they were down in the valley, Piety said to Christiana, this is the place where Christian, your husband, met with that foul fiend Apollyon, and where they had that dreadful fight that they had. I know you cannot but have heard thereof. But be of good courage; as long as you have here Mr. Greatheart to be your guide and conductor, we hope you will fare the better. So when these two had committed the pilgrims unto the conduct of their guide, he went forward, and they went after.

Then said Mr. Greatheart, we need not be so afraid of this valley, for here is nothing to hurt us, unless we procure it to ourselves. 'Tis true Christian did here meet with Apollyon, with whom he also had a sore combat; but that fray was the fruit of those slips that he got in his going down the hill, for they that get slips there must look for combats here. And hence it is that this valley has got so hard a name; for the common people, when they hear that some frightful thing has befallen such a one in such a place, are of opinion that that place is haunted with some foul fiend or evil spirit, when, alas! it is for the fruit of their own doing that such things do befall them there.

This valley of humiliation is of itself as fruitful a place as any the crow flies over; and I am persuaded, if we could hit upon it, we might find somewhere hereabouts something that might give us an account why Christian was so hardly beset in this place.

Then said James to his mother, Lo! yonder stands a pillar, and it looks as if something was written thereon: let us go and see what it is. So they went, and found there written, "Let Christian's slip, before he came hither, and the battles that he met with in this place, be a warning to those that come after." Lo! said their guide, did not I tell you that there was something hereabouts that would give intimation of the reason why Christian was so hard beset in this place? Then turning himself to Christiana, he said, no disparagement to Christian more than to many others whose hap and lot it was; for it is easier going up than down this hill, and that can be said but of few hills in all these parts of the world. But we will leave the good man; he is at rest; he also had a brave victory over his enemy; let Him grant, that dwelleth above, that we fare no worse, when we come to be tried, than he!

But we will come again to this valley of humiliation. It is the best and most fruitful piece of ground in all these parts. It is fat ground, and, as you see, consisteth much in meadows; and if a man was to come here in summer-time, as we do now, if he knew not anything before thereof, and if he also delighted himself in the sight of his eyes, he might see that which would be delightful to him. Behold how green this valley is! also how beautiful with lilies! I have known many laboring men that have got good estates in this valley of humiliation. "For God resisteth the proud, but giveth grace to the humble;" for indeed it is a very fruitful soil, and doth bring forth by handfuls. Some also have wished that the next way to their Father's house were here, that they might be troubled no more with either hills or mountains to go over; but the way is the way, and there's an end.

Now, as they were going along and talking, they espied a boy feeding his father's sheep. The boy was in very mean clothes, but of a fresh and well-favored countenance, and as he sat by himself he sung. "Hark," said Mr. Greatheart, "to what the shepherd's boy saith;" so they hearkened, and he said, —

He that is down needs fear no fall;
  He that is low no pride;
He that is humble ever shall
  Have God to be his guide.
I am content with what I have,
  Little be it or much;
And, Lord! contentment still I crave,
  Because thou savest such.
Fulness to such a burden is,
  That go on pilgrimage:
Here little, and hereafter bliss,
  Is best from age to age.

Then said their guide, do you hear him? I will dare to say this boy lives a merrier life, and wears more of that herb called heart's-ease in his bosom than he that is clad in silk and velvet! but we will proceed in our discourse.

The Golden City.

Now I saw in my dream that by this time the pilgrims were got over the Enchanted Ground, and entering into the country of Beulah, whose air was very sweet and pleasant, the way lying directly through it, they solaced them there for a season. Yea, here they heard continually the singing of birds, and saw every day the flowers appear in the earth, and heard the voice of the turtle in the land. In this country the sun shineth night and day; wherefore it was beyond the Valley of the Shadow of Death, and also out of reach of the Giant Despair; neither could they from this place so much as see Doubting Castle. Here they were within sight of the city they were going to, also here met them some of the inhabitants thereof, for in this land the shining ones commonly walked, because it was upon the borders of Heaven. In this land, also, the contract between the bride and bridegroom was renewed; yea, here, "as the bridegroom rejoiceth over the bride, so did their God rejoice over them." Here they had no want of corn and wine; for in this place they met abundance of what they had sought for in all their pilgrimage. Here they heard voices from out of the city — loud voices — saying, "Say ye to the daughter of Zion, Behold thy salvation cometh. Behold, his reward is with him!" Here all the inhabitants of the country called them "the holy people, the redeemed of the Lord, sought out," &c.

Now, as they walked in this land, they had more rejoicing than in parts more remote from the kingdom to which they were bound; and drawing nearer to the city yet, they had a more perfect view thereof: it was built of pearls and precious stones; also the streets thereof were paved with gold; so that, by reason of the natural glory of the city, and the reflections of the sunbeams upon it, Christian with desire fell sick; Hopeful also had a fit or two of the same disease: wherefore here they lay by it for a little while, crying out, because of their pangs, "If you see my beloved, tell him that I am sick of love." * * *

So I saw that, when they awoke, they addressed themselves to go up to the great city. But, as I said, the reflection of the sun upon the city, for the city was of pure gold, was so extremely glorious, that they could not as yet with open face behold it, but through an instrument made for that purpose. So I saw that, as they went on, there met them two men in raiment that shone like gold; also their faces shone as the light.

These men asked the pilgrims whence they came. They also asked them where they had lodged, what difficulties and dangers, what comforts and pleasures, they had met with in the way? and they told them. Then said the men that met them, You have but two difficulties more to meet with, and then you are in the city.

Christian and his companion then asked the men to go along with them; so they told them that they would. But, said they, you must obtain it by your own faith. So I saw in my dream that they went on together till they came in sight of the gate.

Now, I further saw that betwixt them and the gate was a river, but there was no bridge to go over, and the river was very deep. At the sight, therefore, of this river, the pilgrims were much stunned; but the men that went with them said, You must go through, or you cannot come to the gate.

The pilgrims then began to inquire if there was no other way to the gate? To which they answered, Yes, but there hath not any, save two, to wit, Enoch and Elijah, been permitted to tread that path since the foundation of the world, nor shall, until the last trumpet shall sound. The pilgrims then, especially Christian, began to despond in their minds, and looked this way and that; but no way could be found by them by which they might escape the river. Then they asked the men if the waters were all of a depth? They said, No; yet they could not help them in that case; for, said they, you shall find it deeper or shallower, as you believe in the king of the place.

They then addressed themselves to the water, and, entering, Christian began to sink, and crying out to his good friend Hopeful, he said, I sink in deep waters: the billows go over my head; all the waters go over me. Selah.

Then said the other, Be of good cheer, my brother; I feel the bottom, and it is good. Then said Christian, Ah! my friend, the sorrow of death hath encompassed me about; I shall not see the land that flows with milk and honey. And with that a great darkness and horror fell upon Christian, so that he could not see before him. Also here, in a great measure, he lost his senses, so that he could neither remember nor orderly talk of any of those sweet refreshments that he had met with in the way of his pilgrimage. * * * Then I saw in my dream that Christian was in a muse a while. To whom, also, Hopeful added these words, Be of good cheer; Jesus Christ maketh thee whole: and with that Christian brake out with a loud voice, O! I see him again, and he tells me, "When thou passest through the waters, I will be with thee; and through the rivers, they shall not overflow thee." Then they both took courage; and the enemy was after that as still as a stone, until they were gone over. Christian, therefore, presently found ground to stand upon, and so it followed that the rest of the river was but shallow, but thus they got over.

Edward Hyde, Earl of Clarendon. 1608–1674. (Manual, pp. 225–227.)

From "The History of the Great Rebellion."

156. Character of John Hampden.

Mr. Hampden was a man of much greater cunning, and, it may be, of the most discerning spirit, and of the greatest address and insinuation to bring anything to pass which he desired, of any man of that time, and who laid the design deepest. He was a gentleman of a good extraction, and a fair fortune; who, from a life of great pleasure and license, had on a sudden retired to extraordinary sobriety and strictness, and yet retained his usual cheerfulness and affability; which, together with the opinion of his wisdom and justice, and the courage he had shown in opposing the ship-money, raised his reputation to a very great height, not only in Buckinghamshire, where he lived, but generally throughout the kingdom. He was not a man of many words, and rarely begun the discourse, or made the first entrance upon any business that was assumed; but a very weighty speaker; and after he had heard a full debate, and observed how the house was like to be inclined, took up the argument, and shortly, and clearly, and craftily so stated it, that he commonly conducted it to the conclusion he desired; and if he found he could not do that, he was never without the dexterity to divert the debate to another time, and to prevent the determining anything in the negative, which might prove inconvenient in the future. * * * *

He was rather of reputation in his own country, than of public discourse, or fame in the kingdom, before the business of ship-money; but then he grew the argument of all tongues, every man inquiring who and what he was, that durst, at his own charge, support the liberty and property of the kingdom, and rescue his country, as he thought, from being made a prey to the court. His carriage, throughout this agitation, was with that rare temper and modesty, that they who watched him narrowly to find some advantage against his person, to make him less resolute in his cause, were compelled to give him a just testimony. He was of that rare affability and temper in debate, and of that seeming humility and submission of judgment, as if he brought no opinion of his own with him, but a desire of information and instruction; yet he had so subtle a way of interrogating, and, under the notion of doubts, insinuating his objections, that he infused his own opinions into those from whom he pretended to learn and receive them. And even with them who were able to preserve themselves from his infusions, and discerned those opinions to be fixed in him, with which they could not comply, he always left the character of an ingenious and conscientious person. He was, indeed, a very wise man, and of great parts, and possessed with the most absolute spirit of popularity, and the most absolute faculties to govern the people, of any man I ever knew.

In the first entrance into the troubles, he undertook the command of a regiment of foot, and performed the duty of a colonel, upon all occasions, most punctually. He was very temperate in diet, and a supreme governor over all his passions and affections, and had thereby a great power over other men's. He was of an industry and vigilance not to be tired out, or wearied by the most laborious; and of parts not to be imposed upon by the subtle or sharp; and of a personal courage equal to his best parts: so that he was an enemy not to be wished, wherever he might have been made a friend; and as much to be apprehended where he was so, as any man could deserve to be. And therefore his death was no less pleasing to the one party, than it was condoled in the other.

---

157. Execution of Montrose.

As soon as he had ended his discourse, he was ordered to withdraw; and after a short space, was brought in, and told by the chancellor, "that he was, on the morrow, being the one-and-twentieth of May, 1650, to be carried to Edinburgh cross, and there to be hanged on a gallows thirty foot high, for the space of three hours, and then to be taken down, and his head to be cut off upon a scaffold, and hanged on Edinburgh tollbooth; and his legs and arms to be hanged up in other public towns of the kingdom, and his body to be buried at the place where he was to be executed, except the kirk should take off his excommunication; and then his body might be buried in the common place of burial." He desired "that he might say somewhat to them," but was not suffered, and so was carried back to the prison. * * *

The next day they executed every part and circumstance of that barbarous sentence, with all the inhumanity imaginable; and he bore it with all the courage and magnanimity, and the greatest piety, that a good Christian could manifest. He magnified the virtue, courage, and religion of the last king, exceedingly commended the justice and goodness, and understanding of the present king, and prayed "that they might not betray him as they had done his father." When he had ended all he meant to say, and was expecting to expire, they had yet one scene more to act of their tyranny. The hangman brought the book that had been published of his truly heroic actions, whilst he had commanded in that kingdom, which book was tied in a small cord that was put about his neck. The marquis smiled at this new instance of their malice, and thanked them for it, and said, "he was pleased that it should be there, and was prouder of wearing it than ever he had been of the garter;" and so renewing some devout ejaculations, he patiently endured the last act of the executioner.

Thus died the gallant Marquis of Montrose, after he had given as great a testimony of loyalty and courage as a subject can do, and performed as wonderful actions in several battles, upon as great inequality of numbers, and as great disadvantages in respect of arms, and other preparations for war, as have been performed in this age. He was a gentleman of a very ancient extraction, many of whose ancestors had exercised the highest charges under the king in that kingdom, and had been allied to the crown itself. He was of very good parts, which were improved by a good education: he had always a great emulation, or rather a great contempt of the Marquis of Argyle (as he was too apt to contemn those he did not love), who wanted nothing but honesty and courage to be a very extraordinary man, having all other good talents in a great degree. Montrose was in his nature fearless of danger, and never declined any enterprise for the difficulty of going through with it, but exceedingly affected those which seemed desperate to other men, and did believe somewhat to be in himself which other men were not acquainted with, which made him live more easily towards those who were, or were willing to be, inferior to him (towards whom he exercised wonderful civility and generosity), than with his superiors or equals. He was naturally jealous, and suspected those who did not concur with him in the way, not to mean so well as he. He was not without vanity, but his virtues were much superior, and he well deserved to have his memory preserved and celebrated amongst the most illustrious persons of the age in which he lived.

---

158. Izaak Walton. 1593–1683. (Manual, p. 227.)

From "The Complete Angler."

Fishing.

But turn out of the way a little, good scholar, towards yonder high honeysuckle hedge; there we'll sit and sing whilst this shower falls so gently upon the teeming earth, and gives yet a sweeter smell to the lovely flowers that adorn these verdant meadows.

Look, under that broad beech-tree, I sat down when I was last this way a-fishing, and the birds in the adjoining grove seemed to have a friendly contention with an echo, whose dead voice seemed to live in a hollow tree, near to the brow of that primrose-hill; there I sat viewing the silver streams glide silently towards their centre, the tempestuous sea; yet sometimes opposed by rugged roots and pebble stones, which broke their waves, and turned them into foam: and sometimes I beguiled time by viewing the harmless lambs, some leaping securely in the cool shade, whilst others sported themselves in the cheerful sun, and saw others craving comfort from the swollen udders of their bleating dams. As I thus sat, these and other sights had so fully possessed my soul with content, that I thought, as the poet has happily expressed it,

> 'Twas for that time lifted above earth,
> And possessed joys not promised in my birth.

As I left this place, and entered into the next field, a second pleasure entertained me; it was a handsome milkmaid that had not yet attained so much age and wisdom as to load her mind with any fears of many things that will never be, as too many men too often do; but she cast away all care, and sung like a nightingale: her voice was good, and the ditty fitted for it: it was that smooth song which was made by Kit Marlow, now at least fifty years ago; and the milkmaid's mother sung an answer to it, which was made by Sir Walter Raleigh in his younger days.

They were old-fashioned poetry, but choicely good; I think much better than the strong lines that are now in fashion in this critical age. Look yonder! on my word, yonder they both be a-milking again. I will give her the chub, and persuade them to sing those two songs to us.

CONTENTMENT.

I knew a man that had health and riches, and several houses, all beautiful and ready furnished, and would often trouble himself and family to be removing from one house to another; and being asked by a friend why he removed so often from one house to another, replied, "It was to find content in some of them." But his friend, knowing his temper, told him, "If he would find content in any of his houses, he must leave himself behind him; for content will never dwell but in a meek and quiet soul." And this may appear, if we read and consider what our Saviour says in St. Matthew's Gospel, for He there says, "Blessed be the merciful, for they shall obtain mercy. Blessed be the pure in heart, for they shall see God. Blessed be the poor in spirit, for theirs is the kingdom of heaven. And blessed be the meek, for they shall possess the earth." Not that the meek shall not also obtain mercy, and see God, and be comforted, and at last come to the kingdom of heaven; but, in the mean time, he, and he only, possesses the earth, as he goes toward that kingdom of heaven, by being humble and cheerful, and content with what his good God has allotted him. He has no turbulent, repining, vexatious thoughts that he deserves better; nor is vexed when he sees others possessed of more honor or more riches than his wise God has allotted for his share; but he possesses what he has with a meek and contented quietness, such a quietness as makes his very dreams pleasing, both to God and himself.

John Evelyn. 1620–1706. (Manual, p. 229.)

159. St. Paul's Cathedral and the Fire of London. (Diary.)

At my return I was infinitely concern'd to find that goodly church St. Paules now a sad ruine, and that beautiful portico — for structure comparable to any in Europe, as not long before repair'd by the king — now rent in pieces, flakes of vast stone split asunder, and nothing remaining intire but the inscription in the architrave, showing by whom it was built, which had not one letter of it defac'd. It was astonishing to see what immense stones the heat had in a manner calcin'd, so that all y[e] ornaments, columns, freezes, and projectures of massie Portland stone flew off, even to y[e] very roofe, where a sheet of lead covering a great space was totally melted; the ruins of the vaulted roofe falling, broke into St. Faith's, which being filled with the magazines of bookes belonging to y[e] stationers, and carried thither for safety, they were all consum'd, burning for a weeke following. It is also observable that the lead over y[e] alter at y[e] east end was untouch'd, and among the divers monuments the body of one bishop remain'd intire. Thus lay in ashes that most venerable church, one of the most antient pieces of early piety in y[e] Christian world, besides neere 100 more. The lead, yron worke bells, plate, &c., melted; the exquisitely wrought Mercers Chapell, the sumptuous Exchange, y[e] august fabriq of Christ Christ, all y[e] rest of the Companies Halls, sumptuous buildings, arches, all in dust; the fountaines dried up and ruin'd, whilst the very waters remain'd boiling; the vorago's of subterranean cellars, wells, and dungeons, formerly warehouses, still burning in stench and dark clouds of smoke, so that in five or six miles, in traversing about, I did not see one load of timber unconsum'd, nor many stones but what calcin'd white as snow. The people who now walk'd about y[e] ruines appear'd like men in a dismal desart, or rather in some greate citty laid waste by a cruel enemy, to which was added the stench that came from some poore creatures bodies, beds, &c.

Samuel Pepys. 1632–1703. (Manual, p. 229.)

160. Mr. Pepys quarrels with his Wife. (Diary.)

May 11, 1667.—My wife being dressed this day in fair hair, did make me so mad, that I spoke not one word to her, though I was ready to burst with anger. After that, Creed and I into the Park, and walked, a most pleasant evening, and so took coach, and took up my wife, and in my way home discovered my trouble to my wife for her white locks, swearing several times, which I pray God forgive me for, and bending my fist, that I would not endure it. She, poor wretch, was surprised with it, and made me no answer all the way home;

but there we parted, and I to the office late, and then home, and without supper to bed, vexed.

12. (Lord's Day.) — Up and to my chamber, to settle some accounts there, and by and by down comes my wife to me in her night-gown, and we begun calmly, that, upon having money to lace her gown for second mourning, she would promise to wear white locks no more in my sight, which I, like a severe fool, thinking not enough, begun to except against, and made her fly out to very high terms and cry, and in her heat, told me of keeping company with Mrs. Knipp, saying, that if I would promise never to see her more — of whom she had more reason to suspect than I had heretofore of Pembleton — she would never wear white locks more. This vexed me, but I restrained myself from saying anything, but do think never to see this woman — at least, to have here more; and so all very good friends as ever. My wife and I bethought ourselves to go to a French house to dinner, and so inquired out Monsieur Robins, my perriwigg-maker, who keeps an ordinary, and in an ugly street in Covent Garden did find him at the door, and so we in; and in a moment almost had the table covered, and clean glasses, and all in the French manner, and a mess of potage first, and then a piece of bœuf-à-la-mode, all exceeding well seasoned, and to our great liking; at least it would have been anywhere else but in this bad street, and in a perriwigg-maker's house; but to see the pleasant and ready attendance that we had, and all things so desirous to please, and ingenious in the people, did take me mightily. Our dinner cost us 6*s.*

CHAPTER XIII.

THE SECOND REVOLUTION.

John Locke. 1632–1704. (Manual, pp. 249–254.)

From the "Essay on the Human Understanding." Book II., Ch. 7.

161. Uses of Pleasure and Pain.

3. The infinitely wise Author of our being, having given us the power over several parts of our bodies, to move or keep them at rest as we think fit, and also, by the motion of them, to move ourselves and other contiguous bodies, in which consist all the actions of our body; having also given a power to our minds, in several instances, to choose, amongst its ideas, which it will think on, and to pursue the inquiry of this or that subject with consideration and attention, to excite us to these actions of thinking and motion that we are capable of, has been pleased to join to several thoughts and several sensations a perception of delight. If this were wholly separated from all our outward sensations and inward thoughts, we should have no reason to prefer one thought or action to another, negligence to attention, or motion to rest, and so we should neither stir our bodies nor employ our minds, but let our thoughts (if I may so call it) run adrift, without any direction or design, and suffer the ideas of our minds, like unregarded shadows, to make their appearances there, as it happened, without attending to them; in which state man, however furnished with faculties of understanding and will, would be a very idle, inactive creature, and pass his time only in a lazy, lethargic dream. It has, therefore, pleased our wise Creator to annex to several objects, and the ideas which we receive from them, as also to several[1] of our thoughts, a concomitant pleasure, and that in several objects, to several degrees, that those faculties which he had endowed us with might not remain wholly idle and unemployed by us.

4. Pain has the same efficacy and use to set us on work that pleasure has, we being as ready to employ our faculties to avoid that as to pursue this; only this is worth our consideration, that pain is often produced by the same objects and ideas that produce pleasure in us. This their near conjunction, which makes us often feel pain in the

1 Distinct, or different; an obsolete use of the word *several*.

sensations where we expected pleasure, gives us new occasion of admiring the wisdom and goodness of our Maker, who, designing the preservation of our being, has annexed pain to the application of many things to our bodies, to warn us of the harm that they will do, and as advices to withdraw from them. But he, not designing our preservation barely, but the preservation of every part and organ in its perfection, hath in many cases annexed pain to those very ideas which delight us. Thus heat, that is very agreeable to us in one degree, by a little greater increase of it proves no ordinary torment; and the most pleasant of all sensible objects, light itself, if there be too much of it, if increased beyond a due proportion to our eyes, causes a very painful sensation, which is wisely and favorably so ordered by nature, that when any object does, by the vehemency of its operation, disorder the instruments of sensation, whose structures cannot but be very nice and delicate, we might, by the pain, be warned to withdraw before the organ be quite put out of order, and so be unfitted for its proper function for the future. The consideration of those objects that produce it may well persuade us that this is the end or use of pain; for though great light be insufferable to our eyes, yet the highest degree of darkness does not at all disease them, because that, causing no disorderly motion in it, leaves that curious organ unharmed in its natural state. But yet excess of cold as well as heat pains us, because it is equally destructive to that temper which is necessary to the preservation of life, and the exercise of the several functions of the body, and which consists in a moderate degree of warmth, or, if you please, a motion of the insensible parts of our bodies, confined within certain bounds.[1]

[1] It is worthy of remark that, in this passage, Locke clearly anticipates the recent doctrine that "heat is a mode of motion."

---

162. ISAAC BARROW. 1630–1677. (Manual, pp. 254–256.)

GOD.

The first excellency peculiar to the Christian doctrine I observe to be this; that it assigneth a true, proper, and complete character or notion of God; complete, I mean, not absolutely, but in respect to our condition and capacity; such a notion as agreeth thoroughly with what the best reason dictateth, the works of nature declare, ancient tradition doth attest, and common experience doth intimate, concerning God; such a character as is apt to breed highest love and reverence in men's hearts towards him, to engage them in the strictest practice of duty and obedience to him. It ascribeth unto him all conceivable perfections of nature in the highest degree; it asserteth unto him all his due rights and prerogatives; it commendeth and justifieth to us all his actions and proceedings. For in his essence it representeth him one, eternal, perfectly simple and pure, omnipresent, omniscient, omnipotent, independent, impassible, and immutable; as also, according to his essential disposition of will and natural manner of acting, most absolute and free, most good and benign, most holy and just, most veracious and constant; it acknowledgeth him the maker and upholder of all beings, of what nature and what degree soever, both material and immaterial, visible and invisible; it attributeth to him supreme majesty and authority over all. It informeth us that he framed this visible world with especial regard to our use and benefit; that he preserveth it with the same gracious respect; that he governeth us with a particular care and providence, viewing all the thoughts, and ordering all the actions, of men to good ends, general or particular. It declareth him in his dealings with rational creatures very tender and careful of their good, exceeding beneficent and merciful towards them, compassionate of their evils, placable for their offences, accessible and inclinable to help them at their entreaty, or in their need, yet nowise fond or indulgent to them, not enduring them to proceed in perverse or wanton courses, but impartially just, and inflexibly severe towards all iniquity obstinately pursued; it, in short, describeth him most amiable in his goodness, most terrible in his justice, most glorious and venerable in all his ways of providence.

What is Wit?

To the question what the thing we speak of is, or what this facetiousness doth import? I might reply, as Democritus did to him that asked the definition of a man, 'Tis that which we all see and know: any one better apprehends what it is by acquaintance than I can inform him by description. It is indeed a thing so versatile and multiform, appearing in so many shapes, so many postures, so many garbs, so variously apprehended by several eyes and judgments, that it seemeth no less hard to settle a clear and certain notion thereof, than to make a portrait of Proteus, or to define the figure of a fleeting air. Sometimes it lieth in pat allusion to a known story, or in seasonable application of a trivial saying, or in forging an apposite tale: sometimes it playeth in words and phrases, taking advantage from the ambiguity of their sense, or the affinity of their sound: sometimes it is wrapped in a dress of humorous expression: sometimes it lurketh under an odd similitude: sometimes it is lodged in a sly question, in a smart answer, in a quirkish reason, in a shrewd imitation, in cunningly diverting, or cleverly retorting an objection: sometimes it is couched in a bold scheme of speech, in a tart irony, in a lusty hyperbole, in a startling metaphor, in a plausible reconciling of contradictions, or in acute nonsense: sometimes a scenical representation of persons or things, a counterfeit speech, a mimical look or gesture passeth for it: sometimes an affected simplicity, sometimes a presumptuous bluntness, giveth it being: sometimes it riseth from a lucky hitting upon what is strange, sometimes from a crafty wresting obvious matter to the purpose: often it consisteth in one knows not what, and springeth up one can hardly tell how. Its ways are unaccountable and inexplicable, being answerable to the numberless rovings of fancy and windings of language. It is, in short, a manner of speaking out of the simple and plain way (such as reason teacheth and proveth things by), which, by a pretty surprising uncouthness in conceit or expression, doth affect and amuse the fancy, stirring in it some wonder, and breeding some delight thereto.

JOHN TILLOTSON. 1630–1694. (Manual, p. 256.)

163. HAPPINESS IS GOODNESS.

Another most considerable and essential ingredient of happiness is goodness, without which, as there can be no true majesty and greatness, so neither can there be any felicity or happiness. Now goodness is a generous disposition of mind to communicate and diffuse itself, by making others partakers of its happiness in such degrees as they are capable of it, and as wisdom shall direct. For he is not so happy as may be, who hath not the pleasure of making others so, and of seeing them put into a happy condition by his means, which is the highest pleasure, I had almost said pride, but I may truly say glory, of a good and great mind. For by such communications of himself, an immense and all-sufficient being doth not lessen himself, or put anything out of his power, but doth rather enlarge and magnify himself; and does, as I may say, give great ease and delight to a full and fruitful being, without the least diminution of his power and happiness. For the cause and original of all other beings can make nothing so independent upon itself as not still to maintain his interest in it, to have it always under his power and government; and no being can rebel against his Maker, without extreme hazard to himself.

Perfect happiness doth imply the exercise of all other virtues, which are suitable to so perfect a being, upon all proper and fitting occasions; that is, that so perfect a being do nothing that is contrary to or unbecoming his holiness and righteousness, his truth and faithfulness, which are essential to a perfect being; and for such a being to act contrary to them in any case, would be to create disquiet and disturbance to itself. For this is a certain rule, and never fails, that nothing can act contrary to its own nature without reluctancy and displeasure, which in moral agents is that which we call guilt; for guilt is nothing else but the trouble and disquiet which ariseth in one's mind, from the consciousness of having done something which is contrary to the perfective principles of his being, that is, something that doth not become him, and which, being what he is, he ought not to have done; which we cannot imagine ever to befall so perfect and immutable a being as God is.

Perfect happiness implies in it the settled and secure possession of all those excellences and perfections; for if any of these were liable to fail, or be diminished, so much would be taken off from perfect and complete happiness. If the Deity were subject to any change or impairment of his condition, so that either his knowledge, or power, or wisdom, or goodness, or any other perfection, could any ways decline or fall off, there would be a proportionate abatement of happiness. And from all those do result, in the last place, infinite contentment and satisfaction, pleasure and delight, which is the very essence of happiness.

Infinite contentment and satisfaction in this condition. And well may happiness be contented with itself; that is, with such a condition, that he that is possessed of it, can neither desire it should be better, nor have any cause to fear it should be worse.

Pleasure and delight, which is something more than contentment; for one may be contented with an affliction, and painful condition, in which he is far from taking any pleasure or delight. "No affliction is joyous for the present but grievous," as the apostle speaks. But there cannot be a perfect happiness without pleasure in our condition. Full pleasure is a certain mixture of love and joy, hard to be expressed in words, but certainly known by inward sense and experience.

Robert South. 1633–1716. (Manual, p. 257.)

164. The State of Man before the Fall.

The understanding, the noblest faculty of the mind, was then sublime, clear, and aspiring, and as it were the soul's upper region, lofty and serene, free from the vapors and disturbances of the inferior affections. It was the leading, controlling faculty; all the passions wore the colors of reason; it did not so much persuade as command; it was not consul, but dictator. Discourse was then almost as quick as intuition; it was nimble in proposing, firm in concluding; it could sooner determine than now it can dispute. Like the sun, it had both light and agility; it knew no rest but in motion; no quiet but in activity. It did not so properly apprehend as irradiate the object; not so much find as make things intelligible. It arbitrated upon the several reports of sense, and all the varieties of imagination; not, like a drowsy judge, only hearing, but also directing their verdict. In short, it was vegete,[1] quick, and lively; open as the day, untainted as the morning, full of the innocence and sprightliness of youth; it gave the soul a bright and full view into all things; and was not only a window, but itself the prospect. Adam came into the world a philosopher, which sufficiently appeared by his writing the nature of things upon their names; he could view essences in themselves, and read forms without the comment of their respective properties; he could see consequents yet dormant in their principles, and effects yet unborn

[1] Vigorous.

in the womb of their causes; his understanding could almost pierce into future contingents, his conjectures improving even to prophecy, or the certainties of prediction; till his fall, he was ignorant of nothing but sin; or, at least, it rested in the notion, without the smart of the experiment. Could any difficulty have been proposed, the resolution would have been as early as the proposal; it could not have had time to settle into doubt. Like a better Archimedes, the issue of all his inquiries was an "I have found it, I have found it!" — the offspring of his brain, without the sweat of his brow. Study was not then a duty, night-watchings were needless; the light of reason wanted not the assistance of a candle. This is the doom of fallen man, to labor in the fire, to seek truth in the deep, to exhaust his time, and to impair his health, and perhaps to spin out his days and himself into one pitiful controverted conclusion. There was then no poring, no struggling with memory, no straining for invention; his faculties were quick and expedite; they answered without knocking, they were ready upon the first summons; there was freedom and firmness in all their operations. I confess it is as difficult for us, who date our ignorance from our first being, and were still bred up with the same infirmities about us with which we were born, to raise our thoughts and imaginations to those intellectual perfections that attended our nature in the time of innocence, as it is for a peasant bred up in the obscurities of a cottage to fancy in his mind the unseen splendors of a court. But by rating positives by their privatives, and other acts of reason, by which discourse supplies the want of the reports of sense, we may collect the excellency of the understanding then by the glorious remainders of it now, and guess at the stateliness of the building by the magnificence of its ruins. All those arts, rarities, and inventions, which vulgar minds gaze at, the ingenious pursue, and all admire, are but the relics of an intellect defaced with sin and time. We admire it now only as antiquaries do a piece of old coin, for the stamp it once bore, and not for those vanishing lineaments and disappearing draughts that remain upon it at present. And certainly that must needs have been very glorious the decays of which are so admirable. He that is comely when old and decrepit, surely was very beautiful when he was young. An Aristotle was but the rubbish of an Adam, and Athens but the rudiments of Paradise.

WILLIAM SHERLOCK. 1678–1761. (Manual, p. 258.)

165. CHARITY.

The Gospel, though it has left men in possession of their ancient rights, yet has it enlarged the duties of love and compassion, and taught rich men to consider the poor not only as servants but as brethren, and to look on themselves not only as the masters, but as the patrons and protectors of the needy. On this view, the industrious poor are entitled to the rich man's charity; since, in the candor of the Gospel, we ought to assist our poor neighbors, not only to live, but to live comfortably: and an honest, laborious poverty has charms in it to draw relief from any rich man who has the heart of a Christian or even the bowels of nature. Mean families, though, perhaps, they may subsist by their work, yet go through much sorrow to earn their bread: if they complain not, they are more worthy of regard; their silent suffering and their contented resignation to Providence, entitle them to the more compassion; and there is a pleasure, not to be described in words, which the rich man enjoys, when he makes glad the heart of such patient sufferers, and, by his liberality, makes them for a time forget their poverty and distress; that even, with respect to the present enjoyments, the words are verified, "It is more blessed to give than to receive."

ROBERT BOYLE. 1627–1691. (Manual, p. 261.)

FROM THE TREATISE "ON THE STYLE OF THE HOLY SCRIPTURES."

166. PRACTICAL SUFFICIENCY OF THE GREAT PRINCIPLES OF MORALS.

Whereas, as the condition of a monarch, who is possessed but of one kingdom or province, is preferable to that of a geographer, though he be able to discourse theoretically of the dimensions, situation, and motion, or stability of the whole terrestrial globe, to carve it into zones, climates, and parallels, to enumerate the various names and etymologies of its various regions, and give an account of the extent, the confines, the figure, the divisions, &c., of all the dominions and provinces of it; so the actual possession of one virtue is preferable to the bare speculative knowledge of them all. Their master, Aristotle, hath herein been more plain and less pedantic, who (by the favor of his interpreters) hath not been nice in the method of his ethics. And, indeed, but little theory is essentially requisite to the being virtuous, provided it be duly understood, and cordially put in practice: reason and discretion sufficing, analogically, to extend and apply it to the particular occurrences of life (which otherwise being so near infinite as to be indefinite, are not so easily specifiable in rules); as the view of the single pole-star directs the heedful pilot, in almost all the various courses of navigation. And the systems of moralists may (in this particular) not unfitly be compared to heaven, where there are luminaries and stars obvious to all eyes, that diffuse beams sufficient to light us in most ways; and as I, that, with modern astronomers, by an excellent telescope, have beheld perhaps near a hundred stars in the Pleiades, where common eyes see but six; and have often discerned in the Milky Way, and other pale parts of the firmament, numberless little stars generally unseen, receive yet from heaven no more light useful to travel by, than other men enjoy; so there are certain grand principles and maxims in the ethics, which both are generally conspicuous, and generally afford men much light and much direction; but the numerous little notions (admit them truths) suggested by scholarship to ethical writers, and by them to us, though the speculation be not unpleasant, afford us very little peculiar light to guide our actions by.

JOHN HOWE. 1630–1705.

FROM "THE LIVING TEMPLE."

167. THE TEMPLE IN RUINS.

That God hath withdrawn himself, and left this his temple desolate, we have many sad and plain proofs before us. The stately ruins are visible to every eye, that bear in their front (yet extant) this doleful inscription — "Here God once dwelt." Enough appears of the admirable frame and structure of the soul of man, to show the divine presence did some time reside in it; more than enough of vicious deformity, to proclaim he is now retired and gone. The lamps are extinct, the altar overturned; the light and love are now vanished, which did, the one shine with so heavenly brightness, the other burn with so pious fervor; the golden candlestick is displaced, and thrown away as a useless thing, to make room for the throne of the prince of darkness; the sacred incense, which sent rolling up in clouds its rich perfumes, is exchanged for a poisonous, hellish vapor, and here is, "instead of a sweet savor, a stench." The comely order of this house is turned all into confusion; "the beauties of holiness" into noisome impurities; the "house of prayer into a den of thieves," and that of the worst and most horrid kind; for every lust is a thief, and every theft sacrilege: continual rapine and robbery are committed upon holy things. The noble powers which were designed and dedicated to divine contemplation and delight, are alienated to the service of the most despicable idols, and employed unto vilest intuitions and embraces; to behold and admire lying vanities, to indulge and cherish lust and wickedness. What have not the enemies done wickedly in the sanctuary? How have they broken down the carved work thereof, and that too with axes and hammers, the noise whereof was not to be heard in building, much less in the demolishing, this sacred frame! Look upon the fragment of that curious sculpture which once adorned the palace of that great king; the relics of common notions; the lively prints of some undefaced truth; the fair ideas of things; the yet legible precepts that relate to practice. Behold! with what accuracy the broken pieces show these to have been engraven by the finger of God, and how they now lie torn and scattered, one in this dark corner, another in that, buried in heaps of dirt and rubbish! There is not now a system, an entire table of coherent truths to be found, or a frame of holiness, but some shivered parcels. And if any, with great toil and labor, apply themselves to draw out here one piece, and there another, and set them together, they serve rather to show how exquisite the divine workmanship was in the original composition, than for present use to the excellent purposes for which the whole was first designed.

Gilbert Burnet. 1643–1715. (Manual, p. 262.)

168. Character of William III.

He had a thin and weak body, was brown-haired, and of a clear and delicate constitution. He had a Roman eagle nose, bright and sparkling eyes, a large front, and a countenance composed to gravity and authority. All his senses were critical and exquisite. He was always asthmatical; and the dregs of the small-pox falling on his lungs, he had a constant deep cough. His behavior was solemn and serious, seldom cheerful, and but with a few. He spoke little, and very slowly, and most commonly with a disgusting dryness, which was his character at all times, except in a day of battle; for then he was all fire, though without passion. He was then everywhere, and looked to everything. He had no great advantage from his education. De Witt's discourses were of great use to him; and he, being apprehensive of the observation of those who were looking narrowly into everything he said or did, had brought himself under an habitual caution that he could never shake off, though, in another sense, it proved as hurtful as it was then necessary to his affairs. He spoke Dutch, French, English, and German equally well; and he understood the Latin, Spanish, and Italian; so that he was well fitted to command armies composed of several nations. He had a memory that amazed all about him, for it never failed him. He was an exact observer of men and things. His strength lay rather in a true discerning and sound judgment than in imagination or invention. His designs were always great and good; but it was thought he trusted too much to that, and that he did not descend enough to the humors of his people to make himself and his notions more acceptable to them. This, in a government that has so much of freedom in it as ours, was more necessary than he was inclined to believe. His reservedness grew on him; so that it disgusted most of those who served him. But he had observed the errors of too much talking more than those of too cold a silence. He did not like contradiction, nor to have his actions censured; but he loved to employ and favor those who had the arts of complaisance; yet he did not love flatterers. His genius lay chiefly in war, in which his courage was more admired than his conduct. Great errors were often committed by him; but his heroical courage set things right, as it inflamed those who were about him. He was too lavish of money on some occasions, both in his buildings and to his favorites; but too sparing in rewarding services, or in encouraging those who brought intelligence. He was apt to take ill impressions of people, and these stuck long with him; but he never carried them to indecent revenges. He gave too much way to his own humor almost in everything, not excepting that which related to his own health. He knew all foreign affairs well, and understood the state of every court in Europe very particularly. He instructed his own ministers himself; but he did not apply enough to affairs at home. He believed the truth of the Christian religion very firmly, and he expressed a horror of atheism and blasphemy; and though there was much of both in his court, yet it was always denied to him and kept out of his sight. He was most exemplarily decent and devout in the public exercises of the worship of God; only on week days he came too seldom to them. He was an attentive hearer of sermons, and was constant in his private prayers and in reading the Scriptures; and when he spoke of religious matters, which he did not often, it was with a becoming gravity. His indifference as to the forms of church government, and his being zealous for toleration, together with his cold behavior towards the clergy, gave them generally very ill impressions of him. In his deportment towards all about him, he seemed to make little distinction between the good and the bad, and those who served well or those who served him ill.

SIR ISAAC NEWTON. 1642–1727. (Manual, p. 260.)

FROM A "LETTER TO LOCKE."

169. EFFECT OF AN EXPERIMENT UPON LIGHT.

The observation you mention with Boyle's book of colors, I once made upon myself, with the hazard of my eyes. The manner was this; I looked a very little while upon the sun in the looking-glass with my right eye, and then turned my eyes into a dark corner of my chamber, and winked, to observe the impression made, and the circles of colors which encompassed it, and how they decayed by degrees, and at last vanished. This I repeated a second and a third time.

At the third time, when the phantasm of light and colors about it was almost vanished, intending my fancy upon them to see their last appearance, I found to my amazement that they began to return, and by little and little to become as lively and vivid as when I had newly looked upon the sun. But when I ceased to intend my fancy upon them, they vanished again. After this I found, that as often as I went into the dark and intended my mind upon them, as when a man looks earnestly to see anything which is difficult to be seen, I could make the phantasm return without looking any more upon the sun; and the oftener I made it return, the more easily I could make it return again. And at length, by only repeating this, without looking any more upon the sun, I made such an impression on my eyes, that if I looked upon the clouds, or a book, or any bright object, I saw upon it a round bright shape like the sun; and, which is still stranger, though I looked on the sun with my right eye only, and not with my left, yet my fancy began to make the impression upon my left eye as well as upon my right; for if I shut my right eye, and looked upon a book or the clouds with my left eye, I could see the spectrum of the sun almost as plain as with my right eye, if I did but intend my fancy a little while upon it; for at first, if I shut my right eye, and looked with my left, the spectrum of the sun did not appear till I intended my fancy upon it; but by repeating, this appeared every time more easily; and now, in a few hours' time, I had brought my eyes to such a pass, that I could look upon no bright object with either eye but I saw the sun before me, so that I durst neither write nor read; but to recover the use of my eyes, shut myself up in my chamber, made dark, for three days together, and used all means to divert my imagination from the sun; for if I thought upon him, I presently saw his picture, though I was in the dark. But by keeping in the dark, and employing my mind about other things, I began in three or four days to have some use of my eyes again, and by forbearing a few days longer to look upon bright objects, recovered them pretty well; though not so well but that, for some months after, the spectrum of the sun began to return as often as I began to meditate upon the phenomenon, even though I lay in bed in midnight, with my curtains drawn. But now I have been very well for many years, though I am apt to think, that if I durst venture my eyes, I could still make the phantasm return by the power of my fancy.

CHAPTER XIV.

POPE, SWIFT, AND THE POETS IN THE REIGNS OF QUEEN ANNE, GEORGE I., AND GEORGE II.

ALEXANDER POPE. 1688–1744. (Manual, pp. 265–272.)

170. FROM THE "ESSAY ON CRITICISM."

PRIDE.

Of all the causes which conspire to blind
Man's erring judgment, and misguide the mind,
What the weak head with strongest bias rules,
Is Pride, the never-failing vice of fools.
Whatever Nature has in worth denied,
She gives in large recruits of needful Pride!
For as in bodies, thus in souls, we find
What wants in blood and spirits, swelled with wind.
Pride, where Wit fails, steps in to our defence,
And fills up all the mighty void of sense.
If once right reason drives that cloud away
Truth breaks upon us with resistless day.
Trust not yourself; but, your defects to know,
Make use of every friend — and every foe.
A little learning is a dangerous thing!
Drink deep, or taste not the Pierian spring:
There shallow draughts intoxicate the brain,
And drinking largely sobers us again.
Fired at first sight with what the Muse imparts,
In fearless youth we tempt the heights of Arts,
While, from the bounded level of our mind,
Short views we take, nor see the lengths behind;
But more advanced, behold with strange surprise
New distant scenes of endless science rise!
So pleased at first the towering Alps we try,
Mount o'er the vales, and seem to tread the sky:
Th' eternal snows appear already past,
And the first clouds and mountains seem the last:

But, those attained, we tremble to survey
The growing labors of the lengthened way;
Th' increasing prospect tires our wandering eyes,
Hills peep o'er hills, and Alps on Alps arise!

Sound an Echo to the Sense.

'Tis not enough no harshness gives offence,
The sound must seem an Echo to the sense:
Soft is the strain when Zephyr gently blows,
And the smooth stream in smoother numbers flows;
But when loud surges lash the sounding shore,
The hoarse, rough verse should like the torrent roar.
When Ajax strives some rock's vast weight to throw,
The line too labors, and the words move slow:
Not so when swift Camilla scours the plain,
Flies o'er th' unbending corn, and skims along the main.

---

171. From the "Essay on Man."

The Scale of Being.

Far as Creation's ample range extends,
The scale of sensual, mental powers ascends:
Mark how it mounts to Man's imperial race,
From the green myriads in the peopled grass;
What modes of sight betwixt each wide extreme,
The mole's dim curtain, and the lynx's beam:
Of smell, the headlong lioness between,
And hound sagacious on the tainted green;
Of hearing, from the life that fills the flood,
To that which warbles through the vernal wood;
The spider's touch, how exquisitely fine!
Feels at each thread, and lives along the line:
In the nice bee, what sense, so subtly true,
From poisonous herbs extracts the healing dew?
How Instinct varies in the grovelling swine,
Compared, half-reasoning elephant, with thine!
'Twixt that, and Reason, what a nice barrier!
Forever separate, yet forever near!
Remembrance and Reflection, how allied;
What thin partitions Sense from Thought divide!
And Middle natures, how they long to join,
Yet never pass the insuperable line!
Without this just gradation, could they be
Subjected, these to those, or all to thee?
The powers of all, subdued by thee alone,
Is not thy Reason all these powers in one?

OMNIPRESENCE OF THE DEITY.

All are but parts of one stupendous whole,
Whose body Nature is, and God the soul;
That, changed through all, and yet in all the same,
Great in the earth, as in th' ethereal frame,
Warms in the sun, refreshes in the breeze,
Glows in the stars, and blossoms in the trees;
Lives through all life, extends through all extent,
Spreads undivided, operates unspent;
Breathes in our soul, informs our mortal part,
As full, as perfect, in a hair as heart;
As full, as perfect, in vile Man that mourns,
As the rapt Seraph that adores and burns;
To Him, no high, no low, no great, no small;
He fills, He bounds, connects, and equals all.

ADDRESS TO BOLINGBROKE.

Come then, my Friend, my Genius, come along;
O master of the poet and the song!
And while the Muse now stoops, or now ascends,
To Man's low passions, or their glorious ends,
Teach me, like thee, in various nature wise,
To fall with dignity, with temper rise;
Formed by thy converse, happily to steer
From grave to gay, from lively to severe;
Correct with spirit, eloquent with ease,
Intent to reason, or polite to please.
O! while, along the stream of time, thy name
Expanded flies, and gathers all its fame,
Say, shall my little bark attendant sail,
Pursue the triumph, and partake the gale?
When statesmen, heroes, kings, in dust repose,
Whose sons shall blush their fathers were thy foes,
Shall then this verse to future age pretend
Thou wert my guide, philosopher, and friend?
That, urged by thee, I turned the tuneful art
From sounds to things, from fancy to the heart;
For wit's false mirror held up nature's light;
Showed erring pride, whatever is, is right?
That reason, passion, answer one great aim;
That true self-love and social are the same;
That VIRTUE only makes our bliss below;
And all our knowledge is, OURSELVES TO KNOW?

FROM "THE RAPE OF THE LOCK."

172. DESCRIPTION OF BELINDA.

Not with more glories, in th' ethereal plain,
The sun first rises o'er the purpled main,
Than issuing forth, the rival of his beams,
Launched on the bosom of the silver Thames.
Fair Nymphs and well-dressed Youths around her shone,
But every eye was fixed on her alone.
On her white breast a sparkling cross she wore,
Which Jews might kiss, and Infidels adore.
Her lively looks a sprightly mind disclose,
Quick as her eyes, and as unfixed as those.
Favors to none, to all she smiles extends;
Oft she rejects, but never once offends.
Bright as the sun, her eyes the gazers strike,
And, like the sun, they shine on all alike.
Yet graceful ease, and sweetness void of pride,
Might hide her faults, if Belles had faults to hide;
If to her share some female errors fall,
Look on her face, and you'll forget them all.
This Nymph, to the destruction of mankind,
Nourished two Locks, which graceful hung behind
In equal curls, and well conspired to deck,
With shining ringlets, the smooth ivory neck.
Love in these labyrinths his slaves detains,
And mighty hearts are held in slender chains.
With hairy springes we the birds betray;
Slight lines of hair surprise the finny prey;
Fair tresses man's imperial race insnare,
And beauty draws us with a single hair.

---

173. THE DYING CHRISTIAN TO HIS SOUL.

Vital spark of heavenly flame,
Quit, O quit, this mortal frame!
Trembling, hoping, lingering, flying—
O the pain, the bliss of dying!
Cease, fond Nature, cease thy strife,
And let me languish into life!

Hark! they whisper; Angels say,
Sister spirit, come away.
What is this absorbs me quite?
Steals my senses, shuts my sight?
Drowns my spirits, draws my breath?
Tell me, my soul, can this be death?

The world recedes; it disappears!
Heaven opens on my eyes! my ears
With sounds seraphic ring:
Lend, lend your wings! I mount! I fly!
O Grave! where is thy Victory?
O Death! where is thy Sting?

JONATHAN SWIFT. 1667–1745. (Manual, pp. 272–381.)

174. COUNTRY HOSPITALITY.

Those inferior duties of life, which the French call *les petites morales*, or the smaller morals, are with us distinguished by the name of good manners or breeding. This I look upon, in the general notion of it, to be a sort of artificial good sense, adapted to the meanest capacities, and introduced to make mankind easy in their commerce with each other. Low and little understandings, without some rules of this kind, would be perpetually wandering into a thousand indecencies and irregularities in behavior; and in their ordinary conversation, fall into the same boisterous familiarities that one observes among them where intemperance has quite taken away the use of their reason. In other instances it is odd to consider, that for want of common discretion, the very end of good breeding is wholly perverted; and civility, intended to make us easy, is employed in laying chains and fetters upon us, in debarring us of our wishes, and in crossing our most reasonable desires and inclinations.

This abuse reigns chiefly in the country, as I found to my vexation when I was last there, in a visit I made to a neighbor about two miles from my cousin. As soon as I entered the parlor, they put me into the great chair that stood close by a huge fire, and kept me there by force until I was almost stifled. Then a boy came in a great hurry to pull off my boots, which I in vain opposed, urging that I must return soon after dinner. In the mean time, the good lady whispered her eldest daughter, and slipped a key into her hand; the girl returned instantly with a beer glass half full of *aqua mirabilis* and syrup of gillyflowers. I took as much as I had a mind for, but madam vowed I should drink it off; for she was sure it would do me good after coming out of the cold air; and I was forced to obey, which absolutely took away my stomach. When dinner came in, I had a mind to sit at a distance from the fire; but they told me it was as much as my life was worth, and sat me with my back just against it. Although my appetite was quite gone, I was resolved to force down as much as I could, and desired the leg of a pullet. "Indeed, Mr. Bickerstaff," says the lady, "you must eat a wing, to oblige me; and so put a couple upon my plate. I was persecuted at this rate during the whole meal: as often as I called for small beer, the master tipped the wink, and the servant brought me a brimmer of October.

Some time after dinner, I ordered my cousin's man, who came with me, to get ready the horses; but it was resolved I should not stir that night; and when I seemed pretty much bent upon going, they ordered the stable door to be locked, and the children hid my cloak and boots. The next question was, What would I have for supper? I said, I never eat anything at night; but was at last, in my own defence, obliged to name the first thing that came into my head. After three hours, spent chiefly in apologies for my entertainment, insinuating to me, "That this was the worst time of the year for provisions; that they were at a great distance from any market; that they were afraid I should be starved; and that they knew they kept me to my loss;" the lady went, and left me to her husband; for they took special care I should never be alone. As soon as her back was turned, the little misses ran backward and forward every moment, and constantly as they came in, or went out, made a courtesy directly at me, which, in good manners, I was forced to return with a bow, and "your humble servant, pretty miss." Exactly at eight, the mother came up, and discovered, by the redness of her face, that supper was not far off. It was twice as large as the dinner, and my persecution doubled in proportion. I desired at my usual hour to go to my repose, and was conducted to my chamber by the gentleman, his lady, and the whole train of children. They importuned me to drink something before I went to bed; and, upon my refusing, at last left a bottle of stingo, as they call it, for fear I should wake and be thirsty in the night.

I was forced in the morning to rise and dress myself in the dark, because they would not suffer my kinsman's servant to disturb me at the hour I desired to be called. I was now resolved to break through all measures to get away; and, after sitting down to a monstrous breakfast of cold beef, mutton, neat's tongues, venison pasty, and stale beer, took leave of the family. But the gentleman would needs see me part of the way, and carry me a short cut through his own ground, which he told me would save half a mile's riding. This last piece of civility had like to have cost me dear, being once or twice in danger of my neck by leaping over his ditches, and at last forced to alight in the dirt, when my horse, having slipped his bridle, ran away, and took us up more than an hour to recover him again.

From "Gulliver's Travels."

175. The Academy of Legado.

In the school of political projectors I was but ill entertained; the professors appearing, in my judgment, wholly out of their senses, which is a scene that never fails to make me melancholy. These unhappy people were proposing schemes for persuading monarchs to choose favorites upon the scores of their wisdom, capacity, and virtue; of teaching ministers to consult the public good; of rewarding merit, great abilities, and eminent services; of instructing princes to know their true interest, by placing it on the same foundation with that of their people; of choosing for employments persons qualified to exercise them; with many other wild, impossible chimeras, that never entered before into the heart of man to conceive; and confirmed in me the old observation, "That there is nothing so extravagant and irrational, which some philosophers have not maintained for truth."

I heard a very warm debate between two professors, about the most commodious and effectual ways and means of raising money without grieving the subject. The first affirmed, "The justest method would be, to lay a certain tax upon vices and folly; and the sum fixed upon every man to be rated, after the fairest manner, by a jury of his neighbors." The second was of an opinion directly contrary: "To tax those qualities of body and mind for which men chiefly value themselves, the rate to be more or less according to the degrees of excelling, the decision whereof should be left entirely to their own breast." The highest tax was upon men who are the greatest favorites of the other sex. Wit, valor, and politeness were likewise proposed to be largely taxed, and collected in the same manner, by every person's giving his own word for the quantum of what he possessed. But, as to honor, justice, wisdom, and learning, they should not be taxed at all, because they are qualifications of so singular a kind, that no man will either allow them in his neighbor, or value them in himself.

The women were proposed to be taxed according to their beauty and skill in dressing, wherein they had the same privilege with the men, to be determined by their own judgment. But constancy, chastity, good sense, and good nature, were not rated, because they would not bear the charge of collecting.

He gave it for his opinion that whoever could make two ears of corn or two blades of grass grow where only one grew before, would deserve better of his mankind, and do more essential service to his country, than this whole race of politicians put together. — *Ibid.*

---

176. THOUGHTS ON VARIOUS SUBJECTS.

When a true genius appeareth in the world, you may know him by this infallible sign, that the dunces are all in confederacy against him.

It is in disputes as in armies, where the weaker side setteth up false lights, and maketh a great noise, that the enemy may believe them to be more numerous and strong than they really are.

I have known some men possessed of good qualities, which were very serviceable to others, but useless to themselves; like a sundial on the front of a house, to inform the neighbors and passengers, but not the owner within.

The power of fortune is confessed only by the miserable, for the happy impute all their success to prudence and merit.

Ambition often puts men upon doing the meanest offices: so, climbing is performed in the same posture with creeping.

Censure is the tax a man payeth to the public for being eminent.

No wise man ever wished to be younger.

An idle reason lessens the weight of the good ones you gave before.

Complaint is the largest tribute heaven receives, and the sincerest part of our devotion.

To be vain is rather a mark of humility than pride. Vain men delight in telling what honors have been done them, what great company they have kept, and the like; by which they plainly confess that these honors were more than their due, and such as their friends would not believe if they had not been told: whereas a man truly proud thinks the greatest honors below his merit, and consequently scorns to boast. I therefore deliver it as a maxim, that whoever desires the character of a proud man, ought to conceal his vanity.

Matthew Prior. 1664–1721. (Manual, p. 282.)

177. The Chameleon.

As the Chameleon who is known
To have no colors of his own;
But borrows from his neighbor's hue
His white or black, his green or blue;
And struts as much in ready light,
Which credit gives him upon sight,
As if the rainbow were in tail
Settled on him and his heirs male;
So the young 'squire, when first he comes
From country school to Will's or Tom's,
And equally, in truth, is fit
To be a statesman, or a wit;
Without one notion of his own,
He saunters wildly up and down,
Till some acquaintance, good or bad,
Takes notice of a staring lad,
Admits him in among the gang;
They jest, reply, dispute, harangue:
He acts and talks, as they befriend him,
Smeared with the colors which they lend him,
  Thus, merely as his fortune chances,
His merit or his vice advances.
  If haply he the sect pursues,
That read and comment upon news;

He takes up their mysterious face;
He drinks his coffee without lace;
This week his mimic tongue runs o'er
What they have said the week before;
His wisdom sets all Europe right,
And teaches Marlborough when to fight.
  Or if it be his fate to meet
With folks who have more wealth than wit;
He loves cheap port, and double bub;
And settles in the Hum-drum club:
He learns how stocks will fall or rise;
Holds poverty the greatest vice;
Thinks wit the bane of conversation,
And says that learning spoils a nation.
  But if, at first, he minds his hits,
And drinks champaign among the wits;
Five deep he toasts the towering lasses;
Repeats you verses wrote on glasses;
Is in the chair; prescribes the law;
And lies with those he never saw.

JOHN GAY. 1688–1732. (Manual, p. 283.)

178. THE HARE AND MANY FRIENDS.

Friendship, like love, is but a name,
Unless to one you stint the flame.
The child whom many fathers share,
Hath seldom known a father's care.
'Tis thus in friendships; who depend
On many, rarely find a friend.
  A Hare who, in a civil way,
Complied with everything, like Gay,
Was known to all the bestial train
Who hunt the wood, or graze the plain;
Her care was never to offend,
And every creature was her friend.
  As forth she went at early dawn,
To taste the dew-besprinkled lawn,
Behind she hears the hunter's cries,
And from the deep-mouthed thunder flies.
She starts, she stops, she pants for breath;
She hears the near approach of death:
She doubles to mislead the hound,
And measures back her mazy ground;
Till, fainting, in the public way,

Half dead with fear, she gasping lay.
What transport in her bosom grew,
When first the horse appeared in view!
"Let me," says she, "your back ascend,
And owe my safety to a friend.
You know my feet betray my flight;
To friendship every burden's light."
The horse replied, "Poor honest Puss,
It grieves my heart to see you thus:
Be comforted, relief is near,
For all your friends are in the rear."
She next the stately bull implored;
And thus replied the mighty lord;
"Since every beast alive can tell
That I sincerely wish you well,
I may, without offence, pretend
To take the freedom of a friend.
Love calls me hence; a favorite cow
Expects me near yon barley-mow;
And, where a lady's in the case,
You know all other things give place.
To leave you thus would seem unkind:
But see, the goat is just behind."
The goat remarked her pulse was high,
Her languid head, her heavy eye:
"My back," says she, "may do you harm:
The sheep's at hand, and wool is warm."
The sheep was feeble, and complained,
"His sides a load of wool sustained;"
Said he was slow, confessed his fears,
"For hounds eat sheep as well as hares."
She now the trotting calf addressed,
To save from death a friend distressed:
"Shall I," says he, "of tender age,
In this important case engage?
Older and abler passed you by;
How strong are those! how weak am I!
Should I presume to bear you hence,
Those friends of mine may take offence,
Excuse me, then; you know my heart;
But dearest friends, alas! must part.
How shall we all lament! adieu;
For see, the hounds are just in view."

THOMAS PARNELL. 1679–1718. (Manual, p. 285.)

179. HYMN TO CONTENTMENT.

Lovely, lasting peace of mind!
Sweet delight of human kind!
Heavenly born, and bred on high,
To crown the favorites of the sky
With more of happiness below,
Than victors in a triumph know!
Whither, O whither art thou fled,
To lay thy meek contented head;
What happy region dost thou please
To make the seat of calms and ease!
  Ambition searches all its sphere
Of pomp and state, to meet thee there.
Increasing avarice would find
Thy presence in its gold enshrined.
The bold adventurer ploughs his way
Through rocks amidst the foaming sea,
To gain thy love; and then perceives
Thou wert not in the rocks and waves.
The silent heart, which grief assails,
Treads soft and lonesome o'er the vales,
Sees daisies open, rivers run,
And seeks (as I have vainly done)
Amusing thought; but learns to know
That solitude's the nurse of woe.
No real happiness is found
In trailing purple o'er the ground:
Or in a soul exalted high,
To range the circuit of the sky,
Converse with stars above, and know
All nature in its forms below;
The rest it seeks, in seeking dies,
And doubts at last, for knowledge, rise.
  Lovely, lasting peace, appear;
This world itself, if thou art here,
Is once again with Eden blest,
And man contains it in his breast.
  'Twas thus, as under shade I stood,
I sung my wishes to the wood,
And, lost in thought, no more perceived
The branches whisper as they waved:
It seemed as all the quiet place
Confessed the presence of his grace.
  When thus she spoke — Go rule thy will,

Bid thy wild passions all be still,
Know God — and bring thy heart to know
The joys which from religion flow:
Then every grace shall prove its guest,
And I'll be there to crown the rest.
  Oh! by yonder mossy seat,
In my hours of sweet retreat,
Might I thus my soul employ,
With sense of gratitude and joy:
Raised as ancient prophets were,
In heavenly vision, praise, and prayer;
Pleasing all men, hurting none,
Pleased and blessed with God alone:
Then while the gardens take my sight,
With all the colors of delight;
While silver waters glide along,
To please my ear, and court my song:
I'll lift my voice, and tune my string,
And thee, great source of nature, sing.
  The sun that walks his airy way,
To light the world, and give the day;
The moon that shines with borrowed light;
The stars that gild the gloomy night;
The seas that roll unnumbered waves;
The wood that spreads its shady leaves;
The field whose ears conceal the grain,
The yellow treasure of the plain;
All of these, and all I see,
Should be sung, and sung by me:
They speak their Maker as they can,
But want and ask the tongue of man.
  Go search among your idle dreams,
Your busy or your vain extremes;
And find a life of equal bliss,
Or own the next begun in this.

Edward Young. 1681–1765. (Manual, p. 285.)

From the "Night Thoughts."

180. Procrastination.

Be wise to-day: 'tis madness to defer;
Next day the fatal precedent will plead;
Thus on, till wisdom is pushed out of life.
Procrastination is the thief of time;
Year after year it steals till all are fled,
And to the mercies of a moment leaves

The vast concerns of an eternal scene.
If not so frequent, would not this be strange?
That 'tis so frequent, *this* is stranger still.
Of man's miraculous mistakes, this bears
The palm, "That all men are about to live," —
Forever on the brink of being born.
All pay themselves the compliment to think
They one day shall not drivel: and their pride
On this reversion takes up ready praise;
At least, their own; their *future* selves applaud.
How excellent that life — they *ne'er* will lead!
Time lodged in their *own* hands is *folly's* vails;
That lodged in *fate's*, to *wisdom* they consign;
The thing they can't but *purpose*, they *postpone*.
'Tis not in *folly*, not to scorn a fool;
And scarce in human *wisdom*, to do more.
All promise is poor dilatory man,
And that through every stage: when young, indeed,
In full content we, sometimes, nobly rest,
Unanxious for *ourselves;* and only wish,
As duteous sons, our *fathers* were more wise.
At *thirty* man *suspects* himself a fool;
Knows it at *forty*, and reforms his plan;
At *fifty* chides his infamous delay,
Pushes his prudent purpose to *resolve;*
In all the magnanimity of thought
Resolves; and re-resolves; then, dies the same.
And why? Because he thinks himself immortal.
All men think all men mortal, but themselves;
Themselves, when some alarming shock of fate
Strikes through their wounded hearts the sudden dread.
But their hearts wounded, like the wounded air,
Soon close, where, past the shaft, no trace is found.
As from the *wing*, no scar the sky retains;
The parted wave no furrow from the *keel;* —
So dies in human hearts the thought of death,
E'en with the tender tear which Nature sheds
O'er those we love, — we drop it in their grave.

BISHOP BUTLER. 1692–1752. (Manual, p. 343.)

FROM "THE ANALOGY." CHAP. VIII.

181. EVIDENCE FOR CHRISTIANITY SUFFICIENT.

It is most readily acknowledged that the foregoing treatise is by no means satisfactory; very far from it; but so would any natural institution of life appear, if reduced into a system, together with its evidence. Leaving religion out of the case, men are divided in their opinions, whether our pleasures overbalance our pains; and whether it be, or be not, eligible to live in this world. And were all such controversies settled, which, perhaps, in speculation, would be found involved in great difficulties; and were it determined upon the evidence of reason, as nature has determined it to our hands, that life is to be preserved; yet still, the rules that God has been pleased to afford us, for escaping the miseries of it, and obtaining its satisfactions, the rules, for instance, of preserving health, and recovering it when lost, are not only fallible and precarious, but very far from being exact. Nor are we informed by nature, in future contingencies and accidents, so as to render it at all certain, what is the best method of managing our affairs. What will be the success of our temporal pursuits, in the common sense of the word success, is highly doubtful. And what will be the success of them in the proper sense of the word; *i. e.*, what happiness or enjoyment we shall obtain by them, is doubtful in a much higher degree. Indeed, the unsatisfactory nature of the evidence, with which we are obliged to take up in the daily course of life, is scarce to be expressed. Yet men do not throw away life, or disregard the interests of it, upon account of this doubtfulness. The evidence of religion then being admitted real, those who object against it, as not satisfactory, *i. e.*, as not being what they wish it, plainly forget the very condition of our being; for satisfaction, in this sense, does not belong to such a creature as man. And, which is more material, they forget also the very nature of religion. For, religion presupposes, in all those who will embrace it, a certain degree of integrity and honesty; which it was intended to try whether men have or not, and to exercise in such as have it, in order to its improvement. Religion presupposes this as much, and in the same sense, as speaking to a man presupposes that he understands the language in which you speak; or as warning a man of any danger presupposes that he hath such a regard to himself as that he will endeavor to avoid it. And therefore the question is not at all, Whether the evidence of religion be satisfactory; but Whether it be, in reason, sufficient to prove and discipline that virtue, which it presupposes. Now the evidence of it is fully sufficient for all these purposes of probation; how far soever it is from being satisfactory, as to the purposes of curiosity, or any other: and indeed it answers the purposes of the former in several respects, which it would not do if it were as overbearing as is required.

CHAPTER XV.

THE ESSAYISTS.

JOSEPH ADDISON. 1672–1719. (Manual, pp. 289–296.)

FROM "THE TATLER."

182. THE POLITICAL UPHOLSTERER.

There lived some years since, within my neighborhood, a very grave person, an upholsterer, who seemed a man of more than ordinary application to business. He was a very early riser, and was often abroad two or three hours before any of his neighbors. He had a particular carefulness in the knitting of his brows, and a kind of impatience in all his motions, that plainly discovered he was always intent on matters of importance. Upon my inquiry into his life and conversation, I found him to be the greatest newsmonger in our quarter; that he rose before day to read the "Postman," and that he would take two or three turns to the other end of the town before his neighbors were up, to see if there were any Dutch mails come in. He had a wife and several children, but was much more inquisitive to know what passed in Poland than in his own family, and was in greater pain and anxiety of mind for King Augustus's welfare than that of his nearest relations. He looked extremely thin in a dearth of news, and never enjoyed himself in a westerly wind. This indefatigable kind of life was the ruin of his shop; for about the time that his favorite prince left the crown of Poland, he broke and disappeared.

This man and his affairs had been long out of my mind, till, about three days ago, as I was walking in St. James's Park, I heard somebody at a distance hemming after me; and who should it be but my old neighbor the upholsterer? I saw he was reduced to extreme poverty by certain shabby superfluities in his dress; for, notwithstanding that it was a very sultry day for the time of the year, he wore a loose great-coat and a muff, with a long campaign wig out of curl, to which he had added the ornament of a pair of black garters, buckled under the knee. Upon his coming up to me I was going to inquire into his present circumstances, but was prevented by his asking me, with a whisper, whether the last letters brought any accounts that one might rely upon from Bender? I told him none that I heard of, and asked him whether he had yet married his eldest daughter? He told me no. But pray, says he, tell me sincerely what are your thoughts of the king of Sweden? For though his wife and children were starving, I found his chief concern at present was for this great monarch. I told him that I looked upon him as one of the first heroes of the age. But pray, says he, do you think there is anything in the story of his wound? And finding me surprised at the question, — Nay, says he, I only propose it to you. I answered that I thought there was no reason to doubt of it. But why in the heel, says he, more than in any other part of the body! Because, said, I, the bullet chanced to light there. * * * *

We were now got to the upper end of the Mall, where were three or four very odd fellows sitting together upon the bench. These, I found, were all of them politicians, who used to sun themselves in that place every day about dinner-time. Observing them to be curiosities in their kind, and my friend's acquaintance, I sat down among them. The chief politician of the bench was a great asserter of paradoxes. He told us, with a seeming concern, that by some news he had lately read from Muscovy, it appeared to him that there was a storm gathering in the Black Sea, which might in time do hurt to the naval forces of this nation. To this he added, that for his part, he could not wish to see the Turk driven out of Europe, which he believed could not but be prejudicial to our woollen manufacture. He then told us, that he looked upon those extraordinary revolutions, which had lately happened in those parts of the world, to have risen from two persons who were not much talked of; and those, says he, are Prince Menzikoff and the Duchess of Mirandola. He backed his assertions with so many broken hints, and such a show of depth and wisdom, that we gave ourselves up to his opinions. * * * *

When we had fully discussed this point, my friend the upholsterer began to exert himself upon the present negotiations of peace, in which he deposed princes, settled the bounds of kingdoms, and balanced the power of Europe, with great justice and impartiality.

I at length took my leave of the company, and was going away; but had not gone thirty yards, before the upholsterer hemmed again after me. Upon his advancing towards me, with a whisper, I expected to hear some secret piece of news, which he had not thought fit to communicate on the bench; but, instead of that, he desired me in my ear to lend him half a crown. In compassion to so needy a statesman, and to dissipate the confusion I found he was in, I told him, if he pleased, I would give him five shillings, to receive five pounds of him when the great Turk was driven out of Constantinople; which he very readily accepted, but not before he had laid down to me the impossibility of such an event, as the affairs of Europe now stand.

FROM "THE SPECTATOR."

183. THE VISION OF MIRZA.

On the fifth day of the moon, which, according to the custom of my forefathers, I always keep holy, after having washed myself, and offered up my morning devotions, I ascended the high hills of Bagdad, in order to pass the rest of the day in meditation and prayer. As I was here refreshing myself on the tops of the mountains, I fell into a profound contemplation on the vanity of human life; and passing from one thought to another, surely, said I, man is but a shadow, and life a dream. Whilst I was thus musing, I cast my eyes towards the summit of a rock that was not far from me, where I discovered one in the habit of a shepherd, but who was in reality a being of superior nature. I drew near with profound reverence, and fell down at his feet. The genius smiled upon me with a look of compassion and affability, that familiarized him to my imagination, and at once dispelled all the fears and apprehensions with which I approached him. He lifted me from the ground, and taking me by the hand, "Mirza," said he, "I have heard thee in thy soliloquies; follow me."

He then led me to the highest pinnacle of the rock; and placing me on the top of it, "Cast thy eyes eastward," said he, "and tell me what thou seest." "I see," said I, "a huge valley, and a prodigious tide of water rolling through it." "The valley that thou seest," said he, "is the vale of misery; and the tide of water that thou seest, is part of the great tide of eternity." "What is the reason," said I, "that the tide I see rises out of a thick mist at one end, and again loses itself in a thick mist at the other?" "What thou seest," said he, "is that portion of eternity which is called time measured out by the sun, and reaching from the beginning of the world to its consummation. Examine now," said he, "this sea that is bounded with darkness at both ends, and tell me what thou discoverest in it." "I see a bridge," said I, "standing in the midst of the tide." "The bridge thou seest," said he, "is human life; consider it attentively." Upon a more leisurely survey of it, I found that it consisted of three score and ten entire arches, with several broken arches, which, added to those that were entire, made up the number about a hundred. As I was counting the arches, the genius told me that this bridge consisted at first of a thousand; but that a great flood swept away the rest, and left the bridge in the ruinous condition I now beheld it. "But tell me further," said he, "what thou discoverest on it." "I see multitudes of people passing over it," said I, "and a black cloud hanging on each end of it." As I looked more attentively, I saw several of the passengers dropping through the bridge into the great tide that flowed underneath it; and, upon further examination, perceived there were innumerable trap-doors that lay concealed in the bridge, which the passengers no sooner trod upon, than they fell through them into the tide, and immediately disappeared. These hidden pitfalls were set very thick at the entrance of the bridge, so that throngs of people no sooner broke through the cloud than many fell into them. They grew thinner towards the middle, but multiplied and lay closer together towards the end of the arches that were entire. There were indeed some persons, but their number was very small, that continued a kind of hobbling march on the broken arches, but fell through one after another, being quite tired and spent with so long a walk.

I passed some time in the contemplation of this wonderful structure, and the great variety of objects which it presented. My heart was filled with a deep melancholy, to see several dropping unexpectedly in the midst of mirth and jollity, and catching at everything that stood by them, to save themselves. Some were looking up towards the heavens in a thoughtful posture, and, in the midst of a speculation, stumbled and fell out of sight. Multitudes were very busy in the pursuit of bubbles, that glittered in their eyes, and danced before them; but often, when they thought themselves within the reach of them, their footing failed, and down they sunk. In this confusion of objects, I observed some with scimitars in their hands, and others with urinals, who ran to and fro upon the bridge, thrusting several persons on trap-doors which did not seem to lie in their way, and which they might have escaped had they not been thus forced upon them.

The genius seeing me indulge myself in this melancholy prospect, told me I had dwelt long enough upon it. "Take thine eyes off the bridge," said he, "and tell me if thou seest anything thou dost not comprehend." Upon looking up, "What mean," said I, "those great flights of birds that are perpetually hovering about the bridge, and settling upon it from time to time? I see vultures, harpies, ravens, cormorants, and, among many other feathered creatures, several little winged boys that perch in great numbers upon the middle arches." "These," said the genius, "are envy, avarice, superstition, despair, love, with the like cares and passions that infest human life."

I here fetched a deep sigh. "Alas," said I, "man was made in vain! how is he given away to misery and mortality! tortured in life, and swallowed up in death!" The genius being moved with compassion towards me, bid me quit so uncomfortable a prospect. "Look no more," said he, "on man in the first stage of his existence, in his setting out for eternity; but cast thine eye on that thick mist into which the tide bears the several generations of mortals that fall into it." I directed my sight as I was ordered, and (whether or not the good genius strengthened it with any supernatural force, or dissipated part of the mist that was before too thick for the eye to penetrate) I saw the valley opening at the farther end, and spreading forth into an immense ocean, that had a huge rock of adamant running through the midst of it, and dividing it into two equal parts. The clouds still rested on one half of it, insomuch that I could discover nothing in it; but the other appeared to me a vast ocean, planted with innumerable islands, that were covered with fruits and flowers, and interwoven with a thousand little shining seas that ran among them. I could see persons dressed in glorious habits, with garlands upon their heads, passing among the trees, lying down by the sides of fountains, or resting on beds of flowers. Gladness grew in me at the discovery of so delightful a scene. I wished for the wings of an eagle, that I might fly away to those happy seats; but the genius told me there was no passage to them, except through the gates of death that I saw opening every moment upon the bridge. "The islands," said he, "that lie so fresh and green before thee, and with which the whole face of the ocean appears spotted as far as thou canst see, are more in number than the sands on the seashore. There are myriads of islands behind those which thou here discoverest, reaching further than thine eye, or even thine imagination, can extend itself. These are the mansions of good men after death, who, according to the degree and kinds of virtue in which they excelled, are distributed among these several islands, which abound with pleasure of different kinds and degrees, suitable to the relishes and perfections of those who are settled in them: every island is a paradise accommodated to its respective inhabitants. Are not these, O Mirza, habitations worth contending for? Does life appear miserable, that gives the opportunities of earning such a reward? Is death to be feared, that will convey thee to so happy an existence? Think not man was made in vain, who has such an eternity reserved for him." I gazed with inexpressible pleasure on these happy islands. At length, said I, "Show me now, I beseech thee, the secrets that lie hid under those dark clouds, which cover the ocean on the other side of the rock of adamant." The genius making no answer, I turned about to address myself to him a second time, but I found that he had left me. I then turned again to the vision which I had been so long contemplating; but instead of the rolling tide, the arched bridge, and the happy islands, I saw nothing but the long hollow valley of Bagdad, with oxen, sheep, and camels grazing upon the sides of it.

---

184. REFLECTIONS IN WESTMINSTER ABBEY.

When I look upon the tombs of the great, every emotion of envy dies in me; when I read the epitaphs of the beautiful, every inordinate desire goes out; when I meet with the grief of parents upon a tombstone, my heart melts with compassion; when I see the tomb of the parents themselves, I consider the vanity of grieving for those whom we must quickly follow. When I see kings lying by those who deposed them, when I consider rival wits placed side by side, or the holy men that divided the world with their contests and disputes, I reflect with sorrow and astonishment on the little competitions, factions, and debates of mankind. When I read the several dates of the tombs, of some that died yesterday, and some six hundred years ago, I consider that great day when we shall all of us be contemporaries, and make our appearance together.

FROM "CATO."

185. CATO'S SOLILOQUY ON THE IMMORTALITY OF THE SOUL.

It must be so; — Plato, thou reason'st well,
Else whence this pleasing hope, this fond desire,
This longing after immortality?
Or whence this secret dread and inward horror
Of falling into nought? Why shrinks the soul
Back on herself, and startles at destruction?
— 'Tis the Divinity that stirs within us,
'Tis heaven itself that points out an hereafter,
And intimates Eternity to man.
Eternity! — thou pleasing — dreadful thought!
Through what variety of untried being —
Through what new scenes and changes must we pass!
The wide, th' unbounded prospect lies before me;
But shadows, clouds, and darkness rest upon it.
Here will I hold: — If there's a Power above us
(And that there is all Nature cries aloud
Through all her works), he must delight in Virtue;
And that which he delights in must be happy:
But — when? — or where? — *This* world was made for Cæsar.
I'm weary of conjectures: — This must end them.
[*Laying his hand on his sword.*
Thus I am doubly armed; my death and life,
My bane and antidote are both before me.
This in a moment brings me to an end,
But this informs me I shall never die.
The soul, secured in her existence, smiles
At the drawn dagger, and defies its point.
The stars shall fade away, the sun himself
Grow dim with age, and nature sink in years;
But thou shalt flourish in immortal youth,
Unhurt amid the war of elements,
The wreck of matter, and the crush of worlds.

SIR RICHARD STEELE. 1675–1729. (Manual, p. 291.)

186. THE DREAM.

I was once myself in agonies of grief that are unutterable, and in so great a distraction of mind, that I thought myself even out of the possibility of receiving comfort. The occasion was as follows: When I was a youth in a part of the army which was then quartered at Dover, I fell in love with an agreeable young woman, of a good family in those parts, and had the satisfaction of seeing my addresses kindly received, which occasioned the perplexity I am going to relate.

We were, in a calm evening, diverting ourselves upon the top of a cliff with the prospect of the sea, and trifling away the time in such little fondnesses as are most ridiculous to people in business, and most agreeable to those in love.

In the midst of these our innocent endearments, she snatched a paper of verses out of my hand, and ran away with them. I was following her, when on a sudden the ground, though at a considerable distance from the verge of the precipice, sunk under her, and threw her down from so prodigious a height upon such a range of rocks, as would have dashed her into ten thousand pieces, had her body been made of adamant. It is much easier for my reader to imagine my state of mind upon such an occasion, than for me to express it. I said to myself, It is not in the power of Heaven to relieve me! when I awaked, transported and astonished, to see myself drawn out of an affliction which, the very moment before, appeared to me altogether inextricable.

The impressions of grief and horror were so lively on this occasion, that while they lasted they made me more miserable than I was at the real death of this beloved person, which happened a few months after, at a time when the match between us was concluded; inasmuch as the imaginary death was untimely, and I myself in a sort an accessary; whereas her real decease had at least these alleviations, of being natural and inevitable.

The memory of the dream I have related still dwells so strongly upon me, that I can never read the description of Dover Cliff in Shakspeare's tragedy of King Lear, without a fresh sense of my escape. The prospect from that place is drawn with such proper incidents, that whoever can read it without growing giddy must have a good head, or a very bad one.

SIR WILLIAM TEMPLE. 1628–1699. (Manual, p. 296.)

187. AGAINST EXCESSIVE GRIEF.

(From a Letter addressed to the Countess of Essex on the loss of her only daughter.)

I know no duty in religion more generally agreed on, nor more justly required by God Almighty, than a perfect submission to his will in all things; nor do I think any disposition of mind can either please him more, or becomes us better, than that of being satisfied with all he gives, and contented with all he takes away. None, I am sure, can be of more honor to God, nor of more ease to ourselves. For, if we consider him as our Maker, we cannot contend with him; if as our Father, we ought not to distrust him: so that we may be confident, whatever he does is intended for good; and whatever happens that we interpret otherwise, yet we can get nothing by repining, nor save anything by resisting. * * * *

You will say, perhaps, that one thing was all to you, and your fondness of it made you indifferent to everything else. But this, I doubt, will be so far from justifying you, that it will prove to be your fault, as well as your misfortune. God Almighty gave you all the blessings of life, and you set your heart wholly upon one, and despise or undervalue all the rest: is this his fault or yours? Nay, is it not to be very unthankful to Heaven, as well as very scornful to the rest of the world? is it not to say, because you have lost one thing God has given, you thank him for nothing he has left, and care not what he takes away? is it not to say, since that one thing is gone out of the world, there is nothing left in it which you think can deserve your kindness or esteem? * * * *

Christianity teaches and commands us to moderate our passions; to temper our affections towards all things below; to be thankful for the possession, and patient under the loss, whenever He who gave shall see fit to take away. Your extreme fondness was perhaps as displeasing to God before, as now your extreme affliction is; and your loss may have been a punishment for your faults in the manner of enjoying what you had. It is, at least, pious to ascribe all the ill that befalls us to our own demerits, rather than to injustice in God. And it becomes us better to adore the issues of his providence in the effects, than to inquire into the causes; for submission is the only way of reasoning between a creature and its Maker; and contentment in his will is the greatest duty we can pretend to, and the best remedy we can apply to all our misfortunes.

Lord Shaftesbury. 1671–1713. (Manual, p. 297.)

From "The Moralists."

188. The Deity unfolded in his Works.

How oblique and faintly looks the sun on yonder climates, far removed from him! How tedious are the winters there! How deep the horrors of the night, and how uncomfortable even the light of day! The freezing winds employ their fiercest breath, yet are not spent with blowing. The sea, which elsewhere is scarce confined within its limits, lies here immured in walls of crystal. The snow covers the hills, and almost fills the lowest valleys. How wide and deep it lies, incumbent o'er the plains, hiding the sluggish rivers, the shrubs and trees, the dens of beasts, and mansions of distressed and feeble men! See where they lie confined, hardly secure against the raging cold or the attacks of the wild beasts, now masters of the wasted field, and forced by hunger out of the naked wood. Yet not disheartened (such is the force of human breasts), but thus provided for by art and prudence, the kind compensating gifts of Heaven, men and their herds may wait for a release. For, at length, the sun approaching melts the snow, sets longing men at liberty, and affords them means and time to make provision against the next return of cold. It breaks the icy fetters of the main, where vast sea-monsters pierce through floating islands, with arms which can withstand the crystal rock; whilst others, who of themselves seem great as islands, are by their bulk alone armed against all but man, whose superiority over creatures of such stupendous size and force should make him mindful of his privilege of reason, and force him humbly to adore the great Composer of these wondrous frames, and Author of his own superior wisdom.

But leaving these dull climates, so little favored by the sun, for those happier regions, on which he looks more kindly, making perpetual summer, how great an alteration do we find! His purer light confounds weak-sighted mortals, pierced by his scorching beams. Scarce can they tread the glowing ground. The air they breathe cannot enough abate the fire which burns within their panting breasts. Their bodies melt. O'ercome and fainting, they seek the shade, and wait the cool refreshments of the night. Yet oft the bounteous Creator bestows other refreshments. He casts a veil of clouds before them, and raises gentle gales; favored by which, the men and beasts pursue their labors, and plants refreshed by dews and showers can gladly bear the warmest sunbeams.

And here the varying scene opens to new wonders. We see a country rich with gems, but richer with the fragrant spices it affords. How gravely move the largest of land-creatures on the banks of this fair river! How ponderous are their arms, and vast their strength, with courage, and a sense superior to the other beasts! Yet are they tamed (we see) by mankind, and brought even to fight their battles, rather as allies and confederates than as slaves. * * * *

Now may we see that happy country where precious gums and balsams flow from trees, and nature yields her most delicious fruits. How tame and tractable, how patient of labor and of thirst, are those large creatures, who, lifting up their lofty heads, go led and laden through those dry and barren places! Their shape and temper show them framed by nature to submit to man, and fitted for his service, who from hence ought to be more sensible of his wants, and of the divine bounty thus supplying them.

LORD BOLINGBROKE. 1678–1751. (Manual, p. 298.)

189. THE USE OF HISTORY.

To teach and to inculcate the general principles of virtue, and the general rules of wisdom and good policy which result from such details of actions and characters, comes, for the most part, and always should come, expressly and directly into the design of those who are capable of giving such details; and, therefore, whilst they narrate as historians, they hint often as philosophers: they put into our hands, as it were, on every proper occasion, the end of a clue, that serves to remind us of searching, and to guide us in the search of that truth which the example before us either establishes or illustrates. If a writer neglects this part, we are able, however, to suppy his neglect by our own attention and industry: and when he gives us a good history of Peruvians or Mexicans, of Chinese or Tartars, of Muscovites or Negroes, we may blame him, but we must blame ourselves much more, if we do not make it a good lesson of philosophy. This being the general use of history, it is not to be neglected. Every one may make it who is able to read, and to reflect on what he reads; and every one who makes it will find, in his degree, the benefit that arises from an early acquaintance contracted in this manner with mankind. We are not only passengers or sojourners in this world, but we are absolute strangers at the first steps we make in it. Our guides are often ignorant, often unfaithful. By this map of the country, which history spreads before us, we may learn, if we please, to guide ourselves. In our journey through it, we are beset on every side. We are besieged sometimes, even in our strongest holds. Terrors and temptations, conducted by the passions of other men, assault us; and our own passions, that correspond with these, betray us. History is a collection of the journals of those who have travelled through the same country, and been exposed to the same accidents: and their good and their ill success are equally instructive. In this pursuit of knowledge an immense field is opened to us: general histories, sacred and profane; the histories of particular countries, particular events, particular orders, particular men; memorials, anecdotes, travels. But we must not ramble in this field without discernment or choice, nor even with these must we ramble too long.

---

190. The Patriot King.

The good of the people is the ultimate and true end of government. Governors are therefore appointed for this end, and the civil constitution which appoints them, and invests them with their power, is determined to do so by that law of nature and reason which has determined the end of government, and which admits this form of government as the proper mean of arriving at it. Now the greatest good of a people is their liberty; and in the case here referred to, the people has judged it so, and provided for it accordingly. Liberty is to the collective body, what health is to the individual body: without health no pleasure can be tasted by man, without liberty no happiness can be enjoyed by society. The obligation, therefore, to defend and maintain the freedom of such constitutions, will appear most sacred to a patriot king. Kings who have weak understandings, bad hearts, and strong prejudices. and all these, as it oftens happens, inflamed by

16

their passions, and rendered incurable by their self-conceit and presumption, such kings are apt to imagine, and they conduct themselves so as to make many of their subjects imagine, that the king and the people in free governments are rival powers, who stand in competition with one another, who have different interests, and must of course have different views: that the rights and privileges of the people are so many spoils taken from the right and prerogative of the crown; and that the rules and laws, made for the exercise and security of the former, are so many diminutions of their dignity, and restraints on their power.

A patriot king will see all this in a far different and much truer light. The constitution will be considered by him as one law, consisting of two tables, containing the rule of his government, and the measure of his subjects' obedience; or as one system, composed of different parts and powers, but all duly proportioned to one another, and conspiring by their harmony to the perfection of the whole.

BISHOP BERKELEY. 1684–1753. (Manual, p. 299.)

191. LUXURY THE CAUSE OF NATIONAL RUIN.

Frugality of manners is the nourishment and strength of bodies politic. It is that by which they grow and subsist, until they are corrupted by luxury, — the natural cause of their decay and ruin. Of this we have examples in the Persians, Lacedæmonians, and Romans: not to mention many later governments which have sprung up, continued a while, and then perished by the same natural causes. But these are, it seems, of no use to us: and, in spite of them, we are in a fair way of becoming ourselves another useless example to future ages. * * * *

It is not to be believed, what influence public diversions have on the spirit and manners of a people. The Greeks wisely saw this, and made a very serious affair of their public sports. For the same reason, it will, perhaps, seem worthy the care of our legislature to regulate the public diversions, by an absolute prohibition of those which have a direct tendency to corrupt our morals, as well as by a reformation of the drama; which, when rightly managed, is such a noble entertainment, and gave those fine lessons of morality and good sense to the Athenians of old, and to our British gentry above a century ago; but for these last ninety years, hath entertained us, for the most part, with such wretched things as spoil, instead of improving the taste and manners of the audience. Those who are attentive to such propositions only as may fill their pockets, will probably slight these things as trifles below the care of the legislature. But I am sure, all honest, thinking men must lament to see their country run headlong into all those luxurious follies, which, it is evident, have been fatal to other nations, and will undoubtedly prove fatal to us also, if a timely stop be not put to them.

192. Lady Mary Montagu. 1690–1762. (Manual, p. 300.)

From her Letters.

Vienna, October 1, O. S. 1716.

But now I am speaking of Vienna, I am sure you expect I should say something of the convents: they are of all sorts and sizes; but I am best pleased with that of St. Lawrence, where the ease and neatness they seem to live with, appears to be much more edifying than those stricter orders, where perpetual penance and nastiness must breed discontent and wretchedness. The nuns are all of quality. I think there are to the number of fifty. They have each of them a little cell perfectly clean, the walls of which are covered with pictures more or less fine, according to their quality. A long stone gallery runs by all of them, furnished with the pictures of exemplary sisters; the chapel is extremely neat, and richly adorned. Nothing can be more becoming than the dress of these nuns. It is a white robe, the sleeves of which are turned up with fine white calico, and their head-dress the same, excepting a small veil of black crape that falls behind. They have a lower sort of serving nuns that wait on them as their chamber-maids. They receive all visits of women, and play at ombre in their chambers with permission of their abbess, which is very easy to be obtained. I never saw an old woman so good-natured; she is near fourscore, and yet shows very little signs of decay, being still lively and cheerful. She caressed me as if I had been her daughter, giving me some pretty things of her own work, and sweetmeats in abundance. The grate is not of the most rigid; it is not very hard to put a head through. The young Count of Salamis came to the grate, while I was there, and the abbess gave him her hand to kiss. But I was surprised to find here the only beautiful young woman I have seen at Vienna, and, not only beautiful, but genteel, witty, and agreeable, of a great family, and who had been the admiration of the town. I could not forbear showing my surprise at seeing a nun like her. She made me a thousand obliging compliments, and desired me to come often. "It would be an infinite pleasure to me," said she, sighing, "but I avoid, with the greatest care, seeing any of my former acquaintances; and, whenever they come to our convent, I lock myself in my cell." I observed tears come into her eyes, which touched me extremely, and I began to talk to her in that strain of tender pity she inspired me with.

CHAPTER XVI.

THE GREAT NOVELISTS.

193. DANIEL DEFOE. 1661–1731. (Manual, p. 306.)

FROM "THE GREAT PLAGUE IN LONDON."

Much about the same time I walked out into the fields towards Bow, for I had a great mind to see how things were managed in the river, and among the ships; and as I had some concern in shipping, I had a notion that it had been one of the best ways of securing one's self from the infection, to have retired into a ship; and musing how to satisfy my curiosity in that point, I turned away over the fields, from Bow to Bromley, and down to Blackwall, to the stairs that are there for landing or taking water.

Here I saw a poor man walking on the bank or sea-wall, as they call it, by himself. I walked a while also about, seeing the houses all shut up; at last I fell into some talk, at a distance, with this poor man. First I asked him how people did thereabouts? Alas! sir, says he, almost desolate; all dead or sick: here are very few families in this part, or in that village, pointing at Poplar, where half of them are not dead already, and the rest sick. Then pointing to one house, There they are all dead, said he, and the house stands open; nobody dares go into it. A poor thief, says he, ventured in to steal something, but he paid dear for his theft, for he was carried to the churchyard too, last night. Then he pointed to several other houses. There, says he, they are all dead, the man and his wife and five children. There, says he, they are shut up; you see a watchman at the door, and so of other houses. Why, said I, what do you do here all alone? Why, says he, I am a poor desolate man; it hath pleased God I am not yet visited, though my family is, and one of my children dead. How do you mean then, said I, that you are not visited? Why, says he, that is my house, pointing to a very little low boarded house, and there my poor wife and two children live, said he, if they may be said to live; for my wife and one of the children are visited, but I do not come at them. And with that word I saw the tears run very plentifully down his face; and so they did down mine too, I assure you.

But, said I, why do you not come at them? How can you abandon your own flesh and blood? O, sir, says he, the Lord forbid; I do not abandon them; I work for them as much as I am able; and, blessed be the Lord, I keep them from want. And with that I observed he lifted up his eyes to heaven with a countenance that presently told me I had happened on a man that was no hypocrite, but a serious, religious, good man; and his ejaculation was an expression of thankfulness, that, in such a condition as he was in, he should be able to say his family did not want. Well, said I, honest man, that is a great mercy, as things go now with the poor. But how do you live then, and how are you kept from the dreadful calamity that is now upon us all? Why, sir, says he, I am a waterman, and there is my boat, says he, and the boat serves me for a house; I work in it in the day, and I sleep in it in the night, and what I get I lay it down upon that stone, says he, showing me a broad stone on the other side of the street, a good way from his house; and then, says he, I halloo and call to them till I make them hear, and they come and fetch it.

Well, friend, said I, but how can you get money as a waterman? Does anybody go by water these times? Yes, sir, says he, in the way I am employed there does. Do you see there, says he, five ships lie at anchor? pointing down the river a good way below the town; and do you see, says he, eight or ten ships lie at the chain there, and at anchor yonder? pointing above the town. All those ships have families on board, of their merchants and owners, and such like, who have locked themselves up, and live on board, close shut in, for fear of the infection; and I tend on them to fetch things for them, carry letters, and do what is absolutely necessary, that they may not be obliged to come on shore; and every night I fasten my boat on board one of the ship's boats, and there I sleep by myself; and blessed be God, I am preserved hitherto.

Well, said I, friend, but will they let you come on board after you have been on shore here, when this has been such a terrible place, and so infected as it is?

Why, as to that, said he, I very seldom go up the ship-side, but deliver what I bring to their boat, or lie by the side, and they hoist it on board; if I did, I think they are in no danger from me, for I never go into any house on shore, or touch anybody, no, not of my own family; but I fetch provisions for them.

Nay, said I, but that may be worse, for you must have those provisions of somebody or other; and since all this part of the town is so infected, it is dangerous so much as to speak with anybody; for the village, said I, is, as it were, the beginning of London, though it be at some distance from it.

That is true, added he, but you do not understand me right. I do not buy provisions for them here; I row up to Greenwich, and buy fresh meat there, and sometimes I row down the river to Woolwich, and buy there; then I go to single farm-houses on the Kentish side, where I am known, and buy fowls, and eggs, and butter, and bring to the ships, as they direct me, sometimes one, sometimes the other. I seldom come on shore here; and I came only now to call my wife, and hear how my little family do, and give them a little money which I received last night.

Poor man! said I, and how much hast thou gotten for them?

I have gotten four shillings, said he, which is a great sum, as things go now with poor men; but they have given me a bag of bread too, and a salt fish, and some flesh; so all helps out.

Well, said I, and have you given it them yet?

No, said he, but I have called, and my wife has answered that she cannot come out yet; but in half an hour she hopes to come, and I am waiting for her. Poor woman! says he, she is brought sadly down; she has had a swelling, and it is broke, and I hope she will recover, but I fear the child will die; but it is the Lord! Here he stopt, and wept very much.

Well, honest friend, said I, thou hast a sure comforter, if thou hast brought thyself to be resigned to the will of God; he is dealing with us all in judgment.

O, sir, says he, it is infinite mercy if any of us are spared; and who am I to repine!

---

194. HENRY FIELDING. 1707–1754. (Manual, p. 312.)

FROM "TOM JONES."

Being now provided with all the necessaries of life, I betook myself once again to study, and that with a more ordinate application than I had ever done formerly. The books which now employed my time solely were those, as well ancient as modern, which treat of true philosophy, a word which is by many thought to be the subject only of farce and ridicule. I now read over the works of Aristotle and Plato, with the rest of those inestimable treasures which ancient Greece hath bequeathed to the world.

To this I added another study, compared to which all the philosophy taught by the wisest heathens is little better than a dream, and is indeed as full of vanity as the silliest jester ever pleased to represent it. This is that divine wisdom which is alone to be found in the Holy Scriptures: for those impart to us the knowledge and assurance of things much more worthy our attention, than all which this world can offer to our acceptance; of things which Heaven itself hath condescended to reveal to us, and to the smallest knowledge of which the highest human wit unassisted could never ascend. I began now to think all the time I had spent with the best heathen writers was little more than labor lost: for however pleasant and delightful their lessons may be, or however adequate to the right regulation of our conduct with respect to this world only, yet, when compared with the glory revealed in Scripture, their highest documents will appear as trifling, and of as little consequence as the rules by which children regulate their childish little games and pastime. True it is, that philosophy makes us wiser, but Christianity makes us better men. Philosophy elevates and steels the mind, Christianity softens and sweetens it. The former makes us the objects of human admiration, the latter of divine love. That insures us a temporal, but this an eternal happiness.

TOBIAS GEORGE SMOLLETT. 1721–1771. (Manual, p. 315.)

195. THE SOLDIER'S RETURN.

We set out from Glasgow, by the way of Lanark, the county town of Clydesdale, in the neighborhood of which the whole river Clyde, rushing down a steep rock, forms a very noble and stupendous cascade. Next day we were obliged to halt in a small borough, until the carriage, which had received some damage, should be repaired; and here we met with an incident which warmly interested the benevolent spirit of Mr. Bramble. As we stood at the window of an inn that fronted the public prison, a person arrived on horseback, genteelly though plainly dressed in a blue frock, with his own hair cut short, and a gold-laced hat upon his head. Alighting, and giving his horse to the landlord, he advanced to an old man who was at work in paving the street, and accosted him in these words: "This is hard work for such an old man as you." So saying, he took the instrument out of his hand, and began to thump the pavement. After a few strokes, "Had you never a son," said he, "to ease you of this labor?" "Yes, an' please your honor," replied the senior, "I have three hopeful lads, but at present they are out of the way." "Honor not me," cried the stranger; "it more becomes me to honor your gray hairs. Where are those sons you talk of?" The ancient pavior said, his eldest son was a captain in the East Indies, and the youngest had lately enlisted as a soldier, in hopes of prospering like his brother. The gentleman desiring to know what was become of the second, he wiped his eyes, and owned he had taken upon him his old father's debts, for which he was now in the prison hard by.

The traveller made three quick steps towards the jail; then turning short, "Tell me," said he, "has that unnatural captain sent you nothing to relieve your distresses?" "Call him not unnatural," replied the other, "God's blessing be upon him! he sent me a great deal of money, but I made a bad use of it; I lost it by being security for a gentleman that was my landlord, and was stripped of all I had in the world besides." At that instant a young man, thrusting out his head and neck between two iron bars in the prison-window, exclaimed, "Father! father! if my brother William is in life, that's he." "I am! I am!" cried the stranger, clasping the old man in his arms, and shedding a flood of tears; "I am your son Willy, sure enough!" Before the father, who was quite confounded, could make any return to this tenderness, a decent old woman, bolting out from the door of a poor habitation, cried, "Where is my bairn? where is my dear

Willy?" The captain no sooner beheld her than he quitted his father, and ran into her embrace.

I can assure you, my uncle, who saw and heard everything that passed, was as much moved as any one of the parties concerned in this pathetic recognition. He sobbed, and wept, and clapped his hands, and holloed, and finally ran down into the street. By this time the captain had retired with his parents, and all the inhabitants of the place were assembled at the door. Mr. Bramble, nevertheless, pressed through the crowd, and entering the house, "Captain," said he, "I beg the favor of your acquaintance. I would have travelled a hundred miles to see this affecting scene; and I shall think myself happy if you and your parents will dine with me at the public house." The captain thanked him for his kind invitation, which, he said, he would accept with pleasure; but in the mean time he could not think of eating or drinking while his poor brother was in trouble. He forthwith deposited a sum equal to the debt in the hands of the magistrate, who ventured to set his brother at liberty without further process; and then the whole family repaired to the inn with my uncle, attended by the crowd, the individuals of which shook their townsman by the hand, while he returned their caresses without the least sign of pride or affectation. * * * *

My uncle was so charmed with the character of Captain Brown that he drank his health three times successively at dinner. He said he was proud of his acquaintance; that he was an honor to his country, and had in some measure redeemed human nature from the reproach of pride, selfishness, and ingratitude. For my part I was as much pleased with the modesty as with the filial virtue of this honest soldier, who assumed no merit from his success, and said very little of his own transactions, though the answers he made to our inquiries were equally sensible and laconic.

LAURENCE STERNE. 1713–1768. (Manual, p. 319.)

FROM "TRISTRAM SHANDY."

196. DEATH OF LE FEVRE.

— — In a fortnight or three weeks, added my uncle Toby, smiling — he might march. — He will never march, an' please your honor, in this world, said the corporal. — — He will march, said my uncle Toby, rising up from the side of the bed with one shoe off: — — An' please your honor, said the corporal, he will never march but to his grave: — He shall march, cried my uncle Toby, marching the foot which had a shoe on, though without advancing an inch, — he shall march to his regiment. — — He cannot stand it, said the corporal. — — He shall be supported, said my uncle Toby. — — He'll drop at last, said the corporal, and what will become of his boy? — — He shall not drop, said my uncle Toby, firmly. — Ah welladay, — do what we can for him, said Trim, maintaining his point, — the poor soul will die. He shall not die, by G—d! cried my uncle Toby.

— The Accusing Spirit, which flew up to Heaven's chancery with the oath, blushed as he gave it in — — and the Recording Angel, as he wrote it down, dropped a tear upon the word, and blotted it out forever.[1]

— — My uncle Toby went to his bureau — put his purse into his breeches' pocket, and having ordered the corporal to go early in the morning for a physician — he went to bed, and fell asleep.

The sun looked bright the morning after to every eye in the village but Le Fevre's, and his afflicted son's; the hand of Death pressed heavy upon his eyelids, and hardly could the wheel at the cistern turn round its circle, when my uncle Toby, who had rose up an hour before his wonted time, entered the lieutenant's room, and without preface or apology, sat himself down upon the chair by the bedside, and, independently of all modes and customs, opened the curtain in the manner an old friend and brother officer would have done it, and asked him how he did — how he had rested in the night — what was his complaint — where was his pain — and what he could do to help him? — and without giving him time to answer any one of the inquiries, went on, and told him of the little plan which he had been concerting with the corporal the night before for him.

— You shall go home directly, Le Fevre, said my uncle Toby, to my house — and we'll send for a doctor to see what's the matter — and we'll have an apothecary, — and the corporal shall be your nurse, — and I'll be your servant, Le Fevre.

There was a frankness in my uncle Toby, — not the effect of familiarity, —but the cause of it, which let you at once into his soul, and showed you the goodness of his nature; to this, there was something in his looks, and voice, and manner, superadded, which eternally beckoned to the unfortunate to come and take shelter under him; so that before my uncle Toby had half finished the kind offers he was making to the father, the son had insensibly pressed up close to his knees, and had taken hold of the breast of his coat, and was pulling it towards him. The blood and spirits of Le Fevre, which were waxing cold and slow within him, and were retreating to their last citadel, the heart, rallied back, — the film forsook his eyes for a moment, — he looked up wistfully in my uncle Toby's face — then cast a look upon his boy, — and that ligament, fine as it was, was never broken. — —

Nature instantly ebbed again, — — the film returned to its place — — the pulse fluttered — — stopped — — went on — — throbbed — — stopped again — — moved — — stopped — — shall I go on? — — No.

1 The sentiment of this paragraph has been characterized by an eminent American divine as the most beautiful in English literature.

OLIVER GOLDSMITH. 1728–1774. (Manual, p. 321.)

FROM "THE CITIZEN OF THE WORLD."

197. THE STERN MORALIST.

Though fond of many acquaintances, I desire an intimacy only with a few. The man in black, whom I have often mentioned, is one whose friendship I could wish to acquire, because he possesses my esteem. * * * *

In one of our late excursions into the country, happening to discourse upon the provision that was made for the poor in England, he seemed amazed how any of his countrymen could be so foolishly weak as to relieve occasional objects of charity, when the laws had made such ample provision for their support. In every parish house, says he, the poor are supplied with food, clothes, fire, and a bed to lie on; they want no more, I desire no more myself; yet still they seem discontented. I am surprised at the inactivity of our magistrates, in not taking up such vagrants, who are only a weight upon the industrious. I am surprised that the people are found to relieve them, when they must be at the same time sensible that it, in some measure, encourages idleness, extravagance, and imposture. Were I to advise any man for whom I had the least regard, I would caution him, by all means, not to be imposed upon by their false pretences: let me assure you, sir, they are impostors, every one of them, and rather merit a prison than relief.

He was proceeding in this strain earnestly, to dissuade me from an imprudence of which I am seldom guilty, when an old man, who still had about him the remnants of tattered finery, implored our compassion. He assured us that he was no common beggar, but forced into the shameful profession to support a dying wife, and five hungry children. Being prepossessed against such falsehoods, his story had not the least influence upon me; but it was quite otherwise with the man in black. I could see it visibly operate upon his countenance, and effectually interrupt his harangue. I could easily perceive that his heart burned to relieve the five starving children, but he seemed ashamed to discover his weakness to me. While he thus hesitated between compassion and pride, I pretended to look another way, and he seized this opportunity of giving the poor petitioner a piece of silver, bidding him, at the same time, in order that I should not hear, go work for his bread, and not tease passengers with such impertinent falsehoods for the future.

---

198. A FABLE.

Once upon a time, a Giant and a Dwarf were friends, and kept together. They made a bargain that they would never forsake each other, but go seek adventures. The first battle they fought was with two Saracens, and the Dwarf, who was very courageous, dealt one of the champions a most angry blow. It did the Saracen but very little injury, who, lifting up his sword, fairly struck off the poor Dwarf's arm. He was now in a woful plight; but the Giant coming to his assistance, in a short time left the two Saracens dead on the plain, and the Dwarf cut off the dead man's head out of spite. They then travelled on to another adventure. This was against three bloody-minded Satyrs, who were carrying away a damsel in distress. The Dwarf was not quite so fierce now as before; but for all that, struck the first blow; which was returned by another, that knocked out his eye: but the Giant was soon up with them, and had they not fled, would certainly have killed them every one. They were all very joyful for this victory, and the damsel who was relieved fell in love with the Giant, and married him. They now travelled far, and farther than I can tell, till they met with a company of robbers. The Giant, for the first time, was foremost now; but the Dwarf was not far behind. The battle was stout and long. Wherever the Giant came, all fell before him; but the Dwarf had like to have been killed more than once. At last the victory declared for the two adventurers: but the Dwarf lost his leg. The Dwarf had now lost an arm, a leg, and an eye, while the Giant was without a single wound. Upon which he cried out to his little companion: "My little hero, this is glorious sport; let us get one victory more, and then we shall have honor forever." — "No," cries the Dwarf, who was by this time grown wiser, "no, I declare off; I'll fight no more: for I find in every battle that you get all the honor and rewards, but all the blows fall upon me."

From "The Traveller."

199. France.

To kinder skies, where gentler manners reign,
I turn; and France displays her bright domain.
Gay sprightly land of mirth and social ease,
Pleased with thyself, whom all the world can please,
How often have I led thy sportive choir,
With tuneless pipe, beside the murmuring Loire!
Where shading elms along the margin grew,
And freshened from the wave the zephyr flew;
And haply, though my harsh touch, faltering still,
But mocked all tune, and marred the dancer's skill,
Yet would the village praise my wondrous power,
And dance, forgetful of the noontide hour.
Alike all ages. Dames of ancient days
Have led their children through the mirthful maze;
And the gay grandsire, skilled in gestic lore,
Has frisked beneath the burden of threescore.

So blest a life these thoughtless realms display,
Thus idly busy rolls their world away;
Theirs are those arts that mind to mind endear,
For honor forms the social temper here:
Honor, that praise which real merit gains
Or e'en imaginary worth obtains,
Here passes current; paid from hand to hand,
It shifts in splendid traffic round the land:
From courts, to camps, to cottages it strays,
And all are taught an avarice of praise;
They please, are pleased, they give to get esteem,
Till, seeming blest, they grow to what they seem.
But while this softer art their bliss supplies,
It gives their follies also room to rise;
For praise too dearly loved, or warmly sought,
Enfeebles all internal strength of thought;
And the weak soul, within itself unblest,
Leans for all pleasure on another's breast.
Hence ostentation here, with tawdry art,
Pants for the vulgar praise which fools impart;
Here vanity assumes her pert grimace,
And trims her robes of frieze with copper lace;
Here beggar pride defrauds her daily cheer,
To boast one splendid banquet once a year;
The mind still turns where shifting fashion draws,
Nor weighs the solid worth of self-applause.

FROM "THE DESERTED VILLAGE."

200. THE VILLAGE INN.

Near yonder thorn, that lifts its head on high,
Where once the sign-post caught the passing eye,
Low lies that house where nut-brown draughts inspired,
Where gray-beard mirth and smiling toil retired,
Where village statesmen talked with looks profound,
And news much older than their ale went round;
Imagination fondly stoops to trace
The parlor splendors of that festive place;
The white-washed wall, the nicely sanded floor,
The varnished clock that clicked behind the door;
The chest contrived a double debt to pay,
A bed by night, a chest of drawers by day;
The pictures placed for ornament and use,
The twelve good rules, the royal game of goose;
The hearth, except when winter chilled the day,
With aspen boughs, and flowers, and fennel, gay;

While broken tea-cups, wisely kept for show,
Ranged o'er the chimney, glistened in a row.
 Vain transitory splendors! could not all
Reprieve the tottering mansion from its fall?
Obscure its sinks, nor shall it more impart
An hour's importance to the poor man's heart;
Thither no more the peasant shall repair
To sweet oblivion of his daily care;
No more the farmer's news, the barber's tale,
No more the woodman's ballad shall prevail;
No more the smith his dusky brow shall clear,
Relax his pond'rous strength, and lean to hear;
The host himself no longer shall be found,
Careful to see the mantling bliss go round;
Nor the coy maid, half willing to be prest,
Shall kiss the cup to pass it to the rest.

CHAPTER XVII.

HISTORICAL, MORAL, POLITICAL, AND THEOLOGICAL WRITERS OF THE EIGHTEENTH CENTURY.

ISAAC WATTS. 1674–1728. (Manual, p. 288.)

FROM HIS LYRICS. Book I.

201. THE EARNEST STUDENT.

"Infinite Truth, the life of my desires,
Come from the sky, and join thyself to me:
I'm tired with hearing, and this reading tires;
But never tired of telling thee,
'Tis thy fair face alone my spirit burns to see.

"Speak to my soul, alone; no other hand
Shall mark my path out with delusive art:
All nature, silent in His presence, stand;
Creatures, be dumb at his command,
And leave his single voice to whisper to my heart.

"Retire, my soul, within thyself retire,
Away from sense and every outward show:
Now let my thoughts to loftier themes aspire;
My knowledge now on wheels of fire,
May mount and spread above, surveying all below."

The Lord grows lavish of His heavenly light,
And pours whole floods on such a mind as this:
Fled from the eyes, she gains a piercing sight,
She dives into the infinite,
And sees unutterable things in that unknown abyss.

PHILIP DODDRIDGE. 1702–1751. (Manual, p. 345.)

202. OBLIGATION OF HARMONY AMONG CHRISTIANS.

Among many other good affections which the perusal of this history may naturally inspire, and which I have endeavored often to suggest in the improvements which conclude each section, I cannot forbear mentioning one more; I mean a generous and cordial love to our fellow-Christians of every rank and denomination. I never reflect upon the New Testament in this view, but I find it difficult to conceive how so much of a contrary temper should ever have prevailed amongst such multitudes who have professed religiously to receive it, yea, whose office hath been to interpret and enforce it. To have enlisted under the banner of Jesus, to have felt his love, to have espoused his interest, to labor to serve him, to aspire after the enjoyment of him, should, methinks, appear to every one, even on the slightest reflection, a bond of union too strong to be broken by the different apprehensions that one or another of us may entertain (perhaps, too, after diligent inquiry) concerning the exact sense of some of the doctrines he taught, or the circumstantial forms of some of his institutions. A humble sense of our own weakness, and of the many imperfections of our character, which will never be more deeply felt than when we consider ourselves as standing before our Divine Master, will dispose us to mutual candor, will guard us against the indecency of contending in his presence, and will, as St. Paul, with admirable spirit, expresses it, dispose us to receive one another, as Christ hath received us. Yea, our hearts will be so eagerly desirous of employing our life in serving him to the best purpose we can, that we shall dread the thought of misspending, in our mutual animosities, accusations, and complaints, the time that was given us for ends so much nobler, and which is capable of being employed to the honor of our common Lord, and for the benefit of the church and the world.

EPIGRAM ON HIS FAMILY MOTTO, — "*Dum vivimus vivamus.*"

Live while you live, the epicure would say,
And seize the pleasures of the present day;
Live while you live, the sacred preacher cries,
And give to God each moment as it flies.
Lord, in my view let both united be, —
I live in pleasure when I live to thee.

DAVID HUME. 1711–1776. (Manual, p. 326.)

203. CHARACTER OF QUEEN ELIZABETH.

There are few great personages in history who have been more exposed to the calumny of enemies, and the adulation of friends, than Queen Elizabeth, and yet there is scarce any whose reputation has been more certainly determined by the unanimous consent of posterity. The unusual length of her administration, and the strong features of her character, were able to overcome all prejudices; and obliging her detractors to abate much of their invectives, and her admirers somewhat of their panegyrics, have, at last, in spite of political factions, and, what is more, of religious animosities, produced a uniform judgment with regard to her conduct. Her vigor, her constancy, her magnanimity, her penetration, vigilance, address, are allowed to merit the highest praises, and appear not to have been surpassed by any person who ever filled a throne: a conduct less rigorous, less imperious, more sincere, more indulgent to her people, would have been requisite to form a perfect character. By the force of her mind, she controlled all her more active and stronger qualities, and prevented them from running into excess. Her heroism was exempt from all temerity, her frugality from avarice, her friendship from partiality, her active temper from turbulency and a vain ambition. She guarded not herself with equal care or equal success from lesser infirmities — the rivalship of beauty, the desire of admiration, the jealousy of love, and the sallies of anger.

Her singular talents for government were founded equally on her temper and on her capacity. Endowed with a great command over herself, she soon obtained an uncontrolled ascendant over her people; and while she merited all their esteem by her real virtues, she also enjoyed their affection by her pretended ones. Few sovereigns of England succeeded to the throne in more difficult circumstances; and none ever conducted the government with such uniform success and felicity. Though unacquainted with the practice of toleration, the true secret for managing religious factions, she preserved her people, by her superior prudence, from those confusions in which theological controversies had involved all the neighboring nations; and though her enemies were the most powerful princes of Europe, the most active, the most enterprising, the least scrupulous, she was able by her vigor to make deep impressions on their state; her own greatness meanwhile remained untouched and unimpaired.

The wise ministers and brave warriors who flourished during her reign share the praise of her success; but instead of lessening the applause due to her, they make great addition to it. They owed, all of them, their advancement to her choice; they were supported by her constancy; and with all their ability they were never able to acquire any undue ascendant over her. In her family, in her court, in her kingdom, she remained equally mistress: the force of the tender passions was great over her, but the force of her mind was still superior; and the combat which her victory visibly cost her, serves only to display the firmness of her resolution, and the loftiness of her ambitious sentiments.

The fame of this princess, though it has surmounted the prejudices both of faction and bigotry, yet lies still exposed to another prejudice, which is more durable because more natural, and which, according to the different views in which we survey her, is capable either of exalting beyond measure, or diminishing the lustre of her character. This prejudice is founded on the consideration of her sex. When we contemplate her as a woman, we are apt to be struck with the highest admiration of her great qualities and extensive capacity; but we are also apt to require some more softness of disposition, some greater lenity of temper, some of those amiable weaknesses by which her sex is distinguished. But the true method of estimating her merit is to lay aside all these considerations, and consider her merely as a rational being, placed in authority, and intrusted with the government of mankind. We may find it difficult to reconcile our fancy to her as a wife or a mistress; but her qualities as a sovereign, though with some considerable exceptions, are the object of undisputed applause and approbation.

---

204. On the Middle Station of Life.

The moral of the following fable will easily discover itself without my explaining it. One rivulet meeting another, with whom he had been long united in strictest amity, with noisy haughtiness and disdain thus bespoke him: — "What, brother! still in the same state! still low and creeping! Are you not ashamed when you behold me, who, though lately in a like condition with you, am now become a great river, and shall shortly be able to rival the Danube or the Rhine, provided those friendly rains continue which have favored my banks, but neglected yours?" "Very true," replies the humble rivulet, "you are now, indeed, swollen to a great size; but methinks you are become withal somewhat turbulent and muddy. I am contented with my low condition and my purity."

Instead of commenting upon this fable, I shall take occasion from it to compare the different stations of life, and to persuade such of my readers as are placed in the middle station to be satisfied with it, as the most eligible of all others. These form the most numerous rank of men that can be supposed susceptible of philosophy, and therefore all discourses of morality ought principally to be addressed to them. The great are too much immersed in pleasure, and the poor too much occupied in providing for the necessities of life, to hearken to the calm voice of reason. The middle station, as it is most happy in many respects, so particularly in this, that a man placed in it can, with the greatest leisure, consider his own happiness, and reap a new enjoyment, from comparing his situation with that of persons above or below him.

Agur's prayer is sufficiently noted — "Two things have I required of thee; deny me them not before I die: Remove far from me vanity and lies; give me neither poverty nor riches; feed me with food convenient for me, lest I be full and deny thee, and say, who is the Lord? or lest I be poor, and steal, and take the name of my God in vain." The middle station is here justly recommended, as affording the fullest security for virtue; and I may also add, that it gives opportunity for the most ample exercise of it, and furnishes employment for every good quality which we can possibly be possessed of.

WILLIAM ROBERTSON. 1721–1793. (Manual, p. 328.)

205. EXECUTION OF MARY, QUEEN OF SCOTS.

On Tuesday, the 7th of February, 1587, the two earls arrived at Fotheringay, and demanded access to the queen, read in her presence the warrant for execution, and required her to prepare to die next morning. Mary heard them to the end without emotion, and crossing herself in the name of the Father, and of the Son, and of the Holy Ghost, "That soul," said she, "is not worthy the joys of heaven, which repines because the body must endure the stroke of the executioner; and though I did not expect that the Queen of England would set the first example of violating the sacred person of a sovereign prince, I willingly submit to that which Providence has decreed to be my lot." And laying her hand on a Bible, which happened to be near her, she solemnly protested that she was innocent of that conspiracy which Babington had carried on against Elizabeth's life. She then mentioned the request contained in her letter to Elizabeth, but obtained no satisfactory answer. She entreated with particular earnestness, that now in her last moment, her almoner might be suffered to attend her, and that she might enjoy the consolation of those pious institutions prescribed by her religion. Even this favor, which is usually granted to the vilest criminal, was absolutely denied. * * *

With much difficulty, and after many entreaties, she prevailed on the two earls to allow Melvil, together with three of her men-servants, and two of her maids, to attend her to the scaffold. It was erected in the same hall where she had been tried, raised a little above the floor, and covered, as well as a chair, the cushion, and block, with black cloth. Mary mounted the steps with alacrity, beheld all this apparatus of death with an unaltered countenance, and signing herself with the cross, she sat down in the chair. Beale read the warrant for execution with a loud voice, to which she listened with a careless air, and like one occupied in other thoughts. Then the Dean of Peterborough began a devout discourse, suitable to her present condition, and offered up prayers to Heaven in her behalf; but she declared that she could not in conscience hearken to the one, nor join with the other; and falling on her knees, repeated a Latin prayer. When the Dean had finished his devotions, she, with an audible voice, and in the English tongue, recommended unto God the afflicted state of the church, and prayed for prosperity to her son, and for a long life and peaceable reign to Elizabeth. She declared that she hoped for mercy only through the death of Christ, at the foot of whose image she now willingly shed her blood, and lifting up, and kissing the crucifix, she thus addressed it: "As thy arms, O Jesus, were extended on the cross; so with the outstretched arms of thy mercy receive me, and forgive my sins."

She then prepared for the block, by taking off her veil and upper garments; and one of the executioners rudely endeavoring to assist, she gently checked him, and said, with a smile, that she had not been accustomed to undress before so many spectators, nor to be served by such valets. With calm but undaunted fortitude, she laid her neck on the block; and while one executioner held her hands, the other, at the second stroke, cut off her head, which falling out of its attire, discovered her hair already grown quite gray with cares and sorrows. The executioner held it up still streaming with blood, and the Dean crying out, "So perish all Queen Elizabeth's enemies," the Earl of Kent alone answered, Amen. The rest of the spectators continued silent, and drowned in tears, being incapable, at that moment, of any other sentiments but those of pity or admiration.

Edward Gibbon. 1737–1794. (Manual, p. 329.)

From "His Autobiography."

206. Conception and Completion of his History.

It was at Rome, on the 15th of October, 1764, as I sat musing amidst the ruins of the Capitol, while the barefooted friars were singing vespers in the temple of Jupiter, that the idea of writing the decline and fall of the city first started to my mind. But my original plan was circumscribed to the decay of the city rather than of the empire; and though my reading and reflections began to point towards that object, some years elapsed, and several avocations intervened, before I was seriously engaged in the execution of that laborious work. * *

I have presumed to mark the moment of conception: I shall now commemorate the hour of my final deliverance. It was on the day, or rather night, of the 27th of June, 1787, between the hours of eleven and twelve, that I wrote the last lines of the last page, in a summer-house in my garden. After laying down my pen I took several turns in a *berceau*, or covered walk of acacias, which commands a prospect of the country, the lake, and the mountains. The air was temperate, the sky was serene, the silver orb of the moon was reflected from the waters, and all nature was silent. I will not dissemble the first emotions of joy on recovery of my freedom, and, perhaps, the establishment of my fame. But my pride was soon humbled, and a sober melancholy was spread over my mind, by the idea that I had taken an everlasting leave of an old and agreeable companion, and that, whatsoever might be the future date of my history, the life of the historian must be short and precarious. I will add two facts, which have seldom occurred in the composition of six, or at least of five quartos. 1. My first rough manuscript, without any intermediate copy, has been sent to the press. 2. Not a sheet has been seen by any human eyes, excepting those of the author and the printer: the faults and the merits are exclusively my own.

FROM "THE DECLINE AND FALL OF THE ROMAN EMPIRE."

207. CHARLEMAGNE.

The appellation of *Great* has been often bestowed, and sometimes deserved, but Charlemagne is the only prince in whose favor the title has been indissolubly blended with the name. That name, with the addition of saint, is inserted in the Roman calendar; and the saint, by a rare felicity, is crowned with the praises of the historians and philosophers of an enlightened age. His real merit is doubtless enhanced by the barbarism of the nation and the times from which he emerged: but the apparent magnitude of an object is likewise enlarged by an unequal comparison; and the ruins of Palmyra derive a casual splendor from the nakedness of the surrounding desert. Without injustice to his fame I may discern some blemishes in the sanctity and greatness of the restorer of the western empire. * * * * I shall be scarcely permitted to accuse the ambition of a conqueror; but in a day of equal retribution the sons of his brother Carloman, the Merovingian princes of Aquitain, and the four thousand five hundred Saxons who were beheaded on the same spot, would have something to allege against the justice and humanity of Charlemagne. His treatment of the vanquished Saxons was an abuse of the right of conquest: his laws were not less sanguinary than his arms, and in the discussion of his motives whatever is subtracted from bigotry must be imputed to temper. The sedentary reader is amazed by his incessant activity of mind and body; and his subjects and enemies were not less astonished at his sudden presence at the moment when they believed him at the most distant extremity of the empire; neither peace nor war, nor summer nor winter, were a season of repose; and our fancy cannot easily reconcile the annals of his reign with the geography of his expeditions. But this activity was a national rather than a personal virtue; the vagrant life of a Frank was spent in the chase, in pilgrimage, in military adventures; and the journeys of Charlemagne were distinguished only by a more numerous train and a more important purpose. * * * * I touch with reverence the laws of Charlemagne, so highly applauded by a respectable judge. They compose not a system but a series of occasional and minute edicts, for the correction of abuses, the reformation of manners, the economy of his farms, the care of his poultry, and even the sale of his eggs. He wished to improve the laws and the character of the Franks; and his attempts, however feeble and imperfect, are deserving of praise: the inveterate evils of the times were suspended or mollified by his government; but in his institutions I can seldom discover the general views and the immortal spirit of a legislator, who survives himself for the benefit of posterity. The union and stability of his empire depended on the life of a single man: he imitated the dangerous practice of dividing his kingdoms amongst his sons; and after numerous diets the whole constitution was left to fluctuate between the disorders of anarchy and despotism. His esteem for the piety and knowledge of the clergy tempted him to intrust that aspiring order with temporal dominion and civil jurisdiction; and his son Lewis, when he was stripped and degraded by the bishops, might accuse, in some measure, the imprudence of his father. His laws enforced the imposition of tithes, because the demons had proclaimed in the air that the default of payment had been the cause of the last scarcity.

The literary merits of Charlemagne are attested by the foundation of schools, the introduction of arts, the works which were published in his name, and his familiar connection with the subjects and strangers whom he invited to his court to educate both the prince and the people. His own studies were tardy, laborious, and imperfect; if he spoke Latin and understood Greek, he derived the rudiments of knowledge from conversation rather than from books: and in his mature age the emperor strove to acquire the practice of writing, which every peasant now learns in his infancy. The grammar and logic, the music and astronomy, of the times, were only cultivated as the handmaids of superstition; but the curiosity of the human mind must ultimately tend to its improvement, and the encouragement of learning reflects the purest and most pleasing lustre on the character of Charlemagne. The dignity of his person, the length of his reign, the prosperity of his arms, the vigor of his government, and the reverence of distant nations, distinguish him from the royal crowd; and Europe dates a new era from his restoration of the western empire.

---

208. Mahomet.

According to the tradition of his companions, Mahomet was distinguished by the beauty of his person — an outward gift which is seldom despised, except by those to whom it has been refused. Before he spoke, the orator engaged on his side the affections of a public or private audience. They applauded his commanding presence, his majestic aspect, his piercing eye, his gracious smile, his flowing beard, his countenance that painted every sensation of the soul, and his gestures that enforced each expression of the tongue. In the familiar offices of life he scrupulously adhered to the grave and ceremonious politeness of his country: his respectful attention to the rich and powerful was dignified by his condescension and affability to the poorest citizens of Mecca: the frankness of his manner concealed the artifice of his views; and the habits of courtesy were imputed to personal friendship or universal benevolence. His memory was capacious and retentive, his wit easy and social, his imagination sublime, his judgment clear, rapid, and decisive. He possessed the courage both of thought and action; and although his designs might gradually expand with his success, the first idea which he entertained of his divine mission bears the stamp of an original and superior genius.

The son of Abdallah was educated in the bosom of the noblest race, in the use of the purest dialect of Arabia: and the fluency of his speech was corrected and enhanced by the practice of discreet and seasonable silence. With these powers of eloquence, Mahomet was an illiterate barbarian; his youth had never been instructed in the arts of reading and writing: the common ignorance exempted him from shame or reproach, but he was reduced to a narrow circle of existence, and deprived of those faithful mirrors which reflect to our mind the minds of sages and heroes. Yet the book of nature and of man was open to his view; and some fancy has been indulged in the political and philosophical observations which are ascribed to the Arabian traveller. He compares the nations and religions of the earth; discovers the weakness of the Persian and Roman monarchies; beholds with pity and indignation the degeneracy of the times; and resolves to unite, under one God and one king, the invincible spirit and primitive virtues of the Arabs. Our more accurate inquiry will suggest, that instead of visiting the courts, the camps, the temples of the east, the two journeys of Mahomet into Syria were confined to the fairs of Bostra and Damascus: that he was only thirteen years of age when he accompanied the caravan of his uncle, and that his duty compelled him to return as soon as he had disposed of the merchandise of Cadijah. In these hasty and superficial excursions, the eye of genius might discern some objects invisible to his grosser companions; some seeds of knowledge might be cast upon a fruitful soil; but his ignorance of the Syriac language must have checked his curiosity, and I cannot perceive in the life or writings of Mahomet[1] that his prospect was far extended beyond the limits of the Arabian world.

1 The form of orthography adopted by Gibbon for this name, is, by his own admission, an incorrect one, and no authority whatever can be adduced in its support. *Mahomet* was, however, the spelling at that time so generally employed, that the historian, though aware of its inaccuracy, did not venture to change it.

The more correct form — Mohammed — has now become so much more familiar among scholars, that the former is comparatively rare. In accordance, however, with the principle adopted throughout this work, by which the orthography of each author quoted is retained unaltered, it has been deemed best to make no change in the text of Gibbon, and the name, therefore, stands as he wrote it.

The true form, as derived from the Arabic, is the one given by most of the writers who are acquainted with that language, *Muhammed.* The letter *u*, however, represents the short Arabic sound of the vowel, which is analogous to the short sound of the English *oo* in book. This is best given for practical purposes by the ordinary spelling, Mohammed; which may be considered the established orthography among us.

209. Invention and Use of Gunpowder.

The only hope of salvation for the Greek empire and the adjacent kingdoms, would have been some more powerful weapon, some discovery in the art of war, that should give them a decisive superiority over their Turkish foes. Such a weapon was in their hands; such a discovery had been made in the critical moment of their fate. The chemists of China or Europe had found, by casual or elaborate experiments, that a mixture of saltpetre, sulphur, and charcoal produces, with a spark of fire, a tremendous explosion. It was soon observed, hat if the expansive force were compressed in a strong tube, a ball of stone or iron might be expelled with irresistible and destructive velocity. The precise era of the invention and application of gunpowder is involved in doubtful traditions and equivocal language; yet we may clearly discern that it was known before the middle of the fourteenth century; and that before the end of the same, the use of artillery in battles and sieges, by sea and land, was familiar to the states of Germany, Italy, Spain, France, and England. The priority of nations is of small account; none could derive any exclusive benefit from their previous or superior knowledge; and in the common improvement, they stood on the same level of relative power and military science. Nor was it possible to circumscribe the secret within the pale of the church; it was disclosed to the Turks by the treachery of apostates and the selfish policy of rivals; and the sultans had sense to adopt, and wealth to reward, the talents of a Christian engineer. The Genoese, who transported Amurath into Europe, must be accused as his preceptors; and it was probably by their hands that his cannon was cast and directed at the siege of Constantinople. The first attempt was indeed unsuccessful; but in the general warfare of the age, the advantage was on *their* side who were most commonly the assailants; for a while the proportion of the attack and defence was suspended; and this thundering artillery was pointed against the walls and towers which had been erected only to resist the less potent engines of antiquity. By the Venetians, the use of gunpowder was communicated without reproach to the sultans of Egypt and Persia, their allies against the Ottoman power; the secret was soon propagated to the extremities of Asia; and the advantage of the European was confined to his easy victories over the savages of the New World. If we contrast the rapid progress of this mischievous discovery with the slow and laborious advances of reason, science, and the arts of peace, a philosopher, according to his temper, will laugh or weep at the folly of mankind.

SAMUEL JOHNSON. 1709–1784. (Manual, p. 333.)

210. LETTER TO THE EARL OF CHESTERFIELD.

My Lord, — I have been lately informed, by the proprietor of the "World," that two papers, in which my Dictionary is recommended to the public, were written by your lordship. To be so distinguished, is an honor, which, being very little accustomed to favors from the great, I know not well how to receive, or in what terms to acknowledge.

When, upon some slight encouragement, I first visited your lordship, I was overpowered, like the rest of mankind, by the enchantment of your address, and could not forbear to wish that I might boast myself *Le vainqueur du vainqueur de la terre:*[1] that I might obtain that regard for which I saw the world contending; but I found my attendance so little encouraged, that neither pride nor modesty would suffer me to continue it. When I had once addressed your lordship in public, I had exhausted all the art of pleasing which a retired and uncourtly scholar can possess. I had done all that I could; and no man is well pleased to have his all neglected, be it ever so little.

Seven years, my lord, have now passed since I waited in your outward rooms, or was repulsed from your door; during which time I have been pushing on my work through difficulties, of which it is useless to complain, and have brought it, at last, to the verge of publication, without one act of assistance, one word of encouragement, or one smile of favor. Such treatment I did not expect, for I never had a patron before.

The shepherd in Virgil grew at last acquainted with Love, and found him a native of the rocks.

Is not a patron, my lord, one who looks with unconcern on a man struggling for life in the water, and when he has reached the ground, encumbers him with help? The notice which you have been pleased to take of my labors, had it been early, had been kind; but it has been delayed till I am indifferent, and cannot enjoy it; till I am solitary, and cannot impart it; till I am known, and do not want it. I hope it is no very cynical asperity not to confess obligations where no benefit has been received, or to be unwilling that the public should consider me as owing that to a patron, which Providence has enabled me to do for myself.

Having carried on my work thus far with so little obligation to any favorer of learning, I shall not be disappointed, though I should conclude it, if less be possible, with less; for I have been long wakened from that dream of hope, in which I once boasted myself with so much exultation.

My Lord, your Lordship's most humble,
Most obedient servant,
SAMUEL JOHNSON.

[1] The conqueror of the conqueror of the world.

211. From the Preface to his Dictionary.

In hope of giving longevity to that which its own nature forbids to be immortal, I have devoted this book, the labor of years, to the honor of my country, that we may no longer yield the palm of philology, without a contest, to the nations of the continent. The chief glory of every people arises from its authors: whether I shall add anything by my own writings to the reputation of English literature, must be left to time; much of my life has been lost under the pressures of disease; much has been trifled away; and much has always been spent in provision for the day that was passing over me; but I shall not think my employment useless or ignoble, if, by my assistance, foreign nations and distant ages gain access to the propagators of knowledge, and understand the teachers of truth; if my labors afford light to the repositories of science, and add celebrity to Bacon, to Hooker, to Milton, and to Boyle.

When I am animated by this wish, I look with pleasure on my book, however defective, and deliver it to the world with the spirit of a man that has endeavored well. That it will immediately become popular, I have not promised to myself; a few wild blunders and risible absurdities, from which no work of such multiplicity was ever free, may for a time furnish folly with laughter. and harden ignorance into contempt; but useful diligence will at last prevail, and there can never be wanting some who distinguish desert, who will consider that no dictionary of a living tongue ever can be perfect, since, while it is hastening to publication, some words are budding and some falling away; that a whole life cannot be spent upon syntax and etymology, and that even a whole life would not be sufficient; that he whose design includes whatever language can express, must often speak of what he does not understand; that a writer will sometimes be hurried by eagerness to the end, and sometimes faint with weariness under a task which Scaliger compares to the labors of the anvil and the mine; that what is obvious is not always known, and what is known is not always present; that sudden fits of inadvertency will surprise vigilance, slight avocations will seduce attention, and casual eclipses of the mind will darken learning; and that the writer shall often in vain trace his memory at the moment of need for that which yesterday he knew with intuitive readiness, and which will come uncalled into his thoughts tomorrow

---

From "The Rambler."

212. The Right Improvement of Time.

It is usual for those who are advised to the attainment of any new qualification, to look upon themselves as required to change the general course of their conduct, to dismiss business, and exclude pleasure, and to devote their days and nights to a particular attention. But all common degrees of excellence are attainable at a lower price; he that should steadily and resolutely assign to any science or language those interstitial vacancies which intervene in the most crowded variety of diversion or employment, would find every day new irradiations of knowledge, and discover how much more is to be hoped from frequency and perseverance, than from violent efforts and sudden desires; efforts which are soon remitted when they encounter difficulty, and desires which, if they are indulged too often, will shake off the authority of reason, and range capriciously from one object to another.

The disposition to defer every important design to a time of leisure and a state of settled uniformity, proceeds generally from a false estimate of the human power. If we except those gigantic and stupendous intelligences who are said to grasp a system by intuition, and bound forward from one series of conclusions to another, without regular steps through intermediate propositions, the most successful students make their advances in knowledge by short flights, between each of which the mind may lie at rest. For every single act of progression a short time is sufficient, and it is only necessary, that, whenever that time is afforded, it be well employed.

Few minds will be long confined to severe and laborious meditation; and when a successful attack on knowledge has been made, the student recreates himself with the contemplation of his conquest, and forbears another incursion till the new-acquired truth has become familiar, and his curiosity calls upon him for fresh gratifications. Whether the time of intermission is spent in company or in solitude, in necessary business or in voluntary levities, the understanding is equally abstracted from the object of inquiry; but, perhaps, if it be detained by occupations less pleasing, it returns again to study with greater alacrity than when it is glutted with ideal pleasures, and surfeited with intemperance of application. He that will not suffer himself to be discouraged by fancied impossibilities, may sometimes find his abilities invigorated by the necessity of exerting them in short intervals, as the force of a current is increased by the contraction of its channel.

From some cause like this it has probably proceeded, that, among those who have contributed to the advancement of learning, many have risen to eminence in opposition to all the obstacles which external circumstances could place in their way, amidst the tumult of business, the distresses of poverty, or the dissipations of a wandering and unsettled state. A great part of the life of Erasmus was one continual peregrination; ill supplied with the gifts of fortune, and led from city to city, and from kingdom to kingdom, by the hopes of patrons and preferment, hopes which always flattered and always deceived him, he yet found means, by unshaken constancy, and a vigilant improvement of those hours, which, in the midst of the most restless activity, will remain unengaged, to write more than another in the same condition would have hoped to read. Compelled by want to attendance and solicitation, and so much versed in common life, that he has transmitted to us the most perfect delineation of the manners of his age, he joined to his knowledge of the world such application to books, that he will stand forever in the first rank of literary heroes. How this proficiency was obtained he sufficiently discovers, by informing us, that the "Praise of Folly," one of his most celebrated performances, was composed by him on the road to Italy, lest the hours which he was obliged to spend on horseback should be tattled away without regard to literature.

An Italian philosopher expressed in his motto, that TIME WAS HIS ESTATE; an estate, indeed, which will produce nothing without cultivation, but will always abundantly repay the labors of industry, and satisfy the most extensive desires, if no part of it be suffered to lie waste by negligence, to be overrun with noxious plants, or laid out for show rather than for use.

FROM THE "LIVES OF THE POETS."

213. DRYDEN AND POPE.

Integrity of understanding and nicety of discernment were not allotted in a less proportion to Dryden than to Pope. The rectitude of Dryden's mind was sufficiently shown by the dismission of his poetical prejudices, and the rejection of unnatural thoughts and rugged numbers. But Dryden never desired to apply all the judgment that he had. He wrote, and professed to write, merely for the people; and when he pleased others he contented himself. He spent no time in struggles to rouse latent powers; he never attempted to make that better which was already good, nor often to mend what he must have known to be faulty. He wrote, as he tells us, with very little consideration; when occasion or necessity called upon him, he poured out what the present moment happened to supply, and, when once it had passed the press, ejected it from his mind; for when he had no pecuniary interest he had no further solicitude.

Pope was not content to satisfy; he desired to excel, and therefore always endeavored to do his best: he did not court the candor, but dared the judgment of his reader, and, expecting no indulgence from others, he showed none to himself. He examined lines and words with minute and punctilious observation, and retouched every part with indefatigable diligence till he had left nothing to be forgiven.

For this reason he kept his pieces very long in his hands, while he considered and reconsidered them. The only poems which can be supposed to have been written with such regard to the times as might hasten their publication, were the two satires of "Thirty-eight;" of which Dodsley told me, that they were brought to him by the author, that they might be fairly copied. "Almost every line," he said, "was then written twice over. I gave him a clean transcript, which he sent some time afterwards to me for the press, with almost every line written twice over a second time."

His declaration, that his care for his works ceased at their publication, was not strictly true. His parental attention never abandoned them; what he found amiss in the first edition, he silently corrected in those that followed. He appears to have revised the "Iliad," and freed it from some of its imperfections; and the "Essay on Criticism" received many improvements after its first appearance. It will seldom be found that he altered without adding clearness, elegance, or vigor. Pope had perhaps the judgment of Dryden; but Dryden certainly wanted the diligence of Pope.

In acquired knowledge, the superiority must be allowed to Dryden, whose education was more scholastic, and who, before he became an author, had been allowed more time for study, with better means of information. His mind has a larger range, and he collects his images and illustrations from a more extensive circumference of science. Dryden knew more of man in his general nature, and Pope in his local manners. The notions of Dryden were formed by comprehensive speculation; and those of Pope by minute attention. There is more dignity in the knowledge of Dryden, and more certainty in that of Pope.

Poetry was not the sole praise of either, for both excelled likewise in prose; but Pope did not borrow his prose from his predecessor. The style of Dryden is capricious and varied; that of Pope is cautious and uniform. Dryden observes the motions of his own mind; Pope constrains his mind to his own rules of composition. Dryden is sometimes vehement and rapid; Pope is always smooth, uniform, and gentle. Dryden's page is a natural field rising into inequalities, and diversified by the varied exuberance of abundant vegetation; Pope's is a velvet lawn, shaven by the scythe and levelled by the roller.

Of genius, that power which constitutes a poet; that quality, without which judgment is cold, and knowledge is inert; that energy which collects, combines, amplifies, and animates; the superiority must, with some hesitation, be allowed to Dryden. It is not to be inferred that of this poetical vigor Pope had only a little, because Dryden had more; for every other writer since Milton must give place to Pope; and even of Dryden it must be said, that, if he has brighter paragraphs, he has not better poems. Dryden's performances were always hasty, either excited by some external occasion, or extorted by domestic necessity; he composed without consideration, and published without correction. What his mind could supply at call, or gather in one excursion, was all that he sought, and all that he gave. The dilatory caution of Pope enabled him to condense his sentiments, to multiply his images, and to accumulate all that study might produce, or chance might supply. If the flights of Dryden, therefore, are higher, Pope continues longer on the wing. If of Dryden's fire the blaze is brighter, of Pope's the heat is more regular and constant. Dryden often surpasses expectation, and Pope never falls below it. Dryden is read with frequent astonishment, and Pope with perpetual delight.

FROM THE "JOURNEY TO THE HEBRIDES."

214. REFLECTIONS ON LANDING AT IONA.

We were now treading that illustrious island which was once the luminary of the Caledonian regions, whence savage clans and roving barbarians derived the benefits of knowledge and the blessings of religion. To abstract the mind from all local emotion would be impossible if it were endeavored, and would be foolish if it were possible. Whatever withdraws us from the power of our senses, whatever makes the past, the distant, or the future predominate over the present, advances us in the dignity of thinking beings. Far from me and my friends be such frigid philosophy as may conduct us indifferent and unmoved over any ground which has been dignified by wisdom, bravery, or virtue. That man is little to be envied whose patriotism would not gain force on the plains of Marathon, or whose piety would not grow warmer among the ruins of Iona.

FROM "LONDON."

215. THE FATE OF POVERTY.

By numbers here from shame or censure free,
All crimes are safe but hated poverty.
This, only this, the rigid law pursues,
This, only this, provokes the snarling muse.
The sober trader at a tattered cloak
Wakes from his dream, and labors for a joke.
With brisker air the silken courtiers gaze,
And turn the varied taunt a thousand ways.
Of all the griefs that harass the distressed,
Sure the most bitter is a scornful jest;
Fate never wounds more deep the generous heart,
Than when a blockhead's insult points the dart.
Has Heaven reserved, in pity to the poor,
No pathless waste, or undiscovered shore?
No secret island in the boundless main?
No peaceful desert yet unclaimed by Spain?
Quick let us rise, the happy seats explore,
And bear oppression's insolence no more.
This mournful truth is everywhere confessed,
SLOW RISES WORTH, BY POVERTY DEPRESSED.

FROM THE "VANITY OF HUMAN WISHES."

216. CHARLES XII.

On what foundation stands the warrior's pride,
How just his hopes, let Swedish Charles decide.
A frame of adamant, a soul of fire,
No dangers fright him, and no labors tire;
O'er love, o'er fear, extends his wide domain,
Unconquered lord of pleasure and of pain;
No joys to him pacific sceptres yield,
War sounds the trump, he rushes to the field:
Behold surrounding kings their powers combine,
And one capitulate, and one resign;
Peace courts his hand, but spreads her charms in vain;
"Think nothing gained, "he cries, "till nought remain,
On Moscow's walls till Gothic standards fly,
And all be mine beneath the polar sky."
The march begins in military state,
And nations on his eye suspended wait;
Stern Famine guards the solitary coast,
And Winter barricades the realms of Frost;
He comes, nor want nor cold his course delay;—
Hide, blushing Glory, hide Pultowa's day!
The vanquished hero leaves his broken bands,
And shows his miseries in distant lands;
Condemned, a needy suppliant, to wait,
While ladies interpose, and slaves debate.
But did not Chance at length her error mend?
Did no subverted empire mark his end?
Did rival monarch give the fatal wound?
Or hostile millions press him to the ground?
His fall was destined to a barren strand,
A petty fortress, and a dubious hand;
He left a name, at which the world grew pale,
To point a moral, or adorn a tale.

WILLIAM PITT, EARL OF CHATHAM. 1708–1778.

FROM HIS SPEECHES.

217. SPEECH ON AMERICAN AFFAIRS.

I cannot, my lords, I will not, join in congratulation on misfortune and disgrace. This, my lords, is a perilous and tremendous moment; it is not a time for adulation; the smoothness of flattery cannot save us in this rugged and awful crisis. It is now necessary to instruct the throne in the language of truth. We must, if possible, dispel the delusion and darkness which envelop it: and display, in its full danger and genuine colors, the ruin which is brought to our doors. Can ministers still presume to expect support in their infatuation? Can Parliament be so dead to its dignity and duty, as to give their support to measures thus obtruded and forced upon them? measures, my lords, which have reduced this late flourishing empire to scorn and contempt? But yesterday, and England might have stood against the world; now, none so poor as to do her reverence! The people, whom we at first despised as rebels, but whom we now acknowledge as enemies, are abetted against us, supplied with every military store, their interest consulted, and their ambassadors entertained by our inveterate enemy; — and ministers do not, and dare not, interpose with dignity or effect. The desperate state of our army abroad is in part known. No man more highly esteems and honors the English troops than I do: I know their virtues and their valor: I know they can achieve anything but impossibilities; and I know that the conquest of English America is an impossibility. You cannot, my lords, you cannot conquer America. What is your present situation there? We do not know the worst: but we know that in three campaigns we have done nothing, and suffered much. You may swell every expense, accumulate every assistance, and extend your traffic to the shambles of every German despot; your attempts will be forever vain and impotent; — doubly so, indeed, from this mercenary aid on which you rely; for it irritates, to an incurable resentment, the minds of your adversaries, to overrun them with the mercenary sons of rapine and plunder, devoting them and their possessions to the rapacity of hireling cruelty. * *

But, my lords, who is the man, that, in addition to the disgraces and mischiefs of the war, has dared to authorize and associate to our arms, the tomahawk and scalping-knife of the savage? — to call into civilized alliance, the wild and inhuman inhabitants of the woods? — to delegate to the merciless Indian the defence of disputed rights, and to wage the horrors of his barbarous war against our brethren? My lords, these enormities cry aloud for redress and punishment. But, my lords, this barbarous measure has been defended, not only on the principles of policy and necessity, but also on those of morality; "for it is perfectly allowable," says Lord Suffolk, "to use all the means which God and nature have put into our hands." I am astonished, I am shocked, to hear such principles confessed; to hear them avowed in this house, or in this country. My lords, I did not intend to encroach so much on your attention; but I cannot repress my indignation — I feel myself impelled to speak. My lords, we are called upon as members of this house, as men, as Christians, to protest against such horrible barbarity! — "That God and nature have put into our hands!" What ideas of God and nature that noble lord may entertain, I know not; but I know, that such detestable principles are equally abhorrent to religion and humanity. What! to attribute the sacred sanction of God and nature to the massacres of the Indian scalping-knife! to the savage, torturing and murdering his unhappy victims! Such notions shock every precept of morality, every feeling of humanity, every sentiment of honor. These abominable principles, and this more abominable avowal of them, demand the most decisive indignation. I call upon that right reverend, and this most learned bench, to vindicate the religion of their God, to support the justice of their country. I call upon the bishops to interpose the unsullied sanctity of their lawn; upon the judges to interpose the purity of their ermine, to save us from this pollution. I call upon the honor of your lordships, to reverence the dignity of your ancestors, and to maintain your own. I call upon the spirit and humanity of my country, to vindicate the national character. I invoke the genius of the Constitution. From the tapestry that adorns these walls, the immortal ancestor of this noble lord frowns with indignation at the disgrace of his country. In vain did he defend the liberty, and establish the religion of Britain, against the tyranny of Rome, if these worse than Popish cruelties and inquisitorial practices are endured among us. To send forth the merciless Indian, thirsting for blood! against whom?—your Protestant brethren!—to lay waste their country, to desolate their dwellings, and extirpate their race and name, by the aid and instrumentality of these horrible hellhounds of war!—Spain can no longer boast preeminence in barbarity. She armed herself with bloodhounds to extirpate the wretched natives of Mexico; we, more ruthless, loose those brutal warriors against our countrymen in America, endeared to us by every tie that can sanctify humanity. I solemnly call upon your lordships, and upon every order of men in the state, to stamp upon this infamous procedure the indelible stigma of the public abhorrence. More particularly, I call upon the venerable prelates of our religion, to do away this iniquity; let them perform a lustration to purify the country from this deep and deadly sin.

My lords, I am old and weak, and at present unable to say more; but my feelings and indignation were too strong to have allowed me to say less. I could not have slept this night in my bed, nor even reposed my head upon my pillow, without giving vent to my steadfast abhorrence of such enormous and preposterous principles.

EDMUND BURKE. 1731–1797. (Manual, p. 339.)

FROM THE "ESSAY ON THE SUBLIME AND BEAUTIFUL."

218. SYMPATHY A SOURCE OF THE SUBLIME.

It is by the passion of sympathy that we enter into the concerns of others; that we are moved as they are moved, and are never suffered to be indifferent spectators of almost anything which men can do or suffer. For sympathy must be considered as a sort of substitution, by which we are put into the place of another man, and affected in a good measure as he is affected; so that this passion may either partake of the nature of those which regard self-preservation, and turning upon pain may be a source of the sublime; or it may turn upon ideas of pleasure, and then, whatever has been said of the social affections, whether they regard society in general, or only some particular modes of it, may be applicable here.

It is by this principle chiefly that poetry, painting, and other affecting arts, transfuse their passions from one breast to another, and are often capable of grafting a delight on wretchedness, misery, and death itself. It is a common observation, that objects, which in the reality would shock, are, in tragical and such like representations, the source of a very high species of pleasure. This, taken as a fact, has been the cause of much reasoning. This satisfaction has been commonly attributed, first, to the comfort we receive in considering that so melancholy a story is no more than a fiction; and next, to the contemplation of our own freedom from the evils we see represented. I am afraid it is a practice much too common, in inquiries of this nature, to attribute the cause of feelings which merely arise from the mechanical structure of our bodies, or from the natural frame and constitution of our minds, to certain conclusions of the reasoning faculty on the objects presented to us; for I have some reason to apprehend, that the influence of reason in producing our passions is nothing near so extensive as is commonly believed.

---

219. Close of his Speech to the Electors of Bristol.

Gentlemen, I have had my day. I can never sufficiently express my gratitude to you for having set me in a place wherein I could lend the slightest help to great and laudable designs. If I have had my share in any measure giving quiet to private property and private conscience; if by my vote I have aided in securing to families the best possession, peace; if I have joined in reconciling kings to their subjects, and subjects to their prince; if I have assisted to loosen the foreign holdings of the citizen, and taught him to look for his protection to the laws of his country, and for his comfort to the good-will of his countrymen; — if I have thus taken my part with the best of men in the best of their actions, I can shut the book; — I might wish to read a page or two more — but this is enough for my measure. — I have not lived in vain.

And now, gentlemen, on this serious day, when I come, as it were, to make up my account with you, let me take to myself some degree of honest pride on the nature of the charges that are against me. I do not here stand before you accused of venality or of neglect of duty. It is not said, that, in the long period of my service, I have, in a single instance, sacrificed the slightest of your interests to my ambition or to my fortune. It is not alleged, that, to gratify any anger, or revenge of my own, or of my party, I have had a share in wronging or oppressing any description of men, or any one man in any description. No! the charges against me are all of one kind, that I have pushed the principles of general justice and benevolence too far; farther than a cautious policy would warrant; and farther than the opinions of many would go along with me. In every accident which may happen through life — in pain, in sorrow, in depression, and distress — I will call to mind this accusation, and be comforted.

FROM THE "REFLECTIONS ON THE FRENCH REVOLUTION."

220. MARIE ANTOINETTE, QUEEN OF FRANCE.

It is now sixteen or seventeen years since I saw the Queen of France, then the Dauphiness, at Versailles; and surely never lighted on this orb, which she hardly seemed to touch, a more delightful vision. I saw her just above the horizon, decorating and cheering the elevated sphere she just began to move in — glittering like the morning star, full of life, and splendor, and joy. O, what a revolution! and what a heart must I have to contemplate without emotion that elevation and that fall! Little did I dream, when she added titles of veneration to that enthusiastic, distant, respectful love, that she should ever be obliged to carry the sharp antidote against disgrace concealed in that bosom; little did I dream that I should have lived to see such disasters fallen upon her in a nation of gallant men, in a nation of men of honor and of cavaliers. I thought ten thousand swords must have leaped from their scabbards to avenge even a look that threatened her with insult. But the age of chivalry is gone. That of sophisters, economists, and calculators has succeeded; and the glory of Europe is extinguished forever. Never, never more shall we behold that generous loyalty to rank and sex, that proud submission, that dignified obedience, that subordination of the heart, which kept alive, even in servitude itself, the spirit of an exalted freedom. The unbought grace of life, the cheap defence of nations, the nurse of manly sentiment and heroic enterprise is gone! It is gone, that sensibility of principle, that chastity of honor, which felt a stain like a wound, which inspired courage whilst it mitigated ferocity, which ennobled whatever it touched, and under which vice itself lost half its evil by losing all its grossness.

---

221. FROM THE "IMPEACHMENT OF WARREN HASTINGS."

My lords, you have now heard the principles on which Mr. Hastings governs the part of Asia subjected to the British empire. You have heard his opinion of the mean and depraved state of those who are subject to it. You have heard his lecture upon arbitrary power, which he states to be the constitution of Asia. You hear the application he makes of it; and you hear the practices which he employs to justify it, and who the persons were on whose authority he relies, and whose example he professes to follow. In the first place, your lordships will be astonished at the audacity with which he speaks of his own administration, as if he was reading a speculative lecture on the evils attendant upon some vicious system of foreign government, in which he had no sort of concern whatsoever. And then, when in this speculative way he has established, or thinks he has, the vices of the government, he conceives he has found a sufficient apology for his own crimes. And if he violates the most solemn engagements, if he oppresses, extorts, and robs, if he imprisons, confiscates, banishes, at his sole will and pleasure, when we accuse him for his ill treatment of the people committed to him as a sacred trust, his defence is, — "To be robbed, violated, oppressed, is their privilege — let the constitution of their country answer for it. I did not make it for them. Slaves I found them, and as slaves I have treated them. I was a despotic prince, despotic governments are jealous, and the subjects prone to rebellion. This very proneness of the subject to shake off his allegiance exposes him to continual danger from his sovereign's jealousy, and this is consequent on the political state of Hindostanic governments." He lays it down as a rule, that despotism is the genuine constitution of India; that a disposition to rebellion in the subject, or dependent prince, is the necessary effect of this despotism, and that jealousy and its consequences naturally arise on the part of the sovereign; that the government is everything, and the subject nothing; that the great landed men are in a mean and depraved state, and subject to many evils.

But nothing is more false than that despotism is the constitution of any country in Asia, that we are acquainted with. It is certainly not true of any Mahomedan constitution. But if it were, do your lordships really think that the nation would bear, that any human creature would bear, to hear an English governor defend himself on such principles? or, if he can defend himself on such principles, is it possible to deny the conclusion, that no man in India has a security for anything but by being totally independent of the British government? Here he has declared his opinion, that he is a despotic prince, that he is to use arbitrary power, and of course all his acts are covered with that shield. "*I know*," says he, "*the constitution of Asia only from its practice*." Will your lordships submit to hear the corrupt practices of mankind made the principles of government? No; it will be your pride and glory to teach men intrusted with power, that, in their use of it, they are to conform to principles, and not to draw their principles from the corrupt practice of any man whatever. Was there ever heard, or could it be conceived, that a governor would dare to heap up all the evil practices, all the cruelties, oppressions, extortions, corruptions, briberies of all the ferocious usurpers, desperate robbers, thieves, cheats, and jugglers, that ever had office from one end of Asia to another, and consolidating all this mass of the crimes and absurdities of barbarous domination into one code, establish it as the "whole duty" of an English governor? I believe that till this time so audacious a thing was never attempted by man.

He have arbitrary power! My lords, the East Indian Company have not arbitrary power to give him; the king has no arbitrary power to give him; your lordships have not; nor the Commons; nor the whole legislature. We have no arbitrary power to give; because arbitrary power is a thing which neither any man can hold nor any man can give. No man can lawfully govern himself according to his own will, much less can one person be governed by the will of another. We are all born in subjection, all born equally, high and low, governors and governed, in subjection to one great, immutable, pre-existent law, prior to all our devices, and prior to all our contrivances, paramount to all our ideas and all our sensations, antecedent to our very existence, by which we are knit and connected in the eternal frame of the universe, out of which we cannot stir.

---

222. FROM "A LETTER TO A NOBLE LORD" (Duke of Bedford).

Had it pleased God to continue to me the hopes of succession, I should have been, according to my mediocrity, and the mediocrity of the age I live in, a sort of founder of a family; I should have left a son, who, in all the points in which personal merit can be viewed, in science, in erudition, in genius, in taste, in honor, in generosity, in humanity, in every liberal sentiment, and every liberal accomplishment, would not have shown himself inferior to the Duke of Bedford, or to any of those to whom he traces in his line. His grace very soon would have wanted all plausibility in his attack upon that provision which belonged more to mine than to me. He would soon have supplied every deficiency, and symmetrized every disproportion. It would not have been for that successor to resort to any stagnant wasting reservoir of merit in me, or in any ancestry. He had in himself a salient, living spring, of generous and manly action. Every day he lived he would have repurchased the bounty of the crown, and ten times more, if ten times more he had received. He was made a public creature; and had no enjoyment whatever but in the performance of some duty. At this exigent moment, the loss of a finished man is not easily supplied.

But a Disposer whose power we are little able to resist, and whose wisdom it behooves us not at all to dispute, has ordained it in another manner, and (whatever my querulous weakness might suggest) a far better. The storm has gone over me, and I lie like one of those old oaks which the late hurricane hath scattered about me. I am stripped of all my honors: I am torn up by the roots, and lie prostrate on the earth! There, and prostrate there, I most unfeignedly recognize the divine justice, and in some degree submit to it. But whilst I humble myself before God, I do not know that it is forbidden to repel the attacks of unjust and inconsiderate men. The patience of Job is proverbial. After some of the convulsive struggles of our irritable nature, he submitted himself, and repented in dust and ashes. But even so, I do not find him blamed for reprehending, and with a considerable degree of verbal asperity, those ill-natured neighbors of his, who visited his dunghill to read moral, political, and economical lectures on his misery. I am alone. I have none to meet my enemies in the gate. Indeed, my lord, I greatly deceive myself, if, in this hard season, I would give a peck of refuse wheat for all that is called fame and honor in the world. This is the appetite but of a few. It is a luxury; it is a privilege; it is an indulgence for those who are at their ease. But we are all of us made to shun disgrace, as we are made to shrink from pain, and poverty, and disease. It is an instinct; and, under the direction of reason, instinct is always in the right. I live in an inverted order. They who ought to have succeeded me are gone before me. They who should have been to me as posterity are in the place of ancestors. I owe to the dearest relation (which ever must subsist in memory) that act of piety, which he would have performed to me; I owe it to him to show that he was not descended, as the Duke of Bedford would have it, from an unworthy parent.

The Letters of Junius. 1769–1772. (Manual, p. 341.)

223. To His Grace the Duke of Bedford.

My Lord, — You are so little accustomed to receive any marks of respect or esteem from the public, that if, in the following lines, a compliment or expression of applause should escape me, I fear you would consider it as a mockery of your established character, and, perhaps, an insult to your understanding. You have nice feelings, my lord, if we may judge from your resentments. Cautious, therefore, of giving offence, where you have so little deserved it, I shall leave the illustration of your virtues to other hands. Your friends have a privilege to play upon the easiness of your temper, or possibly they are better acquainted with your good qualities than I am. You have done good by stealth. The rest is upon record. You have still left ample room for speculation, when panegyric is exhausted.

You are, indeed, a very considerable man. The highest rank; a splendid fortune; and a name, glorious till it was yours, were sufficient to have supported you with meaner abilities than I think you possess. From the first you derived a constitutional claim to respect; from the second, a natural extensive authority; the last created a partial expectation of hereditary virtues. The use you have made of these uncommon advantages might have been more honorable to yourself, but could not be more instructive to mankind. We may trace it in the veneration of your country, the choice of your friends, and in the accomplishment of every sanguine hope, which the public might have conceived from the illustrious name of Russell.

The eminence of your station gave you a commanding prospect of your duty. The road which led to honor was open to your view. You could not lose it by mistake, and you had no temptation to depart from it by design. Compare the natural dignity and importance of the richest peer of England; — the noble independence which he might have maintained in Parliament, and the real interest and respect which he might have acquired, not only in Parliament, but through the whole kingdom; compare these glorious distinctions with the ambition of holding a share in government, the emoluments of a place, the sale of a borough, or the purchase of a corporation; and though you may not regret the virtues which create respect, you may see, with anguish, how much real importance and authority you have lost. Consider the character of an independent, virtuous Duke of Bedford; imagine what he might be in this country, then reflect one moment upon what you are. If it be possible for me to withdraw my attention from the fact, I will tell you in theory what such a man might be.

Conscious of his own weight and importance, his conduct in Parliament would be directed by nothing but the constitutional duty of a peer. He would consider himself as a guardian of the laws. Willing to support the just measures of government, but determined to observe the conduct of the minister with suspicion, he would oppose the violence of faction with as much firmness as the encroachments of prerogative. He would be as little capable of bargaining with the minister for places for himself, or his dependants, as of descending to mix himself in the intrigues of opposition. Whenever an important question called for his opinion in Parliament, he would be heard, by the most profligate minister, with deference and respect. His authority would either sanctify or disgrace the measures of government. The people would look up to him as to their protector, and a virtuous prince would have one honest man in his dominions in whose integrity and judgment he might safely confide. If it should be the will of Providence to afflict him with a domestic misfortune, he would submit to the stroke, with feeling but not without dignity. He would consider the people as his children, and receive a generous, heartfelt consolation, in the sympathizing tears and blessings of his country.

Your grace may probably discover something more intelligible in the negative part of this illustrious character. The man I have described would never prostitute his dignity in Parliament by an indecent violence either in opposing or defending a minister. He would not at one moment rancorously persecute, at another basely cringe to the favorite of his sovereign. After outraging the royal dignity with peremptory conditions, little short of menace and hostility, he would never descend to the humility of soliciting an interview with the favorite, and of offering to recover, at any price, the honor of his friendship.

Though deceived perhaps in his youth, he would not, through the course of a long life, have invariably chosen his friends from among the most profligate of mankind. His own honor would have forbidden him from mixing his private pleasures or conversation with jockeys, gamesters, blasphemers, gladiators, or buffoons. He would then have never felt, much less would he have submitted to the humiliating, dishonest necessity of engaging in the interest and intrigues of his dependants, of supplying their vices, or relieving their beggary, at the expense of his country. He would not have betrayed such ignorance, or such contempt of the constitution, as openly to avow, in a court of justice, the purchase and sale of a borough. He would not have thought it consistent with his rank in the state, or even with his personal importance, to be the little tyrant of a little corporation. He would never have been insulted with virtues which he had labored to extinguish, nor suffered the disgrace of a mortifying defeat, which has made him ridiculous and contemptible, even to the few by whom he was not detested. I reverence the afflictions of a good man, — his sorrows are sacred. But how can we take part in the distresses of a man whom we can neither love nor esteem, or feel for a calamity of which he himself is insensible? Where was the father's heart, when he could look for, or find an immediate consolation for the loss of an only son, in consultations and bargains for a place at court, and even in the misery of balloting at the India House!

Adam Smith. 1723–1790. (Manual, p. 342.)

From the "Wealth of Nations."

224. On the Division of Labor.

Observe the accommodation of the most common artificer or day-laborer in a civilized and thriving country, and you will perceive that the number of people of whose industry a part, though but a small part, has been employed in procuring him this accommodation, exceeds all computation. The woollen coat, for example, which covers the day-laborer, as coarse and rough as it may appear, is the produce of the joint labor of a great multitude of workmen. The shepherd, the sorter of the wool, the woolcomber or carder, the dyer, the scribbler, the spinner, the weaver, the fuller, the dresser, with many others, must all join their different arts in order to complete even this homely production. How many merchants and carriers, besides, must have been employed in transporting the materials from some of those workmen to others; who often live in a very distant part of the country! How much commerce and navigation in particular, how many ship-builders, sailors, sail-makers, rope-makers, must have been employed in order to bring together the different drugs made use of by the dyer, which often come from the remotest corners of the world! * *

Were we to examine in the same manner all the different parts of his dress and household furniture, the coarse linen shirt which he wears next his skin, the shoes which cover his feet, the bed which he lies on, and all the different parts which compose it, the kitchen grate at which he prepares his victuals, the coals which he makes use of for that purpose, dug from the bowels of the earth, and brought to him perhaps by a long sea and a long land carriage, all the other utensils of his kitchen, all the furniture of his table, the knives and forks, the earthen or pewter plates upon which he serves up and divides his victuals, the different hands employed in preparing his bread and his beer, the glass window which lets in the heat and the light, and keeps out the wind and the rain, with all the knowledge and art requisite for preparing that beautiful and happy invention, without which these northern parts of the world could scarce have afforded a very comfortable habitation, together with the tools of all the different workmen employed in producing these different conveniences; — if we examine, I say, all these things, and consider what a variety of labor is employed about each of them, we shall be sensible that without the assistance and co-operation of many thousands, the very meanest person in a civilized country could not be provided, even according to what we very falsely imagine, the easy and simple manner in which he is commonly accommodated. Compared, indeed, with the more extravagant luxury of the great, his accommodation must no doubt appear extremely simple and easy; and yet it may be true, perhaps, that the accommodation of an European prince does not always so much exceed that of an industrious and frugal peasant, as the accommodations of the latter exceeds that of many an African king, the absolute master of the lives and liberties of ten thousand naked savages.

WILLIAM PALEY. 1743–1805. (Manual, p. 343.)

FROM THE "HORÆ PAULINÆ."

225. CHARACTER OF PAUL.

Here then we have a man of liberal attainments, and, in other points, of sound judgment, who had addicted his life to the service of the gospel. We see him, in the prosecution of his purpose, travelling from country to country, enduring every species of hardship, encountering every extremity of danger, assaulted by the populace, punished by the magistrates, scourged, beat, stoned, left for dead; expecting, wherever he came, a renewal of the same treatment, and the same dangers; yet, when driven from one city, preaching in the next; spending his whole time in the employment, sacrificing to it his pleasures, his ease, his safety; persisting in this course to old age, unaltered by the experience of perverseness, ingratitude, prejudice, desertion; unsubdued by anxiety, want, labor, persecutions; unwearied by long confinement, undismayed by the prospect of death. Such was Paul. We have his letters in our hands; we have also a history purporting to be written by one of his fellow-travellers, and appearing, by a comparison with these letters, certainly to have been written by some person well acquainted with the transactions of his life. From the letters, as well as from the history, we gather not only the account which we have stated of *him*, but that he was one out of many who acted and suffered in the same manner; and that of those who did so, several had been the companions of Christ's ministry, the ocular witnesses, or pretending to be such, of his miracles and of his resurrection. We moreover find this same person referring in his letters to his supernatural conversion, the particulars and accompanying circumstances of which are related in the history; and which accompanying circumstances, if all or any of them be true, render it impossible to have been a delusion. We also find him positively, and in appropriate terms, asserting that he himself worked miracles, strictly and properly so called, in support of the mission which he executed; the history, meanwhile, recording various passages of his ministry, which come up to the extent of this assertion. The question is, whether falsehood was ever attested by evidence like this. Falsehoods, we know, have found their way into reports, into tradition, into books; but is an example to be met with of a man voluntarily undertaking a life of want and pain, of incessant fatigue, of continual peril; submitting to the loss of his home and country, to stripes and stoning, to tedious imprisonment, and the constant expectation of a violent death, for the sake of carrying about a story of what was false, and what, if false, he must have known to be so?

CHAPTER XVIII.

THE DAWN OF ROMANTIC POETRY.

---

226. ROBERT BLAIR. 1699–1746. (Manual, p. 350.)

FROM "THE GRAVE."

Thrice welcome Death!
That, after many a painful bleeding step,
Conducts us to our home, and lands us safe
On the long-wished-for shore. Prodigious change!
Our bane turned to a blessing! Death, disarmed,
Loses his fellness quite; all thanks to Him
Who scourged the venom out. Sure the last end
Of the good man is peace! How calm his exit!
Night-dews fall not more gently to the ground,
Nor weary, worn-out winds expire so soft.
Behold him! in the evening tide of life,
A life well spent, whose early care it was
His riper years should not upbraid his green:
By unperceived degrees he wears away;
Yet, like the sun, seems larger at his setting!
High in his faith and hopes, look how he reaches
After the prize in view! and, like a bird
That's hampered, struggles hard to get away!
Whilst the glad gates of sight are wide expanded
To let new glories in, the first fair fruits
Of the fast-coming harvest. Then, O, then,
Each earth-born joy grows vile, or disappears,
Shrunk to a thing of nought! O, how he longs
To have his passport signed, and be dismissed!
'Tis done — and now he's happy! The glad soul
Has not a wish uncrowned.

James Thomson. 1700–1748. (Manual, p. 351.)

From "Autumn."

227. Evening in Autumn.

The western sun withdraws the shortened day,
And humid evening, gliding o'er the sky
In her chill progress, to the ground condensed
The vapors throws. Where creeping waters ooze,
Where marshes stagnate, and where rivers wind,
Cluster the rolling fogs, and swim along
The dusky-mantled lawn. Meanwhile the moon,
Full-orbed, and breaking through the scattered clouds,
Shows her broad visage in the crimson east.
Turned to the sun direct, her spotted disk,
Where mountains rise, umbrageous dales descend,
And caverns deep, as optic tube descries,
A smaller earth, gives us his blaze again,
Void of its flame, and sheds a softer day.
Now through the passing cloud she seems to stoop,
Now up the pure cerulean rides sublime.
Wide the pale deluge floats, and streaming mild
O'er the skied mountain to the shadowy vale,
While rocks and floods reflect the quivering gleam,
The whole air whitens with a boundless tide
Of silver radiance, trembling round the world.

From "Winter."

228. Reflections suggested by Winter.

'Tis done! — Dread Winter spreads his latest glooms,
And reigns tremendous o'er the conquered year.
How dead the vegetable kingdom lies!
How dumb the tuneful! Horror wide extends
His desolate domain. Behold, fond man!
See here thy pictured life; pass some few years,
Thy flowering Spring, thy Summer's ardent strength,
Thy sober Autumn fading into age,
And pale concluding Winter comes at last,
And shuts the scene. Ah! whither now are fled
Those dreams of greatness? those unsolid hopes
Of happiness? those longings after fame?
Those restless cares? those busy, bustling days?
Those gay-spent, festive nights? those veering thoughts,
Lost between good and ill, that shared thy life?

All now are vanished! Virtue sole survives,
Immortal never-failing friend of man,
His guide to happiness on high. And see!
'Tis come, the glorious morn! the second birth
Of heaven and earth! awakening Nature hears
The new-creating word, and starts to life,
In every heightened form, from pain and death
Forever free. The great eternal scheme,
Involving all, and in a perfect whole
Uniting, as the prospect wider spreads,
To reason's eye refined, clears up apace.
Ye vainly wise! ye blind presumptuous! now,
Confounded in the dust, adore that Power
And Wisdom oft arraigned: see now the cause,
Why unassuming worth in secret lived,
And died, neglected: why the good man's share
In life was gall and bitterness of soul:
Why the lone widow and her orphans pined
In starving solitude! while Luxury,
In palaces, lay straining her low thought,
To form unreal wants: why heaven-born Truth,
And Moderation fair, wore the red marks
Of Superstition's scourge: why licensed Pain,
That cruel spoiler, that imbosomed foe,
Imbittered all our bliss. Ye good distressed!
Ye noble few! who here unbending stand
Beneath life's pressure, yet bear up a while,
And what your bounded view, which only saw
A little part, deemed evil is no more:
The storms of wintry Time will quickly pass,
And one unbounded Spring encircle all.

---

229. From "The Castle of Indolence."

O mortal man, who livest here by toil,
Do not complain of this thy hard estate;
That like an emmet thou must ever moil
Is a sad sentence of an ancient date,
And, certes, there is for it reason great;
For, though sometimes it makes thee weep and wail,
And curse thy star, and early drudge and late,
Withouten that would come a heavier bale,[1]
Loose life, unruly passions, and diseases pale.

In lowly dale, fast by a river's side,
With woody hill o'er hill encompassed round,

[1] Calamity.

A most enchanting wizard did abide,
Than whom a fiend more fell is nowhere found.
It was, I ween, a lovely spot of ground:
And there a season atween June and May,
Half-prankt with spring, with summer half-imbrowned,
A listless climate made, where, sooth to say,
No living wight could work, ne caréd e'en for play.

Was nought around but images of rest;
Sleep-soothing groves, and quiet lawns between;
And flowery beds that slumberous influence kest,[2]
From poppies breathed; and beds of pleasant green,
Where never yet was creeping creature seen.
Meantime, unnumbered glittering streamlets played,
And hurléd everywhere their waters sheen;
That as they bickered through the sunny glade,
Though restless still themselves, a lulling murmur made.

Joined to the prattle of the purling rills
Were heard the lowing herds along the vale,
And flocks loud bleating from the distant hills,
And vacant shepherds piping in the dale:
And now and then sweet Philomel would wail,
Or stock-doves 'plain amid the forest deep,
That drowsy rustled to the sighing gale;
And still a coil[3] the grasshopper did keep;
Yet all these sounds yblent[4] inclinéd all to sleep.

2 Cast. 3 A murmur, or noise. 4 Blended.

William Shenstone. 1714–1763. (Manual, p. 353.)

230. The Shepherd's Home.

My banks they are furnished with bees,
Whose murmur invites one to sleep;
My grottos are shaded with trees,
And my hills are white over with sheep.
I seldom have met with a loss,
Such health do my fountains bestow;
My fountains are bordered with moss,
Where the harebells and violets blow.

Not a pine in my grove is there seen,
But with tendrils of woodbine is bound;
Not a beech's more beautiful green,
But a sweet-brier entwines it around.

Not my fields, in the prime of the year,
  More charms than my cattle unfold;
Not a brook that is limpid and clear,
  But it glitters with fishes of gold.

One would think she might like to retire
  To the bower I have labored to rear;
Not a shrub that I heard her admire,
  But I hasted and planted it there.
O, how sudden the jessamine strove
  With the lilac to render it gay!
Already it calls for my love
  To prune the wild branches away.

From the plains, from the woodlands, and groves,
  What strains of wild melody flow!
How the nightingales warble their loves
  From thickets of roses that blow!
And when her bright form shall appear,
  Each bird shall harmoniously join
In a concert so soft and so clear,
  As — she may not be fond to resign.

I have found out a gift for my fair,
  I have found where the wood-pigeons breed; —
But let me such plunder forbear,
  She will say 'twas a barbarous deed;
For he ne'er could be true, she averred,
  Who would rob a poor bird of its young;
And I loved her the more when I heard
  Such tenderness fall from her tongue.

I have heard her with sweetness unfold
  How that pity was due to a dove;
That it ever attended the bold,
  And she called it the sister of love.
But her words such a pleasure convey,
  So much I her accent adore,
Let her speak, and whatever she say,
  Methinks I should love her the more.

William Collins. 1721–1759. (Manual, p. 353.)

231. Ode to Fear.

Thou, to whom the world unknown,
With all its shadowy shapes, is shown,
Who seest appalled the unreal scene,
While Fancy lifts the veil between:

Ah, Fear! ah, frantic Fear!
I see — I see thee near.
I know thy hurried step, thy haggard eye!
Like thee I start, like thee disordered fly,
For, lo, what monsters in thy train appear!
Danger, whose limbs of giant mould
What mortal eye can fixed behold?
Who stalks his round, a hideous form,
Howling amidst the midnight storm,
Or throws him on the ridgy steep
Of some loose hanging rock to sleep:
And with him thousand phantoms joined,
Who prompt to deeds accursed the mind:
And those, the fiends, who near allied,
O'er nature's wounds and wrecks preside;
While Vengeance, in the lurid air,
Lifts her red arm, exposed and bare:
On whom that ravening brood of fate,
Who lap the blood of Sorrow, wait;
Who, Fear, this ghastly train can see,
And look not madly wild, like thee?

Mark Akenside. 1721–1770. (Manual, p. 354.)

From "The Pleasures of the Imagination."

232. Genius.

From Heaven my strains begin; from Heaven descends
The flame of genius to the human breast,
And love, and beauty, and poetic joy,
And inspiration. Ere the radiant Sun
Sprang from the east, or 'midst the vault of night
The Moon suspended her serener lamp;
Ere mountains, woods, or streams adorned the globe,
Or Wisdom taught the sons of men her lore;
Then lived th' almighty One; then, deep retired
In his unfathomed essence, viewed the forms,
The forms eternal of created things;
The radiant sun, the moon's nocturnal lamp,
The mountains, woods, and streams, the rolling globe,
And Wisdom's mien celestial. From the first
Of days on them his love divine he fixed,
His admiration: till in time complete,
What he admired, and loved, his vital smile
Unfolded into being. Hence the breath
Of life informing each organic frame;
Hence the green earth, and wild resounding waves;

Hence light and shade alternate; warmth and cold;
And clear autumnal skies, and vernal showers;
And all the fair variety of things.

But not alike to every mortal eye
Is this great scene unveiled. For since the claims
Of social life to different labors urge
The active powers of man; with wise intent
The hand of Nature on peculiar minds
Imprints a different bias, and to each
Decrees its province in the common toil.
To some she taught the fabric of the sphere,
The changeful moon, the circuit of the stars,
The golden zones of Heaven: to some she gave
To weigh the moment of eternal things,
Of time, and space, and fate's unbroken chain;
And will's quick impulse: others by the hand
She led o'er vales and mountains, to explore
What healing virtue swells the tender veins
Of herbs and flowers; or what the beams of morn
Draw forth, distilling from the clifted rind
In balmy tears. But some to higher hopes
Were destined: some within a finer mould
She wrought and tempered with a purer flame.
To these the Sire Omnipotent unfolds
The world's harmonious volume, there to read
The transcript of himself. On every part
They trace the bright impressions of his hand;
In earth, or air, the meadow's purple stores,
The moon's mild radiance, or the virgin's form
Blooming with rosy smiles, they see portrayed
That uncreated Beauty which delights
The Mind supreme. They also feel her charms,
Enamoured: they partake th' eternal joy.

THOMAS GRAY. 1716–1771. (Manual, p. 355.)

233. ELEGY WRITTEN IN A COUNTRY CHURCHYARD.

The curfew tolls the knell of parting day,
  The lowing herd wind slowly o'er the lea,
The ploughman homewards plods his weary way,
  And leaves the world to darkness and to me.

Now fades the glimmering landscape on the sight,
  And all the air a solemn stillness holds,
Save where the beetle wheels his droning flight,
  And drowsy tinklings lull the distant folds:

Save that, from yonder ivy-mantled tower,
  The moping owl does to the moon complain
Of such as, wandering near her secret bower,
  Molest her ancient solitary reign.

Beneath those rugged elms, that yew-tree's shade,
  Where heaves the turf in many a mouldering heap,
Each in his narrow cell forever laid,
  The rude forefathers of the hamlet sleep.

The breezy call of incense-breathing Morn,
  The swallow twittering from the straw-built shed,
The cock's shrill clarion, or the echoing horn,
  No more shall rouse them from their lowly bed.

For them no more the blazing hearth shall burn,
  Or busy housewife ply her evening care;
No children run to lisp their sire's return,
  Or climb his knees, the envied kiss to share.

Oft did the harvest to their sickle yield,
  Their furrow oft the stubborn glebe has broke;
How jocund did they drive their team afield!
  How bowed the woods beneath their sturdy stroke!

Let not Ambition mock their useful toil,
  Their homely joys, and destiny obscure;
Nor Grandeur hear with a disdainful smile
  The short and simple annals of the poor.

The boast of heraldry, the pomp of power,
  And all that beauty, all that wealth e'er gave,
Await alike the inevitable hour:
  The paths of glory lead but to the grave.

Nor you, ye Proud! impute to these the fault,
  If Memory o'er their tomb no trophies raise,
Where, through the long-drawn aisle and fretted vault,
  The pealing anthem swells the note of praise.

Can storied urn or animated bust
  Back to its mansion call the fleeting breath?
Can Honor's voice provoke the silent dust,
  Or Flattery soothe the dull cold ear of death?

Perhaps in this neglected spot is laid
  Some heart once pregnant with celestial fire;
Hands that the rod of empire might have swayed,
  Or waked to ecstasy the living lyre.

But Knowledge to their eyes her ample page,
  Rich with the spoils of Time, did ne'er unroll;
Chill Penury repressed their noble rage,
  And froze the genial current of the soul.

Full many a gem of purest ray serene
  The dark unfathomed caves of ocean bear;
Full many a flower is born to blush unseen,
  And waste its sweetness on the desert air.

Some village Hampden, that with dauntless breast
  The little tyrant of his fields withstood,
Some mute inglorious Milton here may rest,
  Some Cromwell, guiltless of his country's blood.

The applause of listening senates to command,
  The threats of pain and ruin to despise,
To scatter plenty o'er a smiling land,
  And read their history in a nation's eyes,

Their lot forbade; nor circumscribed alone
  Their growing virtues, but their crimes confined
Forbade to wade through slaughter to a throne,
  And shut the gates of Mercy on mankind,

The struggling pangs of conscious Truth to hide,
  To quench the blushes of ingenuous Shame,
Or heap the shrine of Luxury and Pride
  With incense kindled at the Muse's flame.

Far from the madding crowd's ignoble strife,
  Their sober wishes never learned to stray;
Along the cool sequestered vale of life
  They kept the noiseless tenor of their way.

Yet e'en these bones from insult to protect,
  Some frail memorial still erected nigh,
With uncouth rhymes and shapeless sculpture decked,
  Implores the passing tribute of a sigh.

Their name, their years, spelt by th' unlettered Muse,
  The place of fame and elegy supply,
And many a holy text around she strews,
  That teach the rustic moralist to die.

For who, to dumb Forgetfulness a prey,
  This pleasing, anxious being e'er resigned,
Left the warm precincts of the cheerful day,
  Nor cast one longing, lingering look behind?

On some fond breast the parting soul relies,
  Some pious drops the closing eye requires;
E'en from the tomb the voice of Nature cries,
  E'en in our ashes live their wonted fires.

For thee, who, mindful of th' unhonored dead,
  Dost in those lines their artless tale relate,
If chance, by lonely Contemplation led,
  Some kindred spirit shall inquire thy fate,

Haply some hoary-headed swain may say,
  "Oft have we seen him, at the peep of dawn,
Brushing with hasty steps the dews away,
  To meet the sun upon the upland lawn.

"There, at the foot of yonder nodding beech,
  That wreathes its old fantastic root so high,
His listless length at noontide would he stretch,
  And pore upon the brook that babbles by.

"Hard by yon wood, now smiling as in scorn,
  Muttering his wayward fancies, he would rove;
Now drooping, woful, wan, like one forlorn,
  Or crazed with care, or crossed in hopeless love.

"One morn I missed him on the accustomed hill,
  Along the heath, and near his favorite tree;
Another came, nor yet beside the rill,
  Nor up the lawn, nor at the wood, was he:

"The next, with dirges due, in sad array,
  Slow through the churchway-path we saw him borne.
Approach, and read (for thou canst read) the lay
  Graved on the stone beneath yon aged thorn:"

THE EPITAPH.

Here rests his head upon the lap of Earth
  A youth to Fortune and to Fame unknown:
Fair Science frowned not on his humble birth,
  And Melancholy marked him for her own.

Large was his bounty, and his soul sincere;
  Heaven did a recompense as largely send:
He gave to misery all he had — a tear;
  He gained from Heaven — 'twas all he wished — a friend.

No further seek his merits to disclose,
  Or draw his frailties from their dread abode
(There they alike in trembling hope repose),
  The bosom of his Father and his God.

234. On a Distant Prospect of Eton College.

Ye distant spires! ye antique towers!
  That crown the watery glade
Where grateful Science still adores
  Her Henry's holy shade;
And ye that from the stately brow
Of Windsor's heights th' expanse below
  Of grove, of lawn, of mead survey,
Whose turf, whose shade, whose flowers among
Wanders the hoary Thames along
  His silver-winding way:

Ah, happy hills! ah, pleasing shade!
  Ah, fields beloved in vain!
Where once my careless childhood strayed,
  A stranger yet to pain!
I feel the gales that from ye blow
A momentary bliss bestow,
  As, waving fresh their gladsome wing,
My weary soul they seem to soothe,
And, redolent of joy and youth,
  To breathe a second spring.

Say, father Thames! for thou hast seen
  Full many a sprightly race,
Disporting on thy margent green,
  The paths of pleasure trace:
Who foremost now delight to cleave
With pliant arm thy glassy wave?
  The captive linnet which inthrall?
What idle progeny succeed
To chase the rolling circle's speed,
  Or urge the flying ball?

While some, on earnest business bent,
  Their murmuring labors ply,
'Gainst graver hours, that bring constraint,
  To sweeten liberty;
Some bold adventurers disdain
The limits of their little reign,
  And unknown regions dare descry,
Still as they run they look behind,
They hear a voice in every wind,
  And snatch a fearful joy.

Gay Hope is theirs, by Fancy fed,
  Less pleasing when possessed:

The tear forgot as soon as shed,
  The sunshine of the breast;
Theirs buxom health of rosy hue,
Wild wit, invention ever new,
  And lively cheer, of vigor born;
The thoughtless day, the easy night,
The spirits pure, the slumbers light,
  That fly the approach of morn.

Alas! regardless of their doom,
  The little victims play;
No sense have they of ills to come,
  Nor care beyond to-day:
Yet see how all around them wait,
The ministers of human fate,
  And black Misfortune's baleful train!
Ah! show them where in ambush stand,
To seize their prey, the murderous band!
  Ah! tell them they are men!

* * * * * *

To each his sufferings; all are men
  Condemned alike to groan:
The tender for another's pain,
  Th' unfeeling for his own.
Yet ah! why should they know their fate,
Since sorrow never comes too late,
  And happiness too swiftly flies?
Thought would destroy their paradise—
No more! Where ignorance is bliss,
  'Tis folly to be wise.

---

235. The Progress of Poesy.

I.

Awake, Æolian lyre! awake,
  And give to rapture all thy trembling strings!
  From Helicon's harmonious springs
A thousand rills their mazy progress take;
The laughing flowers, that round them blow,
Drink life and fragrance as they flow.
Now the rich stream of music winds along,
Deep, majestic, smooth, and strong,
Through verdant vales and Ceres' golden reign;
Now rolling down the steep amain,
Headlong, impetuous, see it pour;
The rocks and nodding groves rebellow to the roar.

* * * * * *

II.

Woods that wave o'er Delphi's steep,
Isles that crown th' Ægean deep,
Fields that cool Ilissus laves,
Or where Meander's amber waves
In lingering labyrinths creep,
How do your tuneful echoes languish,
Mute but to the voice of Anguish?
Where each old poetic mountain
Inspiration breathed around;
Every shade and hallowed fountain
Murmured deep a solemn sound,
Till the sad Nine, in Greece's evil hour,
Left their Parnassus for the Latian plains,
Alike they scorn the pomp of tyrant Power
And coward Vice, that revels in her chains.
When Latium had her lofty spirit lost,
They sought, O Albion! next thy sea-encircled coast.

III.

Far from the sun and summer-gale,
In thy green lap was Nature's darling laid,
What time, where lucid Avon strayed,
To him the mighty Mother did unveil
Her awful face; the dauntless child
Stretched forth his little arms, and smiled.
This pencil take (she said) whose colors clear
Richly paint the vernal year;
Thine, too, these golden keys, immortal Boy!
This can unlock the gates of Joy,
Of Horror that, and thrilling Fears,
Or ope the sacred source of sympathetic Tears.

Nor second He that rode sublime
Upon the seraph-wings of Ecstasy;
The secrets of th' abyss to spy,
He passed the flaming bounds of place and time;
The living throne, the sapphire-blaze,
Where angels tremble while they gaze,
He saw; but blasted with excess of light,
Closed his eyes in endless night.
Behold where Dryden's less presumptuous car
Wide o'er the fields of glory bear
Two coursers of ethereal race,
With necks in thunder clothed and long-resounding pac

Hark! his hands the lyre explore!
Bright-eyed Fancy, hovering o'er,
  Scatters from her pictured urn
  Thoughts that breathe and words that burn;
But ah! 'tis heard no more.
O lyre divine! what dying spirit
Wakes thee now? though he inherit
Nor the pride nor ample pinion
  That the Theban eagle bear,
Sailing with supreme dominion
  Through the azure deep of air,
Yet oft before his infant eyes would run
  Such forms as glitter in the Muse's ray
With orient hues, unborrowed of the sun;
  Yet shall he mount, and keep his distant way
Beyond the limits of a vulgar fate,
Beneath the good how far — but far above the great.

William Cowper. 1731–1800. (Manual, p. 357.)

From "The Task."

236. On the Receipt of my Mother's Picture out of Norfolk, the Gift of my Cousin, Ann Bodham.

O that those lips had language! Life has passed
With me but roughly since I heard thee last.
Those lips are thine — thy own sweet smile I see,
The same that oft in childhood solaced me;
Voice only fails, else how distinct they say,
"Grieve not, my child; chase all thy fears away!"
The meek intelligence of those dear eyes
(Blest be the art that can immortalize,
The art that baffles Time's tyrannic claim
To quench it) here shines on me still the same.
  Faithful remembrancer of one so dear,
O welcome guest, though unexpected here!
Who bidd'st me honor with an artless song,
Affectionate, a mother lost so long.
I will obey, not willingly alone,
But gladly, as the precept were her own:
And, while that face renews my filial grief,
Fancy shall weave a charm for my relief,
Shall steep me in Elysian reverie,
A momentary dream, that thou art she.
  My mother! when I learned that thou wast dead,
Say, wast thou conscious of the tears I shed?
Hovered thy spirit o'er thy sorrowing son,
Wretch even then, life's journey just begun?

Perhaps thou gav'st me, though unfelt, a kiss;
Perhaps a tear, if souls can weep in bliss:
Ah, that maternal smile! it answers, Yes.
I heard the bell tolled on thy burial day,
I saw the hearse that bore thee slow away,
And, turning from my nursery window, drew
A long, long sigh, and wept a last adieu!
But was it such? — It was. — Where thou art gone
Adieus and farewells are a sound unknown.
May I but meet thee on that peaceful shore,
The parting word shall pass my lips no more!
Thy maidens, grieved themselves at my concern,
Oft gave me promise of thy quick return.
What ardently I wished, I long believed,
And, disappointed still, was still deceived.
By expectation every day beguiled,
Dupe of to-morrow even from a child.
Thus many a sad to-morrow came and went,
Till, all my stock of infant sorrows spent,
I learned at last submission to my lot,
But, though I less deplored thee, ne'er forgot.
  Where once we dwelt our name is heard no more;
Children not thine have trod my nursery floor;
And where the gardener Robin, day by day,
Drew me to school along the public way,
Delighted with my bawble coach, and wrapped
In scarlet mantle warm, and velvet cap, —
'Tis now become a history but little known,
That once we called the pastoral house our own.
Short-lived possession! but the record fair,
That memory keeps of all thy kindness there,
Still outlives many a storm, that has effaced
A thousand other themes less deeply traced.
Thy nightly visits to my chamber made,
That thou might'st know me safe and warmly laid;
Thy morning bounties ere I left my home;
The biscuit, or confectionery plum;
The fragrant waters on my cheeks bestowed
By thy own hand, till fresh they shone and glowed, —
All this, and more endearing still than all,
Thy constant flow of love, that knew no fall,
Ne'er roughened by those cataracts and breaks,
That humor interposed too often makes;
All this still legible in memory's page,
And still to be so to my latest age,
Adds joy to duty, makes me glad to pay
Such honors to thee as my numbers may;

Perhaps a frail memorial, but sincere,
Not scorned in Heaven, though little noticed here.
Could Time, his flight reversed, restore the hours,
When playing with thy vesture's tissued flowers,
The violet, the pink, the jessamine,
I pricked them into paper with a pin,
And thou wast happier than myself the while,
Wouldst softly speak, and stroke my head, and smile.
Could those few pleasant days again appear,
Might one wish bring them, would I wish them here?
I would not trust my heart — the dear delight
Seems so to be desired, perhaps I might.
But no — what here we call our life is such,
So little to be loved, and thou so much,
That I should ill requite thee to constrain
Thy unbound spirit into bonds again.
Thou, as a gallant bark from Albion's coast
(The storms all weathered and the ocean crossed)
Shoots into port at some well-havened isle,
Where spices breathe and brighter seasons smile,
There sits quiescent on the floods, that show
Her beauteous form reflected clear below,
While airs impregnated with incense play
Around her, fanning light her streamers gay, —
So thou, with sails how swift! hast reached the shore,
"Where tempests never beat, nor billows roar;"[1]
And thy loved consort on the dangerous tide
Of life long since has anchored by thy side.
But me, scarce hoping to attain that rest,
Always from port withheld, always distressed, —
Me howling blasts drive devious, tempest-tossed,
Sails ripped, seams opening wide, and compass lost,
And day by day some current's thwarting force
Sets me more distant from a prosperous course.
Yet, O, the thought, that thou art safe, and he!
That thought is joy, arrive what may to me.
My boast is not that I deduce my birth
From loins enthroned and rulers of the earth;
But higher far my proud pretensions rise —
The son of parents passed into the skies.
And now, farewell — Time unrevoked has run
His wonted course; yet what I wished is done.
By contemplation's help, not sought in vain,
I seem t' have lived my childhood o'er again,
To have renewed the joys that once were mine,
Without the sin of violating thine;

[1] Garth.

And, while the wings of fancy still are free,
And I can view this mimic show of thee,
Time has but half succeeded in his theft —
Thyself removed, thy power to soothe me left.

237. Mercy to Animals.

I would not enter on my list of friends
(Though graced with polished manners and fine sense,
Yet wanting sensibility) the man
Who needlessly sets foot upon a worm.
An inadvertent step may crush the snail
That crawls at evening in the public path;
But he that has humanity, forewarned,
Will tread aside, and let the reptile live.
The creeping vermin, loathsome to the sight,
And charged, perhaps, with venom, that intrudes,
A visitor unwelcome into scenes
Sacred to neatness and repose, the alcove,
The chamber, or refectory, may die:
A necessary act incurs no blame.
Not so when, held within their proper bounds,
And guiltless of offence, they range the air,
Or take their pastime in the spacious field;
There they are privileged; and he that hunts
Or harms them there, is guilty of a wrong,
Disturbs the economy of Nature's realm,
Who, when she formed, designed them an abode.
The sum is this: If man's convenience, health,
Or safety interfere, his rights and claims
Are paramount, and must extinguish theirs.
Else they are all — the meanest things that are —
As free to live, and to enjoy that life,
As God was free to form them at the first,
Who in His sovereign wisdom made them all.
Ye, therefore, who love mercy, teach your sons
To love it too.

238. Pleasures of a Winter Evening.

Now stir the fire, and close the shutters fast,
Let fall the curtains, wheel the sofa round,
And, while the bubbling and loud-hissing urn
Throws up a steamy column, and the cups,
That cheer but not inebriate, wait on each,
So let us welcome peaceful evening in,
Not such his evening who, with shining face,

Sweats in the crowded theatre, and, squeezed
And bored with elbow-points through both his sides,
Outscolds the ranting actor on the stage;
Nor his, who patient stands till his feet throb,
And his head thumps, to feed upon the breath
Of patriots, bursting with heroic rage,
Or placemen, all tranquillity and smiles,
This folio of four pages, happy work!
Which not e'en critics criticise; that holds
Inquisitive attention, while I read,
Fast bound in chains of silence, which the fair,
Though eloquent themselves, yet fear to break;
What is it, but a map of busy life,
Its fluctuations, and its vast concerns?
Here runs the mountainous and craggy ridge,
That tempts Ambition. On the summit see
The seals of office glitter in his eyes;
He climbs, he pants, he grasps them! At his heels,
Close at his heels, a demagogue ascends,
And with a dexterous jerk soon twists him down,
And wins them, but to lose them in his turn.
Here rills of oily eloquence, in soft
Meanders, lubricate the course they take;
The modest speaker is ashamed and grieved
To engross a moment's notice; and yet begs,
Begs a propitious ear for his poor thoughts,
However trivial all that he conceives.
Sweet bashfulness! it claims at least this praise:
The dearth of information and good sense,
That it foretells us, always comes to pass.
Cataracts of declamation thunder here;
There forests of no meaning spread the page,
In which all comprehension wanders lost;
While fields of pleasantry amuse us there
With merry descants on a nation's woes,
The rest appears a wilderness of strange
But gay confusion; roses for the cheeks,
And lilies for the brows of faded age,
Teeth for the toothless, ringlets for the bald,
Heaven, earth, and ocean, plundered of their sweets,
Nectareous essences, Olympian dews,
Sermons, and city feasts, and favorite airs,
Ethereal journeys, submarine exploits,
And Katterfelto, with his hair on end
At his own wonders, wondering for his bread.
'Tis pleasant, through the loopholes of retreat,
To peep at such a world; to see the stir

Of the great Babel, and not feel the crowd;
To hear the roar she sends through all her gates
At a safe distance, where the dying sound
Falls a soft murmur on th' uninjured ear.
Thus sitting, and surveying thus at ease
The globe and its concerns, I seem advanced
To some secure and more than mortal height,
That liberates and exempts me from them all.

FROM THE "TIROCINIUM."

239. THE PLAY-PLACE OF EARLY DAYS.

Be it a weakness, it deserves some praise,
We love the play-place of our early days;
The scene is touching, and the heart is stone,
That feels not at that sight, and feels at none.
The wall on which we tried our graving skill,
The very name we carved subsisting still;
The bench on which we sat while deep employed,
Though mangled, hacked, and hewed, not yet destroyed;
The little ones, unbuttoned, glowing hot,
Playing our games, and on the very spot;
As happy as we once, to kneel and draw
The chalky ring, and knuckle down at taw;
To pitch the ball into the grounded hat,
Or drive it devious with a dexterous pat;
The pleasing spectacle at once excites
Such recollection of our own delights,
That, viewing it, we seem almost t' obtain
Our innocent sweet simple years again.

---

240. THE DIVERTING HISTORY OF JOHN GILPIN.

John Gilpin was a citizen
  Of credit and renown,
A train-band Captain eke was he
  Of famous London town.

John Gilpin's spouse said to her dear—
  Though wedded we have been
These twice ten tedious years, yet we
  No holiday have seen.

To-morrow is our wedding-day,
  And we will then repair
Unto the Bell at Edmonton
  All in a chaise and pair.

My sister and my sister's child,
  Myself, and children three,
Will fill the chaise; so you must ride
  On horseback after we.

He soon replied — I do admire
  Of womankind but one,
And you are she, my dearest dear,
  Therefore it shall be done.

I am a linen-draper bold,
  As all the world doth know,
And my good friend the calender
  Will lend his horse to go.

Quoth Mistress Gilpin — That's well said;
  And, for that wine is dear,
We will be furnished with our own,
  Which is both bright and clear.

John Gilpin kissed his loving wife;
  O'erjoyed was he to find
That, though on pleasure she was bent,
  She had a frugal mind.

The morning came, the chaise was brought,
  But yet was not allowed
To drive up to the door, lest all
  Should say that she was proud.

So three doors off the chaise was stayed,
  Where they did all get in;
Six precious souls, and all agog
  To dash through thick and thin.

Smack went the whip, round went the wheels,
  Were never folk so glad,
The stones did rattle underneath,
  As if Cheapside were mad.

John Gilpin, at his horse's side,
  Seized fast the flowing mane,
And up he got, in haste to ride,
  But soon came down again:

For saddle-tree scarce reached had he,
  His journey to begin,
When, turning round his head, he saw
  Three customers come in.

So down he came; for loss of time,
  Although it grieved him sore,
Yet loss of pence, full well he knew,
  Would trouble him much more.

'Twas long before the customers
  Were suited to their mind,
When Betty, screaming, came down stairs —
  "The wine is left behind!"

Good lack! quoth he — yet bring it me,
  My leathern belt likewise,
In which I bear my trusty sword,
  When I do exercise.

Now Mistress Gilpin (careful soul!)
  Had two stone bottles found,
To hold the liquor that she loved,
  And keep it safe and sound.

Each bottle had a curling ear,
  Through which the belt he drew,
And hung a bottle on each side,
  To make his balance true.

Then, over all, that he might be
  Equipped from top to toe,
His long red cloak, well brushed and neat,
  He manfully did throw.

Now see him mounted once again
  Upon his nimble steed,
Full slowly pacing o'er the stones,
  With caution and good heed.

But finding soon a smoother road
  Beneath his well-shod feet,
The snorting beast began to trot,
  Which galled him in his seat.

So, Fair and softly, John he cried,
  But John he cried in vain;
That trot became a gallop soon,
  In spite of curb and rein.

So, stooping down, as needs he must
  Who cannot sit upright,
He grasped the mane with both his hands,
  And eke with all his might.

His horse, who never in that sort
  Had handled been before,
What thing upon his back had got
  Did wonder more and more.

Away went Gilpin, neck or nought,
  Away went hat and wig;
He little dreamt, when he set out,
  Of running such a rig.

The wind did blow, the cloak did fly,
  Like streamer long and gay,
Till, loop and button failing both,
  At last it flew away.

Then might all people well discern
  The bottles he had slung;
A bottle swinging at each side,
  As hath been said or sung.

The dogs did bark, the children screamed,
  Up flew the windows all;
And every soul cried out — Well done!
  As loud as he could bawl.

Away went Gilpin — who but he?
  His fame soon spread around, —
He carries weight! he rides a race!
  'Tis for a thousand pound!

And, still, as fast as he drew near,
  'Twas wonderful to view,
How in a trice the turnpike men
  Their gates wide open threw!

And now, as he went bowing down
  His reeking head full low,
The bottles twain, behind his back,
  Were shattered at a blow.

Down ran the wine into the road,
  Most piteous to be seen,
Which made his horse's flanks to smoke
  As they had basted been.

But still he seemed to carry weight,
  With leathern girdle braced;
For all might see the bottle-necks
  Still dangling at his waist.

Thus all through merry Islington,
  These gambols he did play,
And till he came unto the Wash
  Of Edmonton so gay.

And there he threw the Wash about
  On both sides of the way,
Just like unto a trundling mop,
  Or a wild goose at play.

At Edmonton, his loving wife
  From balcony espied
Her tender husband, wondering much
  To see how he did ride.

Stop, stop, John Gilpin! — Here's the house —
  They all at once did cry;
The dinner waits, and we are tired:
  Said Gilpin — So am I!

But yet his horse was not a whit
  Inclined to tarry there;
For why? — his owner had a house
  Full ten miles off, at Ware.

So, like an arrow swift he flew,
  Shot by an archer strong;
So did he fly — which brings me to
  The middle of my song.

Away went Gilpin out of breath,
  And sore against his will,
Till at his friend's the calender's
  His horse at last stood still.

The calender, amazed to see
  His neighbor in such trim,
Laid down his pipe, flew to the gate,
  And thus accosted him: —

What news? what news? your tidings tell;
  Tell me you must and shall —
Say why bareheaded you are come,
  Or why you come at all?

Now Gilpin had a pleasant wit,
  And loved a timely joke,
And thus unto the calender
  In merry guise he spoke: —

I came because your horse would come;
  And, if I well forebode,
My hat and wig will soon be here;
  They are upon the road.

The calender, right glad to find
  His friend in merry pin,
Returned him not a single word,
  But to the house went in.

Whence straight he came with hat and wig;
  A wig that flowed behind,
A hat not much the worse for wear,
  Each comely in its kind.

He held them up, and in his turn
  Thus showed his ready wit, —
My head is twice as big as yours,
  They therefore needs must fit.

But let me scrape the dirt away,
  That hangs upon your face;
And stop and eat, for well you may
  Be in a hungry case.

Said John — It is my wedding-day,
  And all the world would stare,
If wife should dine at Edmonton,
  And I should dine at Ware.

So, turning to his horse, he said —
  I am in haste to dine;
'Twas for your pleasure you came here,
  You shall go back for mine.

Ah! luckless speech, and bootless boast!
  For which he paid full dear;
For, while he spake, a braying ass
  Did sing most loud and clear;

Whereat his horse did snort, as he
  Had heard a lion roar,
And galloped off with all his might,
  As he had done before.

Away went Gilpin, and away
  Went Gilpin's hat and wig;
He lost them sooner than at first,
  For why? they were too big.

Now Mistress Gilpin, when she saw
  Her husband posting down
Into the country far away,
  She pulled out half-a-crown;

And thus unto the youth she said,
  That drove them to the Bell —
This shall be yours when you bring back
  My husband safe and well.

The youth did ride, and soon did meet
  John coming back amain;
Whom in a trice he tried to stop,
  By catching at his rein;

But not performing what he meant,
  And gladly would have done,
The frighted steed he frighted more,
  And made him faster run.

Away went Gilpin, and away
  Went postboy at his heels,
The postboy's horse right glad to miss
  The lumb'ring of the wheels.

Six gentlemen upon the road,
  Thus seeing Gilpin fly,
With postboy scamp'ring in the rear,
  They raised the hue and cry: —

Stop thief! stop thief! — a highwayman!
  Not one of them was mute;
And all and each that passed that way
  Did join in the pursuit.

And now the turnpike gates again
  Flew open in short space;
The toll-men thinking, as before,
  That Gilpin rode a race.

And so he did, and won it too,
  For he got first to town;
Nor stopped till where he first got up
  He did again get down.

Now let us sing — Long live the king,
  And Gilpin, long live he;
And, when he next doth ride abroad,
  May I be there to see!

241. William Falconer. 1730–1769. (Manual, p. 359.)

From "The Shipwreck."

In vain the cords and axes were prepared,
For now th' audacious seas insult the yard;
High o'er the ship they throw a horrid shade,
And o'er her burst in terrible cascade.
Uplifted on the surge, to heaven she flies,
Her shattered top half-buried in the skies,
Then headlong, plunging, thunders on the ground,
Earth groans! air trembles! and the deeps resound!
Her giant bulk the dread concussion feels,
And quivering with the wound, in torment reels;
So reels, convulsed with agonizing throes,
The bleeding bull beneath the murd'rer's blows.—
Again she plunges! hark! a second shock
Tears her strong bottom on the marble rock!
Down on the vale of death, with dismal cries,
The fated victims, shuddering, roll their eyes
In wild despair; while yet another stroke,
With deep convulsion, rends the solid oak;
Till like the mine, in whose infernal cell
The lurking demons of destruction dwell,
At length asunder torn, her frame divides,
And crashing spreads in ruin o'er the tides.

Erasmus Darwin. 1731–1802. (Manual, p. 360.)

From "The Botanic Garden."

242. Steel.

Hail, adamantine Steel! magnetic Lord!
King of the prow, the ploughshare, and the sword!
True to the pole, by thee the pilot guides
His steady helm amid the struggling tides;
Braves with broad sail th' immeasurable sea,
Cleaves the dark air, and asks no star but thee.—
By thee the ploughshare rends the matted plain,
Inhumes in level rows the living grain;
Intrusive forests quit the cultured ground,
And Ceres laughs, with golden fillets crowned.—
O'er restless realms, when scowling Discord flings
Her snakes, and loud the din of battle rings;
Expiring strength and vanquished courage feel
Thy arm resistless, adamantine Steel!

James Macpherson. 1738–1796. (Manual, p. 361.)

243. The Songs of Selma.

Star of descending night! fair is thy light in the west! thou liftest thy unshorn head from thy cloud; thy steps are stately on thy hill. What dost thou behold in the plain? The stormy winds are laid. The murmur of the torrent comes from afar. Roaring waves climb the distant rock. The flies of evening are on their feeble wings; the hum of their course is on the field. What dost thou behold, fair light? But thou dost smile and depart. The waves come with joy around thee: they bathe thy lovely hair. Farewell, thou silent beam! let the light of Ossian's soul arise!

And it does arise in its strength! I behold my departed friends. Their gathering is on Lora, as in the days of other years. Fingal comes like a watery column of mist; his heroes are around. And see the bards of song, gray-haired Ullin! stately Ryno! Alpin with the tuneful voice! the soft complaint of Minona! How are ye changed, my friends, since the days of Selma's feast, when we contended, like gales of spring, as they fly along the hill, and bend by turns the feebly whistling grass!

Minona came forth in her beauty, with downcast look and tearful eye. Her hair flew slowly on the blast, that rushed unfrequent from the hill. The souls of the heroes were sad when she raised the tuneful voice. Often had they seen the grave of Salgar, the dark dwelling of white-bosomed Colma. Colma left alone on the hill, with all her voice of song! Salgar promised to come; but the night descended around. Hear the voice of Colma, when she sat alone on the hill!

Colma. — It is night; I am alone, forlorn on the hill of storms. The wind is heard in the mountain. The torrent pours down the rock. No hut receives me from the rain; forlorn on the hill of winds!

Rise, moon, from behind thy clouds! Stars of the night, arise! Lead me, some light, to the place, where my love rests from the chase alone! his bow near him, unstrung! his dogs panting around him. But here I must sit alone by the rock of the mossy stream. The stream and the wind roar aloud. I hear not the voice of my love. Why delays my Salgar, why the chief of the hill, his promise? Here is the rock, and here the tree! here is the roaring stream! Thou didst promise with night to be here. Ah, whither is my Salgar gone? With thee I would fly from my father; with thee from my brother of pride. Our race have long been foes; we are no foes, O Salgar!

Cease a little while, O wind! stream, be thou silent a while! let my voice be heard around. Let my wanderer hear me! Salgar, it is Colma who calls. Here is the tree, and the rock. Salgar, my love! I am here. Why delayest thou thy coming? Lo! the calm moon comes forth. The flood is bright in the vale. The rocks are gray on the steep. I see him not on the brow. His dogs come not before him, with tidings of his near approach. Here I must sit alone!

Who lie on the heath beside me? Are they my love and my brother? Speak to me, O my friends! To Colma they give no reply. Speak to me; I am alone! My soul is tormented with fears! Ah, they are dead! Their swords are red from the fight. O my brother, my brother, why hast thou slain my Salgar? why, O Salgar, hast thou slain my brother? Dear were ye both to me! What shall I say in your praise? Thou wert fair on the hill among thousands! he was terrible in fight. Speak to me: hear my voice; hear me, sons of my love. They are silent, silent forever! Cold, cold are their breasts of clay! O, from the rock on the hill; from the top of the windy steep, speak, ye ghosts of the dead! speak, I will not be afraid! Whither are ye gone to rest? In what cave of the hill shall I find the departed? No feeble voice is on the gale; no answer half-drowned in the storm!

I sit in my grief! I wait for morning in my tears! Rear the tomb, ye friends of the dead! Close it not till Colma come. My life flies away like a dream; why should I stay behind? Here shall I rest with my friends, by the sounding rock. When night comes on the hill; when the loud winds arise; my ghost shall stand in the blast, and mourn the death of my friends. The hunter shall hear from his booth. He shall fear but love my voice! For sweet shall my voice be for my friends; pleasant were her friends to Colma!

Such was thy song, Minona, softly blushing daughter of Torman. Our tears descended for Colma, and our souls were sad! Ullin came with his harp: he gave the song of Alpin. The voice of Alpin was pleasant; the soul of Ryno was a beam of fire! But they rested in the narrow house; their voice had ceased in Selma. Ullin had returned, one day, from the chase, before the heroes fell. He heard their strife on the hill; their song was soft but sad! They mourned the fall of Morar, first of mortal men! His soul was like the soul of Fingal; his sword like the sword of Oscar. But he fell, and his father mourned; his sister's eyes were full of tears. Minona's eyes were full of tears, the sister of car-borne Morar. She retired from the song of Ullin, like the moon in the west, when she foresees the shower, and hides her fair head in a cloud. I touched the harp with Ullin; the song of mourning rose!

Ryno. — The wind and the rain are past; calm is the noon of day. The clouds are divided in heaven. Over the green hills flies the inconstant sun. Red through the stony vale comes down the stream of the hill. Sweet are thy murmurs, O stream! but more sweet is the voice I hear. It is the voice of Alpin, the son of song. Why alone on the silent hill? Why complainest thou, as a blast in the wood, as a wave on the lonely shore?

Alpin. — My tears, O Ryno, are for the dead; my voice for those that have passed away. Tall thou art on the hill; fair among the sons of the vale. But thou shalt fall like Morar; the mourner shall sit on the tomb. The hills shall know thee no more; thy bow shall lie in thy hall, unstrung!

Thou wert swift, O Morar! as a roe on the desert; terrible as a meteor of fire. Thy wrath was as the storm. Thy sword in battle, as lightning in the field. Thy voice was a stream after rain; like thunder on distant hills. Many fell by thy arm; they were consumed in the flames of thy wrath. But when thou didst return from war, how peaceful was thy brow! Thy face was like the sun after rain; like the moon in the silence of night; calm as the breast of the lake when the loud wind is laid.

Narrow is thy dwelling now! dark the place of thine abode! With three steps I compass thy grave, O thou who wast so great before. Four stones, with their heads of moss, are the only memorial of thee. A tree with scarce a leaf, long grass which whistles in the wind, mark to the hunter's eye the grave of the mighty Morar. Morar, thou art low indeed. Thou hast no mother to mourn thee; no maid with her tears of love. Dead is she that brought thee forth. Fallen is the daughter of Morglan.

Who on his staff is this? who is this whose head is white with age? whose eyes are red with tears? who quakes at every step? It is thy father, O Morar! the father of no son but thee. He heard of thy fame in war; he heard of foes dispersed. He heard of Morar's renown; why did he not hear of his wound? Weep, thou father of Morar, weep, but thy son heareth thee not. Deep is the sleep of the dead; low their pillow of dust. No more shall he hear thy voice; no more awake at thy call. When shall it be morn in the grave, to bid the slumberer awake? Farewell, thou bravest of men! thou conqueror in the field! but the field shall see thee no more; nor the dark wood be lightened with the splendor of thy steel. Thou hast left no son. The song shall preserve thy name. Future times shall hear of thee; they shall hear of the fallen Morar!

THOMAS CHATTERTON. 1752–1770. (Manual, p. 362.)

244. RESIGNATION.

O God, whose thunder shakes the sky,
  Whose eye this atom globe surveys;
To thee, my only rock, I fly,
  Thy mercy in thy justice praise.

The mystic mazes of thy will,
  The shadows of celestial light,
Are past the power of human skill —
  But what th' Eternal acts is right.

O, teach me in the trying hour,
  When anguish swells the dewy tear,
To still my sorrows, own thy power,
  Thy goodness love, thy justice fear.

If in this bosom aught but thee,
  Encroaching sought a boundless sway,
Omniscience could the danger see,
  And Mercy look the cause away.

Then why, my soul, dost thou complain,
  Why drooping seek the dark recess?
Shake off the melancholy chain,
  For God created all to bless.

But, ah! my breast is human still;
  The rising sigh, the falling tear,
My languid vitals' feeble rill,
  The sickness of my soul declare.

But yet, with fortitude resigned,
  I'll thank th' inflicter of the blow,
Forbid the sigh, compose my mind,
  Nor let the gush of misery flow.

The gloomy mantle of the night,
  Which on my sinking spirit steals,
Will vanish at the morning light,
  Which God, my East, my Sun, reveals.

George Crabbe. 1754–1832. (Manual, p. 364.)

From "The Borough."

245. The Dying Sailor.

Yes! there are real mourners. — I have seen
A fair, sad girl, mild, suffering, and serene;
Attention (through the day) her duties claimed,
And to be useful as resigned she aimed:
Neatly she dressed, nor vainly seemed t' expect
Pity for grief, or pardon for neglect;
But, when her wearied parents sunk to sleep,
She sought her place to meditate and weep:
Then to her mind was all the past displayed,
That faithful memory brings to sorrow's aid:
For then she thought on one regretted youth,
Her tender trust, and his unquestioned truth;

In every place she wandered, where they'd been,
And sadly-sacred held the parting scene,
Where last for sea he took his leave — that place
With double interest would she nightly trace;
For long the courtship was, and he would say,
Each time he sailed, — "This once, and then the day:"
Yet prudence tarried; but, when last he went,
He drew from pitying love a full consent.

Happy he sailed, and great the care she took,
That he should softly sleep, and smartly look;
White was his better linen, and his check
Was made more trim than any on the deck;
And every comfort men at sea can know,
Was hers to buy, to make, and to bestow:
For he to Greenland sailed, and much she told,
How he should guard against the climate's cold,
Yet saw not danger; dangers he'd withstood,
Nor could she trace the fever in his blood:
His messmates smiled at flushings on his cheek,
And he too smiled, but seldom would he speak;
For now he found the danger, felt the pain,
With grievous symptoms he could not explain;
Hope was awakened, as for home he sailed,
But quickly sank, and never more prevailed.

He called his friend, and prefaced with a sigh
A lover message — "*Thomas*, I must die:
Would I could see my *Sally*, and could rest
My throbbing temples on her faithful breast,
And gazing, go! — if not, this trifle take,
And say, till death I wore it for her sake;
Yes! I must die — blow on, sweet breeze, blow on!
Give me one look, before my life be gone,
O! give me that, and let me not despair,
One last fond look — and now repeat the prayer."

He had his wish, had more; I will not paint
The lovers' meeting: she beheld him faint, —
With tender fears, she took a nearer view,
Her terrors doubling as her hopes withdrew;
He tried to smile, and, half succeeding, said,
"Yes! I must die;" and hope forever fled.

Still long she nursed him; tender thoughts, meantime,
Were interchanged, and hopes and views sublime.
To her he came to die, and every day
She took some portion of the dread away:
With him she prayed, to him his Bible read,

Soothed the faint heart, and held the aching head;
She came with smiles the hour of pain to cheer;
Apart, she sighed; alone, she shed the tear;
Then, as if breaking from a cloud, she gave
Fresh light, and gilt the prospect of the grave.

One day he lighter seemed, and they forgot
The care, the dread, the anguish of their lot;
They spoke with cheerfulness, and seemed to think,
Yet said not so — "Perhaps he will not sink;"
A sudden brightness in his look appeared,
A sudden vigor in his voice was heard; —
She had been reading in the book of prayer,
And led him forth, and placed him in his chair;
Lively he seemed, and spoke of all he knew,
The friendly many, and the favorite few;
Nor one that day did he to mind recall,
But she has treasured, and she loves them all;
When in her way she meets them, they appear
Peculiar people — death has made them dear.
He named his friend, but then his hand she prest,
And fondly whispered, "Thou must go to rest!"
"I go," he said; but, as he spoke, she found
His hand more cold, and fluttering was the sound!
Then gazed affrightened; but she caught a last,
A dying look of love, and all was past!

She placed a decent stone his grave above,
Neatly engraved — an offering of her love;
For that she wrought, for that forsook her bed,
Awake alike to duty and the dead;
She would have grieved, had friends presumed to spare
The least assistance — 'twas her proper care.

Here will she come, and on the grave will sit,
Folding her arms, in long abstracted fit;
But, if observer pass, will take her round,
And careless seem, for she would not be found;
Then go again, and thus her hour employ,
While visions please her, and while woes destroy.

Forbear, sweet maid! nor be by fancy led,
To hold mysterious converse with the dead;
For sure at length thy thoughts, thy spirit's pain,
In this sad conflict, will disturb thy brain;
All have their tasks and trials; thine are hard,
But short the time, and glorious the reward;
Thy patient spirit to thy duties give,
Regard the dead, but, to the living, live.

FROM "THE PARISH REGISTER."

246. AN ENGLISH PEASANT.

To pomp and pageantry in nought allied,
A noble peasant, Isaac Ashford, died.
Noble he was, contemning all things mean,
His truth unquestioned, and his soul serene:
Of no man's presence Isaac felt afraid,
At no man's question Isaac looked dismayed:
Shame knew him not, he dreaded no disgrace:
Truth, simple truth, was written in his face;
Yet while the serious thought his soul approved,
Cheerful he seemed and gentleness he loved:
To bliss domestic he his heart resigned,
And, with the firmest, had the fondest mind:
Were others joyful, he looked smiling on,
And gave allowance where he needed none:
Good he refused with future ill to buy,
Nor knew a joy that caused reflection's sigh;
A friend to virtue, his unclouded breast
No envy stung, no jealousy distressed
(Bane of the poor! it wounds their weaker mind,
To miss one favor which their neighbors find):
Yet far was he from stoic pride removed;
He felt humanely, and he warmly loved:
I marked his action when his infant died,
And his old neighbor for offence was tried;
The still tears, stealing down that furrowed cheek,
Spoke pity plainer than the tongue can speak.
If pride were his, 'twas not their vulgar pride,
Who, in their base contempt, the great deride;
Nor pride in learning, though my clerk agreed,
If fate should call him, Ashford might succeed;
Nor pride in rustic skill, although we knew
None his superior, and his equals few:
But if that spirit in his soul had place,
It was the jealous pride that shuns disgrace;
A pride in honest fame, by virtue gained,
In sturdy boys to virtuous labors trained;
Pride in the Power that guards his country's coast,
And all that Englishmen enjoy and boast;
Pride, in a life that slander's tongue defied,
In fact a noble passion, misnamed pride.
I feel his absence in the hours of prayer,
And view his seat, and sigh for Isaac there;
I see no more those white locks, thinly spread

Round the bald polish of that honored head;
Nor more that awful glance on playful wight,
Compelled to kneel and tremble at the sight,
To fold his fingers all in dread the while,
Till Master Ashford softened to a smile;
No more that meek and suppliant look in prayer,
Nor the pure faith (to give it forth), are there;
But he is blessed, and I lament no more,
A wise good man, contented to be poor.

Robert Burns. 1759–1796. (Manual, p. 366.)

247. To Mary in Heaven.

Thou lingering star, with lessening ray,
  That lov'st to greet the early morn,
Again thou usher'st in the day
  My Mary from my soul was torn.
O Mary! dear departed shade!
  Where is thy place of blissful rest?
Seest thou thy lover lowly laid?
  Hear'st thou the groans that rend his breast.

That sacred hour can I forget?
  Can I forget the hallowed grove,
Where by the winding Ayr we met,
  To live one day of parting love?
Eternity will not efface
  Those records dear of transports past;
Thy image at our last embrace!
  Ah, little thought we 'twas our last!

Ayr gurgling kissed his pebbled shore,
  O'erhung with wild woods thickening green:
The fragrant birch, and hawthorn hoar,
  Twined amorous round the raptured scene.
The flowers sprang wanton to be prest,
  The birds sang love on every spray,
Till too, too soon the glowing west
  Proclaimed the speed of wingéd day.

Still o'er these scenes my memory wakes,
  And fondly broods with miser care;
Time.but the impression stronger makes,
  As streams their channels deeper wear.
My Mary, dear departed shade!
  Where is thy place of blissful rest?
Seest thou thy lover lowly laid?
  Hear'st thou the groans that rend his breast?

248. JOHN ANDERSON.

John Anderson my jo, John,
  When we were first acquent,
Your locks were like the raven,
  Your bonnie brow was brent;
But now your brow is beld, John,
  Your locks are like the snaw;
But blessings on your frosty pow,
  John Anderson my jo.

John Anderson my jo, John,
  We clamb the hill thegither;
And mony a canty day, John,
  We've had wi' ane anither.
But we maun totter down, John,
  But hand in hand we'll go:
And sleep thegither at the foot,
  John Anderson my jo.

---

249. BANNOCKBURN.

Robert Bruce's Address to his Army.

Scots, wha hae wi' Wallace bled;
Scots, wham Bruce has aften led;
Welcome to your gory bed,
  Or to glorious victorie!

Now's the day and now's the hour—
See the front o' battle lour;
See approach proud Edward's power—
  Edward! chains and slaverie!

Wha will be a traitor knave?
Wha can fill a coward's grave?
Wha sae base as be a slave?
  Traitor! coward! turn and flee!

Wha for Scotland's king and law
Freedom's sword will strongly draw!
Freeman stand or freeman fa',
  Caledonian! on wi' me!

By oppression's woes and pains!
By our sons in servile chains!
We will drain our dearest veins,
  But they shall be — shall be free!

Lay the proud usurpers low!
Tyrants fall in every foe!
Liberty's in every blow!
  Forward! let us do or die!

---

250. The Banks o' Doon.

Ye flowery banks o' bonnie Doon,
  How can ye bloom sae fair!
How can ye chant, ye little birds,
  And I sae fu' o' care!

Thou'll break my heart, thou bonnie bird,
  That sings upon the bough;
Thou minds't me o' the happy days
  When my fause luve was true.

Thou'lt break my heart, thou bonnie bird,
  That sings beside thy mate;
For sae I sat, and sae I sang,
  And wistna' o' my fate.

Aft hae I roved by bonnie Doon,
  To see the woodbine twine,
And ilka bird sang o' its love,
  And sae did I o' mine.

Wi' lightsome heart I pu'd a rose,
  Frae aff its thorny tree;
And my fause luver staw the rose,
  But left the thorn wi' me.

---

251. The Cotter's Saturday Night.

November chill blaws loud wi' angry sugh;
  The shortening winter-day is near a close;
The miry beasts retreating frae [1] the pleugh;
  The blackening trains o' craws to their repose;
The toil-worn cotter frae his labor goes,
  This night his weekly moil [2] is at an end,
Collects his spades, his mattocks, and his hoes,
  Hoping the morn in ease and rest to spend,
And weary, o'er the moor, his course does hameward bend.

At length his lonely cot appears in view,
  Beneath the shelter of an aged tree;

[1] From. [2] Labor.

Th' expectant wee[3] things, toddlin,[4] stacher[5] through
To meet their dad, wi' flicterin[6] noise an' glee.
His wee bit ingle,[7] blinkin[8] bonnily,
His clean hearth-stane, his thriftie wifie's smile,
The lisping infant prattling on his knee,
Does a'[9] his weary carking[10] cares beguile,
An' makes him quite forget his labor and his toil.

Belyve[11] the elder bairns come drappin in,
At service out, amang the farmers roun';
Some ca'[12] the pleugh, some herd, some tentie[13] rin
A cannie[14] errand to a neebor town:
Their eldest hope, their Jenny, woman grown,
In youthfu' bloom, love sparkling in her e'e,
Comes hame, perhaps, to show a braw[15] new gown,
Or deposit her sair-won[16] penny-fee,[17]
To help her parents dear, if they in hardship be.

Wi' joy unfeigned, brothers and sisters meet,
An' each for other's weelfare kindly spiers;[18]
The social hours, swift-winged, unnoticed fleet;
Each tells the uncos[19] that he sees or hears;
The parents, partial, eye their hopeful years;
Anticipation forward points the view:
The mother, wi' her needle an' her shears,
Gars[20] auld claes look amaist as weel's the new;
The father mixes a' with admonition due.

Their master's and their mistress's command,
The younkers a' are warnéd to obey;
An' mind their labors wi' an eydent[21] hand,
An' ne'er, though out o' sight, to jauk or play:
"An', O! be sure to fear the Lord alway!
An' mind your duty, duly, morn an' night!
Lest in temptation's path ye gang astray.
Implore His counsel and assisting might:
They never sought in vain that sought the Lord aright!"

But hark! a rap comes gently to the door;
Jenny, wha kens the meaning o' the same,
Tells how a neebor lad cam' o' the moor,
To do some errands, and convoy her hame.
The wily mother sees the conscious flame
Sparkle in Jenny's e'e, and flush her cheek;
With heart-struck anxious care, inquires his name,
While Jenny hafflins[22] is afraid to speak;
Weel pleased the mother hears it's nae wild worthless rake.

3 Little. 4 Tottering in their walk. 5 Stagger. 6 Fluttering. 7 Fire. 8 Shining at intervals. 9 All. 10 Consuming. 11 By and by. 12 Drive. 13 Cautious. 14 Kindly, dexterous. 15 Fine, handsome. 16 Sorely won. 17 Wages. 18 Asks. 19 News. 20 Makes. 21 Diligent. 22 Partly.

Wi' kindly welcome Jenny brings him ben;[23]
  A strappan[24] youth, he taks the mother's eye;
Blythe Jenny sees the visit's no ill-ta'en;
  The father cracks[25] of horses, pleughs, and kye.[26]
The youngster's artless heart o'erflows wi' joy,
  But blate[27] an' laithfu',[28] scarce can weel behave:
The mother, wi' a woman's wiles, can spy
  What maks the youth sae bashfu' an' sae grave,
Weel pleased to think her bairn's respected like the lave.[29]

O, happy love! where love like this is found!
  O heartfelt raptures! bliss beyond compare!
I've pacéd much this weary, mortal round,
  And sage experience bids me this declare, —
"If Heaven a draught of heavenly pleasure spare,
  One cordial in this melancholy vale,
'Tis when a youthful, loving, modest pair
  In other's arms breathe out the tender tale,
Beneath the milk-white thorn that scents the evening gale."

Is there, in human form, that bears a heart, —
  A wretch, a villain, lost to love and truth,
That can, with studied, sly, insnaring art,
  Betray sweet Jenny's unsuspecting youth?
Curse on his perjured arts! dissembling smooth!
  Are honor, virtue, conscience, all exiled?
Is there no pity, no relenting ruth,[30]
  Points to the parents fondling o'er their child?
Then paints the ruined maid, and their distraction wild?

But now the supper crowns their simple board!
  The healsome parritch,[31] chief o' Scotia's food:
The soupe[32] their only hawkie[33] does afford,
  That 'yont[34] the hallan[35] snugly chows her cood:
The dame brings forth, in complimental mood,
  To grace the lad, her weel-hained[36] kebbuck,[37] fell,[38]
An' aft he's pressed, an' aft he ca's it good;
  The frugal wifie, garrulous, will tell,
How 'twas a towmond[39] auld,[40] sin[41] lint was i' the bell.[42]

The cheerfu' supper done, wi' serious face,
  They round the ingle form a circle wide;
The sire turns o'er, wi' patriarchal grace,
  The big Ha'-Bible,[43] ance his father's pride;

23 Into the parlor. 24 Tall and handsome. 25 Converses. 26 Kine, cows. 27 Bashful. 28 Reluctant. 29 The rest, the others. 30 Mercy, kind feeling. 31 Oatmeal pudding. 32 Sauce, milk. 33 A pet name for a cow. 34 Beyond. 35 A partition wall in a cottage. 36 Carefully preserved. 37 A cheese. 38 Biting to the taste. 39 Twelve months. 40 Old. 41 Since. 42 Flax was in blossom. 43 The great Bible kept in the hall.

His bonnet reverently is laid aside,
His lyart[44] haffets[45] wearin' thin an' bare;
Those strains that once did sweet in Zion glide,
He wales[46] a portion with judicious care;
And "Let us worship God," he says, wi' solemn air.

They chant their artless notes in simple guise;
They tune their hearts, by far the noblest aim;
Perhaps Dundee's[47] wild warbling measures rise,
Or plaintive Martyrs,[47] worthy of the name;
Or noble Elgin[47] beets the heavenward flame,
The sweetest far of Scotia's holy lays:
Compared with these, Italian trills are tame;
The tickled ears no heartfelt raptures raise;
Nae unison hae they with our Creator's praise.

The priest-like father reads the sacred page,
How Abram was the friend of God on high;
Or, Moses bade eternal warfare wage
With Amalek's ungracious progeny;
Or, how the Royal Bard[48] did groaning lie
Beneath the stroke of Heaven's avenging ire;
Or, Job's pathetic plaint and wailing cry;
Or, rapt Isaiah's wild seraphic fire;
Or other holy seers that tune the sacred lyre.

Perhaps the Christian volume is the theme,
How guiltless blood for guilty man was shed;
How He, who bore in heaven the second name,
Had not on earth whereon to lay his head:
How His first followers and servants sped,
The precepts sage they wrote to many a land:
How he[49] who lone in Patmos[50] banishéd,
Saw in the sun a mighty angel stand,
And heard great Babylon's doom pronounced by Heaven's command.

Then kneeling down to Heaven's Eternal King,
The saint, the father, and the husband prays;
Hope "springs exulting on triumphant wing,"
That thus they all shall meet in future days;
There ever bask in uncreated rays,
No more to sigh, or shed the bitter tear,
Together hymning their Creator's praise,
In such society, yet still more dear,
While circling time moves round in an eternal sphere.

44 Gray. 45 The temples, the sides of the head. 46 Chooses. 47 The names of Scottish psalm-tunes. 48 David. 49 Saint John.
50 An island in the Archipelago, where John is supposed to have written the book of Revelation.

Compared with this, how poor Religion's pride,
  In all the pomp of method and of art,
When men display to congregations wide
  Devotion's every grace, except the heart!
The Power, incensed, the pageant will desert,
  The pompous strain, the sacerdotal stole;[51]
But haply, in some cottage far apart,
  May hear, well pleased, the language of the soul;
And in His book of life the inmates poor enroll.

Then homeward all take off their several way;
  The youngling cottagers retire to rest;
The parent pair their secret homage pay,
  And proffer up to Heaven the warm request
That He, who stills the raven's clamorous nest,
  And decks the lily fair in flowery pride,
Would, in the way His wisdom sees the best,
  For them and for their little ones provide;
But, chiefly, in their hearts with grace divine preside.

From scenes like these old Scotia's grandeur springs,
  That makes her loved at home, revered abroad;
Princes and lords are but the breath of kings,
  "An honest man's the noblest work of God;"
And certes,[52] in fair virtue's heavenly road,
  The cottage leaves the palace far behind:
What is a lordling's pomp? a cumbrous load,
  Disguising oft the wretch of human-kind,
Studied in arts of hell, in wickedness refined!

O Scotia! my dear, my native soil!
  For whom my warmest wish to Heaven is sent!
Long may thy hardy sons of rustic toil
  Be blessed with health, and peace, and sweet content!
And, O! may Heaven their simple lives prevent
  From luxury's contagion, weak and vile!
Then, however crowns and coronets be rent,
  A virtuous populace may rise the while,
And stand, a wall of fire, around their much-loved isle.

O Thou! who poured the patriotic tide
  That streamed through Wallace's undaunted heart,
Who dared to, nobly, stem tyrannic pride,
  Or nobly die, the second glorious part
(The patriot's God peculiarly Thou art,
  His friend, inspirer, guardian, and reward),
O never, never, Scotia's realm desert:
  But still the patriot, and the patriot bard,
In bright succession raise, her ornament and guard!

51 Priestly vestment.

52 Certainly.

JOHN WOLCOTT. 1738–1819. (Manual, p. 370.)

252. THE RAZOR SELLER.

A fellow in a market town,
Most musical, cried razors up and down,
  And offered twelve for eighteen pence;
Which certainly seemed wondrous cheap,
And for the money quite a heap,
  As every man would buy, with cash and sense.

A country bumpkin the great offer heard:
Poor Hodge, who suffered by a broad black beard,
  That seemed a shoe-brush stuck beneath his nose:
With cheerfulness the eighteen pence he paid,
And proudly to himself, in whispers, said,
" This rascal stole the razors, I suppose.

"No matter if the fellow *be* a knave,
Provided that the razors *shave;*
  It certainly will be a monstrous prize."
So home the clown, with his good fortune, went,
Smiling in heart and soul, content,
  And quickly soaped himself to ears and eyes.

Being well lathered from a dish or tub,
Hodge now began with grinning pain to grub,
  Just like a hedger cutting furze:
'Twas a vile razor! — then the rest he tried —
All were impostors. "Ah!" Hodge sighed,
  "I wish my eighteen pence within my purse."

Hodge sought the fellow — found him — and begun:
" P'rhaps, Master Razor-rogue, to you 'tis fun,
  That people flay themselves out of their lives:
You rascal! for an hour have I been grubbing,
Giving my crying whiskers here a scrubbing,
  With razors just like oyster knives.
Sirrah! I tell you, you're a knave,
To cry up razors that can't *shave.*"

"Friend," quoth the razor-man, "I'm not a knave:
  As for the razors you have bought,
  Upon my soul I never thought
That they would *shave.*"
"Not think they'd *shave!*" quoth Hodge, with wondering eyes,
  And voice not much unlike an Indian yell;
"What were they made for then, you dog?" he cries:
  "Made!" quoth the fellow, with a smile, — "to SELL."

Richard Brinsley Sheridan. 1751–1816. (Manual, p. 371.)

From "The School for Scandal."

253. The Old Husband and the Young Wife.

Sir Peter Teazle. But here comes my helpmate! She appears in great good humor. How happy I should be if I could tease her into loving me, though but a little!

Enter Lady Teazle.

Lady Teaz. Lud! Sir Peter, I hope you haven't been quarrelling with Maria? It is not using me well to be ill humored when I am not by.

Sir Pet. Ah, Lady Teazle, you might have the power to make me good humored at all times.

Lady Teaz. I am sure I wish I had; for I want you to be in a charming sweet temper at this moment. Do be good humored now, and let me have two hundred pounds, will you?

Sir Pet. Two hundred pounds; what, a'n't I to be in a good humor without paying for it! But speak to me thus, and i' faith there's nothing I could refuse you. You shall have it; but seal me a bond for the repayment.

Lady Teaz. O, no — there — my note of hand will do as well. [*Offering her hand.*

Sir Pet. And you shall no longer reproach me with not giving you an independent settlement. I mean shortly to surprise you: but shall we always live thus, hey?

Lady Teaz. If you please. I'm sure I don't care how soon we leave off quarrelling, provided you'll own you were tired first.

Sir Pet. Well — then let our future contest be, who shall be most obliging.

Lady Teaz. I assure you, Sir Peter, good nature becomes you. You look now as you did before we were married, when you used to walk with me under the elms, and tell me stories of what a gallant you were in your youth, and chuck me under the chin, you would; and ask me if I thought I could love an old fellow, who would deny me nothing — didn't you?

Sir Pet. Yes, yes, and you were as kind and attentive ——

Lady Teaz. Ay, so I was, and would always take your part, when my acquaintance used to abuse you, and turn you into ridicule.

Sir Pet. Indeed!

Lady Teaz. Ay, and when my cousin Sophy has called you a stiff, peevish old bachelor, and laughed at me for thinking of marrying one who might be my father, I have always defended you, and said, I didn't think you so ugly by any means.

Sir Pet. Thank you,

Lady Teaz. And I dared say you'd make a very good sort of a husband.

Sir Pet. And you prophesied right; and we shall now be the happiest couple ——

Lady Teaz. And never differ again?

Sir Pet. No, never! — though at the same time, indeed, my dear Lady Teazle, you must watch your temper very seriously; for in all our little quarrels, my dear, if you recollect, my love, you always began first.

Lady Teaz. I beg your pardon, my dear Sir Peter; indeed, you always gave the provocation.

Sir Pet. Now see, my angel! take care — contradicting isn't the way to keep friends.

Lady Teaz. Then don't you begin it, my love!

Sir Pet. There, now! you — you are going on. You don't perceive, my love, that you are just doing the very thing which you know always makes me angry.

Lady Teaz. Nay, you know if you will be angry without any reason, my dear ——

Sir Pet. There! now you want to quarrel again.

Lady Teaz. No, I'm sure I don't; but, if you will be so peevish ——

Sir Pet, There now! who begins first?

Lady Teaz. Why, you, to be sure. I said nothing — but there's no bearing your temper.

Sir Pet. No, no, madam; the fault's in your own temper.

Lady Teaz. Ay, you are just what my cousin Sophy said you would be.

Sir Pet. Your cousin Sophy is a forward, impertinent gypsy.

Lady Teaz. You are a great bear, I'm sure, to abuse my relations.

Sir Pet. Now may all the plagues of marriage be doubled on me, if ever I try to be friends with you any more!

Lady Teaz. So much the better.

Sir Pet. No, no, madam: 'tis evident you never cared a pin for me, and I was a madman to marry you — a pert, rural coquette, that had refused half the honest squires in the neighborhood.

Lady Teaz. And I am sure I was a fool to marry you — an old dangling bachelor, who was single at fifty, only because he never could meet with any one who would have him.

Sir Pet. Ay, ay, madam; but you were pleased enough to listen to me: you never had such an offer before.

Lady Teaz. No! didn't I refuse Sir Tivy Terrier, who everybody said would have been a better match? for his estate is just as good as yours, and he has broke his neck since we have been married.

Sir Pet. I have done with you, madam. You are an unfeeling, ungrateful — but there's an end of everything. I believe you capable of everything that is bad. Yes, madam, I now believe the reports relative to you and Charles, madam. Yes, madam, you and Charles are, not without grounds ——

Lady Teaz. Take care, Sir Peter! you had better not insinuate any such thing! I'll not be suspected without cause, I promise you.

Sir Pet. Very well, madam! very well! A separate maintenance as soon as you please. Yes, madam, or a divorce! I'll make an example of myself for the benefit of all old bachelors. Let us separate, madam.

Lady Teaz. Agreed! agreed! And now, my dear Sir Peter, we are of a mind once more; we may be the happiest couple, and never differ again, you know; ha! ha! ha! Well, you are going to be in a passion, I see, and I shall only interrupt you — so, bye, bye? [*Exit.*

Sir Pet. Plagues and tortures! can't I make her angry either! O, I am the most miserable fellow! But I'll not bear her presuming to keep her temper: no! she may break my heart, but she shan't keep her temper. [*Exit.*

CHAPTER XIX.

WALTER SCOTT.

1771–1832. (Manual, pp. 376–395.)

FROM "THE LAY OF THE LAST MINSTREL."

254. DESCRIPTION OF MELROSE ABBEY.

If thou wouldst view fair Melrose aright,
Go visit it by the pale moonlight;
For the gay beams of lightsome day
Gild but to flout the ruins gray.
When the broken arches are black in night,
And each shafted oriel glimmers white;
When the cold light's uncertain shower
Streams on the ruined central tower;
When buttress and buttress, alternately,
Seem framed of ebon and ivory;
When silver edges the imagery,
And the scrolls that teach thee to live and die;
When distant Tweed is heard to rave,
And the owlet to hoot o'er the dead man's grave,
Then go — but go alone the while —
Then view St. David's ruined pile;
And, home returning, soothly swear,
Was never scene so sad and fair!

255. LOVE OF COUNTRY.

Breathes there a man with soul so dead,
Who never to himself hath said,
  This is my own, my native land?
Whose heart hath ne'er within him burned,
As home his footsteps he hath turned
  From wandering on a foreign strand?
If such there breathe, go mark him well;
For him no minstrel raptures swell;
High though his titles, proud his name,
Boundless his wealth as wish can claim;

Despite those titles, power, and pelf,
The wretch, concentred all in self,
Living, shall forfeit fair renown,
And, doubly dying, shall go down
To the vile dust, from whence he sprung,
Unwept, unhonored, and unsung,
O Caledonia! stern and wild,
Meet nurse for a poetic child!
Land of brown heath and shaggy wood,
Land of the mountain and the flood,
Land of my sires! what mortal hand
Can e'er untie the filial band
That knits me to thy rugged strand?
Still as I view each well-known scene,
Think what is now, and what hath been,
Seems as to me, of all bereft,
Sole friends thy woods and streams were left;
And thus I love them better still,
Even in extremity of ill.

FROM "MARMION."

256. PITT AND FOX.

To mute and to material things
New life revolving summer brings:
The genial call dead nature hears,
And in her glory reappears.
But, O! my country's wintry state
What second spring shall renovate?
What powerful call shall bid arise
The buried warlike and the wise!
The mind that thought for Britain's weal,
The hand that grasped the victor's steel?
The vernal sun new life bestows,
E'en on the meanest flower that blows;
But vainly, vainly may he shine,
Where glory weeps o'er Nelson's shrine,
And vainly pierce the solemn gloom
That shrouds, O Pitt, thy hallowed tomb!

* * * * * * *

Hadst thou but lived, though stripped of power,
A watchman on the lonely tower,
Thy thrilling trump had roused the land,
When fraud and danger were at hand;
By thee, as by the beacon-light,
Our pilots had kept course aright;

As some proud column, though alone,
Thy strength had propped the tottering throne.
Now is the stately column broke,
The beacon-light is quenched in smoke,
The trumpet's silver sound is still,
The warder silent on the hill!

O! think how to his latest day,
When Death, just hovering, claimed his prey,
With Palinure's unaltered mood,
Firm at his dangerous post he stood;
Each call for needful rest repelled,
With dying hand the rudder held,
Till, in his fall, with fateful sway,
The steerage of the helm gave way;
Then, while on Britain's thousand plains,
One unpolluted church remains,
Whose peaceful bells ne'er sent around
The bloody tocsin's maddening sound,
But still upon the hallowed day,
Convoke the swains to praise and pray;
While faith and civil peace are dear,
Grace this cold marble with a tear, —
He who preserved them — Pitt, lies here!

Nor yet suppress the generous sigh,
Because his rival slumbers nigh;
Nor be thy *requiescat* dumb,
Lest it be said o'er Fox's tomb, —
For talents mourn, untimely lost,
When best employed and wanted most;
Mourn genius high and lore profound,
And wit that loved to play, not wound;
And all the reasoning powers divine,
To penetrate, resolve, combine;
And feelings keen and fancy's glow, —
They sleep with him who sleeps below;
And, if thou mourn'st they could not save
From error him who owns this grave,
Be every harsher thought suppressed,
And sacred be the last long rest.
Here, where the end of earthly things
Lays heroes, patriots, bards, and kings;
Where stiff the hand, and still the tongue,
Of those who fought, and spoke, and sung:
Here, where the fretted aisles prolong
The distant notes of holy song,
As if some angel spoke again,

All peace on earth, good will to men;
If ever from an English heart,
O! here let prejudice depart,
And partial feeling cast aside,
Record, that Fox a Briton died!
When Europe crouched to France's yoke,
And Austria bent, and Prussia broke,
And the firm Russian's purpose brave
Was bartered by a timorous slave;
Even then dishonor's peace he spurned,
The sullied olive-branch returned,
Stood for his country's glory fast,
And nailed her colors to the mast!
Heaven, to reward his firmness, gave
A portion in this honored grave;
And never held marble in its trust,
Of two such wondrous men the dust.
With more than mortal powers endowed,
How high they soared above the crowd!
Theirs was no common party race,
Jostling by dark intrigue for place;
Like fabled gods, their mighty war
Shook realms and nations in its jar;
Beneath each banner proud to stand,
Looked up the noblest of the land;
Till through the British world were known
The names of Pitt and Fox alone.

---

257. The Parting of Douglas and Marmion.

The train from out the castle drew,
But Marmion stopped to bid adieu:
"Though something I might plain," he said,
  "Of cold respect to stranger guest,
  Sent hither by your king's behest,
While in Tantallon's towers I staid;
Part we in friendship from your land,
And, noble earl, receive my hand."
But Douglas round him drew his cloak,
Folded his arms, and thus he spoke:—
"My manors, halls, and bowers shall still
Be open, at my sovereign's will,
To each one whom he lists, howe'er
Unmeet to be the owner's peer.
My castles are my king's alone,
From turret to foundation stone—
The hand of Douglas is his own,

And never shall in friendly grasp
The hand of such as Marmion clasp."

Burned Marmion's swarthy cheek like fire,
And shook his very frame for ire,
  And — "This to me!" he said, —
"An 'twere not for thy hoary beard,
Such hand as Marmion's had not spared
  To cleave the Douglas' head!
And, first, I tell thee, haughty peer,
He, who does England's message here,
Although the meanest in her state,
May well, proud Angus, be thy mate:
And, Douglas, more I tell thee here,
  Even in thy pitch of pride,
Here, in thy hold, thy vassals near
(Nay, never look upon your lord,
And lay your hands upon your sword), —
  I tell thee, thou'rt defied!
And if thou said'st, I am not peer
To any lord in Scotland here,
Lowland or Highland, far or near,
  Lord Angus, thou hast lied!" —
On the earl's cheek the flush of rage
O'ercame the ashen hue of age:
Fierce he broke forth, — "And dar'st thou then
To beard the lion in his den,
  The Douglas in his hall?
And hop'st thou hence unscathed to go? —
No, by Saint Bride of Bothwell, no! —
Up drawbridge, grooms — what, warder, ho!
  Let the portcullis fall."
Lord Marmion turned, — well was his need, —
And dashed the rowels in his steed,
Like arrow through the archway sprung,
The ponderous grate behind him rung:
To pass there was such scanty room,
The bars, descending, razed his plume.

The steed along the drawbridge flies,
Just as it trembled on the rise;
Not lighter does the swallow skim
Along the smooth lake's level brim:
And when Lord Marmion reached his band,
He halts, and turns with clinchéd hand,
And shout of loud defiance pours,
And shook his gauntlet at the towers.
"Horse! horse!" the Douglas cried, "and chase"
But soon he reined his fury's pace;

"A royal messenger he came,
Though most unworthy of the name,—
A letter forged! Saint Jude to speed!
Did ever knight so foul a deed?
At first in heart it liked me ill,
When the king praised his clerkly skill.
Thanks to Saint Bothan, son of mine,
Save Gawain, ne'er could pen a line:
So swore I, and I swear it still,
Let my boy-bishop fret his fill.—
Saint Mary mend my fiery mood!
Old age ne'er cools the Douglas' blood,
I thought to slay him where he stood.
'Tis pity of him, too," he cried:
"Bold can he speak, and fairly ride:
I warrant him a warrior tried."—
With this his mandate he recalls,
And slowly seeks his castle's halls.

---

258. The Death of Marmion.

With that, straight up the hill there rode
  Two horsemen drenched with gore,
And in their arms, a helpless load,
  A wounded knight they bore.
His hand still strained the broken brand:
His arms were smeared with blood and sand:
Dragged from among the horses' feet,
With dinted shield, and helmet beat,
The falcon-crest and plumage gone,
Can that be haughty Marmion! . . . .
Young Blount his armor did unlace,
And, gazing on his ghastly face,
  Said—"By St. George, he's gone!
That spear-wound has our master sped,
And see the deep cut on his head!
  Good night to Marmion."—
"Unnurtured Blount!—thy brawling cease:
He opes his eyes," said Eustace, "peace!"

When, doffed his casque, he felt free air,
Around 'gan Marmion wildly stare:—
"Where's Harry Blount! Fitz-Eustace where?
Linger ye here, ye hearts of hare!
Redeem my pennon, charge again!
Cry—'Marmion to the rescue!'—Vain!
Last of my race, on battle plain
That shout shall ne'er be heard again!—

Yet my last thought is England's:—fly,
  To Dacre bear my signet-ring;
  Tell him his squadrons up to bring.—
Fitz-Eustace, to Lord Surrey hie:
  Tunstall lies dead upon the field;
  His life-blood stains the spotless shield:
  Edmund is down:—my life is reft;—
  The Admiral alone is left.
  Let Stanley charge with spur of fire,—
  With Chester charge, and Lancashire,
  Full upon Scotland's central host,
  Or victory and England's lost.—
  Must I bid twice?—hence, varlets! fly!
  Leave Marmion here alone—to die."—
  They parted, and alone he lay;
  Clare drew her from the sight away,
  Till pain wrung forth a lowly moan,
  And half he murmured,—"Is there none,
    Of all my halls have nurst,
  Page, squire, or groom, one cup to bring
  Of blessed water, from the spring,
    To slake my dying thirst!"

O Woman! in our hours of ease,
Uncertain, coy, and hard to please,
And variable as the shade
By the light quivering aspen made;
When pain and anguish wring the brow,
A ministering angel thou!—
Scarce were the piteous accents said,
When, with the Baron's casque, the maid,
  To the nigh streamlet ran:
Forgot were hatred, wrongs, and fears;
The plaintive voice alone she hears,
  Sees but the dying man.
She stooped her by the runnel's side,
  But in abhorrence backward drew;
For, oozing from the mountain wide,
Where raged the war, a dark red tide
  Was curdling in the streamlet blue.
Where shall she turn?—behold her mark
  A little fountain-cell,
Where water, clear as diamond-spark,
  In a stone basin fell.
Above, some half-worn letters say,
"Drink . weary . pilgrim . drink . and . pray .
For . the . kind . soul . of . Sybil . Grey .
  Who . built . this . cross . and . well."

She filled the helm, and back she hied,
And with surprise and joy espied
  A Monk supporting Marmion's head;
A pious man, whom duty brought
To dubious verge of battle fought,
  To shrive the dying, bless the dead.
Deep drank Lord Marmion of the wave.

* * * * * *

With fruitless labor, Clara bound,
And strove to stanch, the gushing wound:
The Monk, with unavailing cares,
Exhausted all the Church's prayers;
Ever, he said, that, close and near,
A lady's voice was in his ear,
And that the priest he could not hear,
  For that she ever sung,
"*In the lost battle, borne down by the flying,*
Where mingles war's rattle with groans of the dying!"
  So the notes rung;
"Avoid thee, Fiend! — with cruel hand
Shake not the dying sinner's sand! —
O look, my son, upon yon sign
Of the Redeemer's grace divine;
  O think on faith and bliss! —
By many a death-bed I have been,
And many a sinner's parting seen,
  But never aught like this." —
The war, that for a space did fail,
Now trebly thundering swelled the gale,
  And — STANLEY! was the cry; —
A light on Marmion's visage spread,
  And fired his glazing eye:
With dying hand, above his head
He shook the fragment of his blade,
  And shouted, "Victory!
Charge, Chester, charge! On, Stanley, on!"
Were the last words of Marmion.

FROM "THE LADY OF THE LAKE."

259. ELLEN — THE LADY OF THE LAKE.

But scarce again his horn he wound,
When lo! forth starting at the sound,
From underneath an agéd oak
That slanted from the islet rock,
A damsel guider of its way,
A little skiff shot to the bay.

With head upraised, and look intent,
And eye and ear attentive bent,
And locks flung back, and lips apart,
Like monument of Grecian art,
In listening mood she seemed to stand,
The guardian Naiad of the strand.

And ne'er did Grecian chisel trace
A Nymph, a Naiad, or a Grace
Of finer form, or lovelier face!
What though the sun, with ardent frown,
Had slightly tinged her cheek with brown —
What though no rule of courtly grace
To measured mood had trained her pace —
A foot more light, a step more true,
Ne'er from the heath-flower dashed the dew;
E'en the slight harebell raised its head,
Elastic from her airy tread:
What though upon her speech there hung
The accents of the mountain tongue —
Those silver sounds, so soft, so dear,
The listener held his breath to hear!

A chieftain's daughter seemed the maid;
Her satin snood, her silken plaid,
Her golden brooch, such birth betrayed.
And seldom was a snood amid
Such wild luxuriant ringlets hid,
Whose glossy black to shame might bring
The plumage of the raven's wing;
And seldom o'er a breast so fair
Mantled a plaid with modest care;
And never brooch the folds combined
Above a heart more good and kind.
Her kindness and her worth to spy,
You need but gaze on Ellen's eye;
Not Katrine, in her mirror blue,
Gives back the shaggy banks more true,
Than every free-born glance confessed
The guileless movements of her breast;
Whether joy danced in her dark eye,
Or woe or pity claimed a sigh,
Or filial love was glowing there,
Or meek devotion poured a prayer,
Or tale of injury called forth
The indignant spirit of the North.

One only passion unrevealed
With maiden pride the maid concealed,
Yet not less purely felt the flame; —
O need I tell that passion's name!

---

260. Paternal Affection.

Some feelings are to mortals given,
With less of earth in them than heaven;
And if there be a human tear
From passion's dross refined and clear,
A tear so limpid and so meek,
It would not stain an angel's cheek,
'Tis that which pious fathers shed
Upon a duteous daughter's head!

From "The Antiquary."

261. Sunset and the Approach of a Storm.

As Sir Arthur and Miss Wardour paced along, enjoying the pleasant footing afforded by the cool moist hard sand, Miss Wardour could not help observing, that the last tide had risen considerably above the usual water-mark. Sir Arthur made the same observation, but without its occurring to either of them to be alarmed at the circumstance. The sun was now resting his huge disk upon the edge of the level ocean, and gilded the accumulation of towering clouds through which he had travelled the livelong day, and which now assembled on all sides, like misfortunes and disasters around a sinking empire and falling monarch. Still, however, his dying splendor gave a sombre magnificence to the massive congregation of vapors, forming out of their unsubstantial gloom, the show of pyramids and towers, some touched with gold, some with purple, some with a hue of deep and dark red. The distant sea, stretched beneath this varied and gorgeous canopy, lay almost portentously still, reflecting back the dazzling and level beams of the descending luminary, and the splendid coloring of the clouds amidst which he was setting. Nearer to the beach the tide rippled onwards in waves of sparkling silver, that imperceptibly, yet rapidly, gained upon the sand.

With a mind employed in admiration of the romantic scene, or perhaps on some more agitating topic, Miss Wardour advanced in silence by her father's side, whose recently offended dignity did not stoop to open any conversation. Following the windings of the beach, they passed one projecting point or headland of rock after another, and now found themselves under a huge and continued extent of the precipices by which that iron-bound coast is in most places defended. Long projecting reefs of rock, extending under water, and only evincing their existence by here and there a peak entirely bare, or by the breakers which foamed over those that were partially covered, rendered Knockwinnock bay dreaded by pilots and ship-masters. The crags which rose between the beach and the main land, to the height of two or three hundred feet, afforded in their crevices shelter for unnumbered sea-fowl, in situations seemingly secured by their dizzy height from the rapacity of man. Many of these wild tribes, with the instinct which sends them to seek the land before a storm arises, were now winging towards their nests with the shrill and dissonant clang which announces disquietude and fear. The disk of the sun became almost totally obscured ere he had altogether sunk below the horizon, and an early and lurid shade of darkness blotted the serene twilight of a summer evening. The wind began next to arise; but its wild and moaning sound was heard for some time, and its effects became visible on the bosom of the sea, before the gale was felt on shore. The mass of waters, now dark and threatening, began to lift itself in larger ridges, and sink in deeper furrows, forming waves that rose high in foam upon the breakers, or burst upon the beach with a sound resembling distant thunder.

FROM "THE HEART OF MID-LOTHIAN."

262. DESCRIPTION OF RICHMOND.

The carriage rolled rapidly onwards through fertile meadows, ornamented with splendid old oaks, and catching occasionally a glance of the majestic mirror of a broad and placid river. After passing through a pleasant village, the equipage stopped on a commanding eminence, where the beauty of English landscape was displayed in its utmost luxuriance. Here the Duke alighted, and desired Jeanie to follow him. They paused for a moment on the brow of a hill, to gaze on the unrivalled landscape which it presented. A huge sea of verdure, with crossing and intersecting promontories of massive and tufted groves, was tenanted by numberless flocks and herds, which seemed to wander unrestrained and unbounded through the rich pastures. The Thames, here turreted with villas, and there garlanded with forests, moved on slowly and placidly, like the mighty monarch of the scene, to whom all its other beauties were but accessories, and bore on its bosom a hundred barks and skiffs, whose white sails and gayly fluttering pennons gave life to the whole.

FROM "IVANHOE."

263. REBECCA DESCRIBES THE SIEGE TO THE WOUNDED IVANHOE.

"And I must lie here like a bedridden monk," exclaimed Ivanhoe, "while the game that gives me freedom or death is played out by the hand of others! — Look from the window once again, kind maiden, but beware that you are not marked by the archers beneath — Look out once more, and tell me if they yet advance to the storm."

With patient courage, strengthened by the interval which she had employed in mental devotion, Rebecca again took post at the lattice, sheltering herself, however, so as not to be visible from beneath.

"What dost thou see, Rebecca?" again demanded the wounded knight.

"Nothing but the cloud of arrows flying so thick as to dazzle mine eyes, and to hide the bowmen who shoot them."

"That cannot endure," said Ivanhoe; "if they press not right on to carry the castle by pure force of arms, the archery may avail but little against stone walls and bulwarks. Look for the Knight of the Fetterlock, fair Rebecca, and see how he bears himself; for as the leader is, so will his followers be."

"I see him not," said Rebecca.

"Foul craven!" exclaimed Ivanhoe; "does he blench from the helm when the wind blows highest?"

"He blenches not! he blenches not!" said Rebecca. "I see him now; he leads a body of men close under the outer barrier of the barbican. — They pull down the piles and palisades; they hew down the barriers with axes. — His high black plume floats abroad over the throng, like a raven over the field of the slain. — They have made a breach in the barriers — they rush in — they are thrust back! — Front-de-Bœuf heads the defenders; I see his gigantic form above the press. They throng again to the breach, and the pass is disputed hand to hand, and man to man. God of Jacob! it is the meeting of two fierce tides — the conflict of two oceans moved by adverse winds!"

She turned her head from the lattice, as if unable longer to endure a sight so terrible.

"Look forth again, Rebecca," said Ivanhoe, mistaking the cause of her retiring; "the archery must in some degree have ceased, since they are now fighting hand to hand. — Look again; there is now less danger."

Rebecca again looked forth, and almost immediately exclaimed, "Holy prophets of the law! Front-de-Bœuf and the Black Knight fight hand to hand on the breach, amid the roar of their followers, who watch the progress of the strife. — Heaven strike with the cause of the oppressed and of the captive!" She then uttered a loud shriek, and exclaimed, "He is down! — he is down!"

"Who is down?" cried Ivanhoe; "for our dear Lady's sake, tell me which has fallen?"

"The Black Knight," answered Rebecca, faintly; then instantly again shouted with joyful eagerness — "But no — but no! — the name of the Lord of Hosts be blessed! — he is on foot again, and fights as if there were twenty men's strength in his single arm — His sword is broken — he snatches an axe from a yeoman — he presses Front-de-Bœuf with blow on blow — The giant stoops and totters like an oak under the steel of the woodman — he falls — he falls!"

"Front-de-Bœuf?" exclaimed Ivanhoe.

"Front-de-Bœuf!" answered the Jewess; "his men rush to the rescue, headed by the haughty Templar — their united force compels the champion to pause — They drag Front-de-Bœuf within the walls."

"The assailants have won the barriers, have they not?" said Ivanhoe.

"They have — they have!" exclaimed Rebecca — "and they press the besieged hard upon the outer wall; some plant ladders, some swarm like bees, and endeavor to ascend upon the shoulders of each other — down go stones, beams, and trunks of trees upon their heads, and as fast as they bear the wounded to the rear, fresh men supply their places in the assault — Great God! hast thou given men thine own image, that it should be thus cruelly defaced by the hands of their brethren!"

"Think not of that," said Ivanhoe; "this is no time for such thoughts — Who yield? — who push their way?"

"The ladders are thrown down," replied Rebecca, shuddering; "the soldiers lie grovelling under them like crushed reptiles — The besieged have the better."

"Saint George strike for us!" exclaimed the knight; "do the false yeomen give way?"

"No!" exclaimed Rebecca, "they bear themselves right yeomanly — the Black Knight approaches the postern with his huge axe — the thundering blows which he deals, you may hear them above all the din and shouts of the battle — Stones and beams are hailed down on the bold champion — he regards them no more than if they were thistle-down or feathers!"

"By Saint John of Acre," said Ivanhoe, raising himself joyfully on his couch, "methought there was but one man in England that might do such a deed!"

"The postern gate shakes," continued Rebecca; "it crashes — it is splintered by his blows — they rush in — the outwork is won — O God! — they hurl the defenders from the battlements — they throw them into the moat — O men, if ye be indeed men, spare them that can resist no longer!"

"The bridge — the bridge which communicates with the castle — have they won that pass?" exclaimed Ivanhoe.

"No," replied Rebecca, "the Templar has destroyed the plank on which they crossed — few of the defenders escaped with him into the castle — the shrieks and cries which you hear tell the fate of the others — Alas! I see it is still more difficult to look upon victory than upon battle."

CHAPTER XX.

BYRON, MOORE, SHELLEY, KEATS, AND CAMPBELL.

LORD BYRON. 1788–1824. (Manual, pp. 396–404.)

FROM "CHILDE HAROLD."

264. THE EVE OF THE BATTLE OF WATERLOO.

There was a sound of revelry by night,
And Belgium's capital had gathered then
Her Beauty and her Chivalry, and bright
The lamps shone o'er fair women and brave men;
A thousand hearts beat happily; and when
Music arose with its voluptuous swell,
Soft eyes looked love to eyes which spake again,
And all went merry as a marriage bell;
But hush! hark! a deep sound strikes like a rising knell!

Did ye not hear it? — No; 'twas but the wind,
Or the car rattling o'er the stony street;
On with the dance! let joy be unconfined;
No sleep till morn, when Youth and Pleasure meet
To chase the glowing Hours with flying feet —
But hark! — that heavy sound breaks in once more,
As if the clouds its echo would repeat;
And nearer, clearer, deadlier than before!
Arm! Arm! it is — it is — the cannon's opening roar! [1]

Within a windowed niche of that high hall
Sate Brunswick's fated chieftain; he did hear
That sound the first amidst the festival,
And caught its tone with Death's prophetic ear;
And when they smiled because he deemed it near,
His heart more truly knew that peal too well
Which stretched his father on a bloody bier,
And roused the vengeance blood alone could quell;
He rushed into the field, and, foremost fighting, fell.[2]

[1] The sound of the cannon decided the Duke of Wellington to appear at the ball, where he remained till three o'clock in the morning, that he might calm, by his apparent indifference, the fears of his supporters in Brussels, and depress the hopes of the well-wishers to the French.

[2] The Duke of Brunswick was killed at Quatre Bras on the 16th of June. His father received the wounds, of which he afterwards died, at the battle of Jena, in 1806.

Ah! then and there was hurrying to and fro,
And gathering tears, and tremblings of distress,
And cheeks all pale, which but an hour ago
Blushed at the praise of their own loveliness;
And there were sudden partings, such as press
The life from out young hearts, and choking sighs
Which ne'er might be repeated; who could guess
If ever more should meet those mutual eyes,
Since upon night so sweet such awful morn could rise!

And there was mounting in hot haste: the steed,
The mustering squadron, and the clattering car,
Went pouring forward with impetuous speed,
And swiftly forming in the ranks of war;
And the deep thunder peal on peal afar;
And near, the beat of the alarming drum
Roused up the soldier ere the morning star;
While thronged the citizens with terror dumb,
Or whispering, with white lips — "The foe! They come! they come!"

---

265. Rome.

O Rome! my country! city of the soul!
The orphans of the heart must turn to thee,
Lone mother of dead empires! and control
In their shut breasts their petty misery.
What are our woes and sufferance? Come and see
The cypress, hear the owl, and plod your way
O'er steps of broken thrones and temples, ye,
Whose agonies are evils of a day —
A world is at our feet as fragile as our clay.

The Niobe of nations! there she stands,
Childless and crownless, in her voiceless woe;
An empty urn within her withered hands,
Whose holy dust was scattered long ago;
The Scipios' tomb contains no ashes now;
The very sepulchres lie tenantless
Of their heroic dwellers: dost thou flow,
Old Tiber! through a marble wilderness?
Rise, with thy yellow waves, and mantle her distress.

---

266. The Gladiator.

I see before me the Gladiator lie:
He leans upon his hand — his manly brow
Consents to death, but conquers agony,

And his drooped head sinks gradually low —
And through his side the last drops, ebbing slow
From the red gash, fall heavy, one by one,
Like the first of a thunder-shower; and now
The arena swims around him — he is gone,
Ere ceased the inhuman shout which hailed the wretch who won.

He heard it, but he heeded not — his eyes
Were with his heart, and that was far away;
He recked not of the life he lost nor prize,
But where his rude hut by the Danube lay,
There were his young barbarians all at play,
There was their Dacian mother — he, their sire,
Butchered to make a Roman holiday;
All this rushed with his blood — Shall he expire
And unavenged? — Arise! ye Goths, and glut your ire!

---

267. The Ocean.

There is a pleasure in the pathless woods,
There is a rapture on the lonely shore,
There is society, where none intrudes,
By the deep Sea, and music in its roar:
I love not Man the less, but Nature more,
From these our interviews, in which I steal
From all I may be, or have been before,
To mingle with the Universe, and feel
What I can ne'er express, yet cannot all conceal.

Roll on, thou deep and dark blue Ocean — roll!
Ten thousand fleets sweep over thee in vain;
Man marks the earth with ruin — his control
Stops with the shore; upon the watery plain
The wrecks are all thy deed, nor doth remain
A shadow of man's ravage, save his own,
When, for a moment, like a drop of rain,
He sinks into thy depths with bubbling groan,
Without a grave, unknelled, uncoffined, and unknown.

His steps are not upon thy paths, — thy fields
Are not a spoil for him, — thou dost arise
And shake him from thee; the vile strength he wields
For earth's destruction thou dost all despise,
Spurning him from thy bosom to the skies,
And send'st him, shivering in thy playful spray
And howling, to his Gods, where haply lies
His petty hope in some near port or bay,
And dashest him again to earth: — there let him lay.

The armaments which thunderstrike the walls
Of rock-built cities, bidding nations quake,
And monarchs tremble in their capitals,
The oak leviathans, whose huge ribs make
Their clay creator the vain title take
Of lord of thee, and arbiter of war, —
These are thy toys, and, as the snowy flake,
They melt into thy yeast of waves, which mar
Alike the Armada's pride or spoils of Trafalgar.

Thy shores are empires, changed in all save thee —
Assyria, Greece, Rome, Carthage, what are they?
Thy waters washed them power while they were free,
And many a tyrant since; their shores obey
The stranger, slave, or savage; their decay
Has dried up realms to deserts: — not so thou; —
Unchangeable, save to thy wild waves' play,
Time writes no wrinkle on thine azure brow;
Such as creation's dawn beheld, thou rollest now.

Thou glorious mirror, where the Almighty's form
Glasses itself in tempests; in all time, —
Calm or convulsed, in breeze or gale or storm,
Icing the pole, or in the torrid clime
Dark heaving — boundless, endless, and sublime,
The image of eternity, the throne
Of the Invisible; even from out thy slime
The monsters of the deep are made; each zone
Obeys thee; thou go'st forth, dread, fathomless, alone.

And I have loved thee, Ocean! and my joy
Of youthful sports was on thy breast to be
Borne, like thy bubbles, onward: from a boy
I wantoned with thy breakers — they to me
Were a delight; and if the freshening sea
Made them a terror — 'twas a pleasing fear,
For I was as it were a child of thee,
And trusted to thy billows far and near,
And laid my hand upon thy mane — as I do here.

FROM "THE GIAOUR."

268. MODERN GREECE.

Clime of the unforgotten brave!
Whose land from plain to mountain-cave
Was Freedom's home or Glory's grave!
Shrine of the mighty! can it be,
That this is all remains of thee?

Approach, thou craven crouching slave:
  Say, is not this Thermopylæ?
These waters blue that round you lave,
  O servile offspring of the free,
Pronounce what sea, what shore is this?
The gulf, the rock of Salamis!
These scenes, their story not unknown,
Arise, and make again your own;
Snatch from the ashes of your sires
The embers of their former fires;
And he who in the strife expires
Will add to theirs a name of fear
That Tyranny shall quake to hear,
And leave his sons a hope, a fame,
They too will rather die than shame:
For Freedom's battle once begun,
Bequeathed by bleeding Sire to Son,
Though baffled oft is ever won.
Bear witness, Greece, thy living page!
Attest it many a deathless age!
While kings, in dusty darkness hid,
Have left a nameless pyramid,
Thy heroes, though the general doom
Hath swept the column from their tomb,
A mightier monument command,
The mountains of their native land!
There points thy Muse to stranger's eye
The graves of those that cannot die!
'Twere long to tell, and sad to trace,
Each step from splendor to disgrace;
Enough — no foreign foe could quell
Thy soul, till from itself it fell;
Yes! Self-abasement paved the way
To villain-bonds and despot sway.

---

269. The Flight of the Giaour.

On — on he hastened, and he drew
My gaze of wonder as he flew:
Though like a demon of the night
He passed, and vanished from my sight,
His aspect and his air impressed
A troubled memory on my breast,
And long upon my startled ear
Rung his dark courser's hoofs of fear.
He spurs his steed; he nears the steep,
That, jutting, shadows o'er the deep;

He winds around; he hurries by:
The rock relieves him from mine eye;
For well I ween unwelcome he
Whose glance is fixed on those that flee;
And not a star but shines too bright
On him who takes such timeless flight.
He wound along; but ere he passed
One glance he snatched, as if his last,
A moment checked his wheeling steed,
A moment breathed him from his speed,
A moment on his stirrup stood —
Why looks he o'er the olive wood?

He stood — some dread was on his face,
Soon Hatred settled in its place:
It rose not with the reddening flush
Of transient Anger's hasty blush,
But pale as marble o'er the tomb,
Whose ghastly whiteness aids its gloom.
His brow was bent, his eye was glazed;
He raised his arm, and fiercely raised,
And sternly shook his hand on high,
As doubting to return or fly;
Impatient of his flight delayed,
Here loud his raven charger neighed —
Down glanced that hand, and grasped his blade;
That sound had burst his waking dream,
As Slumber starts at owlet's scream.
The spur hath lanced his courser's sides;
Away, away, for life he rides.
'Twas but an instant he restrained
That fiery barb so sternly reined;
'Twas but a moment that he stood,
Then sped as if by death pursued;
But in that instant o'er his soul
Winters of Memory seemed to roll,
And gather in that drop of time
A life of pain, an age of crime.
O'er him who loves, or hates, or fears,
Such moment pours the grief of years:
What felt *he* then, at once opprest
By all that most distracts the breast?
That pause, which pondered o'er his fate,
O, who its dreary length shall date!
Though in Time's record nearly nought,
It was Eternity to Thought!

From "The Bride of Abydos."

270. The Crime of the East.

Know ye the land where the cypress and myrtle
  Are emblems of deeds that are done in their clime?
Where the rage of the vulture, the love of the turtle,
  Now melt into sorrow, now madden to crime!
Know ye the land of the cedar and vine,
Where the flowers ever blossom, the beams ever shine;
Where the light wings of Zephyr, oppressed with perfume,
Wax faint o'er the gardens of Gúl[1] in her bloom;
Where the citron and olive are fairest of fruit,
And the voice of the nightingale never is mute:
Where the tints of the earth, and the hues of the sky,
In color though varied, in beauty may vie,
And the purple of ocean is deepest in dye;
Where the virgins are soft as the roses they twine,
And all, save the spirit of man, is divine?
'Tis the clime of the East; 'tis the land of the Sun —
Can he smile on such deeds as his children have done?
O! wild as the accents of lovers' farewell
Are the hearts which they bear, and the tales which they tell.

1 The Rose.

From "The Corsair."

271. A Ship in full Sail.

How gloriously her gallant course she goes!
Her white wings flying — never from her foes —
She walks the waters like a thing of life,
And seems to dare the elements to strife.
Who would not brave the battle-fire, the wreck,
To move the monarch of her peopled deck?

---

272. Remorse.

There is a war, a chaos of the mind,
When all its elements convulsed — combined —
Lie dark and jarring with perturbéd force,
And gnashing with impenitent Remorse;
That juggling fiend — who never spake before —
But cries, "I warned thee!" when the deed is o'er.
No single passion, and no ruling thought
That leaves the rest as once unseen, unsought;

But the wild prospect when the soul reviews —
All rushing through their thousand avenues.
Ambition's dreams expiring, love's regret,
Endangered glory, life itself beset;
The joy untasted, the contempt or hate
'Gainst those who fain would triumph in our fate;
The hopeless past, the hasting future driven
Too quickly on to guess if hell or heaven;
Deeds, thoughts, and words, perhaps remembered not
So keenly till that hour, but ne'er forgot;
Things light or lovely in their acted time,
But now to stern reflection each a crime;
The withering sense of evil unrevealed,
Not cankering less because the more concealed —
All, in a word, from which all eyes must start,
That opening sepulchre — the naked heart
Bares with its buried woes, till Pride awake,
To snatch the mirror from the soul — and break.

---

273. FROM "THE PRISONER OF CHILLON."

Lake Leman lies by Chillon's walls:
A thousand feet in depth below
Its massy waters meet and flow;
Thus much the fathom-line was sent
From Chillon's snow-white battlement,
Which round about the wave inthralls:
A double dungeon wall and wave
Have made — and like a living grave.
Below the surface of the lake
The dark vault lies wherein we lay,
We heard it ripple night and day;
Sounding o'er our heads it knocked;
And I have felt the winter's spray
Wash through the bars when winds were high
And wanton in the happy sky;
And then the very rock hath rocked,
And I have felt it shake, unshocked,
Because I could have smiled to see
The death that would have set me free.

FROM "MANFRED."

274. MANFRED'S SOLILOQUY ON THE JUNGFRAU.

My mother Earth!
And thou, fresh breaking Day, and you, ye Mountains,
Why are ye beautiful? I cannot love ye.

And thou, the bright eye of the universe,
That open'st over all, and unto all
Art a delight — thou shin'st not on my heart.
And you, ye crags, upon whose extreme edge
I stand, and on the torrent's brink beneath
Behold the tall pines dwindled as to shrubs
In dizziness of distance; when a leap,
A stir, a motion, even a breath, would bring
My breast upon its rocky bosom's bed
To rest forever — wherefore do I pause?
I feel the impulse — yet I do not plunge;
I see the peril — yet do not recede;
And my brain reels — and yet my foot is firm:
There is a power upon me which withholds,
And makes it my fatality to live;
If it be life to wear within myself
This barrenness of spirit, and to be
My own soul's sepulchre, for I have ceased
To justify my deeds unto myself —
The last infirmity of evil. Ay,
Thou wingéd and cloud-cleaving minister,
[*An eagle passes.*
Whose happy flight is highest into heaven,
Well mayst thou swoop so near me — I should be
Thy prey, and gorge thine eaglets; thou art gone
Where the eye cannot follow thee; but thine
Yet pierces downward, onward, or above,
With a pervading vision. — Beautiful!
How beautiful is all this visible world!
How glorious in its action and itself!
But we, who name ourselves its sovereigns, we,
Half dust, half deity, alike unfit
To sink or soar, with our mixed essence make
A conflict of its elements, and breathe
The breath of degradation and of pride,
Contending with low wants and lofty will,
Till our mortality predominates,
And men are — what they name not to themselves,
And trust not to each other. Hark! the note,
[*The Shepherd's pipe in the distance is heard.*
The natural music of the mountain reed —
For here the patriarchal days are not
A pastoral fable — pipes in the liberal air,
Mixed with the sweet bells of the sauntering herd;
My soul would drink those echoes. — O that I were
The viewless spirit of a lovely sound,
A living voice, a breathing harmony,
A bodiless enjoyment — born and dying
With the blest tone which made me!

275. THE COLISEUM.

The stars are forth, the moon above the tops
Of the snow-shining mountains. — Beautiful!
I linger yet with Nature, for the Night
Hath been to me a more familiar face
Than that of man; and in her starry shade
Of dim and solitary loveliness,
I learned the language of another world.
I do remember me, that in my youth,
When I was wandering — upon such a night
I stood within the Coliseum's wall,
'Midst the chief relics of almighty Rome;
The trees which grew along the broken arches
Waved dark in the blue midnight, and the stars
Shone through the rents of ruin; from afar
The watch-dog bayed beyond the Tiber; and
More near from out the Cæsars' palace came
The owl's long cry, and, interruptedly,
Of distant sentinels the fitful song
Begun and died upon the gentle wind.
Some cypresses beyond the time-worn breach
Appeared to skirt th' horizon, yet they stood
Within a bowshot. Where the Cæsars dwelt,
And dwell the tuneless birds of night, amidst
A grove which springs through levelled battlements,
And twines its roots with the imperial hearths,
Ivy usurps the laurel's place of growth;
But the gladiators' bloody Circus stands,
A noble wreck in ruinous perfection,
While Cæsar's chambers, and the Augustan halls,
Grovel on earth in indistinct decay.
And thou didst shine, thou rolling moon, upon
All this, and cast a wide and tender light,
Which softened down the hoar austerity
Of rugged desolation, and filled up,
As 'twere anew, the gaps of centuries;
Leaving that beautiful which still was so,
And making that which was not, till the place
Became religion, and the heart ran o'er
With silent worship of the great of old, —
The dead, but sceptred sovereigns, who still rule
Our spirits from their urns.

276. The Isles of Greece.

The isles of Greece, the isles of Greece!
  Where burning Sappho loved and sung,
Where grew the arts of war and peace,
  Where Delos rose, and Phœbus sprung!
Eternal summer gilds them yet,
But all, except their sun, is set.

The Scian and the Teian muse,
  The hero's harp, the lover's lute,
Have found the fame your shores refuse;
  Their place of birth alone is mute
To sounds which echo farther west
Than your sires' "Islands of the Blest."

The mountains look on Marathon —
  And Marathon looks on the sea;
And musing there an hour alone,
  I dreamed that Greece might still be free;
For standing on the Persians' grave,
I could not deem myself a slave.

A king sate on the rocky brow
  Which looks o'er sea-born Salamis;
And ships, by thousands, lay below,
  And men in nations; — all were his!
He counted them at break of day —
And when the sun set where were they?

And where are they? and where art thou,
  My country? On thy voiceless shore
The heroic lay is tuneless now —
  The heroic bosom beats no more!
And must thy lyre, so long divine,
Degenerate into hands like mine?

'Tis something, in the dearth of fame,
  Though linked among a fettered race,
To feel at least a patriot's shame,
  Even as I sing, suffuse my face;
For what is left the poet here?
For Greeks a blush — for Greece a tear.

Must *we* but weep o'er days more blest?
  Must *we* but blush? — Our fathers bled.
Earth! render back from out thy breast
  A remnant of our Spartan dead!
Of the three hundred grant but three,
To make a new Thermopylæ!

What, silent still? and silent all?
  Ah! no; — the voices of the dead
Sound like a distant torrent's fall,
  And answer, "Let one living head,
But one arise, — we come, we come!"
'Tis but the living who are dumb.

In vain — in vain; strike other chords;
  Fill high the cup with Samian wine!
Leave battles to the Turkish hordes,
  And shed the blood of Scio's vine!
Hark! rising to the ignoble call —
How answers each bold Bacchanal!

You have the Pyrrhic dance as yet,
  Where is the Pyrrhic phalanx gone?
Of two such lessons, why forget
  The nobler and the manlier one?
You have the letters Cadmus gave —
Think ye he meant them for a slave?
* * * * * *
Trust not for freedom to the Franks —
  They have a king who buys and sells:
In native swords, and native ranks,
  The only hope of courage dwells:
But Turkish force, and Latin fraud,
Would break your shield, however broad.

---

277. Armenia.

On my arrival at Venice, in the year 1816, I found my mind in a state which required study, and study of a nature which should leave little scope for the imagination, and furnish some difficulty in the pursuit.

At this period I was much struck — in common, I believe, with every other traveller — with the society of the Convent of St. Lazarus, which appears to unite all the advantages of the monastic institution, without any of its vices.

The neatness, the comfort, the gentleness, the unaffected devotion, the accomplishments, and the virtues of the brethren of the order, are well fitted to strike the man of the world with the conviction that "there is another and a better" even in this life.

These men are the priesthood of an oppressed and a noble nation, which has partaken of the proscription and bondage of the Jews and of the Greeks, without the sullenness of the former or the servility of the latter. This people has attained riches without usury, and all the honors that can be awarded to slavery without intrigue. But they have long occupied, nevertheless, a part of the "House of Bondage," who has lately multiplied her many mansions. It would be difficult, perhaps, to find the annals of a nation less stained with crimes than those of the Armenians, whose virtues have been those of peace, and their vices those of compulsion. But whatever may have been their destiny — and it has been bitter — whatever it may be in future, their country must ever be one of the most interesting on the globe; and perhaps their language only requires to be more studied to become more attractive. If the Scriptures are rightly understood, it was in Armenia that Paradise was placed — Armenia, which has paid as dearly as the descendants of Adam for that fleeting participation of its soil in the happiness of him who was created from its dust. It was in Armenia that the flood first abated, and the dove alighted. But with the disappearance of Paradise itself may be dated almost the unhappiness of the country; for though long a powerful kingdom, it was scarcely ever an independent one, and the satraps of Persia and the pachas of Turkey have alike desolated the region where God created man in his own image.

THOMAS MOORE. 1779–1852. (Manual, pp. 404–411.)

FROM "LALLA ROOKH."

278. PARADISE AND THE PERI.

One morn a Peri at the gate
Of Eden stood, disconsolate;
And as she listened to the Springs
Of Life within, like music flowing,
And caught the light upon her wings
Through the half-open portal glowing,
She wept to think her recreant race
Should e'er have lost that glorious place!
"How happy," exclaimed this child of air,
"Are the holy Spirits who wander there,
'Mid flowers that never shall fade or fall;
Though mine are the gardens of earth and sea,
And the stars themselves have flowers for me,
One blossom of Heaven outblooms them all!
Though sunny the Lake of cool Cashmere,
With its plane-tree isle reflected clear,
And sweetly the founts of that Valley fall;
Though bright are the waters of Sing-su-hay,
And the golden floods that thitherward stray,
Yet — O! 'tis only the Blest can say
How the waters of Heaven outshine them all!

"Go, wing thy flight from star to star,
From world to luminous world, as far
As the universe spreads its flaming wall:
Take all the pleasures of all the spheres,
And multiply each through endless years,
One minute of Heaven is worth them all!"
The glorious Angel, who was keeping
The gates of Light, beheld her weeping!
And, as he nearer drew and listened
To her sad song, a tear-drop glistened
Within his eyelids, like the spray
From Eden's fountain, when it lies
On the blue flower, which — Bramins say —
Blooms nowhere but in Paradise!
"Nymph of a fair but erring line!"
Gently he said — "One hope is thine,
'Tis written in the Book of Fate,
The Peri yet may be forgiven
Who brings to this Eternal gate
The Gift that is most dear to Heaven!
Go seek it, and redeem thy sin —
'Tis sweet to let the Pardoned in!"

* * * * * *

Cheered by this hope she bends her thither; —
Still laughs the radiant eye of Heaven,
Nor have the golden bowers of Even
In the rich West begun to wither; —
When, o'er the vale of Balbec winging
Slowly, she sees a child at play,
Among the rosy wild-flowers singing,
As rosy and as wild as they;
Chasing, with eager hands and eyes,
The beautiful blue damsel-flies,
That fluttered round the jasmine stems,
Like wingéd flowers or flying gems: —
And, near the boy, who tired with play,
Now nestling 'mid the roses lay,
She saw a wearied man dismount
From his hot steed, and on the brink
Of a small imaret's rustic fount
Impatient fling him down to drink.
Then swift his haggard brow he turned
To the fair child, who fearless sat,
Though never yet hath day-beam burned
Upon a brow more fierce than that, —
Sullenly fierce — a mixture dire,
Like thunder-clouds, of gloom and fire!

In which the Peri's eye could read
Dark tales of many a ruthless deed;
The ruined maid — the shrine profaned —
Oaths broken — and the threshold stained
With blood of guests! — *there* written, all,
Black as the damning drops that fall
From the denouncing Angel's pen,
Ere Mercy weeps them out again!

Yet tranquil now that man of crime,
(As if the balmy evening time
Softened his spirit) looked and lay,
Watching the rosy infant's play; —
Though still, whene'er his eye by chance
Fell on the boy's, its lurid glance
  Met that unclouded, joyous gaze,
As torches, that have burnt all night
Through some impure and godless rite,
  Encounter morning's glorious rays.

But hark! the vesper call to prayer,
  As slow the orb of daylight sets,
Is rising sweetly on the air,
  From Syria's thousand minarets!
The boy has started from the bed
Of flowers, where he had laid his head,
And down upon the fragrant sod
  Kneels, with his forehead to the south
Lisping the eternal name of God
  From purity's own cherub mouth,
And looking, while his hands and eyes
Are lifted to the glowing skies,
Like a stray babe of Paradise,
Just lighted on that flowery plain,
And seeking for its home again!
O, 'twas a sight — that Heaven — that Child —
A scene, which might have well beguiled
E'en haughty Eblis of a sigh
For glories lost and peace gone by!

And how felt *he*, the wretched Man
Reclining there — while memory ran
O'er many a year of guilt and strife,
Flew o'er the dark flood of his life,
Nor found one sunny resting-place,
Nor brought him back one branch of grace!
"There *was* a time," he said, in mild,
Heart-humbled tones — "thou blessèd child!

When young and haply pure as thou,
I looked and prayed like thee — but now" —
He hung his head — each nobler aim
  And hope and feeling, which had slept
From boyhood's hour, that instant came
  Fresh o'er him, and he wept — he wept!

Blest tears of soul-felt penitence!
  In whose benign, redeeming flow
Is felt the first, the only sense
  Of guiltless joy that guilt can know.
"There's a drop," said the Peri, "that down from the moon
Falls through the withering airs of June
Upon Egypt's land, of so healing a power,
So balmy a virtue, that e'en in the hour
That drop descends, contagion dies,
And health reanimates earth and skies! —
O, is it not thus, thou man of sin,
  The precious tears of repentance fall?
Though foul thy fiery plagues within,
  One heavenly drop hath dispelled them all!"
And now — behold him kneeling there
By the child's side, in humble prayer,
While the same sunbeam shines upon
The guilty and the guiltless one,
And hymns of joy proclaim through Heaven
The Triumph of a soul Forgiven!

'Twas when the golden orb had set,
While on their knees they lingered yet,
There fell a light, more lovely far
Than ever came from sun or star,
Upon the tear that, warm and meek,
Dewed that repentant sinner's cheek:
To mortal eye this light might seem
A northern flash or meteor beam —
But well the enraptured Peri knew
'Twas a bright smile the Angel threw
From Heaven's gate, to hail that tear
Her harbinger of glory near!

"Joy, joy forever! my task is done —
The Gates are passed, and Heaven is won!
O! am I not happy? I am, I am —
  To thee, sweet Eden! how dark and sad
Are the diamond turrets of Shadukiam,
  And the fragrant bowers of Amberabad!

"Farewell, ye odors of Earth, that die,
Passing away like a lover's sigh;

My feast is now of the Tooba Tree,
Whose scent is the breath of Eternity!

"Farewell, ye vanishing flowers, that shone
In my fairy wreath, so bright and brief, —
O! what are the brightest that e'er have blown,
To the lote-tree, springing by Alla's Throne,
Whose flowers have a soul in every leaf!
Joy, joy forever! my task is done —
The Gates are passed, and Heaven is won!"

---

279. 'Tis the Last Rose of Summer.

'Tis the last rose of summer
Left blooming alone;
All her lovely companions
Are faded and gone;
No flower of her kindred,
No rose-bud, is nigh,
To reflect back her blushes,
Or give sigh for sigh.

I'll not leave thee, thou lone one!
To pine on the stem;
Since the lovely are sleeping,
Go, sleep thou with them.
Thus kindly I scatter
Thy leaves o'er the bed,
Where thy mates of the garden
Lie scentless and dead.

So soon may I follow,
When friendships decay,
And from Love's shining circle
The gems drop away!
When true hearts lie withered,
And fond ones are flown,
O! who would inhabit
This bleak world alone?

---

280. Forget not the Field.

Forget not the field where they perished,
The truest, the last of the brave,
All gone — and the bright hope we cherished
Gone with them, and quenched in their grave!

O, could we from death but recover
  Those hearts as they bounded before,
In the face of high Heaven to fight over
  That combat for freedom once more; —

Could the chain for an instant be riven
  Which Tyranny flung round us then,
No, 'tis not in Man, nor in Heaven,
  To let Tyranny bind it again!

But 'tis past — and, though blazoned in story
  The name of our victor may be,
Accurst is the march of that glory
  Which treads o'er the hearts of the free.

Far dearer the grave or the prison,
  Illumed by one patriot name,
Than the trophies of all, who have risen
  On Liberty's ruins to fame.

---

281. THOSE EVENING BELLS.

Those evening bells! those evening bells!
How many a tale their music tells,
Of youth, and home, and that sweet time
When last I heard their soothing chime!

Those joyous hours are past away!
And many a heart, that then was gay,
Within the tomb now darkly dwells,
And hears no more those evening bells!

And so 'twill be when I am gone;
That tuneful peal will still ring on,
While other bards shall walk these dells,
And sing your praise, sweet evening bells!

---

282. THE TURF SHALL BE MY FRAGRANT SHRINE.

The turf shall be my fragrant shrine;
My temple, Lord! that arch of thine;
My censer's breath the mountain airs,
And silent thoughts my only prayers.

My choir shall be the moonlight waves,
When murmuring homeward to their caves,
Or when the stillness of the sea,
E'en more than music, breathes of Thee!

I'll seek, by day, some glade unknown,
All light and silence, like thy Throne!
And the pale stars shall be, at night,
The only eyes that watch my rite.

Thy Heaven, on which 'tis bliss to look,
Shall be my pure and shining book,
Where I shall read, in words of flame,
The glories of thy wondrous name.

I'll read thy anger in the rack
That clouds awhile the day-beam's track;
Thy mercy in the azure hue
Of sunny brightness breaking through!

There's nothing bright, above, below,
From flowers that bloom to stars that glow,
But in its light my soul can see
Some feature of thy Deity!

There's nothing dark, below, above,
But in its gloom I trace thy Love,
And meekly wait that moment, when
Thy touch shall turn all bright again!

PERCY BYSSHE SHELLEY. 1792–1821. (Manual, pp. 411–415.)

283. FROM "ODE TO A SKYLARK."

Hail to thee, blithe spirit!
  Bird thou never wert,
That from heaven, or near it,
  Pourest thy full heart
In profuse strains of unpremeditated art.

Higher still and higher,
  From the earth thou springest
Like a cloud of fire;
  The blue deep thou wingest,
And singing still dost soar, and soaring ever, singest.

In the golden lightning
  Of the sunken sun,
O'er which clouds are bright'ning,
  Thou dost float and run,
Like an unbodied joy whose race is just begun.

The pale purple even
  Melts around thy flight;
Like a star of heaven,
  In the broad daylight
Thou art unseen, but yet I hear thy shrill delight.

Keen are the arrows
  Of that silver sphere,
Whose intense lamp narrows
  In the white dawn clear,
Until we hardly see, we feel that it is there.

All the earth and air
  With thy voice is loud,
As, when night is bare,
  From one lonely cloud
The moon rains out her beams, and heaven is overflowed.

What thou art we know not;
  What is most like thee?
From rainbow clouds there flow not
  Drops so bright to see,
As from thy presence showers a rain of melody.

Like a poet hidden
  In the light of thought,
Singing hymns unbidden,
  Till the world is wrought
To sympathy with hopes and fears it heeded not.
* * * * * *

---

284. RETURNING SPRING.

Ah, woe is me! Winter is come and gone,
But grief returns with the revolving year;
The airs and streams renew their joyous tone;
The ants, the bees, the swallows, reappear;
Fresh leaves and flowers deck the dead season's bier.
The loving birds now pair in every brake,
And build their mossy homes in field and brere;
And the green lizard, and the golden snake,
Like unimprisoned flames, out of their trance awake.

Through wood and stream and field and hill and ocean,
A quickening life from the earth's heart has burst,
As it has ever done, with change and motion,
From the great morning of the world when first

God dawned on chaos; in its stream immersed,
The lamps of heaven flash with a softer light;
All baser things pant with life's sacred thirst,
Diffuse themselves; and spend in love's delight
The beauty and the joy of their renewéd might.

---

285. The Plain of Lombardy.

Beneath is spread, like a green sea,
The waveless plain of Lombardy,
Bounded by the vaporous air,
Islanded by cities fair;
Underneath day's azure eyes,
Ocean's nursling, Venice, lies, —
A peopled labyrinth of walls,
Amphitrite's destined halls,
Which her hoary sire now paves
With his blue and beaming waves.
Lo! the sun upsprings behind,
Broad, red, radiant, half-reclined
On the level quivering line
Of the waters crystalline;
And before that chasm of light,
As within a furnace bright,
Column, tower, and dome, and spire,
Shine like obelisks of fire,
Pointing with inconstant motion
From the altar of dark ocean
To the sapphire-tinted skies:
As the flames of sacrifice
From the marble shrines did rise,
As to pierce the dome of gold
Where Apollo spoke of old.
Sun-girt City! thou hast been
Ocean's child, and then his queen.
* * * * * * *
Noon descends around me now;
'Tis the noon of autumn's glow,
When a soft and purple mist,
Like a vaporous amethyst,
Or an air-dissolvéd star,
Mingling light and fragrance, far
From the curved horizon's bound
To the point of heaven's profound,
Fills the overflowing sky;
And the plains that silent lie

Underneath; the leaves unsodden,
Where the infant frost has trodden
With his morning-wingéd feet,
Whose bright print is gleaming yet;
And the red and golden vines,
Piercing with their trellised lines
The rough dark skirted wilderness;
The dim and bladed grass, no less,
Pointing from this hoary tower
In the windless air; the flower
Glimmering at my feet; the line
Of the olive-sandalled Apennine,
In the south dimly islanded;
And the Alps, whose snows are spread
High between the clouds and sun;
And of living things each one;
And my spirit, which so long
Darkened this swift stream of song,
Interpenetrated lie
By the glory of the sky;
Be it love, light, harmony,
Odor, or the soul of all,
Which from heaven like dew doth fall,
Or the mind which feeds this verse
Peopling the lone universe.

JOHN KEATS. 1796–1821. (Manual, p. 415.)

286. FROM "ODE TO AUTUMN."

Who hath not seen thee oft amid thy store?
  Sometimes whoever seeks abroad may find
Thee sitting careless on a granary floor,
  Thy hair soft-lifted by the winnowing wind;
Or on a half-reaped furrow sound asleep,
  Drowsed with the fume of poppies, while thy hook
    Spares the next swath and all its twinéd flowers:
And sometimes like a gleaner thou dost keep
  Steady thy laden head across a brook;
  Or by a cider-press, with patient look,
    Thou watchest the last oozings, hours by hours.

Where are the songs of Spring? Ay, where are they?
  Think not of them, thou hast thy music too, —
While barréd clouds bloom the soft dying day,
  And touch the stubble-plains with rosy hue;

Then in a wailful choir the small gnats mourn
  Among the river shallows, borne aloft,
    Or sinking, as the light wind lives or dies;
And full-grown lambs loud bleat from hilly bourn;
  Hedge-crickets sing; and now, with treble soft,
  The redbreast whistles from a garden-croft;
    And gathering swallows twitter in the skies.

---

287. From "Hyperion."

There is a roaring in the bleak-grown pines
When Winter lifts his voice; there is a noise
Among immortals when a God gives sign,
With hushing finger, how he means to load
His tongue with the full weight of utterless thought,
With thunder, and with music, and with pomp:
Such noise is like the roar of bleak-grown pines;
Which, when it ceases in this mountained world,
No other sound succeeds; but ceasing here,
Among these fallen, Saturn's voice therefrom
Grew up like organ, that begins anew
Its strain, when other harmonies, stopped short,
Leave the dinned air vibrating silverly.
Thus grew it up — "Not in my own sad breast,
Which is its own great judge and searcher out,
Can I find reason why ye should be thus:
Not in the legends of the first of days,
Studied from that old spirit-leaved book
Which starry Uranus with finger bright
Saved from the shores of darkness, when the waves
Low-ebbed still hid it up in shallow gloom; —
And the which book ye know I ever kept
For my firm-based footstool: — Ah, infirm!
Not there, nor in sign, symbol, or portent
Of element, earth, water, air, and fire, —
At war, at peace, or inter-quarrelling
One against one, or two, or three, or all
Each several one against the other three,
As fire with air loud warring when rain-floods
Drown both, and press them both against earth's face,
Where, finding sulphur, a quadruple wrath
Unhinges the poor world: — not in that strife,
Wherefrom I take strange lore, and read it deep,
Can I find reason why ye should be thus:
No, nowhere can unriddle, though I search,
And pore on Nature's universal scroll
Even to swooning, why ye, Divinities,

The first-born of all shaped and palpable Gods,
Should cower beneath what, in comparison,
Is untremendous might. Yet ye are here,
O'erwhelmed, and spurned, and battered, ye are here!
O Titans, shall I say 'Arise!' — Ye groan:
Shall I say 'Crouch!' — Ye groan. What can I then?
O Heaven wide! O unseen parent dear!
What can I? Tell me, all ye brethren Gods,
How we can war, how engine our great wrath!
O, speak your counsel now, for Saturn's ear
Is all a-hungered. Thou, Oceanus,
Ponderest high and deep; and in thy face
I see, astonied, that severe content
Which comes of thought and musing: give us help!"

288. ODE ON A GRECIAN URN.

Thou still unravished bride of quietness,
  Thou foster-child of silence and slow time,
Sylvan historian, who canst thus express
  A flowery tale more sweetly than our rhyme:
What leaf-fringed legend haunts about thy shape
  Of deities or mortals, or of both,
    In Tempe or the dales of Arcady?
  What men or gods are these? What maidens loath?
What mad pursuit? What struggle to escape?
    What pipes and timbrels? What wild ecstasy?

Heard melodies are sweet, but those unheard
  Are sweeter; therefore, ye soft pipes, play on;
Not to the sensual ear, but, more endeared,
  Pipe to the spirit ditties of no tone;
Fair youth, beneath the trees, thou canst not leave
  Thy song, nor ever can those trees be bare;
    Bold Lover, never, never canst thou kiss,
Though winning near the goal — yet, do not grieve;
  She cannot fade, though thou hast not thy bliss,
    Forever wilt thou love, and she be fair!

Ah, happy, happy boughs! that cannot shed
  Your leaves, nor ever bid the Spring adieu;
And, happy melodist, unwearied,
  Forever piping songs forever new;
More happy love! more happy, happy love!
  Forever warm and still to be enjoyed,
    Forever panting, and forever young;
All breathing human passion far above,
  That leaves a heart high-sorrowful and cloyed,
    A burning forehead, and a parching tongue.

FROM "ENDYMION."

289. MOONLIGHT.

Eterne Apollo! that thy sister fair
Is of all these the gentlier-mightiest.
When thy gold breath is misting in the west,
She unobservéd steals unto her throne,
And there she sits most meek and most alone;
As if she had not pomp subservient;
As if thine eye, high Poet! was not bent
Towards her with the muses in thine heart;
As if the ministering stars kept not apart,
Waiting for silver-footed messages.
O Moon! the oldest shades 'mong oldest trees
Feel palpitations when thou lookest in:
O Moon! old boughs lisp forth a holier din
The while they feel thine airy fellowship.
Thou dost bless everywhere, with silver lip
Kissing dead things to life. The sleeping kine,
Couched in thy brightness, dream of fields divine:
Innumerable mountains rise, and rise,
Ambitious for the hallowing of thine eyes;
And yet thy benediction passeth not
One obscure hiding-place, one little spot
Where pleasure may be sent: the nested wren
Has thy fair face within its tranquil ken,
And from beneath a sheltering ivy leaf
Takes glimpses of thee; thou art a relief
To the poor patient oyster, where it sleeps
Within its pearly house. — The mighty deeps,
The monstrous sea is thine — the myriad sea!
O Moon! far spooming ocean bows to thee,
And Tellus feels her forehead's cumbrous load.

THOMAS CAMPBELL. 1777–1844. (Manual, p. 416.)

FROM "THE PLEASURES OF HOPE."

290. HOPE BEYOND THE GRAVE.

Unfading HOPE! when life's last embers burn,
When soul to soul, and dust to dust return!
Heaven to thy charge resigns the awful hour!
O, then, thy kingdom comes! Immortal Power!
What though each spark of earth-born rapture fly
The quivering lip, pale cheek, and closing eye!

Bright to the soul thy seraph hands convey
The morning dream of life's eternal day —
Then, then, the triumph and the trance begin,
And all the phœnix spirit burns within!

O, deep-enchanting prelude to repose,
The dawn of bliss, the twilight of our woes!
Yet half I hear the panting spirit sigh,
It is a dread and awful thing to die!
Mysterious worlds, untravelled by the sun,
Where Time's far wandering tide has never run,
From your unfathomed shades and viewless spheres
A warning comes, unheard by other ears.
'Tis Heaven's commanding trumpet, long and loud,
Like Sinai's thunder, pealing from the cloud!
While Nature hears, with terror-mingled trust,
The shock that hurls her fabric to the dust;
And, like the trembling Hebrew, when he trod
The roaring waves, and called upon his God,
With mortal terrors clouds immortal bliss,
And shrieks and hovers o'er the dark abyss!

Daughter of Faith! awake, arise, illume
The dread unknown, the chaos of the tomb;
Melt and dispel, ye spectre-doubts, that roll
Cimmerian darkness o'er the parting soul!
Fly, like the moon-eyed herald of Dismay,
Chased on his night-steed by the star of day!
The strife is o'er — the pangs of Nature close,
And life's last rapture triumphs o'er her woes.
Hark! as the spirit eyes, with eagle gaze,
The noon of Heaven undazzled by the blaze;
On heavenly winds that waft her to the sky,
Float the sweet tones of star-born melody;
Wild as that hallowed anthem sent to hail
Bethlehem's shepherds in the lonely vale,
When Jordan hushed his waves, and midnight still
Watched on the holy towers of Zion hill!

---

291. The Soldier's Dream.

Our bugles sang truce — for the night-cloud had lowered,
  And the sentinel stars set their watch in the sky:
And thousands had sunk on the ground overpowered,
  The weary to sleep, and the wounded to die.

When reposing that night on my pallet of straw,
  By the wolf-scaring fagot that guarded the slain,

At the dead of the night a sweet vision I saw,
And thrice ere the morning I dreamt it again.

Methought from the battle-field's dreadful array,
Far, far I had roamed on a desolate track;
'Twas Autumn — and sunshine arose on the way
To the home of my fathers, that welcomed me back.

I flew to the pleasant fields traversed so oft
In life's morning march, when my bosom was young;
I heard my own mountain-goats bleating aloft,
And knew the sweet strain that the corn-reapers sung.

Then pledged we the wine-cup, and fondly I swore
From my home and my weeping friends never to part;
My little ones kissed me a thousand times o'er,
And my wife sobbed aloud in her fulness of heart.

Stay, stay with us — rest, thou art weary and worn;
And fain was their war-broken soldier to stay:
But sorrow returned with the dawning of morn,
And the voice in my dreaming ear melted away.

---

292. Ye Mariners of England:

A Naval Ode.

Ye Mariners of England!
That guard our native seas;
Whose flag has braved, a thousand years,
The battle and the breeze!
Your glorious standard launch again
To match another foe!
And sweep through the deep,
While the stormy tempests blow;
While the battle rages loud and long,
And the stormy tempests blow.

The spirits of your fathers
Shall start from every wave! —
For the deck it was their field of fame,
And Ocean was their grave:
Where Blake and mighty Nelson fell,
Your manly hearts shall glow,
As ye sweep through the deep,
While the stormy tempests blow;
While the battle rages loud and long,
And the stormy tempests blow.

Britannia needs no bulwark,
No towers along the steep;
Her march is o'er the mountain waves,
Her home is on the deep.
With thunders from her native oak,
She quells the floods below, —
As they roar on the shore,
When the stormy tempests blow:
When the battle rages loud and long,
And the stormy tempests blow.

The meteor flag of England
Shall yet terrific burn;
Till danger's troubled night depart,
And the star of peace return.
Then, then, ye ocean-warriors!
Our song and feast shall flow
To the fame of your name,
When the storm has ceased to blow;
When the fiery fight is heard no more,
And the storm has ceased to blow.

---

293. HOHENLINDEN.

On Linden, when the sun was low,
All bloodless lay th' untrodden snow,
And dark as winter was the flow
Of Iser, rolling rapidly.

But Linden saw another sight,
When the drum beat, at dead of night,
Commanding fires of death to light
The darkness of her scenery.

By torch and trumpet fast arrayed,
Each horseman drew his battle-blade,
And furious every charger neighed,
To join the dreadful revelry.

Then shook the hills with thunder riven,
Then rushed the steed to battle driven,
And louder than the bolts of heaven,
Far flashed the red artillery.

But redder yet that light shall glow
On Linden's hills of stainéd snow,
And bloodier yet the torrent flow
Of Iser, rolling rapidly.

'Tis morn, but scarce yon level sun
Can pierce the war-clouds, rolling dun,
Where furious Frank and fiery Hun
Shout in their sulph'rous canopy.

The combat deepens. On, ye brave,
Who rush to glory, or the grave!
Wave, Munich! all thy banners wave,
And charge with all thy chivalry!

Few, few, shall part where many meet!
The snow shall be their winding-sheet,
And every turf beneath their feet
Shall be a soldier's sepulchre.

CHAPTER XXI.

WORDSWORTH, COLERIDGE, SOUTHEY, AND OTHER MODERN POETS.

William Wordsworth. 1770–1850. (Manual, pp. 420–424.)

From "The Excursion."

294. The Greek Mythology.

In that fair clime, the lonely herdsman, stretched
On the soft grass, through half a summer's day,
With music lulled his indolent repose:
And, in some fit of weariness, if he,
When his own breath was silent, chanced to hear
A distant strain, far sweeter than the sounds
Which his poor skill could make, his fancy fetched,
Even from the blazing chariot of the sun,
A beardless youth,[1] who touched a golden lute,
And filled th' illumined groves with ravishment.
The nightly hunter, lifting up his eyes
Towards the crescent moon, with grateful heart
Called on the lovely wanderer who bestowed
That timely light, to share his joyous sport:
And hence, a beaming goddess[2] with her nymphs,
Across the lawn and through the darksome grove
(Not unaccompanied with tuneful notes,
By echo multiplied from rock or cave),
Swept in the storm of chase, as moon and stars
Glance rapidly along the clouded heaven,
When winds are blowing strong. The traveller slaked
His thirst from rill or gushing fount, and thanked
The Naiad.[3] — Sunbeams, upon distant hills
Gliding apace, with shadows in their train,
Might, with small help from fancy, be transformed
Into fleet Oreads sporting visibly.
The Zephyrs, fanning, as they passed, their wings,
Lacked not, for love, fair objects, whom they wooed
With gentle whisper. Withered boughs grotesque,

1 Phœbus Apollo. 2 Diana.
3 *Naiads*, the nymphs of the springs; *Oreads*, those of the mountains.

Stripped of their leaves and twigs by hoary age,
From depth of shaggy covert peeping forth,
In the low vale, or on steep mountain-side;
And sometimes intermixed with stirring horns
Of the live deer, or goat's depending beard, —
These were the lurking Satyrs, a wild brood
Of gamesome deities; or Pan himself,
The simple shepherd's awe-inspiring god!

---

295. Tintern Abbey.[1]

Five years have passed; five summers with the length
Of five long winters; and again I hear
These waters, rolling from their mountain springs
With a sweet inland murmur. Once again
Do I behold these steep and lofty cliffs,
Which on a wild secluded scene impress
Thoughts of more deep seclusion, and connect
The landscape with the quiet of the sky.
The day is come when I again repose
Here, under this dark sycamore, and view
These plots of cottage ground, these orchard tufts,
Which, at this season, with their unripe fruits,
Are clad in one green hue, and lose themselves
Among the woods and copses, nor disturb
The wild green landscape. Once again I see
These hedgerows, hardly hedgerows, little lines
Of sportive wood run wild; these pastoral farms
Green to the very door; and wreaths of smoke
Sent up in silence from among the trees,
With some uncertain notice, as might seem,
Of vagrant dwellers in the houseless woods,
Or of some hermit's cave, where, by his fire,
The hermit sits alone.
Though absent long,
These forms of beauty have not been to me
As is a landscape to a blind man's eye:
But oft, in lonely rooms, and 'mid the din
Of towns and cities, I have owed to them,
In hours of weariness, sensations sweet,
Felt in the blood, and felt along the heart,
And passing even into my purer mind

[1] This abbey was founded by the Cistercian monks, in 1131. It is now a celebrated ruin, on the west bank of the River Wye, which forms the boundary between the counties of Monmouth and Gloucester, England. It is about five miles above the junction of the Wye and Severn, and eighteen miles north of Bristol.

With tranquil restoration — feelings, too,
Of unremembered pleasure; such, perhaps,
As may have had no trivial influence
On that best portion of a good man's life,
His little, nameless, unremembered acts
Of kindness and of love. Nor less, I trust,
To them I may have owed another gift,
Of aspect more sublime; that blessed mood
In which the burden of the mystery,
In which the heavy and the weary weight
Of all this unintelligible world
Is lightened; that serene and blessed mood
In which the affections gently lead us on,
Until the breath of this corporeal frame,
And even the motion of our human blood
Almost suspended, we are laid asleep
In body, and become a living soul;
While with an eye made quiet by the power
Of harmony and the deep power of joy,
We see into the life of things.

* * * * * * *

For I have learned
To look on nature, not as in the hour
Of thoughtless youth, but hearing oftentimes
The still sad music of humanity,
Nor harsh, nor grating, though of ample power
To chasten and subdue. And I have felt
A presence that disturbs me with the joy
Of elevated thoughts; a sense sublime
Of something far more deeply interfused,
Whose dwelling is the light of setting suns,
And the round ocean, and the living air,
And the blue sky, and in the mind of man;
A motion and a spirit that impels
All thinking things, all objects of all thought,
And rolls through all things. Therefore am I still
A lover of the meadows and the woods
And mountains, and of all that we behold
From this green earth: of all the mighty world
Of eye and ear, both what they half create
And what perceive; well pleased to recognize
In nature, and the language of the sense,
The anchor of my purest thoughts, the nurse,
The guide, the guardian of my heart, and soul
Of all my moral being.

Nor, perchance,
If I were not thus taught, should I the more
Suffer my genial spirits to decay:

For thou art with me here, upon the banks
Of this fair river; thou, my dearest friend,
My dear, dear friend, and in thy voice I catch
The language of my former heart, and read
My former pleasures in the shooting lights
Of thy wild eyes. O! yet a little while
May I behold in thee what I was once,
My dear, dear sister! And this prayer I make,
Knowing that nature never did betray
The heart that loved her; 'tis her privilege,
Through all the years of this our life to lead,
From joy to joy; for she can so inform
The mind that is within us, so impress
With quietness and beauty, and so feed
With lofty thoughts, that neither evil tongues,
Rash judgments, nor the sneers of selfish men,
Nor greetings where no kindness is, nor all
The dreary intercourse of daily life,
Shall e'er prevail against us, or disturb
Our cheerful faith that all which we behold
Is full of blessings. Therefore let the moon
Shine on thee in thy solitary walk!
And let the misty mountain winds be free
To blow against thee; and in after years,
When these wild ecstasies shall be matured
Into a sober pleasure, when thy mind
Shall be a mansion for all lovely forms,
Thy memory be as a dwelling-place
For all sweet sounds and harmonies; O! then,
If solitude, or fear, or pain, or grief,
Should be thy portion, with what healing thoughts
Of tender joy wilt thou remember me,
And these my exhortations! Nor, perchance,
If I should be where I no more can hear
Thy voice, nor catch from thy wild eyes these gleams
Of past existence, wilt thou then forget
That on the banks of this delightful stream
We stood together; and that I, so long
A worshipper of nature, hither came,
Unwearied in that service; rather say
With warmer love, O! with far deeper zeal
Of holier love. Nor wilt thou then forget,
That after many wanderings, many years
Of absence, these steep woods and lofty cliffs,
And this green pastoral landscape, were to me
More dear, both for themselves and for thy sake.

296. To a Skylark.

Up with me! up with me into the clouds!
For thy song, Lark, is strong;
Up with me, up with me into the clouds!
Singing, singing,
With clouds and sky about thee ringing,
Lift me, guide me till I find
That spot which seems so to thy mind!

I have walked through wildernesses dreary,
And to-day my heart is weary;
Had I now the wings of a Faery,
Up to thee would I fly.
There's madness about thee, and joy divine
In that song of thine;
Lift me, guide me high and high
To thy banqueting-place in the sky.

Joyous as morning,
Thou art laughing and scorning;
Thou hast a nest for thy love and thy rest,
And, though little troubled with sloth,
Drunken Lark! thou wouldst be loath
To be such a Traveller as I.
Happy, happy Liver,
With a soul as strong as a mountain River
Pouring out praise to the Almighty Giver,
Joy and jollity be with us both!

Alas! my journey, rugged and uneven,
Through prickly moors or dusty ways must wind;
But hearing thee, or others of thy kind,
As full of gladness and as free of heaven,
I, with my fate contented, will plod on,
And hope for higher raptures, when Life's day is done.

---

297. Portrait.

She was a phantom of delight
When first she gleamed upon my sight;
A lovely apparition, sent
To be a moment's ornament;
Her eyes as stars of twilight fair;
Like twilight's, too, her dusky hair.

But all things else about her drawn
From May-time and the cheerful dawn;
A dancing shape, an image gay,
To haunt, to startle, and waylay.

I saw her, upon nearer view,
A spirit, yet a woman too!
Her household motions light and free,
And steps of virgin liberty;
A countenance in which did meet
Sweet records, promises as sweet;
A creature not too bright or good
For human nature's daily food;
For transient sorrows, simple wiles,
Praise, blame, love, kisses, tears, and smiles.

And now I see with eye serene
The very pulse of the machine;
A being breathing thoughtful breath,
A traveller 'twixt life and death;
The reason firm, the temperate will,
Endurance, foresight, strength, and skill,
A perfect woman, nobly planned,
To warn, to comfort, and command;
And yet a spirit still, and bright
With something of an angel light.

---

298. Milton.

Milton! thou shouldst be living at this hour;
  England hath need of thee; she is a fen
  Of stagnant waters; altar, sword, and pen,
Fireside, the heroic wealth of hall and bower,
Have forfeited their ancient English dower
  Of inward happiness. We are selfish men;
  O! raise us up, return to us again;
And give us manners, virtue, freedom, power.
  Thy soul was like a star, and dwelt apart;
Thou hadst a voice whose sound was like the sea;
Pure as the naked heavens — majestic, free,
So didst thou travel on life's common way
  In cheerful godliness; and yet thy heart
The lowliest duties on herself did lay.

299. We are Seven.

A simple child, dear brother Jim,
  That lightly draws its breath,
And feels its life in every limb,
  What should it know of death?

I met a little cottage girl;
  She was eight years old, she said;
Her hair was thick with many a curl
  That clustered round her head.

She had a rustic woodland air,
  And she was wildly clad;
Her eyes were fair, and very fair—
  Her beauty made me glad.

"Sisters and brothers, little maid,
  How many may you be?"
"How many? Seven in all," she said,
  And wondering looked at me.

"And where are they? I pray you tell."
  She answered, "Seven are we;
And two of us at Conway dwell,
  And two are gone to sea.

"Two of us in the churchyard lie,
  My sister and my brother;
And in the churchyard cottage, I
  Dwell near them, with my mother."

"You say that two at Conway dwell,
  And two are gone to sea,
Yet ye are seven! I pray you tell,
  Sweet maid, how this may be."

Then did the little maid reply,
  "Seven boys and girls are we;
Two of us in the churchyard lie,
  Beneath the churchyard tree."

"You run about, my little maid,
  Your limbs they are alive;
If two are in the churchyard laid,
  Then ye are only five."

"Their graves are green, they may be seen,"
  The little maid replied,
"Twelve steps or more from my mother's door,
  And they are side by side.

"My stockings there I often knit,
  My kerchief there I hem,
And there upon the ground I sit —
  I sit and sing to them.

"And often after sunset, sir,
  When it is light and fair,
I take my little porringer,
  And eat my supper there.

"The first that died was little Jane;
  In bed she moaning lay,
Till God released her of her pain,
  And then she went away.

"So in the churchyard she was laid;
  And all the summer dry,
Together round her grave we played —
  My brother John and I.

"And when the ground was white with snow,
  And I could run and slide,
My brother John was forced to go —
  And he lies by her side."

"How many are you then," said I,
  "If they two are in heaven?"
The little maiden did reply,
  "O master! we are seven."

"But they are dead; those two are dead!
  Their spirits are in heaven!"
'Twas throwing words away; for still,
The little maid would have her will
  And said, "Nay, we are seven!"

300. Criticism of Poetry.

With the young of both sexes, poetry is, like love, a passion; but, for much the greater part of those who have been proud of its power over their minds, a necessity soon arises of breaking the pleasing bondage; or it relaxes of itself; the thoughts being occupied in domestic cares, or the time engrossed by business. Poetry then becomes only an occasional recreation; while to those whose existence passes away in a course of fashionable pleasure, it is a species of luxurious amusement. In middle and declining age, a scattered number of serious persons resort to poetry, as to religion, for a protection against the pressure of trivial employments, and as a consolation for the afflictions of life. And, lastly, there are many, who, having been enamoured of this art in their youth, have found leisure, after youth was spent, to cultivate general literature, in which poetry has continued to be comprehended *as a study.*

Into the above classes the readers of poetry may be divided; critics abound in them all; but from the last only can opinions be collected of absolute value, and worthy to be depended upon, as prophetic of the destiny of a new work. The young, who in nothing can escape delusion, are especially subject to it in their intercourse with poetry. The cause, not so obvious as the fact is unquestionable, is the same as that from which erroneous judgments in this art, in the minds of men of all ages, chiefly proceed; but upon youth it operates with peculiar force. The appropriate business of poetry (which, nevertheless, if genuine, is as permanent as pure science), her appropriate employment, her privilege and her *duty*, is to treat of things not as they *are*, but as they *appear;* not as they exist in themselves, but as they *seem* to exist to the *senses* and to the *passions.* What a world of delusion does this acknowledged principle prepare for the inexperienced! what temptations to go astray are here held forth for them whose thoughts have been little disciplined by the understanding, and whose feelings revolt from the sway of reason! When a juvenile reader is in the height of his rapture with some vicious passage, should experience throw in doubts, or common sense suggest suspicions, a lurking consciousness that the realities of the Muse are but shows, and that her liveliest excitements are raised by transient shocks of conflicting feeling and successive assemblages of contradictory thoughts — is ever at hand to justify extravagance, and to sanction absurdity. But, it may be asked, as these illusions are unavoidable, and, no doubt, eminently useful to the mind as a process, what good can be gained by making observations, the tendency of which is to diminish the confidence of youth in its feelings, and thus to abridge its innocent and even profitable pleasures? The reproach implied in the question could not be warded off, if youth were incapable of being delighted with what is truly excellent; or, if these errors always terminated of themselves in due season. But, with the majority, though their force be abated, they continue through life. Moreover, the fire of youth is too vivacious an element to be extinguished or damped by a philosophical remark; and, while there is no danger that what has been said will be injurious or painful to the ardent and the confident, it may prove beneficial to those who, being enthusiastic, are, at the same time, modest and ingenuous. The intimation may unite with their own misgivings to regulate their sensibility, and to bring in, sooner than it would otherwise have arrived, a more discreet and sound judgment.

If it should excite wonder that men of ability, in later life, whose understandings have been rendered acute by practice in affairs, should be so easily and so far imposed upon when they happen to take up a new work in verse, this appears to be the cause — that, having discontinued their attention to poetry, whatever progress may have been made in other departments of knowledge, they have not, as to this art, advanced in true discernment beyond the age of youth. If, then, a new poem falls in their way, whose attractions are of that kind which would have enraptured them during the heat of youth, the judgment not being improved to a degree that they shall be disgusted, they are dazzled; and prize and cherish the faults for having had power to make the present time vanish before them, and to throw the mind back, as by enchantment, into the happiest season of life. As they read, powers seem to be revived, passions are regenerated, and pleasures restored. The book was probably taken up after an escape from the burden of business, and with a wish to forget the world, and all its vexations and anxieties. Having obtained this wish, and so much more, it is natural that they should make report as they have felt.

If men of mature age, through want of practice, be thus easily beguiled into admiration of absurdities, extravagances, and misplaced ornaments, thinking it proper that their understandings should enjoy a holiday, while they are unbending their minds with verse, it may be expected that such readers will resemble their former selves also in strength of prejudice, and an inaptitude to be moved by the unostentatious beauties of a pure style. In the higher poetry, an enlightened critic chiefly looks for a reflection of the wisdom of the heart and the grandeur of the imagination. Wherever these appear, simplicity accompanies them; magnificence herself, when legitimate, depending upon a simplicity of her own, to regulate her ornaments. But it is a well-known property of human nature, that our estimates are ever governed by comparisons, of which we are conscious with various degrees of distinctness. Is it not, then, inevitable (confining these observations to the effects of style merely) that an eye, accustomed to the glaring hues of diction by which such readers are caught and excited, will for the most part be rather repelled than attracted by an original work, the coloring of which is disposed according to a pure and refined scheme of harmony? It is in the fine arts as in the affairs of life — no man can *serve* (*i. e.* obey with zeal and fidelity) two masters.

Samuel Taylor Coleridge. 1772–1834. (Manual, pp. 425–427.)

301. Genevieve.

Maid of my Love, sweet Genevieve!
In Beauty's light you glide along:
Your eye is like the star of eve,
And sweet your Voice, as Seraph's song.
Yet not your heavenly Beauty gives
This heart with passion soft to glow:
Within your soul a Voice there lives!
It bids you hear the tale of Woe.

When sinking low the Sufferer wan
Beholds no hand outstretched to save,
Fair, as the bosom of the Swan
That rises graceful o'er the wave,
I've seen your breast with pity heave,
And therefore love I you, sweet Genevieve!

---

302. HYMN BEFORE SUNRISE IN THE VALE OF CHAMOUNI.

Hast thou a charm to stay the morning star
In his steep course? So long he seems to pause
On thy bald awful head, O sovran Blanc!
The Arve and Arveiron at thy base
Rave ceaselessly; but thou, most awful form!
Risest from forth thy silent sea of pines,
How silently! Around thee and above
Deep is the air, and dark, substantial, black,
An ebon mass: methinks thou piercest it,
As with a wedge! But when I look again,
It is thine own calm home, thy crystal shrine,
Thy habitation from eternity!
O dread and silent mount! I gazed upon thee,
Till thou, still present to the bodily sense,
Didst vanish from my thought: entranced in prayer,
I worshipped the Invisible alone.

Yet, like some sweet beguiling melody,
So sweet, we know not we are listening to it,
Thou, the mean while, wast blending with my thought,
Yea, with my life, and life's own secret joy;
Till the dilating soul, enrapt, transfused,
Into the mighty vision passing — there,
As in her natural form, swelled vast to heaven.

Awake, my soul! not only passive praise
Thou owest! not alone these swelling tears,
Mute thanks and secret ecstasy! Awake,
Voice of sweet song! Awake, my heart, awake!
Green vales and icy cliffs, all join my hymn.

Thou first and chief, sole Sovran of the Vale!
O struggling with the darkness all the night,
And visited all night by troops of stars,
Or when they climb the sky or when they sink:
Companion of the morning-star at dawn,
Thyself earth's ROSY STAR, and of the dawn
Co-herald! wake, O wake, and utter praise!

Who sank thy sunless pillars deep in earth?
Who filled thy countenance with rosy light?
Who made thee parent of perpetual streams?

And you, ye five wild torrents fiercely glad!
Who called you forth from night and utter death,
From dark and icy caverns called you forth,
Down those precipitous, black, jagged rocks,
Forever shattered, and the same forever?
Who gave you your invulnerable life,
Your strength, your speed, your fury, and your joy,
Unceasing thunder, and eternal foam?
And who commanded (and the silence came),
Here let the billows stiffen and have rest?

Ye ice-falls! ye that from the mountain's brow
Adown enormous ravines slope amain —
Torrents, methinks, that heard a mighty voice,
And stopped at once amid their maddest plunge!
Motionless torrents! silent cataracts!
Who made you glorious as the gates of heaven
Beneath the keen full moon? Who bade the sun
Clothe you with rainbows? Who, with living flowers
Of loveliest blue, spread garlands at your feet?
God! let the torrents, like a shout of nations,
Answer! and let the ice-plains echo, God!
God! sing, ye meadow-streams with gladsome voice!
Ye pine-groves, with your soft and soul-like sounds!
And they too have a voice, yon piles of snow,
And in their perilous fall shall thunder, God!

Ye living flowers that skirt the eternal frost!
Ye wild goats sporting round the eagle's nest!
Ye eagles, playmates of the mountain storm!
Ye lightnings, the dread arrows of the clouds!
Ye signs and wonders of the element!
Utter forth God, and fill the hills with praise!

Thou too, hoar Mount! with thy sky-pointing peaks,
Oft from whose feet the avalanche, unheard,
Shoots downward, glittering through the pure serene,
Into the depth of clouds that veil thy breast —
Thou too, again, stupendous mountain! thou,
That as I raise my head, awhile bowed low
In adoration, upward from thy base
Slow-travelling with dim eyes suffused with tears,
Solemnly seemest, like a vapory cloud,
To rise before me — rise, O ever rise,

Rise like a cloud of incense from the earth!
Thou kingly spirit throned among the hills,
Thou dread ambassador from earth to heaven,
Great hierarch! tell thou the silent sky,
And tell the stars, and tell yon rising sun,
Earth, with her thousand voices, praises God.

---

303. KUBLA KHAN: OR, A VISION IN A DREAM.

In Xanadu did Kubla Khan
A stately pleasure-dome decree:
Where Alph, the sacred river, ran
Through caverns measureless to man
  Down to a sunless sea.
So twice five miles of fertile ground
With walls and towers were girdled round:
And there were gardens bright with sinuous rills
Where blossomed many an incense-bearing tree;
And here were forests ancient as the hills,
Infolding sunny spots of greenery.
But O, that deep romantic chasm which slanted
Down the green hill athwart a cedarn cover!
A savage place! as holy and enchanted
As e'er beneath a waning moon was haunted
By woman wailing for her demon-lover!
And from this chasm, with ceaseless turmoil seething,
As if this earth in fast thick pants were breathing,
A mighty fountain momently was forced:
Amid whose swift half-intermitted burst
Huge fragments vaulted like rebounding hail,
Or chaffy grain beneath the thresher's flail:
And 'mid these dancing rocks at once and ever
It flung up momently the sacred river.
Five miles meandering with a mazy motion
Through wood and dale the sacred river ran,
Then reached the caverns measureless to man,
And sank in tumult to a lifeless ocean:
And 'mid this tumult Kubla heard from far
Ancestral voices prophesying war!

    The shadow of the dome of pleasure
    Floated midway on the waves;
    Where was heard the mingled measure
    From the fountain and the caves.
It was a miracle of rare device,
A sunny pleasure-dome with caves of ice!

A damsel with a dulcimer
In a vision once I saw:
It was an Abyssinian maid,
And on her dulcimer she played,
Singing of Mount Abora.
Could I revive within me
Her symphony and song,
To such a deep delight 'twould win me,
That with music loud and long
I would build that dome in air,
That sunny dome! those caves of ice!
And all who heard should see them there,
And all should cry, Beware! Beware!
His flashing eyes, his floating hair!
Weave a circle round him thrice,
And close your eyes with holy dread,
For he on honey-dew hath fed,
And drunk the milk of Paradìse.

From "The Ancient Mariner."

304. A Calm on the Equator.

The fair breeze blew, the white foam flew,
The furrow followed free;
We were the first that evèr burst
Into that silent sea.

Down dropped the breeze, the sails dropped down,
'Twas sad as sad could be;
And we did speak only to break
The silence of the sea!

All in a hot and copper sky,
The bloody Sun, at noon,
Right up above the mast did stand,
No bigger than the Moon.

Day after day, day after day,
We stuck, nor breath nor motion:
As idle as a painted ship
Upon a painted ocean.

Water, water, everywhere,
And all the boards did shrink;
Water, water, everywhere,
Nor any drop to drink.

The very deep did rot: — O Christ!
That ever this should be!
Yea, slimy things did crawl with legs
Upon the slimy sea.

About, about, in reel and rout
The death-fires danced at night;
The water, like a witch's oils,
Burnt green, and blue, and white.

---

305. The Phantom Ship.

There passed a weary time. Each throat
Was parched, and glazed each eye.
A weary time! a weary time!
How glazed each weary eye,
When, looking westward, I beheld
A something in the sky!

At first it seemed a little speck,
And then it seemed a mist;
It moved and moved, and took at last
A certain shape, I wist.

A speck, a mist, a shape, I wist!
And still it neared and neared:
As if it dodged a water-sprite,
It plunged and tacked and veered.

With throats unslaked, with black lips baked,
We could nor laugh nor wail;
Through utter drought all dumb we stood!
I bit my arm, I sucked the blood,
And cried, A sail, a sail!

With throats unslaked, with black lips baked,
Agape they heard me call:
Gramercy! they for joy did grin,
And all at once their breath drew in,
As they were drinking all.

See! see! (I cried) she tacks no more!
Hither to work us weal;
Without a breeze, without a tide,
She steadies with upright keel!

The western wave was all a-flame.
The day was well nigh done!

Almost upon the western wave
Rested the broad bright Sun;
When that strange shape drove suddenly
Betwixt us and the Sun.

And straight the Sun was flecked with bars,
(Heaven's Mother send us grace!)
As if through a dungeon-grate he peered
With broad and burning face.

Alas! (thought I, and my heart beat loud)
How fast she nears and nears!
Are those her sails that glance in the Sun,
Like restless gossameres?

Are those her ribs through which the Sun
Did peer, as through a grate?
And is that Woman all her crew?
Is that a Death? and are there two?
Is Death that Woman's mate?

Her lips were red, her looks were free,
Her locks were yellow as gold:
Her skin was as white as leprosy,
The Night-mare Life-in-Death was she,
Who thicks man's blood with cold.

The naked hulk alongside came,
And the twain were casting dice;
"The game is done! I've won, I've won!"
Quoth she, and whistles thrice.

The Sun's rim dips; the stars rush out:
At one stride comes the dark;
With far-heard whisper, o'er the sea,
Off shot the spectre-bark.

We listened and looked sideways up!
Fear at my heart, as at a cup,
My life-blood seemed to sip!
The stars were dim, and thick the night,
The steersman's face by his lamp gleamed white;
From the sails the dew did drip —
Till clomb above the eastern bar
The hornéd Moon, with one bright star,
Within the nether tip.

FROM "THE FRIEND."

306. TRUTH.

Monsters and madmen canonized, and Galileo blind in a dungeon! It is not so in our times. Heaven be praised, that in this respect, at least, we are, if not better, yet *better off* than our forefathers. But to what and to whom (under Providence) do we owe the improvement? To any radical change in the moral affections of mankind in general? In order to answer this question in the affirmative, I must forget the infamous empirics whose advertisements pollute and disgrace all our newspapers, and almost *paper* the walls of our cities; and the vending of whose poisons and poisonous drams (with shame and anguish be it spoken) supports a shop in every market-town! I must forget that other opprobrium of the nation, that *mother vice*, the lottery! I must forget that a numerous class plead *prudence* for keeping their fellow-men ignorant and incapable of intellectual enjoyments, and the *revenue* for upholding such temptations as men so ignorant will not withstand — yes! that even senators and officers of state hold forth the *revenue* as a sufficient plea for upholding, at every fiftieth door throughout the kingdom, temptations to the most pernicious vices. * * * * No! let us not deceive ourselves. Like the man who used to pull off his hat with great demonstration of respect whenever he spoke of himself, we are fond of styling our own the *enlightened age*, though, as Jortin, I think, has wittily remarked, the *golden* age would be more appropriate.

To whom, then, do we owe our ameliorated condition? To the successive few in every age (more, indeed, in one generation than in another, but relatively to the mass of mankind always few), who, by the intensity and permanence of their action, have compensated for the limited sphere within which it is at any one time intelligible, and whose good deeds posterity reverence in their results, though the mode in which we repair the inevitable waste of time, and the style of our additions, too generally furnish a sad proof how little we understand the principles.

Still, however, there are truths so self-evident, or so immediately and palpably deduced from those that are, or are acknowledged for such, that they are at once intelligible to all men who possess the common advantages of the social state; although by sophistry, by evil habits, by the neglect, false persuasions, and impostures of an anti-Christian priesthood, joined in one conspiracy with the violence of tyrannical governors, the understandings of men may become so darkened, and their consciences so lethargic, that there may arise a necessity for the republication of these truths, and this, too, with a voice of loud alarm and impassioned warning. Such were the doctrines proclaimed by the first Christians to the pagan world: such were the lightnings flashed by Wicklif, Huss, Luther, Calvin, Zuinglius,

Latimer, and others, across the papal darkness; and such in our own times, the agitating truths with which Thomas Clarkson and his excellent confederates, the Quakers, fought and conquered the legalized banditti of men-stealers, the numerous and powerful perpetrators and advocates of rapine, murder, and (of blacker guilt than either) slavery. Truths of this kind being indispensable to man, considered as a moral being, are above all expedience, all accidental consequences: for, as sure as God is holy and man immortal, there can be no evil so great as the ignorance or disregard of them. It is the very madness of mock prudence to oppose the removal of a poisoned dish on account of the pleasant sauces or nutritious viands which would be lost with it! The dish contains destruction to that for which alone we ought to wish the palate to be gratified, or the body to be nourished.

The prejudices of one age are condemned even by the prejudiced of the succeeding ages: for endless are the modes of folly, and the fool joins with the wise in passing sentence on all modes but his own. Who cried out with greater horror against the murderers of the prophets than those who likewise cried out, Crucify him! crucify him! The truth-haters of every future generation will call the truth-haters of the preceding ages by their true names, for even these the stream of time carries onward. In fine, truth, considered in itself, and in the effects natural to it, may be conceived as a gentle spring or water-source, warm from the genial earth, and breathing up into the snow-drift that is piled over and around its outlet. It turns the obstacle into its own form and character, and, as it makes its way, increases its stream. And should it be arrested in its course by a chilling season, it suffers delay, not loss, and awaits only for a change in the wind to awaken and again roll onward.

---

307. Advantage of Method.

What is that which first strikes us, and strikes us at once, in a man of education; and which, among educated men, so instantly distinguishes the man of superior mind, that (as was observed with eminent propriety of the late Edmund Burke) "we cannot stand under the same archway, during a shower of rain, without finding him out"? Not the weight or novelty of his remarks; not any unusual interest of facts communicated by him: for we may suppose both the one and the other precluded by the shortness of our intercourse, and the triviality of the subjects. The difference will be impressed and felt though the conversation should be confined to the state of the weather or the pavement. Still less will it arise from any peculiarity in his words and phrases; for if he be, as we now assume, a *well*-educated man, as well as a man of superior powers, he will not fail to follow the golden rule of Julius Cæsar, and, unless where new things necessitate new terms, he will avoid an unusual word as a rock. It must have been among the earliest lessons of his youth that the breach of this precept, at all times hazardous, becomes ridiculous in the topics of ordinary conversation. There remains but one other point of distinction possible; and this must be, and in fact is, the true cause of the impression made on us. It is the unpremeditated and evidently habitual *arrangement* of his words, grounded on the habit of foreseeing, in each integral part, or (more plainly) in every sentence, the whole that he then intends to communicate. However irregular and desultory his talk, there is METHOD in the fragments.

Listen, on the other hand, to an ignorant man, though perhaps shrewd and able in his particular calling; whether he be describing or relating. We immediately perceive that his memory alone is called into action, and that the objects and events recur in the narration in the same order, and with the same accompaniments, however accidental or impertinent, as they had first occurred to the narrator. The necessity of taking breath, the efforts of recollection, and the abrupt rectification of its failures, produce all his pauses, and, with the exception of the "*and then*," the "*and there*," and the still less significant "*and so*," they constitute likewise all his connections. Our discussion, however, is confined to method, as employed in the formation of the understanding and in the constructions of science and literature. It would, indeed, be superfluous to attempt a proof of its importance in the business and economy of active or domestic life. From the cotter's hearth, or the workshop of the artisan, to the palace, or the arsenal, the first merit, that which admits neither substitute nor equivalent, is, that *everything is in its place*. Where this charm is wanting, every other merit either loses its name or becomes an additional ground of accusation and regret. Of one by whom it is eminently possessed, we say proverbially he is like clock-work. The resemblance extends beyond the point of regularity, and yet falls short of the truth. Both do, indeed, at once divide and announce the silent and otherwise indistinguishable lapse of time. But the man of methodical industry and honorable pursuits does more: he realizes its ideal divisions, and gives a character and individuality to its moments. If the idle are described as killing time, he may be justly said to call it into life and moral being, while he makes it the distinct object not only of the consciousness, but of the conscience. He organizes the hours, and gives them a soul; and that, the very essence of which is to fleet away, and evermore *to have been*, he takes up into his own permanence, and communicates to it the imperishableness of a spiritual nature. Of the good and faithful servant whose energies, thus directed, are thus methodized, it is less truly affirmed that he lives in time than that time lives in him. His days, months, and years, as the stops and punctual marks in the records of duties performed, will survive the wreck of worlds, and remain extant when time itself shall be no more.

Robert Southey. 1774–1843. (Manual, pp. 427–431.)

308. The Battle of Blenheim.[1]

It was a summer evening,
  Old Kaspar's work was done,
And he before his cottage-door
  Was sitting in the sun:
And by him sported on the green
His little grandchild Wilhelmine.

She saw her brother Peterkin
  Roll something large and round,
Which he beside the rivulet,
  In playing there, had found;
He came to ask what he had found,
That was so large, and smooth, and round.

Old Kaspar took it from the boy,
  Who stood expectant by;
And then the old man shook his head,
  And with a natural sigh,
"'Tis some poor fellow's skull," said he,
"Who fell in the great victory.

"I find them in the garden,
  For there's many here about;
And often, when I go to plough,
  The ploughshare turns them out!
For many thousand men," said he,
"Were slain in that great victory."

"Now tell us what 'twas all about,"
  Young Peterkin, he cries:
While little Wilhelmine looks up,
  With wonder-waiting eyes:
"Now tell us all about the war,
  And what they killed each other for."

"It was the English," Kaspar cried,
  "Who put the French to rout;
But what they killed each other for,
  I could not well make out.
But everybody said," quoth he,
  "That 'twas a famous victory.

1 A battle fought near the village of Blenheim, Bavaria, August 2, 1704, in which the English Duke of Marlborough gained a victory over the French and Bavarians. It is called by the French the Battle of Hochstedt.

"My father lived at Blenheim then,
  Yon little stream hard by;
They burnt his dwelling to the ground,
  And he was forced to fly;
So with his wife and child he fled,
Nor had he where to rest his head.

"With fire and sword, the country round
  Was wasted far and wide;
And many a childing mother then,
  And new-born baby, died;
But things like that, you know, must be
  At every famous victory.

"They say it was a shocking sight
  After the field was won;
For many thousand bodies here
  Lay rotting in the sun;
But things like that, you know, must be
After a famous victory.

"Great praise the Duke of Marlbro' won,
  And our good prince, Eugene."
"Why, 'twas a very wicked thing!"
  Said little Wilhelmine.
"Nay — nay — my little girl," quoth he,
  "It was a famous victory.

"And everybody praised the duke,
  Who this great fight did win."
"And what good came of it at last?"
  Quoth little Peterkin.
"Why, that I cannot tell," said he,
"But 'twas a famous victory."

---

309. THE EVENING RAINBOW.

Mild arch of promise! on the evening sky
Thou shinest fair, with many a lovely ray,
Each in the other melting. Much mine eye
Delights to linger on thee; for the day,
Changeful and many-weathered, seemed to smile,
Flashing brief splendor through its clouds awhile,
That deepened dark anon, and fell in rain:
But pleasant it is now to pause, and view
Thy various tints of frail and watery hue,
And think the storm shall not return again.

310. Lord William and Edmund.

No eye beheld when William plunged
  Young Edmund in the stream:
No human ear but William's heard
  Young Edmund's drowning scream.

"I bade thee with a father's love
  My orphan Edmund guard —
Well, William, hast thou kept thy charge?
  Now take thy due reward."

He started up, each limb convulsed
  With agonizing fear —
He only heard the storm of night —
  'Twas music to his ear!

When lo! the voice of loud alarm
  His inmost soul appalls —
"What, ho! Lord William, rise in haste!
  The water saps thy walls!"

He rose in haste — beneath the walls
  He saw the flood appear;
It hemmed him round — 'twas midnight now —
  No human aid was near.

He heard the shout of joy! for now
  A boat approached the wall:
And eager to the welcome aid
  They crowd for safety all.

"My boat is small," the boatman cried,
  "'Twill bear but one away;
Come in, Lord William, and do ye
  In God's protection stay."

The boatman plied the oar, the boat
  Went light along the stream; —
Sudden Lord William heard a cry,
  Like Edmund's dying scream!

The boatman paused — "Methought I heard
  A child's distressful cry!"
"'Twas but the howling winds of night,"
  Lord William made reply.

"Haste — haste — ply swift and strong the oar;
  Haste — haste across the stream!"
Again Lord William heard a cry,
  Like Edmund's dying scream!

"I heard a child's distressful scream,"
  The boatman cried again.
"Nay, hasten on — the night is dark —
  And we should search in vain."

"O God! Lord William, dost thou know
  How dreadful 'tis to die?
And canst thou, without pity, hear
  A child's expiring cry?

"How horrible it is to sink
  Beneath the chilly stream:
To stretch the powerless arms in vain!
  In vain for help to scream!"

The shriek again was heard: it came
  More deep, more piercing loud.
That instant, o'er the flood, the moon
  Shone through a broken cloud;

And near them they beheld a child;
  Upon a crag he stood,
A little crag, and all around
  Was spread the rising flood.

The boatman plied the oar, the boat
  Approached his resting-place;
The moonbeam shone upon the child,
  And showed how pale his face.

"Now reach thy hand," the boatman cried,
  "Lord William, reach and save!"
The child stretched forth his little hands,
  To grasp the hand he gave.

Then William shrieked; — the hand he touched
  Was cold, and damp, and dead!
He felt young Edmund in his arms,
  A heavier weight than lead!

"Help! help! for mercy, help!" he cried,
  "The waters round me flow."
"No — William — to an infant's cries
  No mercy didst thou show."

The boat sunk down — the murderer sunk
  Beneath th' avenging stream;
He rose — he screamed — no human ear
  Heard William's drowning scream.

311. From the "Life of Nelson."

It had been part of Nelson's prayer, that the British fleet might be distinguished by humanity in the victory which he expected. Setting an example himself, he twice gave orders to cease firing on the Redoubtable, supposing that she had struck, because her guns were silent; for, as she carried no flag, there was no means of instantly ascertaining the fact. From this ship, which he had thus twice spared, he received his death. A ball fired from her mizzen-top, which, in the then situation of the two vessels, was not more than fifteen yards from that part of the deck where he was standing, struck the epaulet on his left shoulder, about a quarter after one, just in the heat of action. He fell upon his face, on the spot which was covered with his poor secretary's blood. Hardy, who was a few steps from him, turning round, saw three men raising him up. "They have done for me at last, Hardy," said he. "I hope not," cried Hardy. "Yes!" he replied; "my back-bone is shot through." Yet even now, not for a moment losing his presence of mind, he observed, as they were carrying him down the ladder, that the tiller-ropes, which had been shot away, were not yet replaced, and ordered that new ones should be rove immediately; then, that he might not be seen by the crew, he took out his handkerchief, and covered his face and his stars. Had he but concealed these badges of honor from the enemy, England, perhaps, would not have had cause to receive with sorrow the news of the battle of Trafalgar. The cockpit was crowded with wounded and dying men, over whose bodies he was with some difficulty conveyed, and laid upon a pallet in the midshipmen's berth. It was soon perceived, upon examination, that the wound was mortal. This, however, was concealed from all except Captain Hardy, the chaplain, and the medical attendants. He himself being certain, from the sensation in his back, and the gush of blood he felt momently within his breast, that no human care could avail him, insisted that the surgeon should leave him, and attend to those to whom he might be useful; "for," said he, "you can do nothing for me." All that could be done was to fan him with paper, and frequently to give him lemonade to alleviate his intense thirst. He was in great pain, and expressed much anxiety for the event of the action, which now began to declare itself. As often as a ship struck, the crew of the Victory hurrahed; and at every hurrah, a visible expression of joy gleamed in the eyes and marked the countenance of the dying hero. But he became impatient to see Hardy; and as that officer, though often sent for, could not leave the deck, Nelson feared that some fatal cause prevented him, and repeatedly cried, "Will no one bring Hardy to me? he must be killed! he is surely dead!" An hour and ten minutes elapsed from the time when Nelson received his wound, before Hardy could come to him. They shook hands in silence; Hardy in vain struggling to suppress the feelings of that most painful and yet sublimest moment.

"Well, Hardy," said Nelson, "how goes the day with us?" "Very well," replied Hardy; "ten ships have struck, but five of the van have tacked, and show an intention to bear down upon the Victory. I have called two or three of our fresh ships round, and have no doubt of giving them a drubbing." "I hope," said Nelson, "none of our ships have struck." Hardy answered, "there was no fear of that." Then, and not till then, Nelson spoke of himself. "I am a dead man, Hardy," said he; "I am going fast: it will be all over with me soon. Come nearer to me. Let my dear Lady Hamilton have my hair, and all other things belonging to me." Hardy observed, that he hoped Mr. Beatty could yet hold out some prospect of life. "O! no," he replied, "it is impossible. My back is shot through. Beatty will tell you so." Hardy then, once more, shook hands with him, and with a heart almost bursting, hastened upon deck.

By this time all feeling below the breast was gone; and Nelson, having made the surgeon ascertain this, said to him, "You know I am gone. I know it. I feel something rising in my breast," putting his hand on his left side, "which tells me so." And upon Beatty's inquiring whether his pain was very great, he replied, "so great that he wished he was dead. Yet," said he, in a lower voice, "one would like to live a little longer too!" And after a few minutes, in the same under-tone, he added, "What would become of poor Lady Hamilton, if she knew my situation!" Next to his country she occupied his thoughts. Captain Hardy, some fifty minutes after he had left the cockpit, returned; and, again taking the hand of his dying friend and commander, congratulated him on having gained a complete victory. How many of the enemy were taken he did not know, as it was impossible to perceive them distinctly; but fourteen or fifteen at least. "That's well," cried Nelson, "but I bargained for twenty." And then, in a stronger voice, he said, "Anchor, Hardy; anchor." Hardy, upon this, hinted that Admiral Collingwood would take upon himself the direction of affairs. "Not while I live, Hardy," said the dying Nelson, ineffectually endeavoring to raise himself from the bed: "do you anchor." His previous orders for preparing to anchor had shown how clearly he foresaw the necessity of this. Presently, calling Hardy back, he said to him, in a low voice, "Don't throw me overboard;" and he desired that he might be buried by his parents, unless it should please the king to order otherwise. * * * * His articulation now became difficult! but he was distinctly heard to say, "Thank God, I have done my duty!" These words he repeatedly pronounced; and they were the last words which he uttered. He expired at thirty minutes after four, — three hours and a quarter after he had received his wound.

The death of Nelson was felt in England as something more than a public calamity: men started at the intelligence, and turned pale, as if they had heard of the loss of a dear friend. An object of our admiration and affection, of our pride and of our hopes, was suddenly taken from us; and it seemed as if we had never till then known how deeply we loved and reverenced him. What the country had lost in its great naval hero — the greatest of our own and of all former times — was scarcely taken into the account of grief. So perfectly, indeed, had he performed his part, that the maritime war, after the battle of Trafalgar, was considered at an end. The fleets of the enemy were not merely defeated, but destroyed; new navies must be built, and a new race of seamen reared for them, before the possibility of their invading our shores could again be contemplated. It was not, therefore, from any selfish reflection upon the magnitude of our loss that we mourned for him: the general sorrow was of a higher character. The people of England grieved that funeral ceremonies, and public monuments, and posthumous rewards, were all which they could now bestow upon him whom the king, the legislature, and the nation would have alike delighted to honor; whom every tongue would have blessed; whose presence in every village through which he might have passed would have wakened the church-bells, have given schoolboys a holiday, have drawn children from their sports to gaze upon him, and "old men from the chimney corner" to look upon Nelson ere they died. The victory of Trafalgar was celebrated, indeed, with the usual forms of rejoicing, but they were without joy; for such already was the glory of the British navy, through Nelson's surpassing genius, that it scarcely seemed to receive any addition from the most signal victory that ever was achieved upon the seas; and the destruction of this mighty fleet, by which all the maritime schemes of France were totally frustrated, hardly appeared to add to our security or strength; for, while Nelson was living to watch the combined squadrons of the enemy, we felt ourselves as secure as now, when they were no longer in existence.

SAMUEL ROGERS. 1763–1855. (Manual, p. 432.)

312. GINEVRA.

She was an only child — her name Ginevra, —
The joy, the pride of an indulgent father;
And in her fifteenth year became a bride,
Marrying an only son, Francesco Doria,
Her playmate from her birth, and her first love.

Just as she looks there in her bridal dress,
She was all gentleness, all gayety,
Her pranks the favorite theme of every tongue.
But now the day was come, the day, the hour;
Now frowning, smiling, for the hundredth time,
The nurse, that ancient lady, preached decorum;
And, in the lustre of her youth, she gave
Her hand, with her heart in it, to Francesco.

Great was the joy; but at the nuptial feast,
When all sate down, the bride herself was wanting,
Nor was she to be found! Her father cried,
"'Tis but to make a trial of our love!"
And filled his glass to all; but his hand shook,
And soon from guest to guest the panic spread.
'Twas but that instant she had left Francesco,
Laughing, and looking back, and flying still,
Her ivory tooth imprinted on his finger.
But now, alas! she was not to be found;
Nor from that hour could anything be guessed,
But that she was not!

Weary of his life,
Francesco flew to Venice, and, embarking,
Flung it away in battle with the Turks.
Orsini lived; and long might you have seen
An old man wandering as in quest of something —
Something he could not find — he knew not what.
When he was gone, the house remained awhile
Silent and tenantless, then went to strangers.

Full fifty years were past and all forgotten,
When on an idle day, a day of search
'Mid the old lumber in the gallery,
That mouldering chest was noticed; and 'twas said,
By one as young, as thoughtless as Ginevra,
"Why not remove it from its lurking-place?"
'Twas done as soon as said; but on the way
It burst, it fell; and lo! a skeleton,
With here and there a pearl, an emerald stone,
A golden clasp, clasping a shred of gold.
All else had perished — save a wedding ring
And a small seal, her mother's legacy,
Engraven with a name, the name of both,
"Ginevra."

There then had she found a grave!
Within that chest had she concealed herself,
Fluttering with joy, the happiest of the happy;
When a spring lock, that lay in ambush there,
Fastened her down forever!

REV. CHARLES WOLFE. 1791–1823. (Manual, p. 432.)

313. THE BURIAL OF SIR JOHN MOORE.[1]

Not a drum was heard, not a funeral note,
  As his corse to the rampart we hurried:
Not a soldier discharged his farewell shot
  O'er the grave where our hero we buried.

We buried him darkly at dead of night,
  The sods with our bayonets turning —
By the struggling moonbeam's misty light,
  And the lantern dimly burning.

No useless coffin enclosed his breast,
  Not in sheet or in shroud we wound him;
But he lay like a warrior taking his rest,
  With his martial cloak around him.

Few and short were the prayers we said,
  And we spoke not a word of sorrow;
But we steadfastly gazed on the face that was dead,
  And we bitterly thought of the morrow.

We thought, as we hollowed his narrow bed,
  And smoothed down his lonely pillow,
That the foe and the stranger would tread o'er his head,
  And we far away on the billow.

Lightly they'll talk of the spirit that's gone,
  And o'er his cold ashes upbraid him —
But little he'll reck, if they let him sleep on
  In the grave where a Briton has laid him.

But half of our heavy task was done
  When the clock struck the hour for retiring;
And we heard the distant and random gun
  That the foe was sullenly firing.

Slowly and sadly we laid him down,
  From the field of his fame fresh and gory;
We carved not a line, and we raised not a stone —
  But we left him alone with his glory.

1 Sir John Moore was mortally wounded by a cannon ball, January 16, 1809, in an action between the English and Spanish forces under his command, and the French under Marshal Soult, on the Heights of Elvina, near Corunna, Spain, and died in the moment of his victory.

JAMES MONTGOMERY. 1771–1854. (Manual, p. 432.)

FROM "THE WEST INDIES."

314. THE LOVE OF COUNTRY AND OF HOME.

There is a land, of every land the pride,
Beloved by heaven, o'er all the world beside ;
Where brighter suns dispense serener light,
And milder moons emparadise the night;
A land of beauty, virtue, valor, truth,
Time-tutored age, and love-exalted youth:
The wandering mariner, whose eye explores
The wealthiest isles, the most enchanting shores,
Views not a realm so bountiful and fair,
Nor breathes the spirit of a purer air;
In every clime the magnet of his soul,
Touched by remembrance, trembles to that pole;
For in this land of heaven's peculiar grace,
The heritage of nature's noblest race,
There is a spot of earth supremely blest,
A dearer, sweeter spot than all the rest;
Where man, creation's tyrant, casts aside
His sword and sceptre, pageantry and pride,
While in his softened looks benignly blend
The sire, the son, the husband, father, friend:
Here woman reigns: the mother, daughter, wife,
Strews with fresh flowers the narrow way of life;
In the clear heaven of her delightful eye,
An angel-guard of loves and graces lie;
Around her knees domestic duties meet,
And fireside pleasures gambol at her feet.
"Where shall that *land*, that *spot of earth*, be found?"
Art thou a man?—a patriot?—look around;
O, thou shalt find, howe'er thy footsteps roam,
That land THY COUNTRY, and that spot THY HOME!

---

315. PRAYER.

Prayer is the soul's sincere desire,
  Uttered or unexpressed;
The motion of a hidden fire
  That trembles in the breast.

Prayer is the burden of a sigh,
  The falling of a tear,
The upward glancing of an eye,
  When none but God is near.

Prayer is the simplest form of speech
  That infant lips can try;
Prayer the sublimest strains that reach
  The Majesty on high.

Prayer is the Christian's vital breath,
  The Christian's native air;
His watchword at the gates of death,
  He enters heaven by prayer.

Prayer is the contrite sinner's voice
  Returning from his ways;
While angels in their songs rejoice,
  And say, "Behold, he prays!"

The saints in prayer appear as one,
  In word, and deed, and mind,
When with the Father and his Son
  Their fellowship they find.

Nor prayer is made on earth alone;
  The Holy Spirit pleads;
And Jesus, on the eternal throne,
  For sinners intercedes.

O Thou, by whom we come to God,
  The Life, the Truth, the Way,
The path of prayer thyself hast trod,
  Lord, teach us how to pray!

Horace Smith. 1780–1849. (Manual, p. 432.)

316. Address to a Mummy.

And thou hast walked about (how strange a story!)
  In Thebes's streets three thousand years ago,
When the Memnonium was in all its glory,
  And time had not begun to overthrow
Those temples, palaces, and piles stupendous,
Of which the very ruins are tremendous!

Speak! for thou long enough hast acted dumby:
  Thou hast a tongue, come, let us hear its tune;
Thou'rt standing on thy legs above ground, mummy!
  Revisiting the glimpses of the moon.
Not like thin ghosts or disembodied creatures,
But with thy bones, and flesh, and limbs, and features.

Tell us — for doubtless thou canst recollect —
  To whom we should assign the Sphinx's fame?
Was Cheops or Cephrenes architect
  Of either Pyramid that bears his name?
Is Pompey's Pillar really a misnomer?
Had Thebes a hundred gates, as sung by Homer?

Perhaps thou wert a mason, and forbidden
  By oath to tell the secrets of thy trade —
Then say, what secret melody was hidden
  In Memnon's statue, which at sunrise played?
Perhaps thou wert a Priest — if so, my struggles
Are vain, for priestcraft never owns its juggles.

Perchance that very hand, now pinioned flat,
  Has hob-a-nobbed with Pharaoh, glass to glass;
Or dropped a halfpenny in Homer's hat,
  Or doffed thine own to let Queen Dido pass,
Or held, by Solomon's own invitation,
A torch at the great Temple's dedication.

I need not ask thee if that hand, when armed,
  Has any Roman soldier mauled and knuckled,
For thou wert dead, and buried, and embalmed,
  Ere Romulus and Remus had been suckled:
Antiquity appears to have begun
Long after thy primeval race was run.

Thou couldst develop, if that withered tongue
  Might tell us what those sightless orbs have seen,
How the world looked when it was fresh and young,
  And the great deluge still had left it green;
Or was it then so old, that history's pages
Contained no record of its early ages?

Still silent, incommunicative elf!
  Art sworn to secrecy? then keep thy vows;
But prythee tell us something of thyself,
  Reveal the secrets of thy prison-house;
Since in the world of spirits thou hast slumbered,
What hast thou seen — what strange adventures numbered?

Since first thy form was in this box extended,
  We have, above ground, seen some strange mutations;
The Roman empire has begun and ended,
  New worlds have risen — we have lost old nations,
And countless kings have into dust been humbled,
Whilst not a fragment of thy flesh has crumbled.

Didst thou not hear the pother o'er thy head,
  When the great Persian conqueror, Cambyses,
Marched armies o'er thy tomb with thundering tread,
  O'erthrew Osiris, Orus, Apis, Isis,
And shook the pyramids with fear and wonder,
When the gigantic Memnon fell asunder?

If the tomb's secrets may not be confessed,
  The nature of thy private life unfold:
A heart has throbbed beneath that leathern breast,
  And tears adown that dusky cheek have rolled;
Have children climbed those knees and kissed that face?
What was thy name and station, age and race?

Statue of flesh — immortal of the dead!
  Imperishable type of evanescence!
Posthumous man, who quitt'st thy narrow bed,
  And standest undecayed within our presence,
Thou wilt hear nothing till the judgment morning,
When the great trump shall thrill thee with its warning.

Why should this worthless tegument endure,
  If its undying guest be lost forever?
O, let us keep the soul embalmed and pure
  In living virtue, that, when both must sever,
Although corruption may our frame consume,
The immortal spirit in the skies may bloom.

George Canning. 1770–1827.

FROM "THE ANTIJACOBIN."

317. The Friend of Humanity and the Knife-Grinder.

Friend of Humanity.

Needy Knife-grinder, whither are you going?
Rough is your road, your wheel is out of order;
Bleak blows the blast — your hat has got a hole in't
          So have your breeches.

Weary Knife-grinder, little think the proud ones,
Who, in their coaches, roll along the turnpike-
Road, what hard work 'tis crying all day, "Knives and
          Scissors to grind, O!"

Tell me, Knife-grinder, how came you to grind knives?
Did some rich man tyrannically use you?
Was it the squire or parson of the parish,
          Or the attorney?

Was it the squire, for killing of his game? or
Covetous parson, for his tithes distraining?
Or roguish lawyer, made you lose your little
All in a lawsuit?

(Have you not read the Rights of Man, by Tom Paine?)
Drops of compassion tremble on my eyelids,
Ready to fall, as soon as you have told your
Pitiful story.

Knife-Grinder.

Story! God bless you, I have none to tell, Sir;
Only last night, a-drinking at the Chequers,
This poor old hat and breeches, as you see, were
Torn in a scuffle.

Constables came up for to take me into
Custody; they took me before the justice;
Justice Oldmixon put me in the parish
Stocks for a vagrant.

I should be glad to drink your honor's health in
A pot of beer, if you will give me sixpence;
But, for my part, I never love to meddle
With politics, Sir.

Friend of Humanity.

I give thee sixpence! I will see thee hanged first —
Wretch, whom no sense of wrongs can rouse to vengeance —
Sordid, unfeeling, reprobate, degraded,
Spiritless outcast!

[*Kicks the Knife-grinder, overturns his wheel, and exit in a transport of republican enthusiasm and universal philanthropy.*]

JOHN WILSON. 1785–1854. (Manual, p. 469.)

318. FROM "THE CITY OF THE PLAGUE."

Together will ye walk through long, long streets,
All standing silent as a midnight church.
You will hear nothing but the brown-red grass
Rustling beneath your feet; the very beating
Of your own hearts will awe you; the small voice
Of that vain bawble, idly counting time,

Will speak a solemn language in the desert.
Look up to Heaven, and there the sultry clouds,
Still threatening thunder, lower with grim delight,
As if the Spirit of the Plague dwelt there,
Darkening the city with the shadows of death.
Know ye that hideous hubbub? Hark, far off
A tumult like an echo! On it comes,
Weeping and wailing, shrieks and groaning prayer;
And, louder than all, outrageous blasphemy.
The passing storm hath left the silent streets.
But are these houses near you tenantless?
Over your heads, from a window, suddenly
A ghastly face is thrust, and yells of death
With voice not human. Who is he that flies,
As if a demon dogged him on his path?
With ragged hair, white face, and bloodshot eyes,
Raving, he rushes past you; till he falls,
As if struck by lightning, down upon the stones,
Or, in blind madness, dashed against the wall,
Sinks backward into stillness. Stand aloof,
And let the Pest's triumphant chariot
Have open way advancing to the tomb.
See how he mocks the pomp and pageantry
Of earthly kings! a miserable cart,
Heaped up with human bodies; dragged along
By pale steeds, skeleton-anatomies!
And onwards urged by a wan meagre wretch,
Doomed never to return from the foul pit,
Whither, with oaths, he drives his load of horror.
Would you look in? Gray hairs and golden tresses,
Wan shrivelled cheeks that have not smiled for years,
And many a rosy visage smiling still;
Bodies in the noisome weeds of beggary wrapped,
With age decrepit, and wasted to the bone;
And youthful frames, august and beautiful,
In spite of mortal pangs, — there lie they all,
Embraced in ghastliness! But look not long,
For haply, 'mid the faces glimmering there,
The well-known cheek of some belovéd friend
Will meet thy gaze, or some small snow-white hand,
Bright with the ring that holds her lover's hair.
Let me sit down beside you. I am faint
Talking of horrors that I looked upon
At last without a shudder.

JOHN GIBSON LOCKHART. 1794–1854.

319. ZARA'S EAR-RINGS.[1]

"My ear-rings! my ear-rings! they've dropped into the well,
And what to say to Muça, I cannot, cannot tell." —
'Twas thus, Granada's fountain by, spoke Albuharez' daughter, —
"The well is deep, far down they lie, beneath the cold blue water —
To me did Muça give them, when he spake his sad farewell,
And what to say when he comes back, alas! I cannot tell.

"My ear-rings! my ear-rings! they were pearls in silver set,
That when my Moor was far away, I ne'er should him forget,
That I ne'er to other tongue should list, nor smile on other's tale,
But remember he my lips had kissed, pure as those ear-rings pale —
When he comes back and hears that I have dropped them in the well,
O, what will Muça think of me, I cannot, cannot tell.

"My ear-rings! my ear-rings! he'll say they should have been,
Not of pearl and silver, but of gold and glittering sheen,
Of jasper and of onyx, and of diamond shining clear,
Changing to the changing light, with radiance insincere —
That changeful mind unchanging gems are not befitting well —
Thus will he think, — and what to say, alas! I cannot tell.

"He'll think when I to market went, I loitered by the way;
He'll think a willing ear I lent to all the lads might say;
He'll think some other lover's hand among my tresses noosed,
From the ears where he had placed them, my rings of pearl unloosed;
He'll think when I was sporting so beside this marble well,
My pearls fell in, — and what to say, alas! I cannot tell.

"He'll say I am a woman, and we are all the same;
He'll say I loved when he was here to whisper of his flame —
But when he went to Tunis my virgin troth had broken,
And thought no more of Muça, and cared not for his token.
My ear-rings! my ear-rings! O, luckless, luckless well!
For what to say to Muça, alas! I cannot tell.

"I'll tell the truth to Muça, and I hope he will believe —
That I have thought of him at morning, and thought of him at eve:
That musing on my lover, when down the sun was gone,
His ear-rings in my hand I held, by the fountain all alone:
And that my mind was o'er the sea, when from my hand they fell,
And that deep his love lies in my heart, as they lie in the well."

[1] A Moorish Ballad.

ROBERT POLLOK. 1790–1827. (Manual, p. 433.)

FROM "THE COURSE OF TIME."

320. THE GENIUS OF BYRON.

He touched his harp, and nations heard, entranced;
As some vast river of unfailing source,
Rapid, exhaustless, deep, his numbers flowed,
And oped new fountains in the human heart.
Where Fancy halted, weary in her flight,
In other men, his, fresh as morning, rose,
And soared untrodden heights, and seemed at home,
Where angels bashful looked. Others, though great,
Beneath their argument seemed struggling whiles;
He, from above descending, stooped to touch
The loftiest thought; and proudly stooped, as though
It scarce deserved his verse. With Nature's self
He seemed an old acquaintance, free to jest
At will with all her glorious majesty.
He laid his hand upon "the Ocean's mane,"
And played familiar with his hoary locks;
Stood on the Alps, stood on the Apennines,
And with the thunder talked as friend to friend;
And wove his garland of the lightning's wing,
In sportive twist, the lightning's fiery wing,
Which, as the footsteps of the dreadful God,
Marching upon the storm in vengeance, seemed;
Then turned, and with the grasshopper, who sung
His evening song beneath his feet, conversed.
Suns, moons, and stars, and clouds, his sisters were;
Rocks, mountains, meteors, seas, and winds, and storms,
His brothers, younger brothers, whom he scarce
As equals deemed. All passions of all men,
The wild and tame, the gentle and severe;
All thoughts, all maxims, sacred and profane;
All creeds, all seasons, Time, Eternity;
All that was hated, and all that was dear,
All that was hoped, all that was feared, by man,
He tossed about, as tempest-withered leaves;
Then, smiling, looked upon the wreck he made.
With terror now he froze the cowering blood,
And now dissolved the heart in tenderness;
Yet would not tremble, would not weep himself;
But back into his soul retired, alone,
Dark, sullen, proud, gazing contemptuously
On hearts and passions prostrate at his feet.

FELICIA DOROTHEA HEMANS. 1793–1835. (Manual, p. 432.)

321. THE TREASURES OF THE DEEP.

What hidest thou in thy treasure-caves and cells,
Thou hollow-sounding and mysterious Main? —
Pale glistening pearls, and rainbow-colored shells,
Bright things which gleam unrecked of, and in vain. —
Keep, keep thy riches, melancholy Sea!
We ask not such from thee.

Yet more, the Depths have more! What wealth untold
Far down, and shining through their stillness, lies!
Thou hast the starry gems, the burning gold,
Won from ten thousand royal Argosies. —
Sweep o'er thy spoils, thou wild and wrathful Main!
Earth claims not these again!

Yet more, the Depths have more! Thy waves have rolled
Above the cities of a world gone by!
Sand hath filled up the palaces of old,
Sea-weed o'ergrown the halls of revelry!
Dash o'er them, Ocean! in thy scornful play—
Man yields them to decay!

Yet more! the Billows and the Depths have more!
High hearts and brave are gathered to thy breast!
They hear not now the booming waters roar,
The battle-thunders will not break their rest; —
Keep thy red gold and gems, thou stormy grave —
Give back the true and brave!

Give back the lost and lovely! those for whom
The place was kept at board and hearth so long,
The prayer went up through midnight's breathless gloom,
And the vain yearning woke 'midst festal song!
Hold fast thy buried isles, thy towers o'erthrown, —
But all is not thine own!

To thee the love of woman hath gone down,
Dark flow thy tides o'er manhood's noble head,
O'er youth's bright locks and beauty's flowery crown: —
Yet must thou hear a voice — Restore the Dead!
Earth shall reclaim her precious things from thee —
Restore the Dead, thou Sea!

Thomas Hood. 1798–1845. (Manual, p. 434.)

322. The Bridge of Sighs.

One more unfortunate,
  Weary of breath,
Rashly importunate,
  Gone to her death!

Take her up tenderly,
  Lift her with care,
Fashioned so slenderly,
  Young, and so fair.

Look at her garments
Clinging like cerements;
  Whilst the wave constantly
Drips from her clothing;
  Take her up instantly,
Loving, not loathing.

Touch her not scornfully;
Think of her mournfully,
  Gently, and humanly;
Not of the stains of her;
All that remains of her
  Now is pure womanly.

Make no deep scrutiny
Into her mutiny
  Rash and undutiful;
Past all dishonor,
Death has left on her
  Only the beautiful.

Still, for all slips of hers,
  One of Eve's family,
Wipe those poor lips of hers,
  Oozing so clammily.

Loop up her tresses,
  Escaped from the comb,
Her fair auburn tresses,
Whilst wonderment guesses,
  Where was her home?
  Who was her father?
  Who was her mother?

Had she a sister?
Had she a brother?
Or was there a dearer one
Still, or a nearer one
Yet, than all other?

Alas! for the rarity
Of Christian charity
Under the sun!
O! it was pitiful —
Near a whole city full,
Home had she none!

Sisterly, brotherly,
Fatherly, motherly,
Feelings had changed;
Love, by harsh evidence
Thrown from its eminence,
Even God's providence
Seeming estranged.

When the lamps quiver
So far in the river,
With many a light
From many a casement,
From garret to basement,
She stood, with amazement,
Houseless by night.

The bleak wind of March
Made her tremble and shiver,
But not the dark arch,
Or the black flowing river.
Mad, from life's history,
Glad, to death's mystery,
Swift to be hurled
Anywhere! anywhere
Out of the world!

In she plunged boldly,
No matter how coldly
The rough river ran;
Over the brink of it,
Picture it — think of it,
Dissolute man!
Lave in it — drink of it
Then, if you can.

Take her up tenderly,
  Lift her with care,
Fashioned so slenderly,
  Young, and so fair.

Ere her limbs frigidly
Stiffen too rigidly,
  Decently, kindly
Smooth and compose them;
And her eyes, close them,
  Staring so blindly!

Dreadfully staring
  Through muddy impurity,
As when with the daring,
Last look of despairing,
  Fixed on futurity.

Perishing gloomily,
Spurned by contumely,
Bold inhumanity,
Burning insanity,
  Into her rest;
Cross her hands humbly,
As if praying dumbly,
  Over her breast!
Owning her weakness,
  Her evil behavior,
And leaving, with meekness,
  Her sins to her Saviour.

---

323. The Death-Bed.

We watched her breathing through the night,
  Her breathing soft and low,
As in her breast the wave of life
  Kept surging to and fro.

So silently we seemed to speak,
  So slowly moved about,
As we had lent her half our powers
  To eke her being out.

Our very hopes belied our fears,
  Our fears our hopes belied,—
We thought her dying when she slept,
  And sleeping when she died.

For when the morn came, dim and sad,
  And chill with early showers,
Her quiet eyelids closed — she had
  Another morn than ours.

ELIZABETH BARRETT BROWNING. —— -1861. (Manual, p. 435.)

324. COWPER'S GRAVE.

It is a place where poets crowned may feel the heart's decaying,
It is a place where happy saints may weep amid their praying;
Yet let the grief and humbleness as low as silence languish,
Earth surely now may give her calm to whom she gave her anguish.
O poets! from a maniac's tongue, was poured the deathless singing;
O Christians! at your cross of hope, a hopeless hand was clinging;
O men! this man in brotherhood your weary paths beguiling,
Groaned inly while he taught you peace, and died while ye were smiling.
And now what time ye all may read through dimming tears his story,
How discord on the music fell, and darkness on the glory;
And how, when, one by one, sweet sounds and wandering lights departed,
He wore no less a loving face, because so broken-hearted.
He shall be strong to sanctify the poet's high vocation,
And bow the meekest Christian down in meeker adoration;
Nor ever shall he be, in praise, by wise or good forsaken;
Named softly as the household name of one whom God hath taken!

THOMAS BABINGTON MACAULAY. 1800–1859.

325. THE BATTLE OF IVRY.[1]

[Henry the Fourth, on his accession to the French crown, was opposed by a large part of his subjects, under the Duke of Mayenne, with the assistance of Spain and Savoy. In March, 1590, he gained a decisive victory over that party at Ivry. Before the battle, he addressed his troops, "My children, if you lose sight of your colors, rally to my white plume — you will always find it in the path to honor and glory." His conduct was answerable to his promise. Nothing could resist his impetuous valor, and the Leaguers underwent a total and bloody defeat. In the midst of the rout, Henry followed, crying, "Save the French!" and his clemency added a number of the enemies to his own army.]

Now glory to the Lord of Hosts, from whom all glories are!
And glory to our Sovereign Liege, King Henry of Navarre!

1 Pronounced *E-vree.* Ivry-la-Bataille is in the Department of Eure, seventeen miles South-east of Evreux.

Now let there be the merry sound of music and the dance,
Through thy cornfields green, and sunny vines, O pleasant land of
France.
And thou, Rochelle, our own Rochelle, proud city of the waters,
Again let rapture light the eyes of all thy mourning daughters.
As thou wert constant in our ills, be joyous in our joy,
For cold, and stiff, and still are they who wrought thy walls annoy.
Hurrah! hurrah! a single field hath turned the chance of war;
Hurrah! hurrah! for Ivry, and King Henry of Navarre.

O, how our hearts were beating, when at the dawn of day,
We saw the army of the League drawn out in long array;
With all its priest-led citizens, and all its rebel peers,
And Appenzel's stout infantry, and Egmont's Flemish spears.
There rode the brood of false Lorraine, the curses of our land!
And dark Mayenne was in the midst, a truncheon in his hand;
And, as we looked on them, we thought of Seine's empurpled flood,
And good Coligni's hoary hair all dabbled with his blood;
And we cried unto the living God, who rules the fate of war,
To fight for his own holy Name and Henry of Navarre.

The king is come to marshal us, in all his armor drest,
And he has bound a snow-white plume upon his gallant crest:
He looked upon his people, and a tear was in his eye;
He looked upon the traitors, and his glance was stern and high.
Right graciously he smiled on us, as rolled from wing to wing,
Down all our line, in deafening shout, "God save our lord, the King!
And if my standard-bearer fall, as fall full well he may, —
For never saw I promise yet of such a bloody fray, —
Press where ye see my white plume shine, amidst the ranks of war,
And be your oriflamme, to-day, the helmet of Navarre."

Hurrah! the foes are moving! Hark to the mingled din
Of fife, and steed, and trump, and drum, and roaring culverin!
The fiery Duke is pricking fast across Saint Andre's plain,
With all the hireling chivalry of Guelders and Almayne.
Now by the lips of those ye love, fair gentlemen of France,
Charge for the golden lilies now, upon them with the lance!
A thousand spurs are striking deep, a thousand spears in rest,
A thousand knights are pressing close behind the snow-white crest;
And in they burst, and on they rushed, while, like a guiding star,
Amidst the thickest carnage, blazed the helmet of Navarre.

Now God be praised, the day is ours! Mayenne hath turned his rein,
D'Aumale hath cried for quarter — the Flemish Count is slain,
Their ranks are breaking like thin clouds before a Biscay gale;
The field is heaped with bleeding steeds, and flags, and cloven mail;
And then we thought on vengeance, and all along our van,
"Remember St. Bartholomew," was passed from man to man;

But out spake gentle Henry then, "No Frenchman is my foe;
Down, down with every foreigner; but let your brethren go."
O, was there ever such a knight, in friendship or in war,
As our sovereign lord, King Henry, the soldier of Navarre!

Ho, maidens of Vienna! Ho, matrons of Lucerne!
Weep, weep, and rend your hair, for those who never shall return:
Ho, Philip, send for charity thy Mexican pistoles,
That Antwerp monks may sing a mass for thy poor spearmen's souls!
Ho, gallant nobles of the League, look that your arms be bright!
Ho, burghers of St. Genevieve, keep watch and ward to-night!
For our God hath crushed the tyrant, our God hath raised the slave,
And mocked the counsel of the wise, and the valor of the brave.
Then glory to his holy Name, from whom all glories are;
And glory to our sovereign lord, King Henry of Navarre.

CHAPTER XXII.

LETTER WRITERS AND MODERN ESSAYISTS, WITH PROSE WRITERS OF THE NINETEENTH CENTURY.

Horace Walpole. 1717–1797. (Manual, p. 437.)

326. Letter to Sir Horace Mann.

Arlington Street, March 17, 1757.

Admiral Byng's tragedy was completed on Monday — a perfect tragedy, for there were variety of incidents, villany, murder, and a hero! His sufferings, persecutions, aspersions, disturbances, nay, the revolutions of his fate, had not in the least unhinged his mind; his whole behavior was natural and firm. A few days before, one of his friends standing by him, said, "Which of us is tallest?" He replied, "Why this ceremony? I know what it means; let the man come and measure me for my coffin." He said, that being acquitted of cowardice, and being persuaded on the coolest reflection that he had acted for the best, and should act so again, he was not unwilling to suffer. He desired to be shot on the quarter-deck, not where common malefactors are; came out at twelve, sat down in a chair, for he would not kneel, and refused to have his face covered, that his countenance might show whether he feared death; but being told that it might frighten his executioners, he submitted,[1] gave the signal at once, received one shot through the head, another through the heart, and fell. Do cowards live or die thus? Can that man want spirit who only fears to terrify his executioners? Has the aspen Duke of Newcastle lived thus? Would my Lord Hardwicke die thus, even supposing he had nothing on his conscience?

This scene is over! what will be the next is matter of great uncertainty. The new ministers are well weary of their situation; without credit at court, without influence in the House of Commons, undermined everywhere, I believe they are too sensible not to desire to be delivered of their burden, which those who increase yet dread to take on themselves. Mr. Pitt's health is as bad as his situation; confidence between the other factions almost impossible; yet I believe their impatience will prevail over their distrust. The nation expects a change every day, and being a nation, I believe, desires it; and being the English nation, will condemn it the moment it is made. We

1 Admiral Byng, on the morning of his execution, took his usual draught for the scurvy.

are trembling for Hanover, and the Duke [of Cumberland] is going to command the army of observation. These are the politics of the week: the diversions are balls, and the two Princes frequent them; but the eldest nephew [afterwards George III.] remains shut up in a room, where, as desirous as they are of keeping him, I believe he is now and then incommode. The Duke of Richmond has made two balls on his approaching wedding with Lady Mary Bruce (Mr. Conway's[2] daughter-in-law): it is the perfectest match in the world; youth, beauty, riches, alliances, and all the blood of all the kings from Robert Bruce to Charles II. They are the prettiest couple in England, except the father-in-law and mother.

As I write so often to you, you must be content with shorter letters, which, however, are always as long as I can make them. *This* summer will not contract our correspondence. Adieu! my dear Sir.

2 Lady Mary Bruce was only daughter of Charles, last Earl of Ailesbury, by Caroline his third wife, daughter of General John Campbell, afterwards Duke of Argyll. Lady Ailesbury married to her second husband, Colonel Henry Seymour Conway, only brother of Francis, Earl of Hertford.

William Cowper. 1731–1800. (Manual, p. 359.)

327. Letter to the Rev. John Newton.

August 21, 1780.

The following occurrence ought not to be passed over in silence, in a place where so few notable ones are to be met with. Last Wednesday night, while we were at supper, between the hours of eight and nine, I heard an unusual noise in the back parlor, as if one of the hares was entangled, and endeavoring to disengage herself. I was just going to rise from table, when it ceased. In about five minutes, a voice on the outside of the parlor door inquired if one of my hares had got away. I immediately rushed into the next room, and found that my poor favorite Puss had made her escape. She had gnawed in sunder the strings of a lattice work, with which I thought I had sufficiently secured the window, and which I preferred to any other sort of blind, because it admitted plenty of air. From thence I hastened to the kitchen, where I saw the redoubtable Thomas Freeman, who told me, that having seen her, just after she had dropped into the street, he attempted to cover her with his hat, but she screamed out, and leaped directly over his head. I then desired him to pursue as fast as possible, and added Richard Coleman to the chase, as being nimbler, and carrying less weight than Thomas; not expecting to see her again, but desirous to learn, if possible, what became of her. In something less than an hour, Richard returned, almost breathless, with the following account. That soon after he began to run, he left Tom behind him, and came in sight of a most numerous hunt of men, women, children, and dogs; that he did his best to keep back the dogs, and presently outstripped the crowd, so that the race was at last disputed between himself and Puss; — she ran right through the town, and down the lane that leads to Dropshort; a little before she came to the house, he got the start and turned her; she pushed for the town again, and soon after she entered it, sought shelter in Mr. Wagstaff's tanyard, adjoining to old Mr. Drake's. Sturges's harvest men were at supper, and saw her from the opposite side of the way. There she encountered the tanpits full of water; and while she was struggling out of one pit, and plunging into another, and almost drowned, one of the men drew her out by the ears, and secured her. She was then well washed in a bucket, to get the lime out of her coat, and brought home in a sack at ten o'clock.

This frolic cost us four shillings, but you may believe we did not grudge a farthing of it. The poor creature received only a little hurt in one of her claws, and in one of her ears, and is now almost as well as ever.

I do not call this an answer to your letter, but such as it is I send it, presuming upon that interest which I know you take in my minutest concerns, which I cannot express better than in the words of Terence a little varied — *Nihil mei a te alienum putas.*

Yours, my dear friend,

W. C.

---

328. To Lady Hesketh.

Feb. 27, 1786.

My Dearest Cousin,

* * * * Now for Homer, and the matters to Homer appertaining. Sephus and I are of opinions perfectly different on the subject of such an advertisement as he recommends. The only proper part for me is not to know that such a man as Pope has ever existed. I am so nice upon this subject that in that note in the specimen, in which I have accounted for the anger of Achilles (which, I believe, I may pay myself the compliment to say was never accounted for before), I have not even so much as hinted at the perplexity in which Pope was entangled when he endeavored to explain it, nor at the preposterous and blundering work that he has made with it. No, my dear, as I told you once before, my attempt has itself a loud voice, and speaks a most intelligible language. Had Pope's translation been good, or had I thought it such, or had I not known that it is admitted by all whom a knowledge of the original qualifies to judge of it, to be a very defective one, I had never translated myself one line of Homer. Dr. Johnson is the only modern writer who has spoken of it in terms of approbation, at least the only one that I have met with. And his praise of it is such as convinces me, intimately acquainted as I am with Pope's performance, that he talked at random, that either he had never examined it by Homer's, or never since he was a boy. For I would undertake to produce numberless passages from it, if need were, not only ill translated, but meanly written. It is not therefore for me, convinced as I am of the truth of all I say, to go forth into the

world holding up Pope's translation with one hand as a work to be extolled, and my own with the other as a work still wanted. It is plain to me that I behave with sufficient liberality on the occasion if, neither praising nor blaming my predecessor, I go right forward, and leave the world to decide between us.

Now, to come nearer to myself. Poets, my dear (it is a secret I have lately discovered), are born to trouble; and of all poets, translators of Homer to the most. Our dear friend, the General, whom I truly love, in his last letter mortified me not a little. I do not mean by suggesting lines that he thought might be amended, for I hardly ever wrote fifty lines together that I could not afterwards have improved, but by what appeared to me an implied censure on the whole, or nearly the whole quire that I sent to you. It was a great work, he said; — it should be kept long in hand; — years, if it were possible; that it stood in need of much amendment, that it ought to be made worthy of me, that he could not think of showing it to Maty, that he could not even think of laying it before Johnson and his friend in its present condition. Now, my dear, understand thou this: if there lives a man who stands clear of the charge of careless writing, I am that man. I might prudently, perhaps, but I could not honestly, admit that charge: it would account in a way favorable to my own ability for many defects of which I am guilty, but it would be disingenuous and untrue. The copy which I sent to you was almost a new, I mean a second, translation, as far as it went. With the first I had taken pains, but with the second I took more. I weighed many expressions, exacted from myself the utmost fidelity to my author, and tried all the numbers upon my own ear again and again. If therefore, after all this care, the execution be such as in the General's account it seems to be, I appear to have made shipwreck of my hopes at once. He said, indeed, that the similes delighted him, and the catalogue of the ships surpassed his expectations: but his commendation of so small a portion of the whole affected me rather painfully, as it seemed to amount to an implied condemnation of the rest. I have been the more uneasy because I know his taste to be good, and by the selection that he made of lines that he thought should be altered, he proved it such. I altered them all, and thanked him, as I could very sincerely, for his friendly attention. Now what is the present state of my mind on this subject? It is this. I do not myself think ill of what I have done, nor at the same time so foolishly well as to suppose that it has no blemishes. But I am sadly afraid that the General's anxiety will make him extremely difficult to be pleased: I fear that he will require of me more than any other man would require, or than he himself would require of any other writer. What I can do to give him satisfaction, I am perfectly ready to do; but it is possible for an anxious friend to demand more than my ability could perform. Not a syllable of all this, my dear, to him, or to any other creature. — Mum!

Yours most truly,

WM. COWPER.

THOMAS DE QUINCEY. 1785–1859. (Manual, p. 472.)

FROM "THE ENGLISH OPIUM EATER."

329. INTERVIEW WITH A MALAY.

One day a Malay knocked at my door. What business a Malay could have to transact among English mountains, I canot conjecture; but possibly he was on his road to a sea-port, about forty miles distant. The servant who opened the door to him was a young girl born and bred among the mountains, who had never seen an Asiatic dress of any sort: his turban, therefore, confounded her not a little; and, as it turned out that his attainments in English were exactly of the same extent as hers in the Malay, there seemed to be an impassable gulf fixed between all communication of ideas, if either party had happened to possess any. In this dilemma, the girl recollecting the reputed learning of her master (and, doubtless, giving me credit for a knowledge of all the languages of the earth, besides, perhaps, a few of the lunar ones), came and gave me to understand that there was a sort of demon below, whom she clearly imagined that my art could exorcise from the house. I did not immediately go down; but when I did, the group which presented itself, arranged as it was by accident, though not very elaborate, took hold of my fancy and my eye in a way that none of the statuesque attitudes exhibited in the ballets at the opera-house, though so ostentatiously complex, had ever done. In a cottage kitchen, but panelled on the wall with dark wood that from age and rubbing resembled oak, and looking more like a rustic hall of entrance than a kitchen, stood the Malay — his turban and loose trousers of dingy white relieved upon the dark panelling: he had placed himself nearer to the girl than she seemed to relish, though her native spirit of mountain intrepidity contended with the feelings of simple awe which her countenance expressed as she gazed upon the tiger-cat before her. And a more striking picture there could not be imagined than the beautiful English face of the girl, and its exquisite fairness, together with her erect and independent attitude, contrasted with the sallow and bilious skin of the Malay, enamelled or veneered with mahogany by marine air; his small, fierce, restless eyes, thin lips, slavish gestures and adorations. Half hidden by the ferocious-looking Malay was a little child from a neighboring cottage, who had crept in after him, and was now in the act of reverting its head and gazing upwards at the turban and the fiery eyes beneath it, whilst with one hand he caught at the dress of the young woman for protection. My knowledge of the Oriental tongues is not remarkably extensive, being, indeed, confined to two words — the Arabic word for barley and the Turkish for opium (*madjoon*), which I have learnt from Anastasius. And as I had neither a Malay dictionary nor even Adelung's *Mithridates*, which might have helped me to a few words, I addressed him in some lines from the Iliad, considering that, of such languages as I possessed, Greek, in point of longitude, came geographically nearest to an Oriental one. He worshipped me in a most devout manner, and replied in what I suppose was Malay. In this way I saved my reputation with my neighbors, for the Malay had no means of betraying the secret. He lay down upon the floor for about an hour, and then pursued his journey. On his departure, I presented him with a piece of opium. To him, as an Orientalist, I concluded that opium must be familiar; and the expression of his face convinced me that it was. Nevertheless I was struck with some little consternation when I saw him suddenly raise his hand to his mouth, and (in the school-boy phrase) bolt the whole, divided into three pieces, at one mouthful. The quantity was enough to kill three dragoons and their horses, and I felt some alarm for the poor creature; but what could be done? I had given him the opium in compassion for his solitary life, on recollecting that, if he had travelled on foot from London, it must be nearly three weeks since he could have exchanged a thought with any human being. I could not think of violating the laws of hospitality by having him surged and drenched with an emetic, and thus frightening him into a notion that we were going to sacrifice him to some English idol. No, there was clearly no help for it; he took his leave, and for some days I felt anxious; but as I never heard of any Malay being found dead, I became convinced that he was used to opium, and that I must have done him the service I designed, by giving him one night of respite from the pains of wandering.

---

330. Opium Dreams.

All this, and much more than I can say, the reader must enter into, before he can comprehend the unimaginable horror which these dreams of Oriental imagery and mythological tortures impressed upon me. Under the connecting feeling of tropical heat and vertical sunlights, I brought together all creatures, birds, beasts, reptiles, all trees and plants, usages and appearances, that are found in all tropical regions, and assembled them together in China or Hindostan.

From kindred feelings, I soon brought Egypt and her gods under the same law. I was stared at, hooted at, grinned at, chattered at, by monkeys, by paroquets, by cockatoos. I ran into pagodas, and was fixed for centuries at the summit, or in secret rooms. I was the idol; I was the priest; I was worshipped; I was sacrificed. I fled from the wrath of Brama through all the forests of Asia. Vishnu hated me; Seeva lay in wait for me. I came suddenly upon Isis and Osiris. I had done a deed, they said, which the ibis and the crocodile trembled at. Thousands of years I lived and was buried in stone coffins, with mummies and sphinxes, in narrow chambers at the heart of eternal pyramids. I was kissed, with cancerous kisses, by crocodiles, and was laid, confounded with all unutterable abortions, amongst reeds and Nilotic mud.

Some slight abstraction I thus attempt of my Oriental dreams, which filled me always with such amazement at the monstrous scenery, that horror seemed absorbed for a while in sheer astonishment. Sooner or later came a reflux of feeling that swallowed up the astonishment, and left me, not so much in terror, as in hatred and abomination of what I saw. Over every form, and threat, and punishment, and dim sightless incarceration, brooded a killing sense of eternity and infinity. Into these dreams only it was, with one or two slight exceptions, that any circumstances of physical horror entered. All before had been moral and spiritual terrors. But here the main agents were ugly birds, or snakes, or crocodiles, especially the last. The cursed crocodile became to me the object of more horror than all the rest. I was compelled to live with him, and (as was always the case in my dreams) for centuries. Sometimes I escaped, and found myself in Chinese houses. All the feet of the tables, sofas, &c., soon became instinct with life: the abominable head of the crocodile, and his leering eyes, looked out at me, multiplied into ten thousand repetitions; and I stood loathing and fascinated. So often did this hideous reptile haunt my dreams, that many times the very same dream was broken up in the very same way. I heard gentle voices speaking to me (I hear everything when I am sleeping), and instantly I awoke; it was broad noon, and my children were standing, hand in hand, at my bedside, come to show me their colored shoes, or new frocks, or to let me see them dressed for going out. No experience was so awful to me, and at the same time so pathetic, as this abrupt translation from the darkness of the infinite to the gaudy summer air of highest noon, and from the unutterable abortions of miscreated gigantic vermin to the sight of infancy and innocent human natures.

* * * * * * *

Then suddenly would come a dream of far different character, — a tumultuous dream, — commencing with a music such as now I often heard in sleep — music of preparation and of awakening suspense. The undulations of fast-gathering tumults were like the opening of the Coronation Anthem; and, like *that*, gave the feeling of a multitudinous movement, of infinite cavalcades filing off, and the tread of innumerable armies. The morning was come of a mighty day — a day of crisis and of ultimate hope for human nature, then suffering mysterious eclipse, and laboring in some dread extremity. Somewhere, but I knew not where — somehow, but I knew not how — by some beings, but I knew not by whom — a battle, a strife, an agony, was travelling through all its stages — was evolving itself, like the catastrophe of some mighty drama, with which my sympathy was the more insupportable, from deepening confusion as to its local scene, its cause, its nature, and its undecipherable issue. I (as is usual in dreams, where, of necessity, we make ourselves central to every movement) had the power, and yet had not the power, to decide it. I had the power, if I could raise myself to will it; and yet again had not the power, for the weight of twenty Atlantics was upon me, or the oppression of inexpiable guilt. "Deeper than ever plummet sounded" I lay inactive. Then, like a chorus, the passion deepened. Some greater interest was at stake, some mightier cause, than ever yet the sword had pleaded, or trumpet had proclaimed. Then came sudden alarms; hurryings to and fro, trepidations of innumerable fugitives; I knew not whether from the good cause or the bad; darkness and lights; tempest and human faces; and, at last, with the sense that all was lost, female forms, and the features that were worth all the world to me; and but a moment allowed — and clasped hands, with heart-breaking partings, and then — everlasting farewells; and, with a sigh, such as the caves of hell sighed when the incestuous mother uttered the abhorred name of Death, the sound was reverberated — everlasting farewells! and again, and yet again reverberated — everlasting farewells!

And I awoke in struggles, and cried aloud, "I will sleep no more!"

SYDNEY SMITH. 1771–1845. (Manual, p. 468.)

331. WIT.

There is an association in men's minds between dulness and wisdom, amusement and folly, which has a very powerful influence in decision upon character, and is not overcome without considerable difficulty. The reason is, that the *outward* signs of a dull man and a wise man are the same, and so are the outward signs of a frivolous man and a witty man; and we are not to expect that the majority will be disposed to look to much *more* than the outward sign. I believe the fact to be, that wit is very seldom the *only* eminent quality which resides in the mind of any man; it is commonly accompanied by many other talents of every description, and ought to be considered as a strong evidence of a fertile and superior understanding. Almost all the great poets, orators, and statesmen of all times, have been witty. Cæsar, Alexander, Aristotle, Descartes, and Lord Bacon, were witty men; so were Cicero, Shakspeare, Demosthenes, Boileau, Pope, Dryden, Fontenelle, Jonson, Waller, Cowley, Solon, Socrates, Dr. Johnson, and almost every man who has made a distinguished figure in the House of Commons . . . The meaning of an extraordinary man is, that he is *eight* men, not one man; that he has as much wit as if he had no sense, and as much sense as if he had no wit; that his conduct is as judicious as if he were the dullest of human beings, and his imagination as brilliant as if he were irretrievably ruined. But when wit is combined with sense and information; when it is softened by benevolence, and restrained by strong principle; when it is in the hands of a man who can use it, and despise it, who can be witty, and something much *better* than witty, who loves honor, justice, decency, good-nature, morality, and religion, ten thousand times better than wit; — wit is *then* a beautiful and delightful part of our nature. There is no more interesting spectacle than to see the effects of wit upon the different characters of men; than to observe it expanding caution, relaxing dignity, unfreezing coldness, — teaching age, and care, and pain, to smile, — extorting reluctant gleams of pleasure from melancholy, and charming even the pangs of grief. It is pleasant to observe how it penetrates through the coldness and awkwardness of society, gradually bringing men nearer together, and, like the combined force of wine and oil, giving every man a glad heart and a shining countenance. Genuine and innocent wit like this is surely the *flavor of the mind!* Man could direct his ways by plain reason, and support his life by tasteless food; but God has given us wit, and flavor, and laughter, and perfumes, to enliven the days of man's pilgrimage, and to "charm his pained steps over the burning marle."

---

332. From "The Letters of Peter Plymley."

I confess, it mortifies me to the very quick to contrast with our matchless stupidity and inimitable folly the conduct of Bonaparte upon the subject of religious persecution. At the moment when we are tearing the crucifixes from the necks of the Catholics, and washing pious mud from the foreheads of the Hindoos, — at that moment this man is assembling the very Jews in Paris, and endeavoring to give them stability and importance. I shall never be reconciled to mending shoes in America; but I see it must be my lot, and I will then take a dreadful revenge upon Mr. Perceval, if I catch him preaching within ten miles of me. You cannot imagine, you say, that England will ever be ruined and conquered; and for no other reason that I can find, but because it seems so very odd it should be ruined and conquered. Alas! so reasoned, in their time, the Austrian, Russian, and Prussian Plymleys. But the English are brave; so were all these nations. You might get together a hundred thousand men individually brave; but without generals capable of commanding such a machine, it would be as useless as a first-rate man-of-war manned by Oxford clergymen or Parisian shopkeepers. I do not say this to the disparagement of English officers — they have had no means of acquiring experience; but I do say it to create alarm; for we do not appear to me to be half alarmed enough, or to entertain that sense of our danger which leads to the most obvious means of self-defence. As for the spirit of the peasantry, in making a gallant defence behind hedgerows, and through plate-racks and hen-coops, highly as I think of their bravery, I do not know any nation in Europe so likely to be struck with panic as the English; and this from their total unacquaintance with the science of war. Old wheat and beans blazing for twenty miles round; cart-mares shot; sows of Lord Somerville's breed running wild over the country; the minister of the parish sorely wounded; Mrs. Plymley in fits, — all these scenes of war an

Austrian or a Russian has seen three or four times over; but it is now three centuries since an English pig has fallen in a fair battle upon English ground, or a farm-house been rifled.

There is a village (no matter where) in which the inhabitants, on one day in the year, sit down to a dinner prepared at the common expense: by an extraordinary piece of tyranny (which Lord Hawkesbury would call the wisdom of the village ancestors), the inhabitants of three of the streets, about a hundred years ago, seized upon the inhabitants of the fourth street, bound them hand and foot, laid them upon their backs, and compelled them to look on while the rest were stuffing themselves with beef and beer: the next year, the inhabitants of the persecuted street (though they contributed an equal quota of the expense) were treated precisely in the same manner. The tyranny grew into a custom: and (as the manner of our nature is) it was considered as the most sacred of all duties to keep these poor fellows without their annual dinner: the village was so tenacious of this practice, that nothing could induce them to resign it; every enemy to it was looked upon as a disbeliever in Divine Providence, and any nefarious churchwarden who wished to succeed in his election, had nothing to do but to represent his antagonist as an abolitionist, in order to frustrate his ambition, endanger his life, and throw the village into a state of the most dreadful commotion. By degrees, however, the obnoxious street grew to be so well peopled, and its inhabitants so firmly united, that their oppressors, more afraid of injustice, were more disposed to be just. At the next dinner they are unbound, the year after allowed to sit upright, then a bit of bread and a glass of water; till at last, after a long series of concessions, they are emboldened to ask, in pretty plain terms, that they may be allowed to sit down at the bottom of the table, and to fill their bellies as well as the rest. Forthwith a general cry of shame and scandal: "Ten years ago, were you not laid upon your backs? Don't you remember what a great thing you thought it to get a piece of bread? How thankfnl you were for cheese-parings? Have you forgotten that memorable era, when the lord of the manor interfered to obtain for you a a slice of the public pudding? And now, with an audacity only equalled by your ingratitude, you have the impudence to ask for knives and forks, and to request, in terms too plain to be mistaken, that you may sit down to table with the rest, and be indulged even with beef and beer; there are not more than half a dozen dishes which we have reserved for ourselves: the rest has been thrown open to you in the utmost profusion; you have potatoes and carrots, suet dumplings, sops in the pan, and delicious toast and water, in incredible quantities. Beef, mutton, lamb, pork, and veal are ours; and if you were not the most restless and dissatisfied of human beings, you would never think of aspiring to enjoy them."

Is not this, my dainty Abraham, the very nonsense, and the very insult which is talked to and practised upon the Catholics? You are surprised that men who have tasted of partial justice should ask for perfect justice; that he who has been robbed of coat and cloak will not be contented with the restitution of one of his garments. He would be a very lazy blockhead if he were content; and I (who, though an inhabitant of the village, have preserved, thank God, some sense of justice) most earnestly counsel these half-fed claimants to persevere in their just demands till they are admitted to a more complete share of a dinner for which they pay as much as the others; and if they see a little attenuated lawyer squabbling at the head of their opponents, let them desire him to empty his pockets, and to pull out all the pieces of duck, fowl, and pudding which he has filched from the public feast, to carry home to his wife and children.

Francis Jeffrey. 1773–1850. (Manual, p. 468.)

333. English Literature.

Our first literature consisted of saintly legends, and romances of chivalry, — though Chaucer gave it a more national and popular character, by his original descriptions of external nature, and the familiarity and gayety of his social humor. In the time of Elizabeth, it received a copious infusion of classical images and ideas; but it was still intrinsically romantic — serious — and even somewhat lofty and enthusiastic. Authors were then so few in number, that they were looked upon with a sort of veneration, and considered as a kind of inspired persons; — at least they were not yet so numerous as to be obliged to abuse each other, in order to obtain a share of distinction for themselves; — and they neither affected a tone of derision in their writings, nor wrote in fear of derision from others. They were filled with their subjeets, and dealt with them fearlessly in their own way; and the stamp of originality, force, and freedom, is consequently upon almost all their productions. In the reign of James I., our literature, with some few exceptions, touching rather the form than the substance of its merits, appears to us to have reached the greatest perfection to which it has yet attained; though it would probably have advanced still farther in the succeeding reign, had not the great national dissensions which then arose, turned the talent and energy of the people into other channels — first, to the assertion of their civil rights, and afterwards to the discussion of their religious interests. The graces of literature suffered of course in those fierce contentions; and a deeper shade of austerity was thrown upon the intellectual character of the nation. Her genius, however, though less captivating and adorned than in the happier days which preceded, was still active, fruitful, and commanding; and the period of the civil wars, besides the mighty minds that guided the public councils, and were absorbed in public cares, produced the giant powers of Taylor, and

Hobbes, and Barrow — the muse of Milton — the learning of Coke — and the ingenuity of Cowley.

The Restoration introduced a French court — under circumstances more favorable for the effectual exercise of court influence than ever before existed in England; but this of itself would not have been sufficient to account for the sudden change in our literature which ensued. It was seconded by causes of far more general operation. The Restoration was undoubtedly a popular act; — and, indefensible as the conduct of the army and the civil leaders was on that occasion, there can be no question that the severities of Cromwell, and the extravagances of the sectaries, had made republican professions hateful, and religious ardor ridiculous, in the eyes of a great proportion of the people. All the eminent writers of the preceding period, however, had inclined to the party that was now overthrown; and their writings had not merely been accommodated to the character of the government under which they were produced, but were deeply imbued with its obnoxious principles, which were those of their respective authors. When the restraints of authority were taken off, therefore, and it became profitable, as well as popular, to discredit the fallen party, it was natural that the leading authors should affect a style of levity and derision, as most opposite to that of their opponents, and best calculated for the purposes they had in view. The nation, too, was now for the first time essentially divided in point of character and principle, and a much greater proportion were capable both of writing in support of their own notions, and of being influenced by what was written. Add to all this, that there were real and serious defects in the style and manner of the former generation; and that the grace, and brevity, and vivacity of that gayer manner which was now introduced from France, were not only good and captivating in themselves, but had then all the charms of novelty and of contrast; and it will not be difficult to understand how it came to supplant that which had been established of old in the country, — and that so suddenly, that the same generation, among whom Milton had been formed to the severe sanctity of wisdom and the noble independence of genius, lavished its loudest applauses on the obscenity and servility of such writers as Rochester and Wycherly.

This change, however, like all sudden changes, was too fierce and violent to be long maintained at the same pitch; and when the wits and profligates of King Charles had sufficiently insulted the seriousness and virtue of their predecessors, there would probably have been a revulsion towards the accustomed taste of the nation, had not the party of the innovators been reënforced by champions of more temperance and judgment. The result seemed at one time suspended on the will of Dryden — in whose individual person the genius of the English and of the French school of literature may be said to have maintained a protracted struggle. But the evil principle prevailed! Carried by the original bent of his genius, and his familiarity with our older models, to the cultivation of our native style, to which he might have imparted more steadiness and correctness — for in force and in sweetness it was already matchless — he was unluckily seduced by the attractions of fashion, and the dazzling of the dear wit and gay rhetoric in which it delighted, to lend his powerful aid to the new corruptions and refinements; and in fact, to prostitute his great gifts to the purposes of party rage or licentious ribaldry.

The sobriety of the succeeding reigns allayed this fever of profanity; but no genius arose sufficiently powerful to break the spell that still withheld us from the use of our own peculiar gifts and faculties. On the contrary, it was the unfortunate ambition of the next generation of authors, to improve and perfect the new style, rather than to return to the old one; — and it cannot be denied that they did improve it. They corrected its gross indecency — increased its precision and correctness — made its pleasantry and sarcasm more polished and elegant — and spread through the whole of its irony, its narration, and its reflection, a tone of clear and condensed good sense, which recommended itself to all who had, and all who had not any relish for higher beauties.

This is the praise of Queen Anne's wits — and to this praise they are justly entitled. This was left for them to do, and they did it well. They were invited to it by the circumstances of their situation, and do not seem to have been possessed of any such bold or vigorous spirit, as either to neglect or to outgo the invitation. Coming into life immediately after the consummation of a bloodless revolution, effected much more by the cool sense than the angry passions of the nation, they seem to have felt that they were born in an age of reason, rather than of feeling or fancy; and that men's minds, though considerably divided and unsettled upon many points, were in a much better temper to relish judicious argument and cutting satire, than the glow of enthusiastic passion, or the richness of a luxuriant imagination. To those accordingly they made no pretensions; but, writing with infinite good sense, and great grace and vivacity, and, above all, writing for the first time in a tone that was peculiar to the upper ranks of society, and upon subjects that were almost exclusively interesting to them, they naturally figured, at least while the manner was new, as the most accomplished, fashionable, and perfect writers which the world had ever seen; and made the wild, luxuriant, and humble sweetness of our earlier authors appear rude and untutored in the comparison. Men grew ashamed of admiring, and afraid of imitating, writers of so little skill and smartness; and the opinion became general, not only that their faults were intolerable, but that even their beauties were puerile and barbarous, and unworthy the serious regard of a polite and distinguishing age.

These, and similar considerations, will go far to account for the celebrity which those authors acquired in their day; but it is not quite so easy to explain how they should have so long retained their ascendant. One cause undoubtedly was, the real excellence of their productions, in the style which they had adopted. It was hopeless to think of surpassing them in that style; and, recommended as it was, by the felicity of their execution, it required some courage to depart from it, and to recur to another, which seemed to have been so lately abandoned for its sake. The age which succeeded, too, was not the age of courage or adventure. There never was, on the whole, a quieter time than the reigns of the two first Georges, and the greater part of that which ensued. There were two little provincial rebellions indeed, and a fair proportion of foreign war; but there was nothing to stir the minds of the people at large, to rouse their passions, or excite their imaginations — nothing like the agitations of the Reformation in the sixteenth century, or of the civil wars in the seventeenth. They went on, accordingly, minding their old business, and reading their old books, with great patience and stupidity. And certainly there never was so remarkable a dearth of original talent — so long an *interregnum* of native genius — as during about sixty years in the middle of the last century. The dramatic art was dead fifty years before — and poetry seemed verging to a similar extinction. The few sparks that appeared, too, showed that the old fire was burnt out, and that the altar must hereafter be heaped with fuel of another quality. Gray, with the talents rather of a critic than a poet — with learning, fastidiousness, and scrupulous delicacy of taste, instead of fire, tenderness, or invention — began and ended a small school, which we could scarcely have wished to become permanent, admirable in many respects as some of its productions are — being far too elaborate and artificial, either for grace or for fluency, and fitter to excite the admiration of scholars, than the delight of ordinary men. However, he had the merit of not being in any degree French, and of restoring to our poetry the dignity of seriousness, and the tone at least of force and energy. The Whartons, both as critics and as poets, were of considerable service in discrediting the high pretensions of the former race, and in bringing back to public notice the great stores and treasures of poetry which lay hid in the records of our older literature. Akenside attempted a sort of classical and philosophical rapture, which no elegance of language could easily have rendered popular, but which had merits of no vulgar order for those who could study it. Goldsmith wrote with perfect elegance and beauty, in a style of mellow tenderness and elaborate simplicity. He had the harmony of Pope without his quaintness, and his selectness of diction without his coldness and eternal vivacity. And, last of all, came Cowper, with a style of complete originality, — and, for the first time, made it apparent to readers of all descriptions, that Pope and Addison were no longer to be the models of English poetry.

In philosophy and prose writing in general the case was nearly parallel. The name of Hume is by far the most considerable which occurs in the period to which we have alluded. But, though his thinking was English, his style is entirely French; and being naturally of a cold fancy, there is nothing of that eloquence or richness about him which characterizes the writings of Taylor, and Hooker, and Bacon — and continues, with less weight of matter, to please in those of Cowley and Clarendon. Warburton had great powers; and wrote with more force and freedom than the wits to whom he succeeded — but his faculties were perverted by a paltry love of paradox, and rendered useless to mankind by an unlucky choice of subjects, and the arrogance and dogmatism of his temper. Adam Smith was nearly the first who made deeper reasonings and more exact knowledge popular among us; and Junius and Johnson the first who again familiarized us with more glowing and sonorous diction — and made us feel the tameness and poorness of the serious style of Addison and Swift.

CHARLES LAMB. 1775–1834. (Manual, p. 470.)

334. FROM THE "DISSERTATION UPON ROAST PIG."

Mankind, says a Chinese manuscript, which my friend M. was obliging enough to read and explain to me, for the first seventy thousand ages ate their meat raw, clawing or biting it from the living animal, just as they do in Abyssinia to this day. This period is not obscurely hinted at by their great Confucius in the second chapter of his Mundane Mutations, where he designates a kind of golden age by the term Cho-fang, literally the Cooks' holiday. The manuscript goes on to say, that the art of roasting, or rather boiling (which I take to be the elder brother) was accidentally discovered in the manner following. The swine-herd, Ho-ti, having gone out into the woods one morning, as his manner was, to collect mast for his hogs, left his cottage in the care of his eldest son Bo-bo, a great lubberly boy, who being fond of playing with fire, as younkers of his age commonly are, let some sparks escape into a bundle of straw, which kindling quickly, spread the conflagration over every part of their poor mansion, till it was reduced to ashes. Together with the cottage (a sorry antediluvian make-shift of a building, you may think it), what was of much more importance, a fine litter of new-farrowed pigs, no less than nine in number, perished. China pigs have been esteemed a luxury all over the East from the remotest periods that we read of. Bo-bo was in the utmost consternation, as you may think, not so much for the sake of the tenement, which his father and he could easily build up again with a few dry branches, and the labor of an hour or two, at any time, as for the loss of the pigs. While he was thinking what he should say to his father, and wringing his hands over the smoking remnants of one of those untimely sufferers, an odor assailed his nostrils, unlike any scent which he had before experienced. What could it proceed from? — not from the burnt cottage

— he had smelt that smell before — indeed this was by no means the first accident of the kind which had occurred through the negligence of this unlucky young firebrand. Much less did it resemble that of any known herb, weed, or flower. A premonitory moistening at the same time overflowed his nether lip. He knew not what to think. He next stooped down to feel the pig, if there were any signs of life in it. He burnt his fingers, and to cool them he applied them in his booby fashion to his mouth. Some of the crumbs of the scorched skin had come away with his fingers, and for the first time in his life (in the world's life indeed, for before him no man had known it) he tasted — *crackling!* Again he felt and fumbled at the pig. It did not burn him so much now, still he licked his fingers from a sort of habit. The truth at length broke into his slow understanding, that it was the pig that smelt so, and the pig that tasted so delicious; and, surrendering himself up to the new-born pleasure, he fell to tearing up whole handfuls of the scorched skin with the flesh next it, and was cramming it down his throat in his beastly fashion, when his sire entered amid the smoking rafters, armed with retributory cudgel, and finding how affairs stood, began to rain blows upon the young rogue's shoulders, as thick as hailstones, which Bo-bo heeded not any more than if they had been flies. The tickling pleasure, which he experienced in his lower regions, had rendered him quite callous to any inconveniences he might feel in those remote quarters. His father might lay on, but he could not beat him from his pig, till he had fairly made an end of it, when, becoming a little more sensible of his situation, something like the following dialogue ensued.

"You graceless whelp, what have you got there devouring? Is it not enough that you have burnt me down three houses with your dog's tricks, and be hanged to you, but you must be eating fire, and I know not what — what have you got there, I say?"

"O, father, the pig, the pig, do come and taste how nice the burnt pig eats."

The ears of Ho-ti tingled with horror. He cursed his son, and he cursed himself that ever he should beget a son that should eat burnt pig.

Bo-bo, whose scent was wonderfully sharpened since morning, soon raked out another pig, and fairly rending it asunder, thrust the lesser half by main force into the fists of Ho-ti, still shouting out, "Eat, eat, eat the burnt pig, father, only taste — O Lord," — with such like barbarous ejaculations, cramming all the while as if he would choke.

Ho-ti trembled every joint while he grasped the abominable thing, wavering whether he should not put his son to death for an unnatural young monster, when the crackling scorching his fingers, as it had done his son's, and applying the same remedy to them, he in his turn tasted some of its flavor, which, make what sour mouths he would for a pretence, proved not altogether displeasing to him. In conclusion (for the manuscript here is a little tedious) both father and son fairly sat down to the mess, and never left off till they had despatched all that remained of the litter.

Bo-bo was strictly enjoined not to let the secret escape, for the neighbors would certainly have stoned them for a couple of abominable wretches, who could think of improving upon the good meat which God had sent them. Nevertheless, strange stories got about. It was observed that Ho-ti's cottage was burnt down now more frequently than ever. Nothing but fires from this time forward. Some would break out in broad day, others in the night-time. As often as the sow farrowed, so sure was the house of Ho-ti to be in a blaze; and Ho-ti himself, which was the more remarkable, instead of chastising his son, seemed to grow more indulgent to him than ever. At length they were watched, the terrible mystery discovered, and father and son summoned to take their trial at Pekin, then an inconsiderable assize town. Evidence was given, the obnoxious food itself produced in court, and verdict about to be pronounced, when the foreman of the jury begged that some of the burnt pig, of which the culprits stood accused, might be handed into the box. He handled it, and they all handled it, and burning their fingers, as Bo-bo and his father had done before them, and nature prompting to each of them the same remedy, against the face of all the facts, and the clearest charge which judge had ever given, — to the surprise of the whole court, townsfolk, strangers, reporters, and all present, — without leaving the box, or any manner of consultation whatever, they brought in a simultaneous verdict of Not Guilty.

The judge, who was a shrewd fellow, winked at the manifest iniquity of the decision; and, when the court was dismissed, went privily, and bought up all the pigs that could be had for love or money. In a few days his Lordship's town house was observed to be on fire. The thing took wing, and now there was nothing to be seen but fires in every direction. Fuel and pigs grew enormously dear all over the district. The insurance offices one and all shut up shop. People built slighter and slighter every day, until it was feared that the very science of architecture would in no long time be lost to the world. Thus this custom of firing houses continued, till in process of time, says my manuscript, a sage arose, like our Locke, who made a discovery, that the flesh of swine, or indeed of any other animal, might be cooked (*burnt*, as they called it) without the necessity of consuming a whole house to dress it. Then first began the rude form of a gridiron. Roasting by the string, or spit, came in a century or two later, I forget in whose dynasty. By such slow degrees, concludes the manuscript, do the most useful, and seemingly the most obvious arts, make their way among mankind.

335. A Quaker's Meeting.

Still-born Silence! thou that art
Flood-gate of the deeper heart!
Offspring of a heavenly kind!
Frost o' the mouth, and thaw o' the mind!
Secrecy's confidant, and he
Who makes religion mystery!
Admiration's speakingest tongue!
Leave, thy desert shades among,
Reverend hermits' hallowed cells,
Where retired devotion dwells!
With thy enthusiasms come,
Seize our tongues, and strike us dumb.[1]

Reader, wouldst thou know what true peace and quiet mean; wouldst thou find a refuge from the noises and clamors of the multitude; wouldst thou enjoy at once solitude and society; wouldst thou possess the depth of thy own spirit in stillness, without being shut out from the consolatory faces of thy species; wouldst thou be alone, and yet accompanied; solitary, yet not desolate; singular, yet not without some to keep thee in countenance; a unit in aggregate; a simple in composite? — come with me into a Quaker's Meeting.

Dost thou love silence deep as that "before the winds were made?" go not out into the wilderness, descend not into the profundities of the earth; shut not up thy casements; nor pour wax into the little cells of thy ears, with little-faithed self-mistrusting Ulysses. — Retire with me into a Quaker's Meeting.

For a man to refrain even from good words, and to hold his peace, it is commendable; but for a multitude, it is great mastery.

What is the stillness of the desert, compared with this place? what the uncommunicating muteness of fishes? — here the goddess reigns and revels. — "Boreas, and Cesias, and Argestes loud," do not with their inter-confounding uproars more augment the brawl — nor the waves of the blown Baltic with their clubbed sounds — than their opposite (Silence her sacred self) is multiplied and rendered more intense by numbers, and by sympathy. She too hath her deeps, that call unto deeps. Negation itself hath a positive more and less; and closed eyes would seem to obscure the great obscurity of midnight.

There are wounds which an imperfect solitude cannot heal. By imperfect, I mean that which a man enjoyeth by himself. The perfect is that which he can sometimes attain in crowds, but nowhere so absolutely as in a Quaker's Meeting. — Those first hermits did certainly understand this principle when they retired into Egyptian solitudes, not singly, but in shoals, to enjoy one another's want of conversation. The Carthusian is bound to his brethren by this agreeing spirit of incommunicativeness. In secular occasions, what so pleasant as to be reading a book through a long winter evening, with a friend sitting by — say, a wife — he, or she, too (if that be probable), reading an-

1 From "Poems of all Sorts," by Richard Fleckno, 1653.

other, without interruption or oral communication? — can there be no sympathy without the gabble of words? — away with this inhuman, shy, single, shade-and-cavern-haunting solitariness. Give me, Master Zimmerman, a sympathetic solitude.

To pace alone in the cloisters or side aisles of some cathedral, time-striken;

> Or under hanging mountains,
> Or by the fall of fountains;

is but a vulgar luxury, compared with that which those enjoy who come together for the purposes of more complete, abstracted solitude. This is the loneliness "to be felt." — The Abbey Church of Westminster hath nothing so solemn, so spirit-soothing, as the naked walls and benches of a Quaker's Meeting. Here are no tombs, no inscriptions, —

> sands, ignoble things,
> Dropt from the ruined sides of kings, —

but here is something which throws Antiquity herself into the foreground — SILENCE — eldest of things — language of old Night — primitive Discourser — to which the insolent decays of mouldering grandeur have but arrived by a violent, and, as we may say, unnatural progression.

> How reverend is the view of these hushed heads,
> Looking tranquillity!

* * * * * * *

Reader, if you are not acquainted with it, I would recommend to you, above all church-narratives, to read Sewel's History of the Quakers. It is in folio, and is the abstract of the journals of Fox and the primitive Friends. It is far more edifying and affecting than anything you will read of Wesley and his colleagues. Here is nothing to stagger you, nothing to make you mistrust, no suspicion of alloy, no drop or dreg of the worldly or ambitious spirit. You will here read the true story of that much-injured, ridiculed man (who perhaps hath been a by-word in your mouth), James Naylor: what dreadful sufferings, with what patience, he endured even to the boring through of his tongue with red-hot irons without a murmur; and with what strength of mind, when the delusion he had fallen into, which they stigmatized for blasphemy, had given way to clearer thoughts, he could renounce his error in a strain of the beautifullest humility, yet keep his first grounds, and be a Quaker still! — so different from the practice of your common converts from enthusiasm, who, when they apostatize, *apostatize all*, and think they can never get far enough from the society of their former errors, even to the renunciation of some saving truths, with which they had been mingled, not implicated.

Get the Writings of John Woolman by heart; and love the early Quakers.

How far the followers of these good men in our days have kept to the primitive spirit, or in what proportion they have substituted formality for it, the Judge of Spirits can alone determine. I have seen faces in their assemblies upon which the dove sate visibly brooding. Others again I have watched, when my thoughts should have been better engaged, in which I could possibly detect nothing but a blank inanity. But quiet was in all, and the disposition to unanimity, and the absence of the fierce controversial workings. — If the spiritual pretensions of the Quakers have abated, at least they make few pretences. Hypocrites they certainly are not, in their preaching. It is seldom indeed that you shall see one get up amongst them to hold forth. Only now and then a trembling, female, generally *ancient*, voice is heard — you cannot guess from what part of the meeting it proceeds — with a low, buzzing, musical sound, laying out a few words which "she thought might suit the condition of some present," with a quaking diffidence, which leaves no possibility of supposing that anything of female vanity was mixed up, where the tones were so full of tenderness, and a restraining modesty. The men, for what I have observed, speak seldomer. * * * *

More frequently the Meeting is broken up without a word having been spoken. But the mind has been fed. You go away with a sermon not made with hands. You have been in the milder caverns of Trophonius; or as in some den, where that fiercest and savagest of all wild creatures, the TONGUE, that unruly member, has strangely lain tied up and captive. You have bathed with stillness. — O, when the spirit is sore fretted, even tired to sickness of the janglings and nonsense-noises of the world, what a balm and a solace it is to go and seat yourself, for a quiet half hour, upon some undisputed corner of a bench among the gentle Quakers!

Their garb and stillness conjoined, present a uniformity tranquil and herd-like — as in the pasture — "forty feeding like one."

The very garments of a Quaker seem incapable of receiving a soil, and cleanliness in them to be something more than the absence of its contrary. Every Quakeress is a lily, and when they come up in bands to their Whitsun conferences, whitening the easterly streets of the metropolis, from all parts of the United Kingdom, they show like troops of the Shining Ones.

JOHN FOSTER. 1770–1843. (Manual, p. 464.)

FROM THE ESSAY "ON A MAN'S WRITING MEMOIRS OF HIMSELF."

336. BLESSEDNESS OF A VIRTUOUS CHARACTER.

On the other hand, it would be interesting to record, or to hear, the history of a character which has received its form, and reached its maturity, under the strongest operations of religion. We do not know that there is a more beneficent or a more direct mode of the divine agency in any part of the creation than that which "apprehends" a man, as apostolic language expresses it, amidst the unthinking crowd, and leads him into serious reflection, into elevated devotion, into progressive virtue, and finally into a nobler life after death. When he has long been commanded by this influence, he will be happy to look back to its first operations, whether they were mingled in early life almost insensibly with his feelings, or came on him with mighty force at some particular time, and in connection with some assignable and memorable circumstance, which was apparently the instrumental cause. He will trace all the progress of this his better life, with grateful acknowledgment to the sacred power which has advanced him to a decisiveness of religious habit that seems to stamp eternity on his character. In the great majority of things, habit is a greater plague than ever afflicted Egypt; in religious character it is a grand felicity. The devout man exults in the indications of his being fixed and irretrievable. He feels this confirmed habit as the grasp of the hand of God, which will never let him go. From this advanced state he looks with firmness and joy on futurity, and says, I carry the eternal mark upon me that I belong to God; I am free of the universe; and I am ready to go to any world to which He shall please to transmit me, certain that everywhere, in height or depth, he will acknowledge me forever.

Henry Hallam. 1777–1859. (Manual, p. 463.)

From the "View of the State of Europe during the Middle Ages."

337. Evils produced by the Spirit of Chivalry.

The principles of chivalry were not, I think, naturally productive of many evils. For it is unjust to class those acts of oppression or disorder among the abuses of knighthood, which were committed in spite of its regulations, and were only prevented by them from becoming more extensive. The license of times so imperfectly civilized could not be expected to yield to institutions, which, like those of religion, fell prodigiously short in their practical result of the reformation which they were designed to work. Man's guilt and frailty have never admitted more than a partial corrective. But some bad consequences may be more fairly ascribed to the very nature of chivalry. I have already mentioned the dissoluteness which almost unavoidably resulted from the prevailing tone of gallantry. And yet we sometimes find in the writings of those times a spirit of pure but exaggerated sentiment; and the most fanciful refinements of passion are mingled by the same poets with the coarsest immorality. An undue thirst for military renown was another fault that chivalry must have nourished; and the love of war, sufficiently pernicious in any shape, was more founded, as I have observed, on personal feelings of honor, and less on public spirit, than in the citizens of free states. A third reproach may be made to the character of knighthood, that it widened the separation between the different classes of society, and confirmed that aristocratical spirit of high birth, by which the large mass of mankind were kept in unjust degradation. Compare the generosity of Edward III. towards Eustace de Ribaumont at the siege of Calais with the harshness of his conduct towards the citizens. This may be illustrated by a story from Joinville, who was himself imbued with the full spirit of chivalry, and felt like the best and bravest of his age. He is speaking of Henry, Count of Champagne, who acquired, says he, very deservedly, the surname of Liberal, and adduces the following proof of it. A poor knight implored of him on his knees, one day, as much money as would serve to marry his two daughters. One Arthault de Nogent, a rich burgess, willing to rid the count of this importunity, but rather awkward, we must own, in the turn of his argument, said to the petitioner, My lord has already given away so much that he has nothing left. Sir Villain, replied Henry, turning round to him, you do not speak truth in saying that I have nothing left to give, when I have got yourself. Here, Sir Knight, I give you this man, and warrant your possession of him. Then, says Joinville, the poor knight was not at all confounded, but seized hold of the burgess fast by the collar, and told him he should not go till he had ransomed himself. And in the end he was forced to pay a ransom of five hundred pounds. The simple-minded writer, who brings this evidence of the Count of Champagne's liberality, is not at all struck with the facility of a virtue that is exercised at the cost of others.

WILLIAM HAZLITT. 1778–1830. (Manual, p. 474.)

FROM "THE LECTURES ON DRAMATIC LITERATURE."

338. INFLUENCE OF THE TRANSLATION OF THE BIBLE UPON LITERATURE.

The translation of the Bible was the chief engine in the great work. It threw open, by a secret spring, the rich treasures of religion and morality, which had been there locked up as in a shrine. It revealed the visions of the prophets, and conveyed the lessons of inspired teachers to the meanest of the people. It gave them a common interest in a common cause. Their hearts burnt within them as they read. It gave a mind to the people, by giving them common subjects of thought and feeling. It cemented their union of character and sentiment; it created endless diversity and collision of opinion. They found objects to employ their faculties, and a motive in the magnitude of the consequences attached to them, to exert the utmost eagerness in the pursuit of truth, and the most daring intrepidity in maintaining it. Religious controversy sharpens the understandiug by the subtlety and remoteness of the topics it discusses, and embraces the will by their infinite importance. We perceive in the history of this period a nervous masculine intellect. No levity, no feebleness, no indifference, or, if there were, it is a relaxation from the intense activity which gives a tone to its general character. But there is a gravity approaching to piety; a seriousness of impression, a conscientious severity of argument, an habitual fervor and enthusiasm in their method of handling almost every subject. The debates of the schoolmen were sharp and subtle enough; but they wanted interest and grandeur, and were besides confined to a few: they did not affect the general mass of community. But the Bible was thrown open to all ranks and conditions "to run and read," with its wonderful table of contents from Genesis to the Revelation. Every village in England would present the scene so well described in Burns's Cotter's Saturday Night. I cannot think that all this variety and weight of knowledge could be thrown in all at once upon the mind of the people and not make some impression upon it, the traces of which might be discerned in the manners and literature of the age.

Sir William Hamilton. 1788–1856. (Manual, p. 466.)

From "The Discussions on Philosophy."

339. Mathematical Study an insufficient Discipline.

Before entering on details, it is proper here, once for all, to premise, — In the *first* place, that the question does not regard, the *value of mathematical* SCIENCE, *considered in itself, or in its objective results*, but, *the utility of mathematical* STUDY, that is, *in its subjective effect, as an exercise of mind;* and in the second, that the expediency is not disputed, of leaving mathematics, as a coördinate, to find their level among the other branches of academical instruction. It is only contended, that they ought not to be made the principal, far less the exclusive, object of academical encouragement. We speak not now of professional, but of liberal, education; not of that which considers the mind as an instrument for the improvement of science, but of this, which considers science as an instrument for the improvement of mind.

Of all our intellectual pursuits, the study of the mathematical sciences is the one, whose utility as an intellectual exercise, when carried beyond a moderate extent, has been most peremptorily denied by the greatest number of the most competent judges; and the arguments, on which this opinion is established, have hitherto been evaded rather than opposed. Some intelligent mathematicians, indeed, admit all that has been urged against their science, as a principal discipline of the mind; and only contend that it ought not to be extruded from all place in a scheme of liberal education. With these, therefore, we have no controversy. More strenuous advocates of this study, again, maintain that mathematics are of primary importance as a *logical exercise* of reason; but unable to controvert the evidence of its contracted and partial cultivation of the faculties, they endeavor to vindicate the study in general, by attributing its evil influence to some peculiar modification of the science; and thus hope to avoid the loss of the whole, by the vicarious sacrifice of a part. But here, unfortunately, they are not at one. Some are willing to surrender the modern *analysis* as a gymnastic of the mind. They confess, that its very perfection as an instrument of discovery unfits it for an instrument of mental cultivation, its formulæ mechanically transporting the student with closed eyes to the conclusion; whereas the ancient *geometrical* construction, they contend, leads him to the end, more circuitously, indeed, but by his own exertion, and with a clear consciousness of every step in the procedure. Others, on the contrary, disgusted with the tedious and complex operations of *geometry*, recommend the *algebraic* process as that most favorable to the powers of generalization and reasoning; for, concentrating into the narrowest compass the greatest complement of meaning, it obviates, they maintain, all irrelevant distraction, and enables the intellect to operate for a longer continuance, more energetically, securely, and effectually. The arguments in favor of the study thus neutralize each other; and the reasoning of those who deny it more than a subordinate and partial utility, stands not only uncontroverted, but untouched — not only untouched, but admitted. * * * *

The mathematician, as already noticed, is exclusively engrossed with the deduction of inevitable conclusions, from *data* passively received; while the cultivators of the other departments of knowledge, mental and physical, are, for the most part, actively occupied in the quest and scrutiny, in the collection and balancing of probabilities, in order to obtain and purify the facts on which their premises are to be established. *Their* pursuits, accordingly, from the mingled experience of failure and success, have, to them, proved a special logic, a practical discipline — on the one hand, of skill and confidence, on the other, of caution and sobriety: *his*, on the contrary, have not only not trained him to that acute scent, to that delicate, almost instinctive tact, which, in the twilight of probability, the search and discrimination of its finer facts demand; they have gone to cloud his vision, to indurate his touch, to all but the blazing light and iron chain of demonstration, leaving him, out of the narrow confines of his science, either to a passive *credulity* in any premises, or to an absolute *incredulity* in all.

THOMAS CHALMERS. 1780–1847. (Manual, p. 465.)

FROM "THE BRIDGEWATER TREATISE."

340. THE JOY OF GOOD, AND THE MISERY OF EVIL AFFECTIONS.

God is the lover, and, because so, the patron or the rewarder of virtue. He hath so constituted our nature, that in the very flow and exercise of the good affections there shall be the oil of gladness. There is instant delight in the first conception of benevolence; there is sustained delight in its continued exercise; there is consummated delight in the happy, smiling, and prosperous result of it. Kindness, and honesty, and truth, are of themselves, and irrespective of their rightness, sweet unto the taste of the inner man. Malice, envy, falsehood, injustice, irrespective of their wrongness, have, of themselves, the bitterness of gall and wormwood. The Deity hath annexed a high mental enjoyment, not to the consciousness only of good affections, but to the very sense and feeling of good affections. However closely these may follow on each other, — nay, however implicated or blended together they may be at the same moment into one compound state of feeling, — they are not the less distinct, on that account, of themselves. * * * *

In the calm satisfactions of virtue, this distinction may not be so palpable as in the pungent and more vividly felt disquietudes which are attendant on the wrong affections of our nature. The perpetual corrosion of that heart, for example, which frets in unhappy peevishness all the day long, is plainly distinct from the bitterness of that remorse which is felt, in the recollection of its harsh and injurious outbreakings on the innocent sufferers within its reach. It is saying much for the moral character of God, that he has placed a conscience within us, which administers painful rebuke on every indulgence of a wrong affection. But it is saying still more for such being the character of our Maker, so to have framed our mental constitution, that, in the very working of these bad affections, there should be the painfulness of a felt discomfort and discordancy. Such is the make or mechanism of our nature, that it is thwarted and put out of sorts by rage, and envy, and hatred; and this, irrespective of the adverse moral judgments which conscience passes upon them. Of themselves, they are unsavory; and no sooner do they enter the heart, than they shed upon it an immediate distillation of bitterness. Just as the placid smile of benevolence bespeaks the felt comfort of benevolence, so in the frown and tempest of an angry countenance do we read the unhappiness of that man who is vexed and agitated by his own malignant affections, eating inwardly, as they do, on the vitals of his enjoyment. It is therefore that he is often styled, and truly, a self-tormentor, or his own worst enemy.

The Force of Christian Evidence strengthened by the Christianity of the Witnesses.

Tacitus has actually attested the existence of Jesus Christ. Suppose that besides attesting his existence, he had believed in him so far as to become a Christian. Is his testimony to be refused because he gives this evidence of his sincerity? Tacitus asserting the fact, and remaining a heathen, is not so strong an argument as Tacitus asserting the fact and becoming a Christian in consequence of it. Yet the moment the transition is made, — a transition by which, in point of fact, his testimony becomes stronger, — in point of impression it becomes less; and by a delusion common to the infidel and the believer, the argument is held to be weakened by the very circumstance which imparts greater force to it. * * * A direct testimony to the miracles of the New Testament from the mouth of a heathen is not to be expected. We cannot satisfy this demand of the infidel; but we can give him a host of much stronger testimonies than he is in quest of—the testimonies of those men who were heathens, and who embraced a hazardous and a disgraceful profession, under a deep conviction of those facts to which they gave their testimony. "O, but now you land us in the testimony of Christians." This is very true; but it is the very fact of their being Christians, in which the strength of the argument lies. In the Fathers of the Christian church we see men who, if they had not been Christians, would have risen to as high an eminence as Tacitus in the literature of the times; and whose direct testimony as to the Gospel history would, in that case, have been most impressive even to the mind of an infidel. And are these testimonies to be less impressive because they were preceded by conviction and sealed by martyrdom!

THOMAS BABINGTON MACAULAY. 1800–1859. (Manual, p. 461.)

FROM THE "ESSAY ON MILTON."

341. FALLACIOUS DISTRUST OF LIBERTY.

Ariosto tells a pretty story of a fairy, who, by some mysterious law of her nature, was condemned to appear at certain seasons in the form of a foul and poisonous snake. Those who injured her, during the period of her disguise, were forever excluded from participation in the blessings which she bestowed. But to those who, in spite of her loathsome aspect, pitied and protected her, she afterwards revealed herself in the beautiful and celestial form which was natural to her, accompanied their steps, granted all their wishes, filled their houses with wealth, made them happy in love, and victorious in war. Such a spirit is Liberty. At times she takes the form of a hateful reptile. She growls, she hisses, she stings. But woe to those who in disgust shall venture to crush her! And happy are those who, having dared to receive her in her degraded and frightful shape, shall at length be rewarded by her in the time of her beauty and her glory.

There is only one cure for the evils which newly acquired freedom produces—and that cure is freedom! When a prisoner leaves his cell, he cannot bear the light of day; he is unable to discriminate colors, or recognize faces. But the remedy is not to remand him into his dungeon, but to accustom him to the rays of the sun. The blaze of truth and liberty may at first dazzle and bewilder nations which have become half blind in the house of bondage. But let them gaze on, and they will soon be able to bear it. In a few years men learn to reason. The extreme violence of opinion subsides. Hostile theories correct each other. The scattered elements of truth cease to conflict, and begin to coalesce. And at length a system of justice and order is educed out of the chaos.

Many politicians of our time are in the habit of laying it down as a self-evident proposition, that no people ought to be free, till they are fit to use their freedom. The maxim is worthy of the fool in the old story, who resolved not to go into the water till he had learnt to swim! If men are to wait for liberty till they become wise and good in slavery, they may indeed wait forever.

From the "Essay on Barere."

342. Evils of the Reign of Terror.

We could, we think, also show that the evils produced by the Jacobin administration did not terminate when it fell; that it bequeathed a long series of calamities to France and to Europe; that public opinion, which had during two generations been constantly becoming more and more fovorable to civil and religious freedom, underwent, during the days of Terror, a change of which the traces are still to be distinctly perceived. It was natural that there should be such a change, when men saw that those who called themselves the champions of popular rights, had compressed into the space of twelve months more crimes than the kings of France, Merovingian, Carlovingian, and Capetian, had perpetrated in twelve centuries. Freedom was regarded as a great delusion. Men were willing to submit to the government of hereditary princes, of fortunate soldiers, of nobles, of priests, to any government but that of philosophers and philanthropists. Hence the imperial despotism, with its enslaved press and its silent tribune, its dungeons stronger than the old Bastile, and its tribunals more obsequious than the old Parliaments. Hence the restoration of the Bourbons and of the Jesuits, the Chamber of 1815, with its categories of proscription, the revival of the feudal spirit, the encroachments of the clergy, the persecution of the Protestants, the appearance of a new breed of De Montforts and Dominics, in the full light of the nineteenth century.

And so, in politics, it is the sure law that every excess shall generate its opposite; nor does he deserve the name of a statesman, who strikes a great blow without fully calculating the effect of the rebound. But such calculation was infinitely beyond the reach of the authors of the Reign of Terror. Violence and more violence, blood and more blood, made up their whole policy. In a few months, these poor creatures succeeded in bringing about a reaction, of which none of them saw, and of which none of us may see, the close; and, having brought it about, they marvelled at it; they bewailed it; they execrated it; they ascribed it to everything but the real cause — their own immorality, and their own profound incapacity for the conduct of great affairs.

HUGH MILLER. 1802–1856. (Manual, p. 467.)

FROM "THE OLD RED SANDSTONE."

343. THE FUTURE HISTORY OF MAN UPON THE GLOBE.

We pursue our history no further. Its after course is comparatively well known. The huge sauroid fish was succeeded by the equally huge reptile — the reptile by the bird — the bird by the marsupial quadruped; and at length, after races higher in the scale of instinct had taken precedence in succession, the one of the other, the sagacious elephant appeared, as the lord of that latest creation which immediately preceded our own. How natural does the thought seem which suggested itself to the profound mind of Cuvier, when indulging in a similar review! Has the last scene in the series arisen, or has Deity expended his infinitude of resource, and reached the ultimate stage of progression at which perfection can arrive? The philosopher hesitated, and then decided in the negative, for he was too intimately acquainted with the works of the Omnipotent Creator to think of limiting his power; and he could, therefore, anticipate a coming period in which man would have to resign his post of honor to some nobler and wiser creature — the monarch of a better and happier world. How well it is to be permitted to indulge in the expansion of Cuvier's thought, without sharing in the melancholy of Cuvier's feelings — to be enabled to look forward to the coming of a new heaven and a new earth, not in terror, but in hope — to be encouraged to believe in the system of unending progression, but to entertain no fear of the degradation or despotism of man! The adorable Monarch of the future, with all its unsummed perfection, has already passed into the heavens, flesh of our flesh, and bone of our bone, and Enoch and Elias are there with him, — fit representatives of that dominant race, which no other race shall ever supplant or succeed, and to whose onward and upward march the deep echoes of eternity shall never cease to respond.

PLEASURES OF A LIFE OF LABOR.

I was as light of heart the next morning as any of my brother workmen. There had been a smart frost during the night, and the rime lay white on the grass as we passed onwards through the fields; but the sun rose in a clear atmosphere, and the day mellowed, as it advanced, into one of those delightful days of early spring, which give so pleasing an earnest of whatever is mild and genial in the better half of the year. All the workmen rested at midday, and I went to enjoy my half hour alone on a mossy knoll in the neighboring wood, which commands through the trees a wide prospect of the bay and the opposite shore. There was not a wrinkle on the water nor a cloud in the sky, and the branches were as moveless in the calm as if they had been traced on canvas. From a wooded promontory that stretched half way across the frith, there ascended a thin column of smoke. It rose straight as the line of a plummet for more than a thousand yards, and then, on reaching a thinner stratum of air, spread out equally on every side like the foliage of a stately tree. Ben Wyvis rose to the west, white with the yet unwasted snow of winter, and as sharply defined in the clear atmosphere as if all its sunny slopes and blue retiring hollows had been chiselled in marble. A line of snow ran along the opposite hills; all above was white, and all below was purple. They reminded me of the pretty French story, in which an old artist is described as tasking the ingenuity of his future son-in-law, by giving him as a subject for his pencil a flower-piece composed of only white flowers, of which the one half were to bear their proper color, the other half a deep purple hue, and yet all be perfectly natural; and how the young man resolved the riddle and gained his mistress, by introducing a transparent purple vase into the picture, and making the light pass through it on the flowers that were drooping over the edge. I returned to the quarry, convinced that a very exquisite pleasure may be a very cheap one, and that the busiest employments may afford leisure enough to enjoy it.

Jeremy Bentham. 1748–1832. (Manual, p. 473.)

From "The Rationale of Evidence." Works, Vol. VII.

344. Jargon of the English Law.

Every sham science, of which there are so many, makes to itself a jargon, to serve for a cover to its nothingness, and, if wicked, to its wickedness: alchemy, palmistry, magic, judicial astrology, technical jurisprudence. To unlicensed depredators, their own technical language, the cant or flash language, is of use, not only as a cover, but as a bond of union. Lawyers' cant, besides serving them as a cover and as a bond of union, serves them as an instrument, an iron crow or a pick-lock key, for collecting plunder in cases in which otherwise it could not be collected: for applying the principle of nullification, in many a case in which it could not otherwise have been applied.

The best of all good old times, was when the fate of Englishmen was disposed of in French, and in a something that was called Latin. For having been once in use, language, however, is not much the worse, so it be of use no longer. The antiquated notation of time suffices of itself to throw a veil of mystery over the system of procedure. Martin and Hilary, saints forgotten by devotees, are still of use to lawyers. How many a man has been ruined, because his lawyer made a mistake, designed or undesigned, in reckoning by the almanac! First of January, second of January, and so forth, — where is the science there? Not a child of four years old that does not understand it. Octaves, quindecims, and morrows of All Souls, St. Martin, St. Hilary, the Purification, Easter day, the Ascension, and the Holy Trinity; Essoign day, day of Exception, Retorna Brevium day, day of Appearance — alias *Quarto die post* — alias *Dies amoris;* there you have a science. Terms — Michaelmas, Hilary, Easter, and Trinity,[1] each of them about thirty days, no one of them more than one day; there you have not only a science, but a mystery: do as the devils do, believe and tremble.

FROM "LAW AS IT IS," &c. Works, Vol. V.

345. IMPOSSIBILITY OF A KNOWLEDGE OF THE COMMON LAW BY THE PEOPLE.

Scarce any man has the means of knowing a twentieth part of the laws he is bound by. Both sorts of law are kept most happily and carefully from the knowledge of the people: statute law by its shape and bulk; common law by its very essence. It is the Judges (as we have seen) that make the common law. Do you know how they make it? Just as a man makes laws for his dog. When your dog does anything you want to break him of, you wait till he does it, and then beat him for it. This is the way you make laws for your dog: and this is the way the Judges make laws for you and me. They won't tell a man beforehand what it is he should not do — they won't so much as allow of his being told: they lie by till he has done something which they say he should not have done, and then they hang him for it. What way, then, has any man of coming at this dog-law? Only by watching their proceedings: by observing in what cases they have hanged a man, in what cases they have sent him to jail, in what cases they have seized his goods, and so forth. These proceedings they won't publish themselves; and if anybody else publishes them, it is what they call a contempt of court, and a man may be sent to jail for it.

RICHARD WHATELEY. 1787–1856. (Manual, p. 466.)

FROM "THE LECTURES ON POLITICAL ECONOMY."

346. CIVILIZATION FAVORABLE TO MORALITY.

On the whole, then, there seems every reason to believe, that, as a general rule, that advancement in National Prosperity which mankind are, by the Governor of the universe adapted, and impelled to

[1] These barbarous names, in bad Latin or old French, were the legal titles of certain days on which important steps were to be taken in prosecuting a suit; the latter four designated the terms, of three or four weeks each, during which the English courts were wont to sit, at different seasons, for the administration of justice.

promote, must be favorable to moral improvement. Still more does it appear evident, that such a conclusion must be *acceptable* to a pious and philanthropic mind. It is not probable, still less is it desirable, that the Deity should have fitted and destined society to make a continual progress, impeded only by slothful and negligent habits, by war, rapine, and oppression (in short, by violation of divine commands), which progress inevitably tends towards a greater and greater moral corruption.

And yet there are some who appear not only to think, but to *wish* to think, that a condition but little removed from the savage state, — one of ignorance, grossness, and poverty, — unenlightened, semi-barbarous, and stationary, is the most favorable to virtue. You will meet with persons who will be even offended if you attempt to awaken them from their dreams about primitive rural simplicity, and to convince them that the spread of civilization, which they must see has a tendency to spread, does not tend to increase depravity. Supposing their notion true, it must at least, one would think, be a melancholy truth.

It may be said as a reason, not for wishing, but for believing this, that the moral dangers which beset a wealthy community are designed as a trial. Undoubtedly they are; since no state in which man is placed is exempt from trials. And let it be admitted, also, if you will, that the temptations to evil, to which civilized man is exposed, are *absolutely* stronger than those which exist in a ruder state of society; still, if they are also *relatively* stronger — stronger in proportion to the counteracting forces, and stronger than the augmented motives to good conduct — and are such, consequently, that, as society advances in civilization, there is less and less virtue, and a continually decreasing prospect of its being attained — this amounts to something more than a state of trial; it is a distinct provision made by the Deity for the moral degradation of his rational creatures.

This can hardly be a desirable conclusion; but if it be, nevertheless, a true one (and our wishes should not be allowed to bias our judgment), those who hold it, ought at least to follow it up in practice, by diminishing, as far as is possible, the severity of the trial. * * * Let us put away from us "the accursed thing." If national wealth be, in a moral point of view, an evil, let us, in the name of all that is good, set about to diminish it. Let us, as he advises, burn our fleets, block up our ports, destroy our manufactories, break up our roads, and betake ourselves to a life of frugal and rustic simplicity; like Mandeville's bees, who

"flew into a hollow tree,
Blest with content and honesty."

CHAPTER XXIII.

ORATORS.

347. WILLIAM PITT, EARL OF CHATHAM. 1708–1778.

The character of Lord Chatham's eloquence is thus described by Mr. Charles Butler (1750–1832) in his "Reminiscences": —

Of those by whom Lord North was preceded, none, probably, except Lord Chatham, will be remembered by posterity; but the nature of the eloquence of this extraordinary man it is extremely difficult to describe.

No person in his external appearance was ever more bountifully gifted by nature for an orator. In his look and his gesture, grace and dignity were combined, but dignity presided; the "terrors of his beak, the lightnings of his eye," were insufferable. His voice was both full and clear; his lowest whisper was distinctly heard; his middle tones were sweet, rich, and beautifully varied. When he elevated his voice to its highest pitch, the house was completely filled with the volume of the sound. The effect was awful, except when he wished to cheer or animate; he then had spirit-stirring notes, which were perfectly irresistible. He frequently rose, on a sudden, from a very low to a very high key, but it seemed to be without effort. His diction was remarkably simple; but words were never chosen with greater care. He mentioned to a friend that he had read *Bailey's Dictionary* twice, from beginning to end, and that he had perused some of *Dr. Barrow's Sermons* so often as to know them by heart.

His sentiments, too, were apparently simple; but sentiments were never adopted or uttered with greater skill. He was often familiar, and even playful; but it was the familiarity and playfulness of condescension — the lion that dandled with the kid. The *terrible*, however, was his peculiar power. Then the whole house sunk before him. Still he was dignified; and wonderful as was his eloquence, it was attended with this most important effect, that it impressed every hearer with a conviction that there was something in him even finer than his words; that the *man* was infinitely greater than the *orator*. No impression of this kind was made by the eloquence of his son, or his son's antagonist.

But with this great man — for great he certainly was — *manner* did much. One of the fairest specimens which we possess of his lordship's oratory is his speech, in 1776, for the repeal of the Stamp Act.

Most, perhaps, who read the report of this speech in "Almon's Register," will wonder at the effect which it is known to have produced on the hearers; yet the report is tolerably exact, and exhibits, although faintly, its leading features. But they should have seen the *look* of ineffable contempt with which he surveyed the late Mr. Grenville, who sat within one of him, and should have heard him say with that look, "As to the late ministry, every capital measure they have taken has been entirely wrong." They should also have beheld him, when, addressing himself to Mr. Grenville's successors, he said, "As to the present gentlemen — those, at least, whom I have in my eye" — (looking at the bench on which Mr. Conway sat) — "I have no objection; I have never been made a sacrifice by any of them. Some of them have done me the honor to ask my poor opinion before they would engage to repeal the act: they will do me the justice to own, I did advise them to engage to do it; but notwithstanding — (for I love to be explicit) — I cannot give them my confidence. Pardon me, gentlemen" — (bowing to them) — "*confidence* is a plant of *slow* growth." Those who remember the air of condescending protection with which the bow was made, and the look given, when he spoke these words, will recollect how much they themselves, at the moment, were both delighted and awed, and what they themselves then conceived of the immeasurable superiority of the orator over every human being that surrounded him. In the passages which we have cited, there is nothing which an ordinary speaker might not have said; it was the *manner*, and the manner *only*, which produced the effect. * * * *

Once, while he was speaking, Sir William Young called out, "Question, question!" Lord Chatham paused — then, fixing on Sir William a look of inexpressible disgust, exclaimed, "Pardon me, Mr. Speaker, my agitation: — when that member calls for the question, I fear I hear the knell of my country's ruin." * * * *

But the most extraordinary instance of his command of the house, is the manner in which he fixed indelibly on Mr. Grenville the appellation of "the Gentle Shepherd." At this time, a song of Dr. Howard, which began with the words, "Gentle Shepherd, tell me where," — and in which each stanza ended with that line, — was in every mouth. On some occasion, Mr. Grenville exclaimed, "Where is our money? where are our means? I say again, Where are our means? where is our money?" He then sat down, and Lord Chatham paced slowly out of the house, humming the line, "Gentle Shepherd, tell me where." The effect was irresistible, and settled forever on Mr. Grenville the appellation of "the Gentle Shepherd."

A speech of Lord Chatham's is given on page 270.

EDMUND BURKE. 1731–1797.

348. FROM HIS "SPEECH ON CONCILIATION WITH AMERICA," March 22, 1775.

Compare the two. This I offer to give you is plain and simple; the other full of perplexed and intricate mazes. This is mild; that harsh. This is found by experience effectual for its purposes; the other is a new project. This is universal; the other calculated for certain colonies only. This is immediate in its conciliatory operation; the other remote, contingent, full of hazard. Mine is what becomes the dignity of a ruling people; gratuitous, unconditional, and not held out as matter of bargain and sale. I have done my duty in proposing it to you. I have indeed tired you by a long discourse; but this is the misfortune of those to whose influence nothing will be conceded, and who must win every inch of their ground by argument. You have heard me with goodness. May you decide with wisdom! For my part, I feel my mind greatly disburdened by what I have done to-day. I have been the less fearful of trying your patience, because on this subject I mean to spare it altogether in future. I have this comfort, that in every stage of the American affairs I have steadily opposed the measures that have produced the confusion, and may bring on the destruction, of this empire. I now go so far as to risk a proposal of my own. If I cannot give peace to my country, I give it to my conscience.

But what (says the financier) is peace to us without money? Your plan gives us no revenue. No! But it does — for it secures to the subject the power of REFUSAL; the first of all revenues. Experience is a cheat, and fact a liar, if this power in the subject of proportioning his grant, or of not granting at all, has not been found the richest mine of revenue ever discovered by the skill or by the fortune of man. * * * *

I, for one, protest against compounding our demands. I declare against compounding, for a poor limited sum, the immense, ever-growing, eternal debt, which is due to generous government from protected freedom. And so may I speed in the great object I propose to you, as I think it would not only be an act of injustice, but would be the worst economy in the world, to compel the colonies to a sum certain, either in the way of ransom or in the way of compulsory compact.

But to clear up my ideas on this subject, — a revenue from America transmitted hither, — do not delude yourselves; you never can receive it — No, not a shilling. We have experience that from remote countries it is not to be expected. If, when you attempted to extract revenue from Bengal, you were obliged to return in loan what you had taken in imposition, what can you expect from North America? For certainly, if ever there was a country qualified to produce wealth, it is India; or an institution fit for the transmission, it is the East India Company. America has none of these aptitudes. If America gives you taxable objects, on which you lay your duties here, and gives you, at the same time, a surplus by a foreign sale of her commodities to pay the duties on these objects which you tax at home, she has performed her part to the British revenue. But with regard to her own internal establishments, she may, I doubt not she will, contribute in moderation. I say in moderation, for she ought not to be permitted to exhaust herself. She ought to be reserved to a war, the weight of which, with the enemies that we are most likely to have, must be considerable in her quarter of the globe. There she may serve you, and serve you essentially.

For that service, for all service, whether of revenue, trade, or empire, my trust is in her interest in the British constitution. My hold of the colonies is in the close affection which grows from common names, from kindred blood, from similar privileges, and equal protection. These are ties which, though light as air, are as strong as links of iron. Let the colonies always keep the idea of their civil rights associated with your government, they will cling and grapple to you; and no force under heaven will be of power to tear them from their allegiance. But let it be once understood that your government may be one thing, and their privileges another; that these two things may exist without any mutual relation; the cement is gone, the cohesion is loosened, and everything hastens to decay and dissolution. As long as you have the wisdom to keep the sovereign authority of this country as the sanctuary of liberty, the sacred temple consecrated to our common faith, wherever the chosen race and sons of England worship freedom, they will turn their faces towards you. The more they multiply, the more friends you will have; the more ardently they love liberty, the more perfect will be their obedience. Slavery they can have anywhere. It is a weed that grows in every soil. They may have it from Spain, they may have it from Prussia. But until you become lost to all feeling of your true interest and your natural dignity, freedom they can have from none but you. This is the commodity of price, of which you have the monopoly. This is the true act of navigation, which binds to you the commerce of the colonies, and through them secures to you the wealth of the world. Deny them this participation of freedom, and you break that sole bond which originally made, and must still preserve, the unity of the empire. Do not entertain so weak an imagination as that your registers and your bonds, your affidavits and your sufferances, your cockets and your clearances, are what form the great securities of your commerce. Do not dream that your letters of office, and your instructions, and your suspending clauses, are the things that hold together the great contexture of this mysterious whole. These things do not make your government. Dead instruments, passive tools as they are, it is the spirit of the English communion that gives all their life and efficacy to them. It is the spirit of the English constitution, which, infused through the mighty mass, pervades, feeds, unites, invigorates, vivifies, every part of the empire, even down to the minutest member.

FROM HIS SPEECH ON AMERICAN TAXATION.

349. CHARACTER OF LORD CHATHAM'S SECOND ADMINISTRATION, AND OF CHARLES TOWNSHEND, 1774.

Another scene was opened, and other actors appeared on the stage. The state, in the condition I have described it, was delivered into the hands of Lord Chatham — a great and celebrated name; a name that keeps the name of this country respectable in every other on the globe. * * * *

Sir, the venerable age of this great man, his merited rank, his superior eloquence, his splendid qualities, his eminent services, the vast space he fills in the eye of mankind; and, more than all the rest, his fall from power, which, like death, canonizes and sanctifies a great character, will not suffer me to censure any part of his conduct. I am afraid to flatter him; I am sure I am not disposed to blame him. Let those who have betrayed him by their adulation, insult him with their malevolence. But what I do not presume to censure, I may have leave to lament. For a wise man, he seemed to me at that time to be governed too much by general maxims. I speak with the freedom of history, and I hope without offence. One or two of these maxims, flowing from an opinion not the most indulgent to our unhappy species, and surely a little too general, led him into measures that were greatly mischievous to himself; and for that reason, among others, perhaps fatal to his country; measures, the effects of which, I am afraid, are forever incurable. He made an administration so checkered and speckled; he put together a piece of joinery, so crossly indented and whimsically dovetailed; a cabinet so variously inlaid; such a piece of diversified mosaic; such a tessellated pavement without cement; here a bit of black stone, and there a bit of white; patriots and courtiers, king's friends and republicans; whigs and tories; treacherous friends and open enemies; that it was indeed a very curious show; but utterly unsafe to touch, and unsure to stand on. The colleagues whom he had assorted at the same boards, stared at each other, and were obliged to ask, "Sir, your name? — Sir, you have the advantage of me — Mr. Such a one — I beg a thousand pardons —" I venture to say, it did so happen, that persons had a single office divided between them, who had never spoke to each other in their lives; until they found themselves, they knew not how, pigging together, heads and points, in the same truckle-bed.[1]

1 Supposed to allude to the Right Hon. Lord North, and George Cook, Esq., who were made joint paymasters in 1766, on the removal of the Rockingham administration.

Sir, in consequence of this arrangement, having put so much the larger part of his enemies and opposers into power, the confusion was such, that his own principles could not possibly have any effect or influence in the conduct of affairs. If ever he fell into a fit of the gout, or if any other cause withdrew him from public cares, principles directly the contrary were sure to predominate. When he had executed his plan, he had not an inch of ground to stand upon; when he had accomplished his scheme of administration, he was no longer a minister.

When his face was hid but for a moment, his whole system was on a wide sea, without chart or compass. The gentlemen, his particular friends, who, with the names of various departments of ministry, were admitted, to seem as if they acted a part under him, with a modesty that becomes all men, and with a confidence in him, which was justified even in its extravagance by his superior abilities, had never, in any instance, presumed upon any opinion of their own. Deprived of his guiding influence, they were whirled about, the sport of every gust, and easily driven into any port; and as those who joined with them in manning the vessel were the most directly opposite to his opinions, measures, and character, and far the most artful and most powerful of the set, they easily prevailed, so as to seize upon the vacant, unoccupied, and derelict minds of his friends; and instantly they turned the vessel wholly out of the course of his policy. As if it were to insult as well as to betray him, even long before the close of the first session of his administration, when everything was publicly transacted, and with great parade, in his name, they made an act, declaring it highly just and expedient to raise a revenue in America. For even then, sir, even before this splendid orb was entirely set, and while the western horizon was in a blaze with his descending glory, on the opposite quarter of the heavens arose another luminary, and, for his hour, became lord of the ascendant.

This light, too, is passed and set forever. You understand, to be sure, that I speak of Charles Townshend, officially the reproducer of this fatal scheme; whom I cannot even now remember without some degree of sensibility. In truth, sir, he was the delight and ornament of this house, and the charm of every private society which he honored with his presence. Perhaps there never arose in this country, nor in any country, a man of a more pointed and finished wit; and (where his passions were not concerned) of a more refined, exquisite, and penetrating judgment. If it had not so great a stock, as some have had who flourished formerly, of knowledge long treasured up, he knew better by far, than any man I ever was acquainted with, how to bring together within a short time all that was necessary to establish, to illustrate, and to decorate that side of the question he supported. He stated his matter skilfully and powerfully. He particularly excelled in a most luminous explanation and display of his subject. His style of argument was neither trite and vulgar, nor subtle and abstruse. He hit the house just between wind and water. And not being troubled with too anxious a zeal for any matter in question, he was never more tedious, or more earnest, than the preconceived opinions and present temper of his hearers required; to whom he was always in perfect unison. He conformed exactly to the temper of the house; and he seemed to guide, because he was always sure to follow it.

FROM HIS SPEECH ON THE NABOB OF ARCOT'S DEBTS, 1785.

350. INVASION OF THE CARNATIC BY HYDER ALI.[1]

When at length Hyder Ali found that he had to do with men who either would sign no convention, or whom no treaty and no signature could bind, and who were the determined enemies of human intercourse itself, he decreed to make the country possessed by these incorrigible and predestinated criminals a memorable example to mankind. He resolved, in the gloomy recesses of a mind capacious of such things, to leave the whole Carnatic an everlasting monument of vengeance; and to put perpetual desolation as a barrier between him and those against whom the faith which holds the moral elements of the world together was no protection. He became at length so confident of his force, so collected in his might, that he made no secret whatsoever of his dreadful resolution. Having terminated his disputes with every enemy, and every rival, who buried their mutual animosities in their common detestation against the creditors of the nabob of Arcot, he drew from every quarter whatever a savage ferocity could add to his new rudiments in the arts of destruction; and compounding all the materials of fury, havoc, and desolation into one black cloud, he hung for a while on the declivities of the mountains. Whilst the authors of all these evils were idly and stupidly gazing on this menacing meteor, which blackened all their horizon, it suddenly burst, and poured down the whole of its contents upon the plains of the Carnatic. Then ensued a scene of woe, the like of which no eye had seen, no heart conceived, and which no tongue can adequately tell. All the horrors of war before known or heard of, were mercy to that new havoc. A storm of universal fire blasted every field; consumed every house, destroyed every temple. The miserable inhabitants flying from their flaming villages, in part were slaughtered; others, without regard to sex, to age, to the respect of rank, or sacredness of function; fathers torn from children, husbands from wives, enveloped in a whirlwind of cavalry, and amidst the goading spears of drivers, and the trampling of pursuing horses, were swept into captivity, in an unknown and hostile land. Those who were able to evade this tempest fled to the walled cities. But escaping from fire, sword, and exile, they fell into the jaws of famine.

[1] The Carnatic is that region of India lying between the Bay of Bengal and the Western Ghauts, and extending from Cape Comorin to the River Kistna.

The alms of the settlement, in this dreadful exigency, were certainly liberal; and all was done by charity that private charity could do: but it was a people in beggary: it was a nation which stretched out its hands for food. For months together these creatures of sufferance, whose very excess and luxury in their most plenteous days had fallen short of the allowance of our austerest fasts, silent, patient, resigned, without sedition or disturbance, almost without complaint, perished by a hundred a day in the streets of Madras; every day seventy at least laid their bodies in the streets, or on the glacis of Tanjore, and expired of famine in the granary of India. I was going to awake your justice towards this unhappy part of our fellow-citizens, by bringing before you some of the circumstances of this plague of hunger. Of all the calamities which beset and waylay the life of man, this comes the nearest to our heart, and is that wherein the proudest of us all feels himself to be nothing more than he is: but I find myself unable to manage it with decorum; these details are of a species of horror so nauseous and disgusting; they are so degrading to the sufferers and to the hearers; they are so humiliating to human nature itself, that, on better thoughts, I find it more advisable to throw a pall over this hideous object, and to leave it to your general conceptions.

For eighteen months, without intermission, this destruction raged from the gates of Madras to the gates of Tanjore; and so completely did these masters in their art, Hyder Ali, and his more ferocious son, absolve themselves of their impious vow, that when the British armies traversed, as they did the Carnatic for hundreds of miles in all directions, through the whole line of their march did they not see one man, not one woman, not one child, not one four-footed beast of any description whatever. One dead uniform silence reigned over the whole region. With the inconsiderable exceptions of the narrow vicinage of some few forts, I wish to be understood as speaking literally. I mean to produce to you more than three witnesses, above all exception, who will support this assertion in its full extent. That hurricane of war passed through every part of the central provinces of the Carnatic. Six or seven districts to the north and to the south (and these not wholly untouched) escaped the general ravage.

The Carnatic is a country not much inferior in extent to England. Figure to yourself, Mr. Speaker, the land in whose representative chair you sit; figure to yourself the form and fashion of your sweet and cheerful country from Thames to Trent, north and south, and from the Irish to the German sea east and west, emptied and embowelled (may God overt the omen of our crimes!) by so accomplished a desolation. Extend your imagination a little further, and then suppose your ministers taking a survey of this scene of waste and desolation; what would be your thoughts if you should be informed that they were computing how much had been the amount of the excises, how much the customs, how much the land and malt tax, in order that they should charge (take it in the most favorable light) for public service, upon the relics of the satiated vengeance of relentless enemies, the whole of what England had yielded in the most exuberant seasons of peace and abundance? What would you call it? To call it tyranny, sublimed into madness, would be too faint an image; yet this very madness is the principle upon which the ministers at your right hand have proceeded in their estimate of the revenues of the Carnatic, when they were providing, not supply for the establishments of its protection, but rewards for the authors of its ruin.

Extracts from Burke's speeches are also given on pages 272–277.

---

351. Edward, Lord Thurlow. 1732–1806.

"Lord Thurlow," says Mr. Butler, in his 'Reminiscences,' "was at times superlatively great. It was the good fortune of the reminiscent to hear his celebrated reply to the Duke of Grafton during the inquiry into Lord Sandwich's administration of Greenwich Hospital. His Grace's action and delivery, when he addressed the house, were singularly dignified and graceful; but his matter was not equal to his manner. He reproached Lord Thurlow with his plebeian extraction and his recent admission into the peerage: particular circumstances caused Lord Thurlow's reply to make a deep impression on the reminiscent. His lordship had spoken too often, and began to be heard with a civil, but visible impatience. Under these circumstances he was attacked in the manner we have mentioned. He rose from the woolsack, and advanced slowly to the place from which the Chancellor generally addresses the house; then, fixing on the duke the look of Jove when he grasped the thunder, he said, in a loud tone of voice," —

I am amazed at the attack the noble duke has made on me. Yes, my lords [considerably raising his voice], I am amazed at his Grace's speech. The noble duke cannot look before him, behind him, or on either side of him, without seeing some noble peer who owes his seat in this house to successful exertions in the profession to which I belong. Does he not feel that it is as honorable to owe it to these, as to being the accident of an accident? To all these noble lords the language of the noble duke is as applicable and as insulting as it is to myself. But I don't fear to meet it single and alone. No one venerates the peerage more than I do; but, my lords, I must say, that the peerage solicited me, not I the peerage. Nay, more, I can say, and will say, that as a peer of Parliament, as Speaker of this right honorable house, as Keeper of the Great Seal, as Guardian of his Majesty's Conscience, as Lord High Chancellor of England; nay, even in that character alone in which the noble duke would think it an affront to be considered — as a man — I am at this moment as respectable — I beg leave to add, I am at this moment as much respected — as the proudest peer I now look down upon.

"The effect of this speech, both within the walls of Parliament and out of them, was prodigious. It gave Lord Thurlow an ascendency in the house which no Chancellor had ever possessed; it invested him in public opinion with a character of independence and honor; and this, though he was ever on the unpopular side in politics, made him always popular with the people."

William Pitt, the Younger. 1759–1806.

352. From his Speech on the Abolition of the Slave-Trade, April 2, 1792.

I have shown how great is the enormity of this evil, even on the supposition that we take only convicts and prisoners of war. But take the subject in the other way; take it on the grounds stated by the right honorable gentlemen over the way, and how does it stand? Think of EIGHTY THOUSAND persons carried away out of their country by we know not what means! for crimes imputed! for light or inconsiderable faults! for debt perhaps! for the crime of witchcraft! or a thousand other weak and scandalous pretexts! besides all the fraud and kidnapping, the villanies and perfidy, by which the slave-trade is supplied. Reflect on these eighty thousand persons thus annually taken off! There is something in the horror of it that surpasses all the bounds of imagination. Admitting that there exists in Africa something like to courts of justice; yet what an office of humiliation and meanness it is in us, to take upon ourselves to carry into execution the partial, the cruel, iniquitous sentences of such courts, as if we also were strangers to all religion, and to the first principles of justice! But that country, it is said, has been in some degree civilized, and civilized by us. It is said they have gained some knowledge of the principles of justice. What, sir, have they gained principles of justice from us? Their civilization brought about by us! Yes, we give them enough of our intercourse to convey to them the means, and to initiate them in the study, of mutual destruction. We give them just enough of the forms of justice to enable them to add the pretext of legal trials to their other modes of perpetrating the most atrocious iniquity. We give them just enough of European improvements to enable them the more effectually to turn Africa into a ravaged wilderness. Some evidences say that the Africans are addicted to the practice of gambling; that they even sell their wives and children, and ultimately themselves. Are these, then, the legitimate sources of slavery? Shall we pretend that we can thus acquire an honest right to exact the labor of these people? Can we pretend that we have a right to carry away to distant regions men of whom we know nothing by authentic inquiry, and of whom there is every reasonable presumption to think, that those who sell them to us have no right to do so? But the evil does not stop here. I feel that there is not time for me to make all the remarks which the subject deserves, and I refrain from attempting to enumerate half the dreadful consequences of this system. Do you think nothing of the ruin and the miseries in which so many other individuals, still remaining in Africa, are involved, in consequence of carrying off so many myriads of people? Do you think nothing of their families which are left behind? of the connections which are broken? of the friendships, attachments, and relationships that are burst asunder! Do you think nothing of the miseries in consequence, that are felt from generation to generation? of the privation of that happiness which might be communicated to them by the introduction of civilization, and of mental and moral improvement? A happiness which you withhold from them so long as you permit the slave-trade to continue. What do you know of the internal state of Africa? You have carried on a trade to that quarter of the globe from this civilized and enlightened country; but such a trade, that, instead of diffusing either knowledge or wealth, it has been the check to every laudable pursuit. Instead of any fair interchange of commodities; instead of conveying to them, from this highly favored land, any means of improvement; you carry with you that noxious plant by which everything is withered and blasted; under whose shade nothing that is useful or profitable to Africa will ever flourish or take root. Long as that continent has been known to navigators, the extreme line and boundaries of its coasts is all with which Europe is yet become acquainted; while other countries in the same parallel of latitude, through a happier system of intercourse, have reaped the blessings of a mutually beneficial commeree. But as to the whole interior of that continent you are, by your own principles of commerce, as yet entirely shut out: Africa is known to you only in its skirts. Yet even there you are able to infuse a poison that spreads its contagious effects from one end of it to the other, which penetrates to its very centre, corrupting every part to which it reaches. You there subvert the whole order of nature; you aggravate every natural barbarity, and furnish to every man living on that continent motives for committing, under the name and pretext of commerce, acts of perpetual violence and perfidy against his neighbor.

There was a time, sir, which it may be fit sometimes to revive in the remembrance of our countrymen, when even human sacrifices are said to have been offered in this island. But I would peculiarly observe on this day, for it is a case precisely in point, that the very practice of the slave-trade once prevailed among us, Slaves, as we may read in Henry's History of Great Britain, were formerly an established article of our export. "Great numbers," he says, "were exported like cattle, from the British coast, and were to be seen exposed for sale in the Roman market." It does not distinctly appear by what means they were procured; but there was unquestionably no small resemblance, in this particular point, between the case of our ancestors and that of the present wretched natives of Africa — for the historian tells you that "adultery, witchcraft, and debt were probably some of the chief sources of supplying the Roman market with British slaves — that prisoners taken in war were added to the number — and that there might be among them some unfortunate gamesters, who, after having lost all their goods, at length staked themselves, their wives, and their children." Every one of these sources of slavery has been stated, and almost precisely in the same terms, to be at this hour a source of slavery in Africa. And these circumstances, sir, with a solitary instance or two of human sacrifices, furnish the alleged proofs, that Africa labors under a natural incapacity for civilization; that it is enthusiasm and fanaticism to think that she can ever enjoy the knowledge and the morals of Europe; that Providence never intended her to rise above a state of barbarism; that Providence has irrevocably doomed her to be only a nursery for slaves for us free and civilized Europeans. Allow of this principle, as applied to Africa, and I should be glad to know why it might not also have been applied to ancient and uncivilized Britain. Why might not some Roman senator, reasoning on the principles of some honorable gentlemen, and pointing to *British barbarians*, have predicted with equal boldness, "*There* is a people that will never rise to civilization — *there* is a people destined never to be free — a people without the understanding necessary for the attainment of useful arts; depressed by the hand of nature below the level of the human species; and created to form a supply of slaves for the rest of the world." Might not this have been said, according to the principles which we now hear stated, in all respects as fairly and as truly of Britain herself, at that period of her history, as it can now be said by us of the inhabitants of Africa?

We, sir, have long since emerged from barbarism — we have almost forgotten that we were once barbarians — we are now raised to a situation which exhibits a striking contrast to every circumstance by which a Roman might have characterized us, and by which we now characterize Africa. There is indeed one thing wanting to complete the contrast, and to clear us altogether from the imputation of acting, even to this hour, as barbarians; for we continue to this hour a barbarous traffic in slaves; we continue it even yet in spite of all our great and undeniable pretensions to civilization. We were once as obscure among the nations of the earth, as savage in our manners, as debased in our morals, as degraded in our understanding, as these unhappy Africans are at present. But in the laspe of a long series of years, by a progression slow, and for a time almost imperceptible, we have become rich in a variety of acquirements, favored above measure in the gifts of Providence, unrivalled in commerce, pre-eminent in arts, foremost in the pursuits of philosophy and science, and established in all the blessings of civil society: we are in the possession of peace, of happiness, and of liberty; we are under the guidance of a mild and beneficent religion; and we are protected by impartial laws, and the purest administration of justice; we are living under a system of government, which our own happy experience leads us to pronounce the best and wisest which has ever yet been framed; a system which has become the admiration of the world. From all these blessings we must forever have been shut out, had there been any truth in those principles which some gentlemen have not hesitated to lay down as applicable to the case of Africa. Had those principles been true, we ourselves had languished to this hour in that miserable state of ignorance, brutality, and degradation, in which history proves our ancestors to have been immersed. Had other nations adopted these principles in their conduct towards us; had other nations applied to Great Britain the reasoning which some of the senators of this very island now apply to Africa, ages might have passed without our emerging from barbarism; and we, who are enjoying the blessings of British civilization, of British laws, and British liberty, might at this hour have been little superior, either in morals, in knowledge, or refinement, to the rude inhabitants of the coast of Guinea.

If then we feel that this perpetual confinement in the fetters of brutal ignorance would have been the greatest calamity which could have befallen us; if we view with gratitude and exultation the contrast between the peculiar blessings we enjoy and the wretchedness of the ancient inhabitants of Britain; if we shudder to think of the misery which would still have overwhelmed us, had Great Britain continued to the present times to be the mart for slaves to the more civilized nations of the world, through some cruel policy of theirs, God forbid that we should any longer subject Africa to the same dreadful scourge, and preclude the light of knowledge, which has reached every other quarter of the globe, from having access to her coasts?

CHARLES JAMES FOX. 1749–1806.

353. FROM HIS SPEECH ON THE ADDRESS ON THE KING'S SPEECH, NOV. 26, 1778.

You have now two wars before you, of which you must choose one, for both you cannot support. The war against America has hitherto been carried on against her alone, unassisted by any ally; notwithstanding she stood alone, you have been obliged uniformly to increase your exertions, and to push your efforts in the end to the extent of your power, without being able to bring it to any favorable issue: you have exerted all your force hitherto without effect, and you cannot now divide a force found already inadequate to its object. My opinion is for withdrawing your forces from America entirely, for a defensive war you can never think of; a defensive war would ruin this nation at any time, and in any circumstances: an offensive war is pointed out as proper for this country; our situation points it out, and the spirit of the nation impels us to attack rather than defence: attack France, then, for she is your object. The nature of the war with her is quite different: the war against America is against your own countrymen — you have stopped me from saying against your fellow-subjects; that against France is against your inveterate enemy and rival. Every blow you strike in America is against yourselves; it is against all ideas of reconciliation, and against your own interest, though you should be able, as you never will, to force them to submit. Every stroke against France is of advantage to you; the more you lower the scale in which France lays in the balance, the more your own rises, and the more the Americans will be detached from her as useless to them. Even your own victories over America are in favor of France, from what they must cost you in men and money; your victories over France will be felt by her ally. America must be conquered in France; France never can be conquered in America.

The war of the Americans is a war of passion; it is of such a nature as to be supported by the most powerful virtues — love of liberty and of country; and, at the same time, by those passions in the human heart, which give courage, strength, and perseverance to man — the spirit of revenge for the injuries you have done them; of retaliation for the hardships you have inflicted on them; and of opposition to the unjust powers you have exercised over them. Everything combines to animate them to this war, and such a war is without end; for, whatever obstinacy enthusiasm ever inspired man with, you will now find it in America; no matter what gives birth to that enthusiasm, whether the name of religion or of liberty, the effects are the same; it inspires a spirit that is unconquerable, and solicitous to undergo difficulty, danger, and hardship: and as long as there is a man in America, a being formed such as we are, you will have him present himself against you in the field.

The war of France is of another sort; the war of France is a war of interest: it was her interest first induced her to engage in it, and it is by that interest that she will measure its continuance. Turn your face at once against her; attack her wherever she is exposed, crush her commerce wherever you can, make her feel heavy and immediate distress throughout the nation: the people will soon cry out to their government. Whilst the advantages she promises herself are remote and uncertain, inflict present evils and distresses upon her subjects; the people will become discontented and clamorous: she will find the having entered into this business a bad bargain; and you will force her to desert an ally that brings so much trouble and distress, and the advantages of whose alliance may never take effect.

---

354. From his Speech on the Overtures of Peace from the First Consul, Feb. 3, 1800.

Now, sir, what was the conduct of your own allies to Poland? Is there a single atrocity of the French, in Italy, in Switzerland, in Egypt, if you please, more unprincipled and inhuman than that of Russia, Austria, and Prussia, in Poland? What has there been in the conduct of the French to foreign powers; what in the violation of solemn treaties; what in the plunder, devastation, and dismemberment of unoffending countries; what in the horrors and murders perpetrated upon the subdued victims of their rage in any district which they have overrun; worse than the conduct of those three great powers in the miserable, devoted, and trampled-on kingdom of Poland, and who have been, or are, our allies in this war for religion, social order, and the rights of nations? "O! but we regretted the partition of Poland!" Yes, regretted! You regretted the violence, and that is all you did. You united yourselves with the actors; you, in fact, by your acquiescence, confirmed the atrocity. But they are your allies; and though they overran and divided Poland, there was nothing, perhaps, in the manner of doing it, which stamped it with peculiar infamy and disgrace. The hero of Poland, perhaps, was merciful and mild! He was as much superior to Bonaparte in bravery, and in the discipline which he maintained, as he was superior in virtue and humanity! He was animated by the purest principles of Christianity, and was restrained in his career by the benevolent precepts which it inculcates! Was he? Let unforunate Warsaw, and the miserable inhabitants of the suburb of Praga in particular, tell! What do we understand to have been the conduct of this magnanimous hero, with whom, it seems, Bonaparte is not to be compared? He entered the suburb of Praga, the most populous suburb of Warsaw, and there he let his soldiery loose on the miserable, unarmed, and unresisting people! Men, women, and children, nay, infants at the breast, were doomed to one indiscriminate massacre! Thousands of them were inhumanly, wantonly butchered! And for what? Because they had dared to join in a wish to meliorate their own condition as a people, and to improve their constitution, which had been confessed by their own sovereign to be in want of amendment. And such is the hero upon whom the cause of "religion and social order" is to repose! And such is the man whom we praise for his discipline and his virtue, and whom we hold out as our boast and our dependence, while the conduct of Bonaparte unfits him to be even treated with as an enemy!

FROM BUTLER'S "REMINISCENCES."

355. CHARACTER OF MR. FOX AND MR. PITT.

Almost the whole of Mr. Fox's political life was spent in opposition to his Majesty's ministers. It may be said of him, as of Lord North, that he had political adversaries, but no enemy. Good nature, too easily carried to excess, was one of the distinctive marks of his character. In vehemence and power of argument he resembled Demosthenes; but there the resemblance ended. He possessed a strain of ridicule and wit which nature denied to the Athenian; and it was the more powerful, as it always appeared to be blended with argument, and to result from it. To the perfect composition which so eminently distinguishes the speeches of Demosthenes, he had no pretence.

The moment of his grandeur was, when, — after he had stated the argument of his adversary, with much greater strength than his adversary had done, and with much greater than any of his hearers thought possible, — he seized it with the strength of a giant, and tore and trampled on it to destruction. If, at this moment, he had possessed the power of the Athenian over the passions or the imaginations of his hearers, he might have disposed of the House at his pleasure, — but this was denied to him: and, on this account, his speeches fell very short of the effect which otherwise they must have produced.

It is difficult to decide on the comparative merit of him and Mr. Pitt: the latter had not the vehement reasoning or argumentative ridicule of Mr. Fox; but he had more splendor, more imagery, and much more method and discretion. His long, lofty, and reverential panegyrics of the British constitution, his eloquent vituperations of those whom he described as advocating the democratic spirit then let loose on the inhabitants of the earth, and his solemn adjuration of the House to defend and to assist him in defending their all against it, were, in the highest degree, both imposing and conciliating, In addition, he had the command of bitter contemptuous sarcasm, which tortured to madness. This he could expand or compress at pleasure: even in one member of a sentence, he coult inflict a wound that was never healed.

Mr. Fox had a captivating earnestness of tone and manner; Mr. Pitt was more dignified than earnest. The action of Mr. Fox was easy and graceful; Mr. Pitt's cannot be praised. It was an observation of the reporters in the gallery, that it required great exertion to follow Mr. Fox while he was speaking; none to remember what he had said: that it was easy and delightful to follow Mr. Pitt; not so easy to recollect what had delighted them. It may be added, that, in all Mr. Fox's speeches, even when he was most violent, there was an unquestionable indication of good humor which attracted every heart. Where there was such a seeming equipoise of merit, the two last circumstances might be thought to turn the scale: but Mr. Pitt's undeviating circumspection, — sometimes concealed, sometimes ostentatiously displayed, — tended to obtain for him, from the considerate and the grave, a confidence which they denied to his rival.

Henry Grattan. 1750–1820.

356. Attack upon Mr. Flood.

Thus defective in every relationship, whether to constitution, commerce, and toleration, I will suppose this man to have added much private improbity to public crimes; that his probity was like his patriotism, and his honor on a level with his oath; he loves to deliver panegyrics on himself. I will interrupt him, and say, Sir, you are much mistaken if you think that your talents have been as great as your life has been reprehensible; you began your parliamentary career with an acrimony and personality which could have been justified only by a supposition of virtue; after a rank and clamorous opposition, you became on a sudden *silent;* you were silent for seven years; you were silent on the greatest questions, and you were silent for money! In 1773, while a negotiation was pending to sell your talents and your turbulence, you absconded from your duty in Parliament, you forsook your law of Poynings, you forsook the questions of economy, and abandoned all the old themes of your former declamation: you were not at that period to be found in the House; you were seen, like a guilty spirit, haunting the lobby of the House of Commons, watching the moment in which the question should be put, that you might vanish; you were descried with a criminal anxiety, retiring from the scenes of your past glory; or you were perceived coasting the upper benches of this House, like a bird of prey, with an evil aspect and a sepulchral note, meditating to pounce on its quarry:— these ways, they were not the ways of honor, you practised pending a negotiation which was to end either in your sale or your sedition: the former taking place, you supported the rankest measures that ever came before Parliament; the embargo of 1776, for instance. "O, fatal embargo, that breach of law, and ruin of commerce!" You supported the unparalleled profusion and jobbing of Lord Harcourt's scandalous ministry; the address to support the American war; the other address to send four thousand men, which you had yourself declared to be necessary for the defence of Ireland, to fight against the liberties of America, to which you had declared yourself a friend;—you, sir, who delight to utter execrations against the American commissioners of 1778, on account of their hostility to America;—you, sir, who manufacture stage-thunder against Mr. Eden, for his anti-American principles;—you, sir, whom it pleases to chant a hymn to the immortal Hampden;—you, sir, approved of the tyranny exercised against America;—and you, sir, voted four thousand Irish troops to cut the throats of the Americans fighting for their freedom, fighting for your freedom, fighting for the great principle, *liberty;* but you found, at last (and this should be an eternal lesson to men of your craft and cunning), that the king had only dishonored you; the court had bought, but would not trust you; and having voted for the worst measures, you remained, for seven years, the creature of *salary,* without the confidence of government. Mortified at the discovery, and stung by disappointment, you betake yourself to the sad expedients of duplicity; you try the sorry game of a trimmer in your progress to the acts of an incendiary; you give no honest support either to the government or the people; you, at the most critical period of their existence, take no part, you sign no non-consumption agreement, you are no volunteer, you oppose no perpetual mutiny bill, no altered sugar bill; you declare, that you lament that the declaration of right should have been brought forward; and observing, with regard to prince and people, the most impartial treachery and desertion, you justify the suspicion of your sovereign, by betraying the government as you had sold the people: until, at last, by this hollow conduct, and for some other steps, the result of mortified ambition, being dismissed, and another person put in your place, you fly to the ranks of the volunteers, and canvass for mutiny; you announce that the country was ruined by other men during that period in which she had been sold by you. Your logic is, that the repeal of a declaratory law is not the repeal of a law at all, and the effect of that logic is, an English act affecting to emancipate Ireland, by exercising over her the legislative authority of the British Parliament. Such has been your conduct, and at such conduct every order of your fellow-subjects have a right to exclaim! The merchant may say to you — the constitutionalist may say to you — the American may say to you — and I, I now say, and say to your beard, sir, you are not an honest man.

---

357. Speech against Napoleon, May 25, 1815.

The proposition that we should not interfere with the government of other nations is true, but true with qualifications. If the government of any other country contains an insurrectionary principle, as France did, when she offered to aid the insurrection of her neighbors, your interference is warranted; if the government of another country contains the principle of universal empire, as France did, and promulgated, your interference is justifiable. Gentlemen may call this internal government, but I call this conspiracy. If the government of another country maintains a predatory army, such as Bonaparte's, with a view to hostility and conquest, your interference is just. He may call this internal government, but I call this a preparation for war. No doubt he will accompany this with offers of peace, but such offers of peace are nothing more than one of the arts of war, attended, most assuredly, by charging on you the odium of a long and protracted contest, and with much commonplace, and many good saws and sayings of the miseries of bloodshed, and the savings and good husbandry of peace, and the comforts of a quiet life: but if you listen to this, you will be much deceived; not only deceived, but you will be beaten. Again, if the government of another country covers more ground in Europe, and destroys the balance of power, so as to threaten the independence of other nations, this is a cause of your interference. Such was the principle upon which we acted in the best times: such was the principle of the grand alliance, such was the triple alliance, and such the quadruple; and by such principles has Europe not only been regulated, but protected. If a foreign government does any of those acts I have mentioned, we have a cause of war; but if a foreign power does all of them, — forms a conspiracy for universal empire, keeps up an army for that purpose, employs that army to overturn the balance of power, and attempts the conquest of Europe, — attempts, do I say? in a great degree achieves it (for what else was Bonaparte's dominion before the battle of Leipsic?) — and then receives an overthrow; owes its deliverence to treaties which give that power its life, and these countries their security (for what did you get from France but security?) — if this power, I say, avails itself of the conditions in the treaties, which give it colonies, prisoners, and deliverence, and breaks those conditions which give you security, and resumes the same situation which renders this power capable of repeating the same atrocity, — has England, or has she not, a right of war?

Having considered the two questions, — that of ability and that of right, — and having shown that you are justified on either consideration to go to war, let me now suppose that you treat for peace. First, you will have peace upon a war establishment, and then a war without your present allies. It is not certain that you will have any of them, but it is certain that you will not have the same combination, while Bonaparte increases his power by confirmation of his title, and by further preparation; so that you will have a bad peace and a bad war. Were I disposed to treat for peace I would not agree to the amendment, because it disperses your allies and strengthens your enemy, and says to both, we will quit our alliance to confirm Napoleon on the throne of France, that he may hereafter more advantageously fight us, as he did before, for the throne af England.

Gentlemen set forth the pretensions of Bonaparte; gentlemen say, that he has given liberty to the press; he has given liberty to publication, to be afterwards tried and punished according to the present constitution of France, as a military chief pleases; that is to say, he has given liberty to the French to hang themselves. Gentlemen say, he has in his dominions abolished the slave-trade: I am unwilling to deny him praise for such an act; but if we praise him for giving liberty to the African, let us not assist him in imposing slavery on the European. Gentlemen say, will you make war upon character? But the question is, will you trust a government without one? What will you do if you are conquered, say gentlemen? I answer, the very thing you must do if you treat — abandon the Low Countries. But the question is, in which case are you most likely to be conquered — with allies or without them? Either you must abandon the Low Countries, or you must preserve them by arms, for Bonaparte will not be withheld by treaty. If you abandon them, you will lose your situation on the globe; and instead of being a medium of communication and commerce between the new and the old, you will become an anxious station between two fires — the continent of America, rendered hostile by the intrigues of France, and the continent of Europe, possessed by her arms. It then remains for you to determine, if you do not abandon the Low Countries, in what way you mean to defend them — alone or with allies.

Gentlemen complain of the allies, and say, they have partitioned such a country, and transferred such a country, and seized on such a country. What! will they quarrel with their ally, who has possessed himself of a part of Saxony, and shake hands with Bonaparte, who proposes to take possession of England? If a prince takes Venice, we are indignant; but if he seizes on a great part of Europe, and stands covered with the blood of millions, and the spoils of half mankind, our indignation ceases; vice becomes gigantic, conquers the understanding, and mankind begin by wonder, and conclude by worship. The character of Bonaparte is admirably calculated for this effect: he invests himself with much theatrical grandeur; he is a great actor in the tragedy of his own government; the fire of his genius precipitates on universal empire, certain to destroy his neighbors or himself; better formed to acquire empire than to keep it, he is a hero and a calamity, formed to punish France and to perplex Europe.

The authority of Mr. Fox has been alluded to — a great authority, and a great man; his name excites tenderness and wonder. To do justice to that immortal person, you must not limit your view to this country: his genius was not confined to England; it acted three hundred miles off, in breaking the chains of Ireland; it was seen three thousand miles off, in communicating freedom to the Americans; it was visible, I know not how far off, in ameliorating the condition of the Indian; it was discernible on the coast of Africa, in accomplishing the abolition of the slave-trade. You are to measure the magnitude of his mind by parallels of latitude. His heart was as soft as that of a woman, his intellect was adamant; his weaknesses were virtues — they protected him against the hard habit of a politician, and assisted nature to make him amiable and interesting. The question discussed by Mr. Fox in 1792 was, whether you would treat with a revolutionary government; the present is, whether you will confirm a military and a hostile one. You will observe, that when Mr. Fox was ready to treat, the French, it was understood, were to evacuate the Low Countries. If you confirm the present government, you must expect to lose them. Mr. Fox objected to the idea of driving France upon her resources, lest you should make her a military government. The question now is, whether you will make that military government perpetual. I therefore do not think the theory of Mr. Fox can be quoted against us; and the practice of Mr. Fox tends to establish our proposition, for he treated with Bonaparte, and failed. Mr. Fox was tenacious of England, and would never yield an iota of her superiority; but the failure of the attempt to treat was to be found, not in Mr. Fox, but in Bonaparte.

RICHARD BRINSLEY SHERIDAN. 1751–1816.

358. FROM HIS SPEECH AGAINST WARREN HASTINGS IN THE HOUSE OF COMMONS, Feb. 7, 1787.

I recollect to have heard it advanced by some of those admirers of Mr. Hastings, who were not so implicit as to give unqualified applause to his crimes, that they found an apology for the atrocity of them, in the greatness of his mind. To estimate the solidity of such a defence, it would be sufficient merely to consider in what consisted this prepossessing distinction, this captivating characteristic of greatness of mind. Is it not solely to be traced in great actions directed to great ends? In them, and them alone, we are to search for true estimable magnanimity. To them only can we justly affix the splendid title and honors of real greatness. There is indeed another species of greatness, which displays itself in boldly conceiving a bad measure, and undauntedly pursuing it to its accomplishment. But had Mr. Hastings the merit of exhibiting either of these descriptions of greatness? — even of the latter? I see nothing great — nothing magnanimous — nothing open — nothing direct in his measures, or in his mind; — on the contrary, he has too often pursued the worst objects by the worst means. His course was an eternal deviation from rectitude. He either tyrannized or deceived; and was by turns a Dionysius and a Scapin. As well might the writhing obliquity of the serpent be compared to the swift directness of the arrow, as the duplicity of Mr. Hastings' ambition to the simple steadiness of genuine magnanimity. In his mind all was shuffling, ambiguous, dark, insidious, and little: nothing simple, nothing unmixed: all affected plainness, and actual dissimulation; a heterogeneous mass of contradictory qualities; with nothing great but his crimes; and even those contrasted by the littleness of his motives, which at once denoted both his baseness and his meanness, and marked him for a traitor and a trickster. Nay, in his style and writing, there was the same mixture of vicious contrarieties; — the most grovelling ideas were conveyed in the most inflated language; giving mock consequence to low cavils, and uttering quibbles in heroics; so that his compositions disgusted the mind's taste, as much as his actions excited the soul's abhorrence. Indeed this mixture of character seemed, by some unaccountable, but inherent quality, to be appropriated, though in inferior degrees, to everything that concerned his employers. I remember to have heard an honorable and learned gentleman (Mr. Dundas) remark, that there was something in the first frame and constitution of the company, which extended the sordid principles of their origin over all their successive operations; connecting with their civil policy, and even with their boldest achievements, the meanness of a pedler, and the profligacy of pirates. Alike in the political and the military line could be observed *auctioneering ambassadors* and *trading generals*; — and thus we saw a revolution brought about by *affidavits;* an army employed in *executing an arrest;* a town besieged on *a note of hand;* a prince dethroned for the *balance of an account.* Thus it was they exhibited a government, which united the mock majesty of a bloody sceptre and the little *traffic of a merchant's counting-house,* wielding a truncheon with one hand, and *picking a pocket with the other.*

---

359. From his Speech against Warren Hastings in Westminster Hall, June 3, 1788.

The council, in recommending attention to the public in preference to the private letters, had remarked, in particular, that one letter should not be taken as evidence, because it was manifestly and abstractedly private, as it contained in one part the anxieties of Mr. Middleton for the illness of his son. This was a singular argument indeed; and the circumstance, in my mind, merited strict observation, though not in the view in which it was placed by the counsel. It went to show that some at least of those concerned in these transactions, felt the force of those ties, which their efforts were directed to tear asunder; that those who could ridicule the respective attachment of a mother and a son; who would prohibit the reverence of the son to the mother who had given him life; who could deny to *maternal debility* the protection which *filial tenderness* should afford; — were yet sensible of the *straining* of those *chords* by which they were connected. There was something connected with this transaction so wretchedly horrible, and so vilely loathsome, as to excite the most contemptible disgust. If it were not a part of my duty, it would be superfluous to speak of the sacredness of the ties which those aliens to feeling, those apostles to humanity, had thus divided. In such an assembly as that which I have the honor of addressing, there is not an eye but must dart reproof at this conduct; not a heart but must anticipate its condemnation. Filial Piety! It is the primal bond of society — it is that instinctive principle, which, panting for its proper good, soothes, unbidden, each sense and sensibility of man! — it now quivers on every lip! — it now beams from every eye! — it is an emanation of that gratitude, which, softening under the sense of recollected good, is eager to own the vast countless debt it ne'er, alas! can pay, for so many long years of unceasing solicitude, honorable self-denials, life-preserving cares! — it is that part of our practice where duty drops its awe; where reverence refines into love! — it asks no aid of memory! — it needs not the deductions of reason! — preexisting, paramount over all, whether law or human rule, few arguments can increase, and none can diminish it! — it is the sacrament of our nature! — not only the duty, but the indulgence of man — it is his first great privilege — it is amongst his last most endearing delights! — it causes the bosom to glow with reverberated love! — it requites the visitations of nature, and returns the blessings that have been received! — it fires emotion into vital principle — it renders habituated instinct into a master-passion — sways all the sweetest energies of man — hangs over each vicissitude of all that must pass away — aids the melancholy virtues in their last sad tasks of life to cheer the languors of decrepitude and age — explores the thought — elucidates the aching eye — and breathes sweet consolation even in the awful moment of dissolution?

JOHN PHILPOT CURRAN. 1750–1817.

360. FROM HIS SPEECH ON THE TRIAL OF ARCHIBALD HAMILTON ROWAN.

This paper, gentlemen, insists upon the necessity of emancipating the Catholics of Ireland, and that is charged as part of the libel. If they had waited another year, if they had kept this prosecution impending for another year, how much would remain for a jury to decide upon, I should be at a loss to discover. It seems as if the progress of public information was eating away the ground of the prosecution. Since the commencement of the prosecution, this part of the libel has unluckily received the sanction of the legislature. In that interval our Catholic brethren have obtained that admission, which it seems it was a libel to propose; in what way to acccunt for this I am really at a loss. Have any alarms been occasioned by the emancipation of our Catholic brethren? has the bigoted malignity of any individuals been crushed? or has the stability of the government, or that of the country, been weakened? or is one million of subjects stronger than four millions? Do you think that the benefit they received should be poisoned by the sting of vengeance? If you think so, you must say to them, "You have demanded emancipation, and you have got it; but we abhor your persons, we are outraged at your success, and we will stigmatize by a criminal prosecution the adviser of that relief which you have obtained from the voice of your country." I ask you, do you think, as honest men, anxious for the public tranquillity, conscious that there are wounds not yet completely cicatrized, that you ought to speak this language at this time, to men who are too much disposed to think that in this very emancipation they have been saved from their own Parliament by the humanity of their sovereign? Or do you wish to prepare them for the revocation of these improvident concessions? Do you think it wise or humane at this moment to insult them, by sticking up in a pillory the man who dared to stand forth as their advocate? I put it to your oaths; do you think that a blessing of that kind, that a victory obtained by justice over bigotry and oppression, should have a stigma cast upon it by an ignominious sentence upon men bold and honest enough to propose this measure? to propose the redeeming of religion from the abuses of the church, the reclaiming of three millions of men from bondage, and giving liberty to all who had a right to demand it; giving, I say, in the so much censured words of this paper, giving "UNIVERSAL EMANCIPATION!" I speak in the spirit of the British law, which makes liberty commensurate with and inseparable from British soil; which proclaims even to the stranger and sojourner, the moment he sets his foot upon British earth, that the ground on which he treads is holy, and consecrated by the genius of UNIVERSAL EMANCIPATION. No matter in what language his doom may have been pronounced; no matter what complexion, incompatible with freedom, an Indian or an African sun may have burnt upon him; no matter in what disastrous battle his liberty may have been cloven down; no matter with what solemnities he may have been devoted upon the altar of slavery; the first moment he touches the sacred soil of Britain, the altar and the god sink together in the dust; his soul walks abroad in her own majesty; his body swells beyond the measure of his chains, that burst from around him; and he stands redeemed, regenerated, and disinthralled, by the irresistible genius of UNIVERSAL EMANCIPATION.

ROBERT HALL.[1] 1764–1831.

361. THE WAR WITH NAPOLEON.

In other wars we have been a divided people: the effect of our external operations has been in some measure weakened by intestine dissension. When peace has returned, the breach has widened, while parties have been formed on the merits of particular men, or of particular measures. These have all disappeared: we have buried our mutual animosities in a regard to the common safety. The sentiment of self-preservation, the first law which nature has impressed, has absorbed every other feeling; and the fire of liberty has melted down the discordant sentiments and minds of the British empire into one mass, and propelled them in one direction. Partial interests and feelings are suspended, the spirits of the body are collected at the heart, and we are awaiting with anxiety, but without dismay, the discharge of that mighty tempest which hangs upon the skirts of the horizon, and to which the eyes of Europe and of the world are turned in silent and awful expectation. While we feel solicitude, let us not betray dejection, nor be alarmed at the past successes of our enemy, which are more dangerous to himself than to us, since they have raised him from obscurity to an elevation which has made him giddy, and tempted him to suppose everything within his power. The intoxication of his success is the omen of his fall. What though he has carried the flames of war throughout Europe, and gathered as a nest the riches of the nations, while none peeped, nor muttered, nor moved the wing; he has yet to try his fortune in another field; he has yet to contend on a soil filled with the monuments of freedom, enriched with

1 Robert Hall was a Baptist minister, first at Cambridge, and afterwards at Bristol, and may be reckoned among the greatest orators of our country.

the blood of its defenders; with a people who, animated with one soul, and inflamed with zeal for their laws, and for their prince, are armed in defence of all that is dear or venerable, — their wives, their parents, their children, the sanctuary of God, and the sepulchre of their fathers. We will not suppose there is one who will be deterred from exerting himself in such a cause by a pusillanimous regard to his safety, when he reflects that he has already lived too long who has survived the ruin of his country; and that he who can enjoy life after such an event, deserves not to have lived at all. It will suffice us, if our mortal existence, which is at most but a span, be co-extended with that of the nation which gave us birth. We will gladly quit the scene, with all that is noble and august, innocent and holy; and instead of wishing to survive the oppression of weakness, the violation of beauty, and the extinction of everything on which the heart can repose, welcome the shades which will hide from our view such horrors. To form an adequate idea of the duties of this crisis, it will be necessary to raise your minds to a level with your station, to extend your views to a distant futurity, and to consequences the most certain, though most remote. By a series of criminal enterprises, by the successes of guilty ambition, the liberties of Europe have been gradually extinguished; the subjugation of Holland, Switzerland, and the free towns of Germany, has completed that catastrophe; and we are the only people in the eastern hemisphere who are in possession of equal laws and a free constitution. Freedom, driven from every spot on the Continent, has sought an asylum in a country which she always chose for her favorite abode; but she is pursued even here, and threatened with destruction. The inundation of lawless power, after covering the whole earth, threatens to follow us here; and we are most exactly, most critically placed, in the only aperture where it can be successfully repelled — in the Thermopylæ of the universe. As far as the interests of freedom are concerned, — the most important by far of sublunary interests, — you, my countrymen, stand in the capacity of the federal representatives of the human race; for with you it is to determine (under God) in what condition the latest posterity shall be born; their fortunes are intrusted to your care, and on your conduct at this moment depends the color and complexion of their destiny. If liberty, after being extinguished on the Continent, is suffered to expire here, whence is it ever to emerge in the midst of that thick night that will invest it? It remains with you, then, to decide whether that freedom, at whose voice the kingdoms of Europe awoke from the sleep of ages, to run a career of virtuous emulation in everything great and good; the freedom which dispelled the mists of superstition, and invited the nations to behold their God; whose magic touch kindled the rays of genius, the enthusiasm of poetry, and the flame of eloquence; the freedom which poured into our lap opulence and arts. and embellished life with innumerable institutions and improvements, till it became a theatre of wonders; it is for you to decide whether this freedom shall yet survive, or be covered with a funeral pall, and wrapt in eternal gloom. It is not necessary to await your determination. In the solicitude you feel to approve yourselves worthy of such a trust, every thought of what is afflicting in warfare, every apprehension of danger, must vanish, and you are impatient to mingle in the battle of the civilized world. Go, then, ye defenders of your country, accompanied with every auspicious omen; advance with alacrity into the field, where God Himself musters the hosts to war. Religion is too much interested in your success not to lend you her aid; she will shed over this enterprise her selectest influence. While you are engaged in the field, many will repair to the closet, many to the sanctuary; the faithful of every name will employ that prayer which has power with God; the feeble hands, which are unequal to any other weapon, will grasp the sword of the Spirit; and from myriads of humble, contrite hearts, the voice of intercession, supplication, and weeping, will mingle in its ascent to heaven with the shouts of battle and the shock of arms. While you have everything to fear from the success of the enemy, you have every means of preventing that success, so that it is next to impossible for victory not to crown your exertions. The extent of your resources, under God, is equal to the justice of your cause. But should Providence determine otherwise, should you fall in this struggle, should the nation fall, you will have the satisfaction (the purest allotted to man) of having performed your part; your names will be enrolled with the most illustrious dead; while posterity, to the end of time, as often as they revolve the events of this period (and they will incessantly revolve them), will turn to you a reverential eye, while they mourn over the freedom which is entombed in your sepulchre. I cannot but imagine the virtuous heroes, legislators, and patriots, of every age and country, are bending from their elevated seats to witness this contest, as if they were incapable, till it be brought to a favorable issue, of enjoying their eternal repose. Enjoy that repose, illustrious immortals! Your mantle fell when you ascended; and thousands, inflamed with your spirit, and impatient to tread in your steps, are ready "to swear by Him that sitteth upon the throne, and liveth forever and ever," they will protect Freedom in her last asylum, and never desert that cause which you sustained by your labors, and cemented with your blood. And Thou, sole Ruler among the children of men, to whom the shields of the earth belong, "gird on Thy sword, thou Most Mighty," go forth with our hosts in the day of battle! Impart, in addition to their hereditary valor, that confidence of success which springs from Thy presence! Pour into their hearts the spirit of departed heroes! Inspire them with Thine own; and, while led by Thine hand, and fighting under Thy banners, open Thou their eyes to behold in every valley, and in every plain, what the prophet beheld by the same illumination — chariots of fire, and horses of fire! "Then shall the strong man be as tow, and the maker of it as a spark; and they shall both burn together, and none shall quench them."

SIR JAMES MACKINTOSH. 1765–1832.

362. FROM HIS SPEECH IN DEFENCE OF PELTIER FOR A LIBEL ON THE FIRST CONSUL OF FRANCE — BONAPARTE.

Gentlemen, there is one point of view in which this case seems to merit your most serious attention. The real prosecutor is the master of the greatest empire the civilized world ever saw; the defendant is a defenceless, proscribed exile. I consider this case, therefore, as the first of a long series of conflicts between the greatest power in the world and the ONLY FREE PRESS remaining in Europe. Gentlemen, this distinction of the English press is new — it is a proud and a melancholy distinction. Before the great earthquake of the French Revolution had swallowed up all the asylums of free discussion on the Continent, we enjoyed that privilege, indeed, more fully than others, but we did not enjoy it exclusively. In Holland, in Switzerland, in the imperial towns of Germany, the press was either legally or practically free.

But all these have been swallowed up by that fearful convulsion which has shaken the uttermost corners of the earth. They are destroyed, and gone forever! One asylum of free discussion is still inviolate. There is still one spot in Europe where man can freely exercise his reason on the most important concerns of society, where he can boldly publish his judgment on the acts of the proudest and most powerful tyrants. The press of England is still free. It is guarded by the free constitution of our forefathers. It is guarded by the hearts and arms of Englishmen, and I trust I may venture to say that, if it be to fall, it will fall only under the ruins of the British empire. It is an awful consideration, gentlemen. Every other monument of European liberty has perished. That ancient fabric which has been gradually reared by the wisdom and virtue of our fathers, still stands. It stands, thanks be to God! solid and entire — but it stands alone, and it stands in ruins! Believing, then, as I do, that we are on the eve of a great struggle — that this is only the first battle between reason and power — that you have now in your hands, committed to your trust, the only remains of free discussion in Europe, now confined to this kingdom; addressing you, therefore, as the guardians of the most important interests of mankind; convinced that the unfettered exercise of reason depends more on your present verdict than on any other that was ever delivered by a jury, — I trust I may rely with confidence on the issue, — I trust that you will consider yourselves as the advanced guard of liberty, as having this day to fight the first battle of free discussion against the most formidable enemy that it ever encountered.

THOMAS LORD ERSKINE. 1750–1823.

FROM HIS SPEECH ON THE TRIAL OF STOCKDALE.

363. PRINCIPLES OF THE LAW OF LIBEL.

Gentlemen, the question you have therefore to try upon all this matter is extremely simple. It is neither more nor less than this: At a time when the charges against Mr. Hastings were, by the implied consent of the Commons, in every hand and on every table; when, by their managers, the lightning of eloquence was incessantly consuming him, and flashing in the eyes of the public; when every man was, with perfect impunity, saying, and writing, and publishing just what he pleased of the supposed plunderer and devastator of nations, — would it have been criminal in Mr. Hastings himself to remind the public that he was a native of this free land, entitled to the common protection of her justice, and that he had a defence in his turn to offer to them, the outlines of which he implored them in the mean time to receive, as an antidote to the unlimited and unpunished poison in circulation against him? This is, without color or exaggeration, the true question you are to decide. Because I assert, without the hazard of contradiction, that if Mr. Hastings himself could have stood justified or excused in your eyes for publishing this volume in his own defence, the author, if he wrote it *bonâ fide* to defend him, must stand equally excused and justified; and if the author be justified, the publisher cannot be criminal, unless you had evidence that it was published by him with a different spirit and intention from those in which it was written. The question, therefore, is correctly what I just now stated it to be — Could Mr. Hastings have been condemned to infamy for writing this book?

Gentlemen, I tremble with indignation to be driven to put such a question in England. Shall it be endured, that a subject of this country may be impeached by the Commons for the transactions of twenty years; that the accusation shall spread as wide as the region of letters; that the accused shall stand, day after day and year after year, as a spectacle before the public, which shall be kept in a perpetual state of inflammation against him; yet that he shall not, without the severest penalties, be permitted to submit anything to the judgment of mankind in his defence? If this be law (which it is for you to-day to decide), such a man has *no trial.* That great hall, built by our fathers for English justice, is no longer a court, but an altar; and an Englishman, instead of being judged in it by *God and his country*, is *a victim and a sacrifice.*

One word more, gentlemen, and I have done. Every human tribunal ought to take care to administer justice, as we look hereafter to have justice administered to ourselves. Upon the principle on which the attorney-general prays sentence upon my client, God have mercy upon us! Instead of standing before him in judgment with the hopes and consolations of Christians, we must call upon the mountains to cover us; for which of us can present, for omniscient examination, a pure, unspotted, and faultless course? But I humbly expect that the benevolent Author of our being will judge us as I have been pointing out for your example. Holding up the great volume of our lives in his hands, and regarding the general scope of them, if he discovers benevolence, charity, and good-will to man beating in the heart, where he alone can look; if he finds that our conduct, though often forced out of the path by our infirmities, has been in general well directed, his all-searching eye will assuredly never pursue us into those little corners of our lives, much less will his justice select them for punishment, without the general context of our existence, by which faults may be sometimes found to have grown out of virtues, and very many of our heaviest offences to have been grafted by human imperfection upon the best and kindest of our affections. No, gentlemen, believe me, this is not the course of divine justice, or there is no truth in the gospel of Heaven. If the general tenor of a man's conduct be such as I have represented it, he may walk through the shadow of death, with all his faults about him, with as much cheerfulness as in the common paths of life, because he knows that, instead of a stern accuser to expose before the Author of his nature those frail passages, which, like the scored matter in the book before you, checkers the volume of the brightest and best spent life, his mercy will obscure them from the eye of his purity, and our repentance blot them out forever.

---

364. From his Speech on the Trial of Thomas Hardy.

Gentlemen, my whole argument then amounts to no more than this, that before the crime of compassing THE KING'S DEATH can be found *by you, the jury*, whose province it is to judge of its existence, it must be *believed by you* to have existed in point of fact. Before you can adjudge A FACT, you *must believe it*, — not suspect it, or imagine it, or fancy it, — BUT BELIEVE IT; and it is impossible to impress the human mind with such a reasonable and certain belief, as is necessary to be impressed, before a Christian man can adjudge his neighbor to the smallest penalty, much less to the pains of death, without having such evidence as a reasonable mind will accept of, as the infallible test of truth. And what is that evidence? Neither more nor less than that which the constitution has established in the courts for the general administration of justice; namely, that the evidence convinces the jury, beyond all reasonable doubt, that the criminal *intention*, constituting the crime, existed in the mind of the man upon trial, and was the main-spring of his conduct. The rules of evidence, as they are settled by law, and adopted in its general administration, are not to be overruled or tampered with. They are founded in the charities of religion, in the philosophy of nature, in the truths of history, and in the experience of common life; and whoever ventures rashly to depart from them, let him remember that it will be meted to him in the same measure, and that both God and man will judge him accordingly. These are arguments addressed to your reasons and consciences, not to be shaken in upright minds by any precedent, for no precedents can sanctify injustice; if they could, every human right would long ago have been extinct upon the earth. If the State Trials in bad times are to be searched for precedents, what murders may you not commit; what law of humanity may you not trample upon; what rule of justice may you not violate; and what maxim of wise policy may you not abrogate and confound? If precedents in bad times are to be implicitly followed, why should we have heard any evidence at all? You might have convicted without any evidence, for many have been so convicted, and in this manner murdered, even by acts of Parliament. * * * *

In times when the whole habitable earth is in a state of change and fluctuation, when deserts are starting up into civilized empires around you, and when men, no longer slaves to the prejudices of particular countries, much less to the abuses of particular governments, enlist themselves, like the citizens of an enlightened world, into whatever communities their civil liberties may be best protected, it never can be for the advantage of this country to prove, that the strict, unextended letter of her laws, is no security to its inhabitants. On the contrary, when so dangerous a lure is everywhere holding out to emigration, it will be found to be the wisest policy of Great Britain to set up her happy constitution, — the strict letter of her guardian laws, and the proud condition of equal freedom, which her highest and her lowest subjects ought equally to enjoy; — it will be her wisest policy to set up these first of human blessings against those charms of change and novelty which the varying condition of the world is hourly displaying, and which may deeply affect the population and prosperity of our country. In times when the subordination to authority is said to be everywhere but too little felt, it will be found to be the wisest policy of Great Britain to instil into the governed an almost superstitious reverence for the strict security of the laws; which, from their equality of principle, beget no jealousies or discontent; which, from their equal administration, can seldom work injustice; and which, from the reverence growing out of their mildness and antiquity, acquire a stability in the habits and affections of men, far beyond the force of civil obligation; — whereas severe penalties and arbitrary constructions of laws intended for security, lay the foundations of alienation from every human government, and have been the cause of all the calamities that have come, and are coming, upon the earth.

GEORGE CANNING. 1770–1827.

365. FROM HIS SPEECH ON PARLIAMENTARY REFORM.

Dreading, therefore, the danger of total, and seeing the difficulties as well as the unprofitableness of partial alteration, I object to this first step towards a change in the constitution of the House of Commons. There are wild theories abroad. I am not disposed to impute an ill motive to any man who entertains them. I will believe such a man to be as sincere in his conviction of the possibility of realizing his notions of change without risking the tranquillity of the country, as I am sincere in my belief of their impracticability, and of the tremendous danger of attempting to carry them into effect; but for the sake of the world as well as for our own safety, let us be cautious and firm. Other nations, excited by the example of the liberty which this country has long possessed, have attempted to copy our constitution; and some of them have shot beyond it in the fierceness of their pursuit. I grudge not to other nations that share of liberty which they may acquire: in the name of God let them enjoy it! But let us warn them that they lose not the object of their desire by the very eagerness with which they attempt to grasp it. Inheritors and conservators of rational freedom, let us, while others are seeking it in restlessness and trouble, be a steady and shining light to guide their course, not a wandering meteor to bewilder and mislead them.

Let it not be thought that this is an unfriendly or disheartening counsel to those who are either struggling under the pressure of harsh government, or exulting in the novelty of sudden emancipation. It is addressed much rather to those who, though cradled and educated amidst the sober blessings of the British constitution, pant for other schemes of liberty than those which that constitution sanctions — other than are compatible with a just equality of civil rights, or with the necessary restraints of social obligation; of some of whom it may be said, in the language which Dryden puts into the mouth of one of the most extravagant of his heroes, that,

> "They would be free as nature first made man,
> Ere the base laws of servitude began,
> When wild in woods the noble savage ran."

Noble and swelling sentiments! — but such as cannot be reduced into practice. Grand ideas! — but which must be qualified and adjusted by a compromise between the aspirings of individuals and a due concern for the general tranquillity; — must be subdued and chastened by reason and experience, before they can be directed to any useful end! A search after abstract perfection in government may produce, in generous minds, an enterprise and enthusiasm to be recorded by the historian, and to be celebrated by the poet: but such perfection is not an object of reasonable pursuit, because it is not one of possible attainment: and never yet did a passionate struggle after an absolutely unattainable object fail to be productive of misery to an individual — of madness and confusion to a people. As the inhabitants of those burning climates which lie beneath a tropical sun sigh for the coolness of the mountain and the grove, so (all history instructs us) do nations which have basked for a time in the torrent blaze of an unmitigated liberty, too often call upon the shades of despotism, even of military despotism, to cover them. * * * *

Our lot is happily cast in the temperate zone of freedom: the clime best suited to the development of the moral qualities of the human race; to the cultivation of their faculties, and to the security as well as the improvement of their virtues: a clime not exempt, indeed, from variations of the elements, but variations which purify while they agitate the atmosphere that we breathe. Let us be sensible of the advantages which it is our happiness to enjoy. Let us guard with pious gratitude the flame of genuine liberty, that fire from heaven, of which our constitution is the holy depository; and let us not, for the chance of rendering it more intense and more radiant, impair its purity or hazard its extinction!

---

366. Speech at Plymouth in the Year 1823, upon the Occasion of being presented with the Freedom of that Town.

But while we thus control even our feelings by our duty, let it not be said that we cultivate peace, either because we fear, or because we are unprepared, for war; on the contrary, if eight months ago the government did not hesitate to proclaim that the country was prepared for war, if war should be unfortunately necessary, every month of peace that has since passed, has but made us so much the more capable of exertion. The resources created by peace are means of war. In cherishing those resources we but accumulate those means. Our present repose is no more a proof of inability to act, than the state of inertness and inactivity in which I have seen those mighty masses that float in the waters above your town, is a proof they are devoid of strength, and incapable of being fitted out for action. You well know, gentlemen, how soon one of those stupendous masses, now reposing on their shadows in perfect stillness, — how soon, upon any call of patriotism, or of necessity, it would assume the likeness of an animated thing, instinct with life and motion; how soon it would ruffle, as it were, its swelling plumage; how quickly it would put forth all its beauty and its bravery, collect its scattered elements of strength, and awaken its dormant thunder. Such as is one of these magnificent machines when springing from inaction into a display of its might, such is England herself, while apparently passive and motionless she silently concentrates the power to be put forth on an adequate occasion. But God forbid that that occasion should arise. After a war sustained for nearly a quarter of a century, — sometimes single-handed, and with all Europe arranged at times against her or at her side, — England needs a period of tranquillity, and may enjoy it without fear of misconstruction. Long may we be enabled, gentlemen, to improve the blessings of our present situation, to cultivate the arts of peace, to give to commerce, now reviving, greater extension and new spheres of employment, and to confirm the prosperity now generally diffused throughout this island.

LORD BROUGHAM. 1779–1868.

FROM THE SPEECH ON THE REFORM BILL.

367. PERIL OF DENYING JUST REFORMS.

My Lords, I do not disguise the intense solicitude I feel for the event of this debate, because I know full well that the peace of the country is involved in the issue. I cannot look without dismay at the rejection of this measure. But grievous as may be the consequences of a temporary defeat, temporary it can only be; for its ultimate and even speedy success is certain. Nothing can now stop it. Do not suffer yourselves to be persuaded that, even if the present ministers were driven from the helm, any one could steer you through the troubles which surround you without reform. But our successors would take up the task in circumstances far less auspicious. Under them you would be fain to grant a bill, compared with which, the one we now proffer you is moderate indeed. Hear the parable of the Sybil; for it conveys a wise and wholesome moral. She now appears at your gate, and offers you mildly the volumes, the precious volumes, of wisdom and peace. The price she asks is reasonable; to restore the franchise which, without any bargain, you ought voluntarily to give. You refuse her terms, her moderate terms. She darkens the porch no longer. But soon, for you cannot do without her wares, you call her back. Again she comes, but with diminished treasures. The leaves of the book are in part torn away by lawless hands, in part defaced with characters of blood. But the prophetic Maid has risen in her demands; it is Parliaments by the Year; it is Vote by the Ballot; it is Suffrage by the Million! From this you turn away indignant, and for a second time she departs. Beware of her third coming: for the treasure you must have; and what price she may next demand who shall tell? It may be even the mace which rests upon that woolsack. What may follow if your course of obstinacy is persisted in, I cannot take upon me to predict, nor do I wish to conjecture. But this I know, that as sure as man is mortal, and to err is human, justice deferred enhances the price at which you must purchase safety and peace; nor can you expect to gather in another crop than they did who went before you, if you persevere in their utterly abominable husbandry of sowing injustice and reaping rebellion. * *

You are the highest judicature in this realm. It is a judge's first duty never to pronounce sentence, in the most trifling case, without hearing. Will you make this the exception? Are you really prepared to determine, but not to hear, the mighty cause upon which a nation's hopes and fears hang? You are! Then beware of your decision! Rouse not a peace-loving, but resolute people. Alienate not from your body the affections of a whole empire. I counsel you to assist with your uttermost effort in preserving the peace, in upholding and perpetuating the constitution. Therefore I pray and exhort you not to reject this measure. By all you hold dear, by all the ties that bind every one of us to our common order and our common country, I solemnly adjure you, I warn you, I implore you, yes, on my bended knees, I supplicate you, reject not this bill.

FROM THE SPEECH FOR THE IMMEDIATE ABOLITION OF SLAVERY IN THE BRITISH WEST INDIES.

368. SLAVERY OPPOSED TO THE LAW OF NATURE.

I trust that at length the time is come when Parliament will no longer bear to be told that slave-owners are the best lawgivers on slavery; no longer allow an appeal from the British public to such communities as those in which the Smiths and the Grimsdalls are persecuted to death for teaching the Gospel to the negroes, and the Mosses holden in affectionate respect for torture and murder; no longer suffer our voice to roll across the Atlantic in empty warnings and fruitless orders. Tell me not of rights; talk not of the property of the planter in his slaves. I deny the right; I acknowledge not the property. The principles, the feelings of our common nature, rise in rebellion against it. Be the appeal made to the understanding, or to the heart, the sentence is the same that rejects it. In vain you tell me of the laws that sanction such a crime! There is a law above all the enactments of human codes, — the same throughout the world — the same in all times, — such as it was before the daring genius of Columbus pierced the night of ages, and opened to one world the sources of power, wealth, and knowledge, to another, all unutterable woes, — such as it is this day. It is the law written by the finger of God on the heart of man; and by that law, unchangeable and eternal, while men despise fraud, and loath rapine, and abhor blood, they will reject with indignation the wild and guilty fantasy, that man can hold property in man! In vain you appeal to treaties, to covenants between nations: the covenants of the Almighty, whether the Old covenant or the New, denounce such unholy pretensions. To those laws did they of old refer who maintained the African trade. Such treaties did they cite, and not untruly; for by one shameful compact you bartered the glories of Blenheim for the traffic in blood. Yet despite of law and treaty, that infernal traffic is now destroyed, and its votaries put to death like other pirates. How came this change to pass? Not assuredly by Parliament leading the way; but the country at length awoke; the indignation of the people was kindled; it descended in thunder, and smote the traffic, and scattered its guilty profits to the winds. Now, then, let the planters beware — let their assemblies beware — let the government at home beware — let the Parliament beware! The same country is once more awake — awake to the condition of negro slavery; the same indignation kindles in the bosom of the same people; the same cloud is gathering that annihilated the slave trade; and, if it shall descend again, they on whom its crash may fall, will not be destroyed before I have warned them; but I pray that their destruction may turn away from us the more terrible judgments of God.

EDWARD IRVING. 1792–1834.

FROM THE "ORATIONS FOR THE WORD OF GOD."

369. THE OBJECT OF MIRACLES.

There was a time when each revelation of the Word of God had an introduction into this earth which neither permitted men to doubt whence it came, nor wherefore it was sent. If, at the giving of each several truth, a star was not lighted up in heaven, as at the birth of the Prince of Truth, there was done upon the earth a wonder, to make her children listen to the message of their Maker. The Almighty made bare his arm; and, through mighty acts shown by his holy servants, gave demonstration of his truth, and found for it a sure place among the other matters of human knowledge and belief.

But now the miracles of God have ceased, and nature, secure and unmolested, is no longer called on for testimonies to her Creator's voice. No burning bush draws the footsteps to his presence-chamber; no invisible voice holds the ear awake; no hand cometh forth from the obscure to write his purposes in letters of flame. The vision is shut up, and the testimony is sealed, and the word of the Lord is ended, and this solitary volume, with its chapters and verses, is the sum total of all for which the chariot of heaven made so many visits to the earth, and the Son of God himself tabernacled and dwelt among us.

FROM THE "ORATIONS FOR JUDGMENT TO COME."

370. ANTICIPATION OF A FUTURE WORLD OF GLORY.

Yet shall the happy creatures have enough to do, and to enjoy, though there be no misery to comfort, nor evil to stem, nor grief, over whose departure to rejoice. Of how many cheap exquisite joys are these five senses the inlets! and who is he that can look upon the beautiful scenes of the morning, lying in the freshness of the dew, and the joyful light of the risen sun, and not be happy? Cannot God create another world many times more fair? and cast over it a mantle of light many times more lovely? and wash it with purer dew than ever dropped from the eyelids of the morning? Can he not shut up winter in his hoary caverns, or send him howling over another domain? Can he not form the crystal eye more full of sweet sensations, and fill the soul with a richer faculty of conversing with nature, than the most gifted poet did ever possess? Think you the creative function of God is exhausted upon this dark and troublous ball of earth? or that this body and soul of human nature are the masterpiece of his architecture? Who knows what new enchantment of melody, what new witchery of speech, what poetry of conception, what variety of design, and what brilliancy of execution, he may endow the human faculties withal — in what new graces he may clothe nature, with such various enchantment of hill and dale, woodland, rushing streams, and living fountains; with bowers of bliss and Sabbath scenes of peace, and a thousand forms of disporting creatures, so as to make all the world hath beheld to seem like the gross picture with which you catch infants; and to make the Eastern tale of romances, and the most rapt imagination of Eastern poets, like the ignorant prattle and rude structures which first delight the nursery and afterwards ashame our riper years.

www.ingramcontent.com/pod-product-compliance
Lightning Source LLC
LaVergne TN
LVHW020926110826
845150LV00004B/776

* 9 7 8 1 4 2 5 5 5 3 5 2 4 *